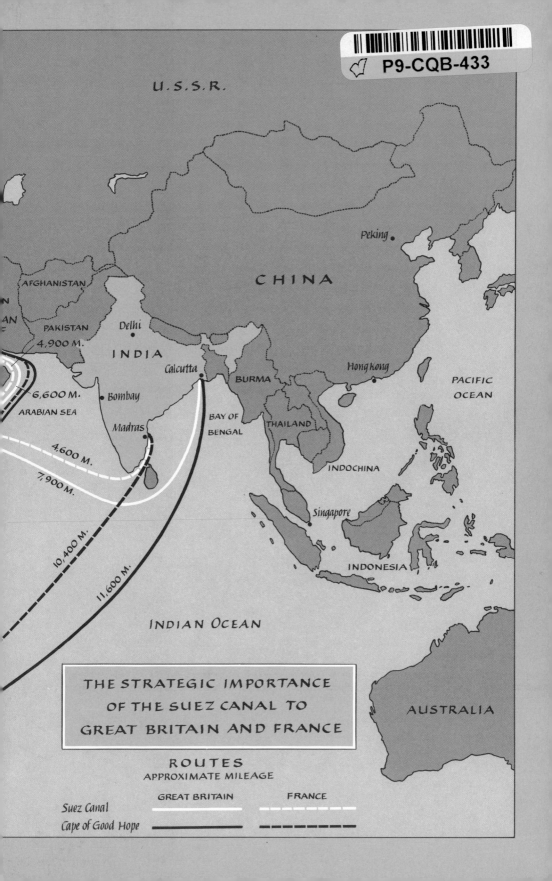

P9-CQB-433

THE STRATEGIC IMPORTANCE
OF THE SUEZ CANAL TO
GREAT BRITAIN AND FRANCE

ROUTES
APPROXIMATE MILEAGE

	GREAT BRITAIN	FRANCE
Suez Canal		
Cape of Good Hope		

Eisenhower Takes America into the Middle East

WARRIORS AT SUEZ

DONALD NEFF

THE LINDEN PRESS / SIMON & SCHUSTER
NEW YORK, 1981

COPYRIGHT © 1981 BY DONALD NEFF
ALL RIGHTS RESERVED
INCLUDING THE RIGHT OF REPRODUCTION
IN WHOLE OR IN PART IN ANY FORM
PUBLISHED BY THE LINDEN PRESS/SIMON & SCHUSTER
A SIMON & SCHUSTER DIVISION OF GULF & WESTERN CORPORATION
SIMON & SCHUSTER BUILDING
1230 AVENUE OF THE AMERICAS
NEW YORK, NEW YORK 10020
THE LINDEN PRESS/SIMON & SCHUSTER AND COLOPHON ARE TRADEMARKS OF
SIMON & SCHUSTER
DESIGNED BY EVE METZ
PHOTO EDITOR: VINCENT VIRGA
MANUFACTURED IN THE UNITED STATES OF AMERICA

10 9 8 7 6 5 4 3 2 1

LIBRARY OF CONGRESS CATALOGING IN PUBLICATION DATA

NEFF, DONALD, 1930–
    WARRIORS AT SUEZ.

    BIBLIOGRAPHY: P.
    INCLUDES INDEX.
    I. EGYPT—HISTORY—INTERVENTION, 1956.   I. TITLE.
DT107.83.N436   962'.053   81-8465
                                AACR2

ISBN 0-671-41010-5

ACKNOWLEDGMENTS

If you have ever wondered about the practical purpose of presidential libraries, the embarking on a major research project will quickly give you the answer. The Dwight D. Eisenhower Library in Abilene, Kansas, is a magnificent example of the worth of these modern pyramids. The archivists patiently sort through millions of pages of documents, catalogue them, index them, and then take on the load of the tedious process of trying to get them declassified. It is a pleasure to work with these conscientious, caring scholars, in particular Supervising Archivist James Leyerzapf and Kathleen Struss, archivist.

The Freedom of Information Act has received glowing compliments in recent years, but if my experience is any guide the act has now fallen to the inroads of the censors and indifferent bureaucrats. For instance, the CIA, more than two years after my first petition, managed to produce exactly four documents from this period in which it was so active. Similarly, the State Department turned over only a modicum of information after great delay and considerable foot-dragging.

But there are happier experiences to recount. Jan Schumacher, a veteran official of the United Nations from its birth until 1980, gathered the valuable and, for the most part, previously unpublished documents covering the 1956 period, and also found photographs to illustrate that era. Without his selfless help—founded upon his unshakable belief that only by the continued existence of a world body that aspires to idealism and rule by law can the world hope to find peace—and the assistance of the

5

U.N. Archivist section, particularly Jack Belwood, the book simply would not be the same.

There were many more who selflessly cheered on the project or in one way or another contributed to its completion: William Brubeck, Ben Gurtizen, Nizar Jwaideh, David Hume Kennerly, William Kirby, Dennis Mullin, Brigid O'Hara-Forster, Richard Emerson Powell, Skip Rosen, Roy Rowen, and Belinda Salzberg; also, Fran Fiorino, Eileen McCarron and Keith Normandeau, for their careful typing of the manuscript; Joelle Attinger and, again, Jan Schumacher, for their patient translation of French; Robbin Reynolds, who believed in the book almost before I did, and especially Joni Evans, who not only bought it but skillfully edited what I produced into as good a read as it could possibly be made to be; and most of all, Abigail Trafford, who read and reread it, improved it, and tolerated the temperamental vagaries that accompanied it.

FOR

GERTRUDE MARIE KESSLER NEFF

AND

The observers and peace-keeping forces of the United
Nations who daily risk their lives in alien lands to
bring justice to the world

CONTENTS

8

CONTENTS

MAPS
   The Gaza Road   *page 34*
   The War   *page 369*
   The Suez Canal, Strategic Routes   *front end leaf*
   Israel and Egypt   *back end leaf*

CAST OF CHARACTERS

AMERICA

George V. Allen, assistant secretary of state
Robert Amory, CIA
Robert B. Anderson, emissary of the President
James J. Angleton, CIA
Arleigh Burke, chief of naval operations
Henry A. Byroade, ambassador to Egypt
Miles Copeland, CIA
Allen Welsh Dulles, director, CIA
John Foster Dulles, secretary of state
Dwight D. Eisenhower, President
Wilbur Crane Eveland, CIA
Herbert Hoover, Jr., under secretary of state
Emmet John Hughes, presidential speech writer
George Humphrey, secretary of the treasury
Henry Cabot Lodge, ambassador to the United Nations
Robert Murphy, under secretary of state for political affairs
Richard M. Nixon, Vice President
Arthur W. Radford, chairman, joint chiefs of staff
Kermit Roosevelt, CIA

BRITAIN

Winston Churchill, former prime minister
Anthony Eden, prime minister
Hugh Gaitskell, leader of the Labour Party
Selwyn Lloyd, foreign secretary
Harold Macmillan, chancellor of the exchequer
Lord Louis Mountbatten, First Sea Lord of the Admiralty
Anthony Nutting, protégé of Eden
Humphrey Trevelyan, ambassador to Egypt

EGYPT

Mahmoud Fawzi, foreign minister
Ahmed Hussein, ambassador to the United States
Gamal Abdel Nasser, president
Mahmoud Yunis, Suez Canal expert

FRANCE

André Beaufre, musketeer deputy commander
Maurice Bourgès-Maunoury, minister of defense
Guy Mollet, premier
Christian Pineau, foreign minister
Abel Thomas, aide to Bourgès-Maunoury

ISRAEL

Menachem Begin, leader of the opposition
David Ben Gurion, prime minister
Moshe Dayan, chief of staff
Abba Eban, ambassador to the United States
Golda Meir, foreign minister
Shimon Peres, protégé of Ben Gurion
Moshe Sharett, former prime minister

SOVIET UNION

Nikolai Bulganin, premier
Nikita Khrushchev, first secretary of the Communist Party

UNITED NATIONS

General E. L. M. Burns, chief of staff in the Middle East
Dag Hammarskjold, secretary-general

When I entered office I knew little of the Middle East. By the end of my time in office I had become like all other old Middle East hands; word had become reality, form and substance had merged.
—HENRY KISSINGER

A land of darkness, as darkness itself; and of the shadow of death, without any order, and where the light is as darkness.
—JOB

PROLOGUE

CONSTRUCTION OF A CANAL at Suez was long a dream of the flourishing European empires. From 1497, when Vasco da Gama valiantly pioneered the route around Africa's Cape of Good Hope, until well into the nineteenth century, the arduous sail around the western bulk of the African continent remained the primary path for European traders and armies seeking the riches of the Orient. The journey was time-consuming and hazardous, endangered by the vagaries of weather and uncertain navigation. From Liverpool, the distance to Calcutta was 11,600 miles, a sail of many anxious weeks; a canal connecting the Mediterranean and the Red Sea would reduce the journey to 7,900 miles. For the French empire, the rewards of a canal were even more alluring. The sail around Africa from Marseilles to India was 10,400 miles; through a canal it would be only 4,600 miles.

The French moved first to secure for themselves a canal across the isthmus of Egypt between the Mediterranean and the waters leading into the inviting Indian Ocean. In the late 1790s, young Napoleon Bonaparte was ordered by France's revolutionary Directory "to cut a canal through the isthmus of Suez, and to take all necessary steps to ensure the free and exclusive use of the Red Sea by French vessels." His orders also included the injunction to "expel the British from all their possessions in the East, wherever they may be." The French plan for a Suez canal was thus intimately linked between a desire to shorten their lucrative Asian trading routes with their ambitions to extend the reaches of their empire at the expense of other colonial powers. It was a linkage of trade and

15

strategic advantage that haunted the imagination of Western leaders for decades to come.

The ambitious French effort failed. Napoleon's chief engineer, Charles le Père, repeated an ancient miscalculation and concluded mistakenly that the Mediterranean and the Red Sea differed in level by more than thirty feet, making a canal impossible. Even if he had been correct, however, the French, torn by revolution and opposed by the powerful British empire, would have had no chance to construct the canal. A month after the French landed in Egypt, Britain's greatest naval hero, Lord Horatio Nelson, sailed into Egyptian waters on August 1, 1798 and sank most of the French fleet, stranding Napoleon and his hapless army. A year later Napoleon managed to elude the British blockade and returned to Paris to become the emperor of France. His army was not so lucky. It languished in the inhospitable land for two more years before Britain, coming to the rescue of the Ottoman empire, which had ruled Egypt since 1517, formed an Anglo-Turkish force and routed the French. Two years after they landed, the British finally departed—but they would return.

• •

The idea of a canal at Suez caught fire in the imagination of Ferdinand de Lesseps, a twenty-seven-year-old French diplomat, when he was posted to Alexandria, then Egypt's capital, as a vice consul in 1832. De Lesseps arrived in Egypt with an inestimable advantage. His father had been posted there as a diplomat thirty years earlier and had befriended Mohammed Ali, an Albanian mercenary who had served with the Anglo-Turkish force in 1801 and had remained to stage a bloody coup and found the dynasty whose great-great-grandson was to be King Farouk. De Lesseps renewed his family's friendship with Ali and, during the five years he served in Egypt, he became close to Ali's teen-age son, Mohammed Said. De Lesseps' dreams of a Suez canal lay dormant until 1854. In September that year Mohammed Said succeeded to the throne and within two months de Lesseps, long since retired from the diplomatic service, traveled to Egypt and received the first of many concessions from his old friend to build the canal.

Fifteen years later, after enormous effort, including the use for a time of forced Egyptian labor, the canal was completed. It was 101 miles long and at its minimum width 196 feet 10 inches. It was opened with great fanfare on November 17, 1869. De Lesseps, accompanying the French Empress Eugénie aboard the imperial yacht *L'Aigle,* led a colorful procession of fifty-one bedecked ships through the canal. Giuseppe Verdi was commissioned to compose the opera *Aida* to commemorate the new waterway. A direct route to the fabulous Orient had finally been opened to European exploitation.

. .

Almost from the beginning Egypt lost its rights to share in the large profits of the canal. The original concessions granted by the canal company, Compagnie Universelle du Canal Maritime de Suez, awarded Egypt 44 percent of the company stock, a 15 percent royalty on net profits and the agreement that Egypt could purchase the company ninety-nine years after the canal's opening. Most of the other shares of the company were held by de Lesseps, French financial syndicates and private French citizens. Six years after the canal opened, the burdens of financing Egypt's 40 percent of the construction costs and his own extravagances forced the Khedive Ismail, who had succeeded Mohammed Said, into a desperate search for money. He decided to sell his share of the canal's stock, and Britain, seeing a chance at last to gain influence over the vital waterway, quickly snapped up the stock for four million British pounds. British Prime Minister Benjamin Disraeli actively encouraged the transaction, explaining to the British people: "I have never recommended this purchase as a financial investment. I have always, and do now recommend it to the country as a political transaction, and one which I believe is calculated to strengthen the empire." In November 1875 Khedive Ismail's 176,602 shares were turned over to Britain in seven large cases and the empire was indeed immeasurably strengthened.

But not Ismail's financial position. His debts, mainly to European powers, were too great. He went bankrupt the next year and found himself having to grant "Dual Control" over his economy to Britain and France in return for their aid. By 1880, the impoverished Khedive Tewfik, who had succeeded Ismail the previous year, was so desperate that he sold his right to 15 percent of net profits to a French group for twenty-two million francs.

Nationalist feelings inside Egypt were stirred by the khedive's profligate surrendering of rights to the canal's profits and the humiliating loss of economic sovereignty. The canal company was already greatly despised by Egyptians, who accurately called it a state within a state because of the dominance of foreigners in its operations and its high-handed methods of operating independently of the Egyptian government. Resentment reached a peak in 1881 when an Egyptian Army colonel, Ahmed

Arabi, staged an uprising against the khedive and thereby opened the door to a totally unexpected occurrence: domination by Britain.

In the decade since the canal's opening, the waterway had become indispensable to Britain. It was already the lifeline to Britain's vastly profitable Asian colonies, particularly India, the "jewel" of the empire. The canal's shorter route reduced shipping costs substantially and cut the distance between Britain and the Orient by as much as a third. Britain was the largest user of the canal with 70 percent of the ships passing through it flying the Union Jack. Colonel Arabi's challenge to the authority of the khedive was a potential threat to the canal's continued operation, and the British moved to crush him.

On August 19, 1882, a British expeditionary force sailed into the canal and quickly defeated Arabi's army. Cairo fell on September 14, and soon British administrators had exclusive control of the country's political and economic institutions, effectively snatching Egypt from the decaying Ottoman empire. The British vowed they would withdraw "as soon as the state of the country, and the organization of proper means for the maintenance of the khedive's authority, will admit of it," in the words of Foreign Secretary Lord Granville.

Nearly three-quarters of a century later, as the decade of the 1950s dawned, they were still there.

• •

The years between the 1880s and the 1950s had not been kind ones for Britain and France. The empires were disintegrating at an accelerating pace, with more than 600 million non-Europeans receiving freedom in the first decade after World War II. But the process was far from over. Six European empires still ruled 172 million people and controlled one-seventh of the world's land mass in the mid-1950s. Britain alone possessed thirty-five colonies, ranging from Nigeria and the Solomons to tiny Malta and Ascension. Half of the vast African continent was still under British dominion.

The prime minister of Britain, handsome Anthony Eden, has been born into the world of empire when England was supreme around the globe. His birth occurred only ten days before Queen Victoria's fabulous Diamond Jubilee, in 1897, a high point of the British empire. The jubilee was celebrated in colonies around the world, but nowhere with the pomp and splendor displayed in London. Representatives of the far-flung colonies strutted in seemingly unending processions through London's streets, Rajput princes and Dayak headhunters, a glory of exotic costumes and flashing colors. The stars of the parade were Britannia's own heroes, like Lord Wolseley of Cairo, whose heralded victory at Tel el Kebir brought English rule to Egypt. The empire spanned a quarter of the world's land mass and nearly a quarter of its people, truly an empire upon which the sun never set. The queen began her joyous Jubilee Day by sending a simple message to her subjects: "From my heart I thank my beloved people. May God bless them." The message was sent around the world. It was impossible for Englishmen of Eden's generation to forget such grandeur, and painful to see its disappearance.

The process of decolonization after World War II was accelerated under the prod of America. The United States was staking out its own self-interested position in the world, at times unavoidably at odds with Britain and France. The country was in its ascendancy, flexing its power, testing its limits, and finding them seemingly nonexistent. It was, exulted Henry Luce in his mass publications, *Time, Life* and *Fortune,* "the American century." Americans did not disagree, nor did European colonialists, though most of them were not happy about it, for each new country that emerged was one less bauble on the glittering necklace of empire, another shock to the once mighty power and prestige of Britain and France.

British Foreign Secretary Selwyn Lloyd expressed some of the resentment that Europeans felt in the mid-1950s in his memoirs written two decades later. "The Americans were, on the face of it, loyal and dependable allies but underneath there was in many Americans' hearts a dislike of colonialism, a resentment of any authority left to us from the great days of our empire, and a pleased smile, only half concealed, at seeing us go down." Lloyd may have been insensitive to the more profound resonances of the unique special relationship between England and America, but his was not a lone voice in the 1950s in what was still called Great Britain.

•   •

It was not only American opposition to colonialism that was causing the dissolution of the empires. They were the victims of two disastrously destructive world wars and the global rise of nationalism. Everywhere colonies were demanding their independence. Whole areas of the world were being transformed by the historic process, none more so than the Middle East.

The region had been the exclusive preserve of Britain and France between the world wars. By 1956 it had nearly all slipped away. Egypt was free of foreign domination for the first time since the Persian conquest more than 2,300 years earlier. Its vibrant new leader, Gamal Abdel Nasser, was challenging colonialism directly and leading the way toward an Arab renaissance. Other Moslem nations, noting his successes, were following suit and shedding their colonial masters. In 1956 alone, Morocco, Sudan and Tunisia gained their freedom. The only steadfast friend Britain had left in the region was Iraq while the only colony France retained was rebel-torn Algeria.

Amid the ferment of the Arab nations was Israel, a vigorous new democracy led by an old "prophet with a gun," as the newspapers called him, David Ben Gurion. Ben Gurion was leading the greatest renewal in Jewish history by molding the first Jewish state in nearly two thousand years. Israel had been born in violence and Ben Gurion was prepared, if need be, to protect it with violence. He was determined to prove that Israel was a permanent fixture in the Middle East.

It was in the midst of such tumultuous change that there occurred a series of galvanizing events that forced the United States to oppose its traditional allies in Britain, France and Israel and brought mankind to the edge of thermonuclear war.

• •

On November 6, 1956, the rising sun disclosed an astonishing sight off the tranquil shores of Egypt. There, spread out in battle array, was the mightiest European invasion force assembled since World War II. Floating gently on the blue waters of the Mediterranean were more than two hundred British and French warships, aircraft carriers and heavy cruisers, a battleship—France's formidable *Jean Bart*—scores of destroyers and frigates, freighters and tankers, and hundreds of tiny landing craft crammed with thousands of soldiers in battle gear. Guns of the powerful ships boomed, their smoke snaking lazily into the clear sky where it obscured the roaring flights of jets and helicopters. In the distance, on the palm-fringed beaches around the Suez Canal, there arose black clouds and the angry flashes and thumps of explosions.

In one dramatic stroke, Nasser had nationalized the canal, and Britain and France were making a last effort to pound Egypt and the Middle East back into subservience to colonialism and thereby guarantee their oil supplies. For the countries of Europe, the Suez Canal had become vital as their lifeline to Middle Eastern oil, which they depended on almost totally to lubricate their industry and propel their transportation. A threat to the canal was a threat to Europe's security. Britain and France thought they perceived such a threat from Egypt's Gamal Abdel Nasser.

Their secret partner in this climactic spasm of colonialism was Israel. Unknown to the rest of the world, an unlikely alliance had been struck between Britain, France and Israel. They had secretly agreed among themselves to attack Egypt without informing the United States. All three countries, for their own reasons, were determined to destroy Nasser.

Confusion was rampant. For it was on the same day as the Anglo-French attack that Russian tanks were slaughtering thousands of people in Hungary. The tentative policy of Russia's new leader, Nikita Khrushchev, to relax Moscow's harsh grip on its satellite nations was coming to a bloody end. So too was the brief attempt of the Hungarians to proclaim their freedom and withdraw from the Soviet orbit.

It was also on November 6 that the American people were voting to re-elect their thirty-fourth President, Dwight David Eisenhower, over Adlai E. Stevenson. The choice had not been a difficult one. Ike had campaigned as the Peace, Progress and Prosperity candidate, and the Americans had enjoyed all of that during his first term. In 1956, inflation was under 1 percent, unemployment stood at 3.7 percent, and the country was producing half of the world's manufactured goods. The federal budget was balanced, however briefly, and America, unlike its European allies, was independent in meeting its own oil needs.

The European powers and Israel that November 6 seemed to Eisenhower almost as culpable as the Soviet Union, and just as threatening to American national interests. They, like the Russians, were using force against a weak nation without justification. The confusion and tension were so great that Chief of Naval Operations Arleigh Burke warned the U.S. Sixth Fleet in the Mediterranean to be ready for any contingency.

"Who's the enemy?" asked the fleet's commander, Vice Admiral Charles R. ("Cat") Brown.

"Don't take any guff from anybody," replied Burke. Later he admitted: "I didn't know who the damned enemy was."

• •

Eisenhower too was confused and worried. While the Soviet Union was indulging in a bloodbath in Hungary, it was loudly protesting the attack on Egypt. The Soviets threatened to rain missiles on London and Paris and to send "volunteers" into the Middle East to save Egypt. The United States, despite its desperate efforts to restrain the Europeans and the Israelis, was inevitably being dragged into the conflict. World War III was suddenly a hideous possibility.

"Our people should be alert in trying to determine Soviet intentions," Eisenhower told CIA Director Allen W. Dulles that day during an emergency White House meeting. "If reconnaissance discloses Soviet air forces on Syrian bases I would think that there would be reason for the British and French to destroy them.

"Are our forces in the Mediterranean equipped with atomic antisubmarine weapons?" he asked.

Then he gave voice to what the world was dreading. "If the Soviets should attack Britain and France directly we would of course be in a major war."

• •

The 1950s are now idealized as a time of contented passivity and innocence in America. They were actually an era of great ferment and change, of social experiment and unparalleled prosperity.

A million families a year were moving off the farms in quest of the new prosperity. A quarter of a million blacks were fleeing the South annually in search of dollars and dignity and the equality so tantalizingly promised by the American dream. The average corporate manager was relocating every two and a half years. The cities, especially the downtowns, were being deserted for the suburbs, those new middle-class oases of prefab homes and, as newcomers belatedly began to realize, often prefab destinies. The man in the gray flannel suit was in fashion. But his children were restless, and he was becoming so too. The whole nation, it seemed, was feeling the itch.

The nature of travel itself was changing and becoming easier and faster. The new Boeing 707 jet was coming on line, replacing the lumbering piston-driven planes with an airliner that was roomier, faster and more comfortable. America's lust for air travel had already manifested itself in the previous five years when passengers on scheduled airlines doubled to 41,623,000. Slower travel by train was already suffering. More than twice the number of Americans were now traveling by plane than rail, accelerating the decay of the nation's neglected railroads.

For short distances, and often even long ones, the automobile had become America's favorite mode of transportation. In 1956 there were sixty-one million cars on the highways, an increase of three million in the past year alone.

Such massive movement and ease of travel had totally unpredicted consequences. Dependence on the car and the jet laid the basis for the country's future dependence on imported oil; at this time the country was totally and blissfully independent in meeting its own oil needs. Socially, the old family ties were replaced helter-skelter by a new morality rooted in mobility. The nuclear family was coming into existence, a rootless and self-centered grouping that was simultaneously sequestered from its parents and its children too as it wandered the nation in search of success and adventure. It was a febrile quest, and it usually took the form of finding new employment. A new job meant more money, a new house in a newer suburb with new friends.

But the price was heavy. Families were sundered and the new neighbors became as casual as acquaintances on the new jets. Life at times was as lonely and aimless as the latest Detroit behemoth hurtling thoughtlessly down the stark new interstate highways with a lone driver inside.

The changes occurring in American life went deep. Even the kind of people Americans were was changing. For the first time in the nation's history white-collar workers performing services and bureaucratic jobs surpassed the number of blue-collar workers actually producing goods. Farming was becoming a big-business enterprise, and the small farmer an anachronism.

The nation was becoming truly middle-class, and spendthrift. A spree of buying and abandoned consumption was sweeping the country in the wake of the new prosperity. Less stringent controls on credit and wider distribution of credit cards facilitated the national splurge. Americans were spending at a profligate rate unimagined by their maimed, cautious Depression-era parents. Between 1952 and 1956, consumer debt shot up 55 percent, to $42.5 billion, as Americans bought that second car, that summer cabin, that new color TV set that was being introduced into the marketplace.

Critic Edmund Wilson was moved to complain that "production, consumption and profit have come to play the role that religion played in our grandfather's generation." But more than that was happening. It was also in 1956 that the Negroes (as they were then called) in Montgomery, Alabama, were locked in a portentous struggle that would still be playing itself out a quarter of a century later. It started with the Negroes boycotting the local bus company because a weary black seamstress had refused to give her seat to a white man. Despite demands from the bus driver and the other passengers, Rosa Parks would not move. The local authorities

23

acted with their usual alacrity and arrested her. The next evening agitated Negroes met in the church of a minister unknown outside of Montgomery to plan a counterattack. They decided on a boycott, which became historic. So too did the minister, twenty-seven-year-old Martin Luther King, Jr.

• •

From self-absorbed Americans, the Suez crisis received comparatively little attention. It was viewed at the time as a foreign matter, involving Europeans and Arabs, Arabs and Israelis, with no obvious direct importance for American interests. The fact that the crisis was an ugly taint on the West's reputation reinforced the indifference, or at least the tendency to ignore it. Eisenhower and Dulles, recognizing its damage to the West's cause, did everything they could to divert attention away from the Suez crisis onto the Soviet's cruel behavior in Hungary. To a surprising degree, they were successful. In the public mind the Suez crisis remains dimly remembered. The period is still thought of in the United States primarily as the time of the Hungarian uprising.

Another reason for the crisis's continuing obscurity was the secrecy that surrounded it. The leading participants in the affair maintained a guilty silence about their scheming for many years. This was especially true of the British, who even a quarter of a century later were still censoring revelations about Suez. Before his death, Lord Louis Mountbatten, First Sea Lord of the Admiralty and a vigorous opponent within the confines of the government of Britain's part in the invasion, finally recorded his criticism for BBC-TV. He requested that the interview be shown only after his death. Mountbatten died tragically in 1979, but as of 1981 the government on one pretext or another has continued to prevent its showing.

The two top British officials involved, Prime Minister Anthony Eden, whose brilliant career would be ruined by the crisis, and Foreign Secretary Selwyn Lloyd, both went to their graves denying that there had been collusion. It was only eleven years after the event that a former British civil servant, Eden protégé Anthony Nutting, admitted in public that indeed Britain, France and Israel had actually ganged up on Egypt. By that time, much of the interest in the United States had long since dissipated and this turning point in history retreated farther into obscurity.

• •

The Suez crisis marked the end of Britain and France as world powers. The two countries entered the affair as colonial giants and emerged from it as faintly disrespectable second-raters. It was now America's turn; the United States was suddenly the superpower arbiter in the Middle East. After Suez, almost by default, the United States assumed, for better or worse, the preeminent position it occupies in the Middle East today.

PART ONE
THE FUSE

February 28, 1955, to December 13, 1955

CHAPTER I

Attackers Will Not Get Away Unpunished

BEN GURION

THERE IS LITTLE at first glance that is remarkable about the Gaza Strip. It is an unprepossessing five-by-twenty-five-mile enclave of sparkling beaches and palm trees, citrus groves, rolling sand dunes, and fields of grain and corn. It lies along the southeastern edge of the Mediterranean Sea astride the route that the great armies of the past trod over the centuries in the unending wars between Egypt and the peoples of the north: Persians, Macedonians, Greeks, Romans, Byzantines, Arabs, Turks, French and British. In the mid-1950s, it was at this little strip that a violent incident profoundly changed the Middle East and the world.

• •

The Gaza Strip protrudes like a probing finger into the southwestern side of Israel, a constant source of worry to Israelis because within its narrow confines was the densest concentration of Arab refugees in the Middle East. Crammed into dusty camps of mud huts with no running water and few comforts were 200,000 Palestinians, more than twice the number of indigenous Gazans, around 80,000, who had been living there before the 1948 war that resulted in the uprooting of the refugees and the creation of Israel. The refugees, resented by the Gazans, still led in 1955 a hand-to-mouth existence, as they had for the past seven years, unable usually to find work in the small strip, depending mainly on the good offices of the United Nations and charitable organizations for their survival. From their dingy camps the refugees could almost see their former homes and fields just across the heavily guarded armistice line in Israel.

29

Their homes were now occupied and their fields sown and harvested by Israelis, a galling and bitter vision.

The daily existence of the dispossessed Palestinians was as bleak as the hopeless future that stretched in front of them. Occasionally two or three of the more restless refugees screwed up their courage and slipped across the frontier into Israel to steal crops and livestock or pillage their former villages. Sometimes they sought revenge. Small gangs from time to time planted bombs and ambushed civilians. But such violence was rare along the Egyptian-Israeli armistice line, though its occasional occurrence was enough to cause tensions along the frontier to flare dangerously high at times.

During the first two months of 1955, tensions were in one of their troughs. It was a period of "comparative tranquility," reported Lieutenant General E. L. M. Burns, the chief of staff of the United Nations Truce Supervision Organization, UNTSO, and the highest-ranking U.N. official in the region.

There had been only four incidents during that period. The year's first came on January 21 when an Egyptian military patrol launched a surprise attack against an Israeli outpost manned by three soldiers. One Israeli was killed and two others wounded. On the same day armed infiltrators attacked two Israelis plowing their fields and killed one and wounded the other. Two of the Palestinians were killed. Eleven days later, an Israeli patrol and an Egyptian military position exchanged fire and one Israeli was wounded while one Egyptian soldier was killed and two others wounded. The only other incident in that period came on February 22 when another Israeli patrol and an Egyptian outpost engaged in a fire fight that left four Egyptian soldiers wounded. Then at the end of February the relative tranquillity was violently shattered.

• •

A crescent moon outlined the distinctive landmark, the slender minaret of a mosque. It marked the way for the Israeli paratroopers, their faces blackened by soot, who were stealthily snaking their way through the orange groves of the Gaza Strip that night of February 28. Their target was a small Egyptian army camp and railroad track on the northern outskirts of the town of Gaza, about two miles inside Egyptian territory. Their orders were to destroy the camp.

The paratroopers, about fifty in all, moved silently toward the camp. When it came into view, they began setting up mortars and machine guns, preparing for battle. Advance teams crawled up to the barbed wire at the perimeter and began quietly snipping the wire. Still others slipped long bangalore torpedoes under the wire, ready to blow passages through its entangling barbs when the attack began.

Though it was only 7 P.M., Private Ahmet Shabar and his squad were already asleep in their tent inside the base when a guard "felt that some strangers were around." The guard challenged them. The answer was rifle fire. Shabar and others, instantly awake and scrambling from the tent, returned the fire.

The Israelis attacked from three sides, blasting the camp with mortars, antitank rockets, hand grenades, machine guns and satchels of TNT. Paratroopers charged into the camp tossing hand grenades and firing their automatics as they ran. Grenades were hurled into the stationmaster's bedroom, wounding his nine-year-old son, and against another house where a seven-year-old boy was killed and his civilian father wounded. Ammunition stored in Private Shabar's tent caught fire and exploded. The wild exchange of fire lit up the night. Tents were burning and heavy explosions shook the ground. Nearly one hundred pounds of TNT were stacked against a stone building and detonated by the paratroopers, totally destroying it. The brick walls of four Nissen huts were blown up and as much as 150 pounds of TNT were used to level a concrete pump house.

From the south, Egyptian reinforcements headed toward the battle in a three-ton truck. Ahmed Mohammed Elisis, the driver, first heard machine-gun fire directed at the truck south of Gaza and then "something exploded on the right side of the road and made a smoke screen and a bright flame. I was unable to keep the truck on the road. The officer beside me was injured. I opened the door and pulled him out and we crawled [away]. I heard heavy machine-gun fire and explosions, then the truck started to burn."

The thirty-three soldiers in the truck desperately tried to escape the deadly Israeli ambush. But they had no chance. The Israelis poured machine-gun fire into the burning vehicle; flames touched off ammunition inside the truck. By the time rescuers could reach the site twenty-two of the Egyptians were dead. All the others were wounded or suffered burns.

Three hours after the start of the attack, the Israeli paratroopers began withdrawing, carrying their dead and wounded. They were guided by searchlights probing the night sky on the other side of the frontier inside Israel. They stumbled through the orange groves and fields, the wounded losing their equipment and leaving trails of blood. Their casualties were eight killed and nine wounded.

31

• •

Daylight disclosed a grisly sight. There were fifteen bodies in the camp and another nineteen persons who had suffered wounds. Pools of blood and gore littered the ground. In one trench, there was an unexploded block of TNT, an Egyptian uniform jacket with bloodstains and another bloody jacket containing a purse with Israeli money. Outside a burned-out tent were three bloody Egyptian caps with bits of brain, three large stains of blood and an empty ammunition parcel bearing Hebrew letters. Along a road were many pools of blood, parts of brain, a dead camel, burned vehicles, two Mills hand grenades and an unexploded bangalore torpedo with Hebrew letters, a 73mm bazooka shell, two kibbutz-type caps, a bloody field water bottle, dirty field dressings, an E. R. Squibb & Sons morphine needle and pieces of toffee marked "Ramat Gan Israel."

At the site where the truck was ambushed, the smoking hulk of the vehicle was riddled with bullet and shrapnel holes. Thirteen helmets had been shot through by bullets. The debris of battle equipment, most of it marked by Hebrew letters, was everywhere.

The tracks of the attackers were easily followed from the battle areas straight back to Israel.

• •

A group of United Nations observers made up of officers from Belgium, Denmark and Sweden condemned Israel in strong language for the attack. "We consider this shocking outrage of extreme gravity and a clear provocation to the Egyptian military forces. Israel must bear the consequences and full responsibility of . . . other aggressions." Though Israel maintained that the attack had only begun as a result of a running fire fight started by Arab infiltrators, the U.N. observers brushed the explanation aside. "This military warlike planned raid doubtless ordered by the Israel authorities shows Israel's complete disregard of the General Armistice Agreement," declared the observers.

General Burns agreed, and characterized the raid as a "prearranged and planned attack ordered by Israel authorities and committed by Israel Regular Army forces." He recommended that the Security Council strongly condemn Israel, which it did under a joint resolution sponsored by three of Israel's friendliest supporters, Britain, France and the United States.

"This was the most serious clash between Egypt and Israel since the armistice had been signed six years before," reported Burns. He was a cool professional soldier from Canada, commander of UNTSO's multinational force of military officers assigned by their various governments to help keep the peace in the region. UNTSO observers came from Europe (including the Soviet Union), and the United States, Africa and Asia, but no Israelis or Arabs were included in order to avoid biased reporting. The function of UNTSO was to watch over the frontiers of Israel with Egypt, Jordan, Lebanon and Syria, to investigate incidents and attempt to dampen tempers and prevent fighting. The effectiveness of their performance depended on their objectivity, and General Burns was a stickler in treating both sides with judicious fairness.

The Gaza raid, observed General Burns, "was a critical event in [the] dismal history" of the Middle East.

• •

The Gaza raid, the bloodiest incident between Egypt and Israel since the 1948 war, changed the nature of the Middle East. The raid helped propel the young and inexperienced leader of Egypt, Gamal Abdel Nasser, from a comparatively obscure lieutenant colonel into a hero of the Arab world. It touched off a desperate arms race between Egypt and Israel. And it transformed the Middle East from an area of parochial conflict between Arabs and Jews into an arena of superpower competition. With the Gaza raid, the countdown to war began.

• •

Nasser since coming to power two and a half years earlier had shown scant interest in the usual Arab expressions of hatred for Israel. When General Burns first met him November 15, 1954, he found the Egyptian leader absorbed by domestic problems. "He told me that it was his desire that there should be no trouble on the northeastern border of Egypt, no disturbances of the six years of quiescence of the armistice regime, no military adventures," recalled Burns. To *New York Times* correspondent Kennett Love, Nasser said: "We want peace in order to spend money that is now being devoted to defense on our economic and social projects."

The month before the raid, Nasser talked only of reforming Egyptian society to noted British Zionist Richard H. S. Crossman, a journalist and Labour member of Parliament. "The Israelis will destroy themselves if they go on spending 60 percent of their budget on armaments," Nasser said. "We are not going to make that mistake." Crossman, though very

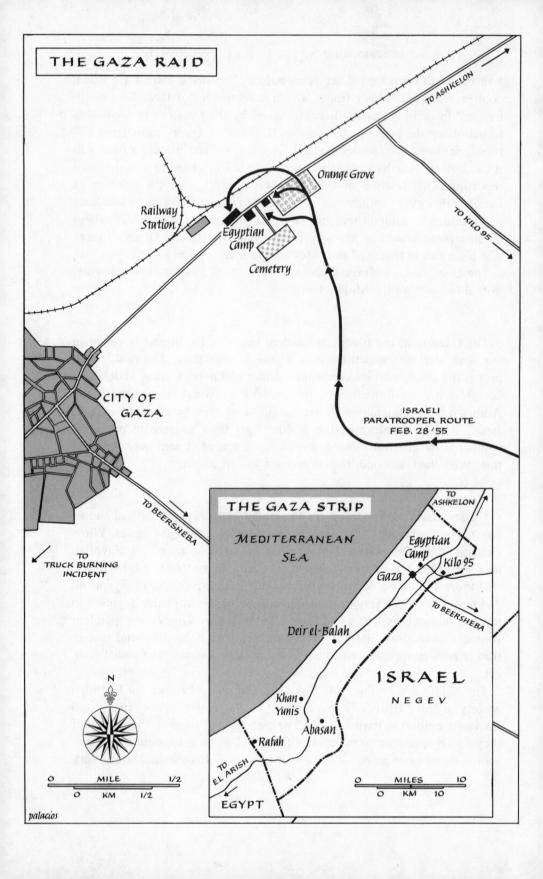

THE GAZA RAID

Railway Station

Orange Grove

Egyptian Camp

Cemetery

CITY OF GAZA

TO ASHKELON

TO KILO 95

ISRAELI PARATROOPER ROUTE FEB. 28 '55

TO BEERSHEBA

TO TRUCK BURNING INCIDENT

N

0 MILE 1/2
0 KM 1/2

palacios

THE GAZA STRIP

MEDITERRANEAN SEA

TO ASHKELON

Egyptian Camp

Kilo 95

Gaza

TO BEERSHEBA

Deir el-Balah

ISRAEL

NEGEV

Khan Yunis

Abasan

Rafah

TO EL ARISH

EGYPT

0 MILES 10
0 KM 10

partial to the Israeli cause, was much taken by the Egyptian leader. He ended his story for the *New Statesman* by expressing the hope that Nasser would survive in power because "so long as he is in power directing his middle-class revolution, Egypt will remain a factor for peace and social development."

• •

The effect of the 1955 raid on Nasser was dramatic. It frightened, humiliated and angered him. Only a few days before, he had visited the troops at Gaza and had assured them that there was no danger of war, that the demarcation line would remain as quiet in the future as it had been in the past. But, General Burns observed, "After that, many of them had been shot in their beds. Never again could he risk telling the troops they had no attack to fear; never again could he let them believe that they could relax their vigilance."

Nasser was faced with the legacy of shame that the Army suffered from the 1948 war when it was defeated by Israeli troops. Resentment then had centered on King Farouk because his corruption had denied the Army needed supplies; now Nasser was confronted by a similar resentment and demands for modern weapons. Before the raid he had been able to fend off requests by the Army for more weapons. Not now. "I made a big effort to convince them to be patient," Nasser told *The New York Times*. "There were assurances from the United States and the United Kingdom that everything would continue quiet. After Gaza, the position changed because reason was on the side of the Army."

The Gaza raid caused other changes in Nasser's policies. Within weeks he decreed that Palestinian volunteers from the Gaza Strip be organized into commando *fedayeen* (self-sacrifice) units for sabotage and terror operations inside Israel. He ordered the Regular Army to train and assist the units, and for the first time, to unleash commando operations against Israel that were fully backed by the might of the government. The day of the lone peasant out marauding for himself was over.

Nasser also made the momentous decision to change the top priority of his government from reforming Egypt's backward society to an urgent quest for weapons. Toward this end, he cast his eyes to Washington.

• •

For the man in the White House in 1955, the Middle East was low on his list of foreign concerns. Dwight D. Eisenhower had been elected two years earlier on his pledge to stop the war in Korea, and, though the fighting had stopped, numerous other problems in Asia demanded his attention, as did the affairs of Europe. But it was America's competitor for world leadership, the Soviet Union, that consumed the most time of Eisenhower and his secretary of state, John Foster Dulles. Both men were profoundly suspicious of the motives and intentions of Communism. The Cold War that had followed World War II was in thaw, but Eisenhower and Dulles still recognized the Soviet Union as the nation's deadliest enemy. Of all the non-Western countries, it was only Russia that possessed missiles and a nuclear arsenal great enough to threaten the United States.

Beside the Soviet Union and the potential lethal threats it posed, the Middle East was of only peripheral interest. Britain traditionally had been the major Western power in the region and it remained so in 1955. It had the greatest influence and was the region's largest supplier of weaponry. London still retained a crown colony in Aden and enjoyed exclusive relations with other states of the Persian Gulf, where it had kept a presence since the early seventeenth century. It maintained a massive military force in the region with troops stationed at bases in Aden, Cyprus, Egypt, Iraq and Libya, plus powerful naval and air units.

America's involvement in the region was minimal. It had profitable oil dealings with Saudi Arabia, Iraq and Kuwait, was warmly disposed toward Nasser in Egypt and gave sympathetic support to Israel. But beyond that it had little direct interest in Middle Eastern affairs. It was not dependent on the region's oil. "We felt that the British should continue to carry a major responsibility for its stability and security," recalled Eisenhower. "The British were intimately familiar with the history, traditions and peoples of the Middle East; we, on the other hand, were heavily involved in Korea, Formosa, Vietnam, Iran, and in this hemisphere."

The United States had prudently refrained from selling large weapons systems to any of the Middle Eastern countries, including Israel, though it sold token amounts to Egypt, Israel, Iraq, Lebanon and Saudi Arabia. Nor did Eisenhower and Dulles plan to sell large amounts. "By no means did we desire to become a main source of arms supply for the region," said Eisenhower. "Even less did we want to damage British influence there, though at times the British seemed suspicious that we did."

Eisenhower's contentment with Britain's leading role was not based totally on his friendly and close relations with Britain. Arms sales to the Middle East were a controversial political issue in Washington. If the United States sold weapons to Israel then the strategically important, oil-rich Arab nations would complain; if it sold to the Arabs, the powerful Jewish lobby and Israel's many American supporters would bring heavy political pressure on the Administration. Eisenhower's solution to this dilemma was typically pragmatic. He let the British do it.

． ．

Such common sense served as Eisenhower's trademark. He was widely regarded as a kindly grandfather figure, a bit inarticulate and above politics, a man who enjoyed golfing and trout fishing over the routine chores of running the government. He was indeed easily bored by political and bureaucratic bickering. But he was also a deceptively shrewd leader. For instance, his seeming inability to speak in whole sentences was more ruse than impediment, a weapon he used to great advantage in his weekly press conferences to avoid sensitive issues. He repeatedly revealed his cunning by remarking to his staff during preparation sessions for press conferences that "I will be evasive" or "Don't worry, if that question comes up I'll just confuse them." Once, when Secretary of State Dulles asked his advice about the wording for a statement on a touchy issue, Ike told him: "I want it so factual as to be uninteresting." In another matter, he ordered Dulles to word a message to a foreign government in "a sympathetic vein" but to keep the text general. "I don't, of course, want to be specific or say anything that might tie our hands later."

Far from being inarticulate, Eisenhower was a smooth writer. He graduated tenth in English in his West Point class of 1915 and before World War II served a tour as the speech writer for General Douglas MacArthur, whom he loathed for his pomposity. He personally edited important government statements and diplomatic messages, and on major speeches he spent an average of twenty to thirty hours reworking them for the right tone and content. But his seeming inarticulateness served him well, and he exploited it. He was able to brag in his memoirs that "by consistently focusing on ideas rather than on phrasing, I was able to avoid causing the nation a serious setback through anything I said in many hours, over eight years, of intensive questioning."

Eisenhower brought a similar combination of cunning and common sense to the other areas of his presidency, especially foreign affairs. His liberal views on tariffs, free trade and aid had less to do with political philosophy than his simple belief that such policies were in America's best interests. "One of the frustrating facts of my daily existence is the seeming inability of our people to understand our position and role in the world and what our own best interests demand of us," he wrote his old boyhood friend Everett E. ("Swede") Hazlett, one of the few men to share Eisenhower's intimate thoughts. "We must understand that our foreign expenditures are investments in America's future. No other nation is exhausting its irreplaceable resources so rapidly as is ours. Unless we are careful to build up and maintain a great group of international friends ready to trade with us, where do we hope to get all the materials that we will one day need as our rate of consumption continues and accelerates?"

He could not understand why such allies as France could not comprehend this transparent fact. "The French are fully capable of the most senseless action just to express their disagreement with others," he wrote Hazlett. "Their basic trouble is that they are still trying to act as if they headed a great empire, all of it, as of old, completely dependent on them." In his diary, he added: "The French—supposed to be our friends —have antagonized almost every Arab in North Africa and will probably be hated for centuries."

• •

The illusory image that the fifties was a period of placidity owed much to the calm and measured way in which Dwight Eisenhower conducted his presidency. Routine and orderliness characterized his Administration. He was in the Oval Office each morning around eight o'clock, took a leisurely lunch and nap in the Mansion, returned to his office in the afternoon and usually left before 6 P.M. He held a press conference weekly during which he addressed the nation's and the world's problems in moderate tones that reassured Americans. On Thursdays there was the meeting of the National Security Council and on Fridays the Cabinet. He presided at both. When Congress was in session, he met weekly with the legislative leaders. At various times during the week he met at least once with his budget experts and the secretary of defense. He and his secretary of state met or talked almost daily, and frequently more often. But if there was no immediate emergency, Ike did not hesitate to embark on a six-week vacation, or pop off to Georgia for some golf and quail shooting, or retire to the seclusion of his beloved farm in Gettysburg.

Eisenhower was an enormously popular President. The American people liked and trusted him, admired his accomplishments in rising from a modest Kansas childhood to become Supreme Commander, Allied Expeditionary Forces during World War II, and delighted in his folksy wisdom and firm control of the government. He was not without his weaknesses, but criticism that he failed to work at his presidential duties was not one of them. At times, it was true, he seemed almost too laid back, too casual and unconcerned, but this was as much a matter of style as of substance. "While I am often urged to be more assertive, to do a little more desk-pounding, to challenge Russia more specifically and harshly, I do not do these things for the simple reason that I think they are unwise," he once explained to a friend. "Possibly I do not always control my temper well, but I do succeed in controlling it in public. And I still believe that a frequent exhibition or a loss of temper is a sure sign of weakness."

Despite such sentiments, Ike had a notorious temper. When the Pentagon leaked a sensitive story to the press against Eisenhower's orders, he exploded to an aide: "I am going to tell [Defense Secretary Charles E.] Wilson this is intolerable and that if he does not do something about it I will take charge of the Defense Department myself!" But such displays of his temper were conducted in private, unobserved by his admiring public.

A shibboleth about Eisenhower's presidency was that he allowed his secretary of state to run the nation's foreign affairs with almost total independence. Nothing could have been further from the truth. Eisenhower kept Dulles on a short leash, though he did grant him considerable latitude in handling the department's day-to-day routine. But when it came to major issues or crises, it was Eisenhower who made the decisions.

Foster Dulles accepted this relationship, and he was careful to coordinate his actions with the President and take his lead from him. This constant consultation ranged over such petty matters as Dulles' seeking the President's permission to show memos to members of Congress to substantive subjects like clearing his speeches with Eisenhower before delivering them. Repeatedly Ike gave Dulles guidance, and even on occasion gently upbraided him about his gruff personality.

To his diary, the President confided: "He is not particularly persuasive in presentation and, at times, seems to have a curious lack of understanding as to how his words and manner may affect another personality. Personally, I like and admire him; my only doubts concerning him lie in the general field of personality, not in his capacity as a student of foreign affairs."

In Britain, where Dulles was never popular, Winston Churchill said that "Foster Dulles is the only case I know of a bull who carries his china shop with him."

39

During talks in Washington with Churchill and Anthony Eden in 1954, Eisenhower privately told Dulles that he had deduced from comments by Eden that the Britisher felt a lack of friendliness from Dulles. Ike advised his secretary of state that "by purely personal little things the matter could be helped." At other times, the President ordered Dulles "not to make the message sound disapproving" or that a message "seems a little cold."

The relationship between Dulles and Eisenhower was never a warm personal one. Dulles retained his high position wholly on the basis of Eisenhower's professional respect for him. Unlike such powerful secretaries of state as Cordell Hull or James Byrnes, Dulles had no personal power base; his only bid for one failed in 1949 when he ran for the U.S. Senate in New York and lost. Dulles was keenly aware that his power was reflective and that he served at the pleasure of the President. As a result, he was scrupulous in keeping Eisenhower minutely informed, and in paying homage to his master.

"You know that it is for us a great honor and privilege to serve you," he wrote Ike in a New Year's note. In another message, he told the President that during a European trip he had been impressed by the "high degree of affection and respect in which you are held by the peoples of Europe. They almost equal our own people in that regard—and that is saying something!"

Eisenhower was aware of course of the belief that he allowed Dulles to run the State Department as something of an independent duchy, and he scoffed at the idea. "No one, none of my Cabinet officials, made as much of an effort to keep in absolute concord as did Dulles," Eisenhower recalled. "He was insistent in knowing exactly what his mission and instructions were."

Dulles, at sixty-seven nearly three years older than Eisenhower, was so highly regarded by the President that early in the Administration he offered to appoint him the Chief Justice of the Supreme Court. Dulles declined, saying his whole life had been aimed at the goal he had achieved when he became secretary of state. Indeed, there did seem something almost predestined about Dulles' ascension to the nation's highest foreign policy position. His grandfather John Watson Foster had been secretary of state in 1892–93 during the last eight months of Benjamin Harrison's Administration, and his uncle, Robert Lansing, held the post under Woodrow Wilson from mid-1915 to 1920. Both men favored their scion with government assignments, providing the young Dulles with early diplomatic experience at the Second Hague Peace Conference in 1907, where he accompanied grandfather John, who was a delegate, and as a young U.S. attorney working on war reparations in Paris after World War I.

Thereafter he had immersed himself in the prestigious Wall Street law firm of Sullivan and Cromwell, where he quickly became a senior partner and head of the firm. He was also an active leader in the Presbyterian Church. The influences of the law and the church combined in Dulles to produce a peculiarly abstract coalescence of high morality and low politics. His 1939 book, *War, Peace and Change,* was judged by one critic to be remarkable mainly for its "high-minded impracticality."

But anyone who sat across the negotiating table from Dulles quickly realized that he was dealing with a formidable bargainer. His years as a highly successful international attorney had made him savvy in the ways of power and money, and he could read the fine print with the best of them. Eisenhower rated him unique in his "technical competence in the diplomatic field. He has spent his life in this work in one form or another, and is a man of great intellectual capacity and moral courage."

Others, experiencing his talents for cold calculation, were more impressed with his nimbleness in the art of realpolitik. Abba Eban, Israel's ambassador to the United States at the time, found him a "complex personality [who] was able to pass from moral elevation to an extraordinary deviousness and back again with little visible transition." His major biographer, Townsend Hoopes, concluded that he had "titanic energy, iron determination and a tactical guile that did not hesitate to mislead and manipulate his allies."

For all his moralistic pronouncements, Dulles did not hesitate to use every subterfuge of the intelligence community to achieve his goals. He was an avid supporter of covert operations by the Central Intelligence Agency, a pursuit that was facilitated by the fact that the agency was headed by his brother, Allen Welsh Dulles. This highly unusual arrangement came about at the start of the Eisenhower Administration when Allen was sworn in as director of the CIA less than two months after Foster took over the State Department. Their dual appointments meant that the two brothers controlled between them America's two most powerful foreign policy establishments.

Allen, four years younger than Foster, was nearly his opposite in personality. He was an easygoing bon vivant who enjoyed good food and wine and had a twinkle in his eye for the ladies. But behind his pipe-smoking, relaxed exterior, he could be every bit as cold and manipulative as his brother. He spent his early career in the State Department's foreign service and as an attorney in Sullivan and Cromwell, but it was as a dashing and highly successful agent for the Office of Strategic Services, the forerunner of the CIA, that he earned his reputation in World War II as one of the nation's great spies.

The Dulles brothers came naturally to their fascination with intelligence matters. It was their uncle, Robert Lansing, who established the first Bureau of Secret Intelligence in the State Department when he was secretary of state in 1916. Over the years between the world wars the Dulles brothers had maintained a loose relationship with U.S. military intelligence, aiding an occasional operation with their high legal and social contacts. In the first two years of the Eisenhower Administration, the brothers, with Eisenhower's consent, conspired in the successful overthrow of Mohammed Mossadegh in Iran and Jacobo Arbenz in Guatemala. "When Foster Dulles couldn't get his way through diplomacy," recalled one of the CIA's top operatives, Kermit Roosevelt, "he turned to the CIA to get it." The brothers worked closely and well together, with Allen out of lifetime habit always deferring to his older brother. This unique relationship gave the CIA greater influence in the upper echelons of the State Department than it ever enjoyed before or since. It was a dangerously unhealthy situation, that contributed to the agency's later abuses.

Foster's best friend was his adoring wife, Janet. They were a self-sufficient couple who had a close relationship that not even the births of three children, two sons and a daughter, were allowed to interfere with. The children were reared by a nanny and later recalled that they grew up feeling their father's world consisted first of his wife, his work, his brother and sister Eleanor, and only last themselves. But Janet saw no faults in him. When she was once asked whether she would help in a biography of him, "warts and all," she replied coolly: "What warts?"

"He knew that if he wasn't right in his opinions on life, he was as right as he could be, and as right as most people he knew," recalled Eleanor. "He had few doubts. He was sure of himself in everything he did. He knew he was a good lawyer. He knew he was a good sailor. He knew he was a good husband."

• •

Dulles presided over the State Department like a patriarch. His handsome office was dominated by two oil paintings, those of his family's two previous secretaries of state. On his spacious desk, near his left hand, lay his well-read Bible. Nearby was Josef Stalin's *Problems of Leninism,* a copy of the Charter of the United Nations and *The Federalist*. He was in the habit of giving new envoys to America *The Federalist* with the explanation that it would help them to understand the country better.

He had been a strong supporter of Israel at its creation, and a force in winning entry into the United Nations for the new state. But over the years of conflict in the Middle East his support cooled and by the time he became secretary of state, in 1953, he was convinced that the preceding Truman Administration had "gone overboard in favor of Israel." A more evenhanded policy was needed in the Middle East, he believed. Eisenhower agreed.

It was in the name of evenhandedness that the Eisenhower Administration refused to sell large amounts of weapons to either Israel or the Arab states. This arrangement was acceptable to supporters of Israel in 1955 because at the time the Jewish state was stronger than any of its Arab neighbors. "There was no question that, should war break out between Israel and Egypt, the latter would be decisively defeated," observed Eisenhower.

But, to the distress of Israeli officials, Eisenhower and Dulles extended their evenhanded policy in arms supplies to other aspects of the Middle East. Dulles traveled to the region in May 1953, only to discover, apparently somewhat to his surprise, that the Arabs were "more fearful of Zionism than of the Communists." That was not welcome news to the new secretary of state, who saw his top priority as the containment of Communism around the globe. Dulles reported on his return to Washington that the Arabs suspected "the United States will back the new state of Israel in aggressive expansion. Our basic political problem . . . is to improve the Moslem states' attitudes toward the Western democracies because our prestige in that area had been in constant decline ever since the war."

Dulles was determined to shatter the Arab suspicion that America leaned over backward to support Israel at the expense of the Arab world. He did not have long to wait for a chance. Shortly after his visit to Tel Aviv, Israel began moving its government offices from that seafront city to Jerusalem. Dulles protested that the move violated the 1947 U.N. Partition Plan, which recognized Jerusalem as an international city to which neither Jews nor Arabs could claim sovereignty. But Israel ignored the warning. The move to Jerusalem continued despite the fact that no nation recognized the city as Israel's capital. Dulles' protests proved useless.

He determined that he would be tougher the next time. When Israel defied U.N. entreaties to stop work on a hydroelectric project that was diverting waters of the Jordan River away from Arab lands, Dulles acted decisively. He ordered U.S. aid stopped. Dulles' peremptory action stunned Israel, which had become used to kid-glove treatment from the Democratic Administration of Harry S. Truman. But despite pleas from Tel Aviv and political pressure from the Jewish lobby, Dulles and Eisenhower refused to relent. Aid remained suspended for more than a month, until October 28, 1953, which was the day after Israel finally caved in and abandoned its ill-conceived project.

The policy of evenhandedness caused other jolts in Israel and made increasingly tense the relationship between the two countries. Relations soured severely in 1954 after Israeli forces attacked the Jordanian town of Nahalin and killed nine and wounded nineteen civilians. The State Department strongly condemned the attack in a speech by Henry Alfred Byroade, the assistant secretary of state for Near Eastern, South Asian and African affairs. He warned Israel shortly after the March 28, 1954, raid to "drop the attitude of conqueror and the conviction that force and a policy of retaliatory killings is the only policy that your neighbors will understand. You should make your deeds correspond to your frequent utterances of the desire for peace."

Byroade followed that on May 1 with a tough warning that Israel should not contemplate engaging in a war of expansion. The Arabs, Byroade declared, "should have the right to know the magnitude of this new state. Their fears are enhanced by the knowledge that the only limitation imposed by statute on immigration into Israel is, in fact, the total number of those of the Jewish faith in the entire world. They see only one result—future attempt at territorial expansion—and hence warfare of serious proportion."

Byroade's harsh warning caused consternation in Israel, but no revision in its policies nor any efforts to define the limits of the Jewish state. This was a serious misreading of Washington's new attitude. Byroade's words were not empty rhetoric. His views accurately mirrored the conclusions of a top-secret State Department study, completed the previous October 29, that outlined the grave problems facing Israel. The study found that Israel was in a deep crisis because "too many people have been admitted too rapidly into a country which possesses almost no natural resources. Whether it will ever be possible to develop a viable economy in Israel is very uncertain." Yet, the study noted, Israel was actively encouraging the Ingathering of the Exiles and Israel's prime minister, David Ben Gurion, had spoken of a target number of two million more immigrants on top of Israel's current population of two million.

"This unrealistic approach can only lead to further economic and financial difficulties and will probably result in additional pressure to expand Israel's frontiers into the rich lands of the Tigris and Euphrates valleys, and northward into the settled lands of Syria," said the study.

"There is a considerable element in the Army, the government, and among the people who feel that the only solution to Israel's problems is territorial expansion. As economic pressure rises, this group is likely to increase in numbers. The situation is serious both for the security of the Near East and for the future of the new state."

By their actions, Eisenhower and Dulles indicated their agreement with the study's general conclusions. But they failed to take into account the special circumstances of Israel, which made it a unique nation of the driven and the persecuted.

• •

The heart of Zionism and the whole reason for the existence of the Jewish state were to provide a haven for the wandering Jew. Despite such worries as expressed in the State Department study, there was no chance that Israel would close its door to Jewish immigrants. Neither Western criticism nor economic distress could bring that about. Immigration was the one subject on which most Israelis generally agreed. Without it, the raison d'être of the state ceased to exist. As Ben Gurion said: "Who is willing and capable of guaranteeing that what happened to us in Europe will not recur? Can the conscience of humanity . . . absolve itself of all responsibility for that holocaust? There is only one security guarantee: a homeland and a state."

Ben Gurion demanded that the gates be thrown open to all Jewish immigrants, and they were. In 1949, 239,576 arrived, nearly a third of the number of Jews already living there. Within four years, 686,748 immigrants had crowded into the tiny country less than the size of New Jersey; with natural increase, the population had soared by 120 percent by 1954.

At first the largest groups came from Eastern Europe, Poland, Russia and Rumania, just as had the early Zionists since the turn of the century. These modern immigrants were the survivors of the horrors of the holocaust seeking refuge and safety and, most of all, a homeland of their own. But then came a new wave of immigrants that the early Zionists had barely even considered in their dreams of populating the Holy Land, the Oriental Jews. Zionism had passed them by, as the centuries had, and World War II had touched them no more than it had the Arabs. But still they came, goaded by rising Arab suspicions, wanderlust and the whispers of Israeli agents who held out the hope of the Promised Land against the fear of Arab persecution.

"Half of the population is now composed of Oriental Jews, many of them near-primitive savages from darkest Arabia who had never sat down to a table," *Time* magazine reported in the mid-1950s. Jews from Europe (Ashkenazim) and from the Orient (Sephardim) were as different in background, education, manner, looks and religious observance as peoples from two different cultures. Those differences thrust as great a challenge on the leaders of Israel as any they faced from the hostility of the surrounding Arabs.

David Ben Gurion was determined to integrate this disparate mass of persecuted mankind from 70 different countries into a unified society. One of the major tools he used was his controversial reprisal policy. In response to any Arab attack, and often even at the mere suspicion of a planned attack, the country hit back with overwhelming force. The policy was bloody and brutal, and brought on Israel frequent international condemnation. But Ben Gurion believed it was the only effective way to protect the Jewish homeland and homogenize its immigrant citizens.

In defending the policy, Ben Gurion cited two reasons. The first, he told his biographer, Michael Bar-Zohar, was the obvious one: deter Arab aggression. "But there's a further reason, an educational and moral reason," added the prime minister. "Look at these Jews. They come from Iraq, from Kurdistan, from North Africa. They come from countries where their blood was unavenged, where it was permissible to mistreat them, torture them, beat them. They have grown used to being helpless victims. Here we have to show them that the Jewish people has a state and an Army that will no longer permit them to be abused. We must straighten their backs and demonstrate that those who attack them will not get away unpunished, that they are citizens of a sovereign state which is responsible for their lives and their safety."

The 1955 Gaza raid was a product of Ben Gurion's policy.

• •

Eisenhower did not believe Ben Gurion's reprisal policy was either right or efficacious and he did not hesitate to condemn its bloody results. Thus he ordered the State Department to join with France and Britain in introducing the resolution condemning Israel for the Gaza raid. He thought the raid, like others by Israel, had been carried out with "merciless severity."

The resolution caused Eisenhower political discomfiture at home, but he continued to believe strongly that the U.S. had to be perceived as a fair and unbiased broker to be influential in the region. He explained his thinking during a telephone call to Foster Dulles on March 16, shortly before the Security Council action. When border raids occur in the Middle East, he told Dulles, "the U.S. is not unilaterally going to determine who is at fault, but wait for some kind of adjudication by the U.N. and then merely do its part." But, he added, "In a general conflict, the U.S. would follow its traditional policy of supporting the aggrieved side and oppose aggression.

"I'm astonished that this could be misunderstood since we've said it several times."

Dulles agreed. "We have accepted the authority of the Tripartite Declaration of the U.K., France and the U.S. that said, 'If there were aggression in the area, we would take action both within and without the U.N. to stop aggression and to support the aggrieved side.' "

"Yes," Eisenhower said emphatically. "But it does not necessarily mean we would put arms in."

• •

Though Eisenhower and Dulles still considered the Middle East a sideshow in America's strategic interests, they were soon to be forced to change their minds. The demand for arms, by Egypt and soon Israel too, was about to make the Middle East the latest area for superpower competition.

CHAPTER II

Helpless and Utterly Depressed

SHARETT

THE GAZA RAID was David Ben Gurion's way of saying he had returned to power in Israel. The aging father of modern Israel had been in desert retirement for the previous year, growing increasingly impatient and pessimistic about the abilities of his successor, Moshe Sharett. For a half century Ben Gurion had fought in the cause of Zionism, and for the first five turbulent years of Israel's existence he had led the nation by a combination of charisma, mystical Zionism, vigor, and enormous determination. He was a wrathful visionary, intolerant of small talk, humorless and hot-tempered, brusque and bullying. More than any individual, Ben Gurion symbolized the vitality and the dreams of Israel, and some of its darker sides too. With his large head, wreathed by an unruly white mane, and his gnarled, stubby-legged body, he looked and often acted like an Old Testament patriarch.

By the autumn of 1953, at sixty-seven years of age, Ben Gurion was worn and drained and, like the prophets of old, he had decided to retire and live in the desert. But he was hesitant to turn over the government to his old colleague Sharett, who since the birth of Israel had been foreign minister. Ben Gurion considered him too weak, too ready to compromise. Force had to be used to demonstrate to the Arabs that Israel was in the Middle East to stay, Ben Gurion believed, and to that end he felt strongly that his retaliatory policy had to be continued. He was resentfully aware that Sharett did not fully share his belief in the efficacy of retaliation, yet it was Sharett who was to succeed him. As his last major act before retiring, the crusty prime minister approved a large, symbolic

48

raid against the Arabs. This one was aimed at Jordan and its small Palestinian village of Qibya, near Tel Aviv, which was suspected of harboring terrorists. A special commando force called Unit 101 had been formed several months earlier under the command of flamboyant Ariel ("Arik") Sharon specifically for such tasks. It was in effect a government-sponsored terror unit, the same one that would carry out the Gaza raid sixteen months later.

The commandos wore neither uniforms nor badges of rank, and they used only weapons that were not Regular Army issue. The purpose was to maintain the fiction that they were not soldiers. This unusual arrangement made it easier for Israel to deny after a raid that the government had been involved. Foreign governments were less incensed by vigilante raids because emotions in the area were so raw that the local government could persuasively argue that it was helpless to prevent every individual act of terror.

Sharon led his commando unit of several hundred men against Qibya at 9:30 P.M. on October 14, 1953. After a brief skirmish in which several Jordanian soldiers were killed, the commandos moved through the town firing their rifles and tossing hand grenades into homes. Panic erupted among the villagers, many of whom were already in bed. Families fled through the streets seeking the safety of nearby villages; many others sought safety under their beds. Soon the shooting stopped and all was dark and quiet, the only sounds the tread of the troopers' heavy nailed boots and the ululation of an Oriental tune coming from a radio in a deserted café. But the raid was not over. The commandos had brought with them twelve hundred pounds of explosives and they now began systematically blowing up homes. Their work took them until 4:30 A.M.

At dawn, the first U.N. military observers arrived at the massacre. In a report to the Security Council, they described the gruesome scene. "Bullet-riddled bodies near the doorways and multiple bullet hits on the doors of the demolished houses indicated that the inhabitants had been forced to remain inside until their homes were blown up over them. Witnesses were uniform in describing their experience as a night of horror, during which Israeli soldiers moved about in their village blowing up buildings, firing into doorways and windows with automatic weapons and throwing hand grenades."

Sixty-six villagers were killed in the attack, nearly three-quarters of them women and children; another seventy-five suffered wounds and severe injuries. Forty-five homes were left in rubble.

Sharon later explained disingenuously that he thought all of the vil-

49

lagers had fled before he ordered the homes destroyed. In fact, most of the deaths occurred when the cowering victims were buried in the debris of their demolished houses.

. .

The Qibya raid was as important inside Israel as the later Gaza raid was to be to the whole of the Middle East. Sharett, who as acting prime minister had opposed the Qibya raid, was alienated from Ben Gurion by it. He was heartsick when he learned of the death toll. "This reprisal is unprecedented in its dimensions and in the offensive power used," he recorded in his diary. "I walked up and down in my room, helpless and utterly depressed by my feeling of impotence. I was simply horrified by Radio Ramallah's broadcast of the destruction of the Arab village. I must underline that when I opposed the action I didn't even remotely suspect such a bloodbath.

"Now the Army wants to know how we [at the Foreign Ministry] are going to explain the issue. I condemned the Qibya affair that exposed us in front of the whole world as a gang of bloodsuckers, capable of mass massacres regardless, it seems, of whether their actions may lead to war. I warned that this stain will stick to us and will not be washed away for many years to come."

Ben Gurion told Sharett that he would go on national radio and explain that the Army was not involved in the slaughter. He would claim it was caused by outraged settlers. "I said that no one in the world will believe such a story and we shall only expose ourselves as liars," noted Sharett in his diary. "But I couldn't seriously demand that the communiqué explicitly affirm the Army's responsibility because this would have made it impossible to condemn the act and we will have ended up approving this monstrous bloodbath."

. .

U.N. observers reported that the raid had been carried out "by a force approximately one half of a battalion from the Israeli Regular Army," but Ben Gurion nonetheless went through with his denial. He spoke on national radio five days later and boldly labeled the U.N. report an "absurd and fantastic allegation." He insisted that the raid had been the work of frontier settlers, "mostly Jewish refugees from Arab countries or survivors of Nazi concentration camps." He declared that frontier settlers had been infuriated by the killings two days before the raid of an Israeli woman and her two children by a hand grenade that was thrown into their home in Tirat Yehuda, presumably by an Arab. But the story did not wash. A raid the size of Qibya obviously could not have been mounted in two days, the U.N. observers reported to the Security Council.

· ·

The Qibya raid symbolized Ben Gurion's rule and touched off cries of condemnation both outside and within Israel. Winston Churchill, a friend of Israel's, personally sent a protest to Ben Gurion. The U.N. Security Council roundly condemned Israel in a unanimous resolution and urged the country to take "vigorous measures to prevent the recurrence of such aggression." John Foster Dulles admonished Israel to display a "decent respect for the opinion of mankind."

But such protests and warnings ignored the national imperatives, as seen by Ben Gurion and his supporters, in Israel in the mid-1950s. The Jews were a majority inside Israel, yet outside of those narrow confines there was a sea of Arabs. In Ben Gurion's eyes, they had to be taught that Israel was an enduring nation, just as the mismatched assortment of Diaspora Jews flocking to the new country had to be made to realize that they no longer were a minority. It was a new experience—the days of persecution were over. Israel was again the land of the Jews, a proud and independent people who had to suffer no more the discrimination of the ghetto or the horrors of the holocaust.

It was in that spirit of assertive independence that the *Jerusalem Post,* an influential Jewish daily published in English, responded to the U.N.'s urging that Israel take vigorous measures to prevent another Qibya. "It would be no cynicism to say that Israel has in fact already taken the vigorous measures required," the newspaper noted smugly.

· ·

Eisenhower deplored Israel's fear-inspired hostility toward the Arabs. He had first detected the attitude when two young Israelis called on him years earlier at the time he was chief of staff of the Army after World War II and they were in search of U.S. weapons. He recalled the moment in his diary while he was President and Israel was complaining about Arab hostility. "The two of them belittled the Arabs in every way. They cited the ease with which the Turkish Empire was dismembered following World War I and in spite of talk about a holy war the Arabs, due to their laziness, shiftlessness, lack of spirit and low morale, did nothing. They boastfully claimed that Israel needed nothing but a few defensive arms,

51

and they would take care of themselves forever and without help of any kind from the United States.

"I told them they were mistaken—that I had talked to many of the Arab leaders, and I was certain they were stirring up a hornet's nest and if they could solve the initial question peacefully and without doing unnecessary violence to the self-respect and interests of the Arabs, they would profit immeasurably in the long run.

"I would like to see those young Israelites today."

• •

Long after the tempest of the 1953 Qibya raid settled down, Ben Gurion admitted to a friend that he had indeed lied about the identity of the raiders. He said he had been afraid if it had become known that they were soldiers then the country would have suffered in the international community, so he had to lie. He tried to explain by way of analogy.

"Have you read Victor Hugo's *Les Misérables?*" Ben Gurion asked his friend. "There's a description in the book of the wanted prisoner's flight from the officer pursuing him. He hides in a room where a nun is seated. The police officer enters the room and asks the nun: 'Have you seen the prisoner?' and she answers: 'No.' Never doubting her word, he leaves the room without conducting a search. As for the nun, she committed no sin in lying because her lie was designed to save human life. A lie like that is measured by a different yardstick."

Sharett did not agree. He confided to his wife, Zipporah: "I would have resigned if it had fallen to me to step before a microphone and broadcast a fictitious account of what happened [at Qibya] to the people of Israel and the whole world."

• •

The raid against Qibya and Ben Gurion's prevarications about it lacerated beyond repair the strained relations between him and Moshe Sharett. It was a fatal split, not only between two men but between the divergent views they represented on how to find peace in the Middle East. It was a rift that resulted in Ben Gurion's fiery vision overwhelming Israel's moderate voices, and it led directly to war.

Ben Gurion and Sharett embodied the struggle in Israel between the voices for unbending Old Testament militancy and those of conciliation. The two men had arrived in Palestine in 1906 from different parts of Eastern Europe and had toiled closely together for establishment of the Zionist state, but by the time of the 1953 Qibya raid they had grown as wide apart as the meanings of their self-chosen Hebrew names. David Gruen of czarist Poland picked Ben Gurion, son of lion; Moshe Shertok of the Ukraine chose Sharett, servant. When Ben Gurion became prime minister at the founding of the new state on May 14, 1948, Sharett became the foreign minister.

The Foreign Ministry was a post for which the mild-mannered intellectual was well suited. Sharett was a gentle man who spoke seven languages and displayed a cautious concern about world opinion and the goodwill of the United Nations. He epitomized the view that "without the U.N. resolution [to form the state of Israel] the state would not have come into being." To which Ben Gurion replied: "The state of Israel exists solely due to the people of Israel, and primarily, due to the Army."

During another argument between the two of them over the importance of having world support, Ben Gurion declared that "our future depends, not on what the *goyim* [non-Jews] say, but on what the Jews do!" Sharett's response: "Correct. But it is also important what the *goyim* do!"

. .

On December 14, 1953, Ben Gurion and his wife, Paula, set out for the tiny kibbutz of Sdeh Boker, in the central Negev desert to begin their life in retirement. During his fourteen months on the kibbutz, Ben Gurion worked as a regular member, plowing, spreading manure and shepherding. The great and the humble journeyed into the desert to call on him, and they found that the pastoral experience had not increased his tolerance of small talk or tamed his temper. Burma's prime minister, U Nu, paid a visit and Ben Gurion avidly engaged him in a discussion of Buddhism. Afterward Ben Gurion snapped: "The man knows nothing about Buddhism."

When he was not shepherding, Ben Gurion indulged himself in his passion, philosophy, reading Spinoza, the Greeks, Buddhist writings and, of course, the Torah. He also kept up a lively correspondence, repeatedly assuring the many Israelis who beseeched him to return to government that he was "happy and content. . . . It is possible to help in building up the country not only by standing at the head of the government." But what he saw transpiring under Sharett's leadership caused him deep concern.

Shortly after the start of 1954, there occurred a series of shocks and setbacks for Israel. In January, reports began circulating that the United States was considering selling weapons to the pro-Western government of Iraq, the only Arab belligerent that had not signed an armistice with

53

Israel. The very next month Iraqi officials began meeting with their counterparts from Turkey and Pakistan for talks about forming a "northern tier" defense pact against the Soviet Union. The talks were aimed at the creation of the American inspired and British-sponsored Baghdad Pact, which Israel violently opposed, since it would make its Arab members eligible for Western weaponry.

In March, the Soviet Union signaled that the brief thaw in its relations with Israel following Josef Stalin's death in 1953 was over. An Israeli demand that the U.N. Security Council direct Egypt to lift its ban against Israeli shipping using the Suez Canal was vetoed by Russia. Egypt had kept the canal closed to Israeli flag ships since 1948 and, despite a U.N. resolution and urgings from the West, continued to maintain the prohibition under the fiction that the two countries were still technically at war despite their armistice. The Egyptians claimed they were justified in ignoring the U.N.'s call because the Jewish state had ignored repeated General Assembly resolutions ordering Tel Aviv to let the 750,000 refugees created by the 1948 war return to their homes inside Israel.

Also in March, on the seventeenth, came more violence. Israel was rocked by its worst massacre since the 1949 armistices. A busload of Israeli vacationers was ambushed at Scorpion Pass in the Negev and eleven civilians were killed and two wounded. The nation demanded retribution. But there was no clear evidence of who had committed the atrocity. The Israeli-Jordanian Mixed Armistice Commission, which was headed by a senior U.N. officer and charged with investigating truce violations, uncovered some evidence that the killings had been done by a gang of Bedouins venting its anger over Israel's forceful expulsion of seven thousand nomads and the closing of their traditional grazing routes across the Negev.* The commission was unable to reach a unanimous finding on the identity of the Scorpion Pass culprits.

Suspicions in Israel centered on Jordan, and national outrage demanded revenge. Despite pleas from U.N. Secretary-General Dag Hammarskjold and John Foster Dulles for Israel to refrain from reprisal, the emotional uproar was too much for Sharett to ignore. He acceded to the near-hysterical popular mood, and on March 28 Israeli night fighters were

---

* The expulsion occurred in the demilitarized zone at El Auja in July 1950 and was carried out "often with great brutality," according to journalist Earl Berger, who lived in Israel in the mid-1950s and was sympathetic to the Zionist cause. "Planes and army personnel carried out the operation, driving the Bedouins before them. Tents, livestock, crops, and possessions were burned." The Israeli action had been taken in the name of security, but the effect on the nomadic tribesmen was to render them destitute.

again on the prowl. They struck Nahalin, and killed nine civilians. It was the only major retaliatory raid during the period of Sharett's premiership.

. .

Far surpassing all other setbacks for Israel during 1954 were the increasing power and popularity of Gamal Abdel Nasser, the leader of the strongest Arab state. Nasser, who was then thirty-six, was making impressive gains in his dealings with the Western powers and in consolidating his rule in Egypt. His relations with the United States were amicable, and with Washington's help he was well on his way toward scoring a historic achievement. His goal was no less than bringing about the removal of all British troops from Egyptian soil for the first time since 1882.

Approximately eighty thousand British troops were stationed on a huge base along the Suez Canal, a source of angry resentment to Egyptians and of considerable contentment to Israel, which regarded the Britishers as a deterrent to an Egyptian attack across the canal. The base sprawled ninety miles along the canal and stretched at points as much as sixty miles westward. During World War II, the base had been the largest staging area in North Africa when it supported fifteen divisions, sixty-five air squadrons and the Royal Navy fleet in the eastern Mediterranean and employed 200,000 Egyptians.

But now, except as a bolster to the imperial illusions of old colonialists in Britain, the base had lost its strategic importance in a world dominated by nuclear weapons. Whatever tactical advantages it retained were negated by fierce Egyptian resentment that manifested itself by terrorists' attacks, sabotage and pilfering. The British responded by enforcing tough security measures against Egyptians. Tensions were so great over the continued presence of the British troops in Egypt that Cairo had sealed off the base from all commercial transactions, sequestering the bored and restless troops inside amidst an alien and angry population.

Despite its marginal importance, the pretensions of empire cast the Suez base into the forefront of the colonialists' imagination. A group of Conservatives in Britain led by Captain Charles Waterhouse and Julian Amery and known as the "Suez Group" ardently campaigned against surrendering the base. Amery thought that Britain had already gone too far in surrendering bases in the Middle East. "We should have held Haifa and the Holy Places and from there guaranteed Israeli and Arab frontiers," declared an unrepentant Amery even a decade later to Hugh Thomas, a distinguished historian of the period. "Hadn't the withdrawal from India been based on the assumption we would stay in Egypt?"

But Eisenhower actively pushed Britain to remove its troops. "I believed that it would be undesirable and impracticable for the British to retain sizable forces permanently in the territory of a jealous and resentful government amid an openly hostile population," he recalled. "Therefore, Secretary Dulles and I encouraged the British . . . gradually to evacuate."

Talks between Britain and Egypt had first begun on April 17, 1953, but soon sputtered to a halt over such issues as the rate of withdrawal of the British troops and the conditions under which they might return. But by the winter of 1954, the excessive costs of the base and its essential impotence in a nuclear age had convinced even Churchill, who opposed a "scuttle" from Egypt, that it was an anachronism. He admitted to a friend that "not even a single soldier is in favor of staying there." New negotiations soon got under way.

• •

Israel was distressed at the prospect of the withdrawal negotiations succeeding. It would mean that the protective shield of British troops along the canal between Israel's and Egypt's major forces would be withdrawn and Nasser's popularity and strength would be greatly enhanced. That was not a prospect that the struggling Jewish nation relished. To prevent it, Aman, Israel Military Intelligence, concocted a devious scheme—without informing Sharett—to launch a secret operation against American and British installations in Egypt. The aim was to make the sabotage appear the work of Egyptian fanatics and thus show that Nasser's government was so fragile that it could not guarantee the operation of the Suez Canal if the British withdrew.

Aman chose a former army officer to head the operation. He was Abraham Seidenwerg, known as Avri Elad, a handsome Austrian-Israeli, twenty-seven years old, blond and blue-eyed, who carried a German passport, and already was stationed in Cairo passing as a former Nazi SS officer and the representative of a German electrical appliance firm. In fact, he was a shifty, dishonored former Israeli major who had been stripped of his rank when he was accused of stealing Arab property. He was out of work and divorced in 1952 when Aman hired him for its sabotage department called Unit 131, trained him for a year and sent him to Cairo in December 1953 under the name Paul Frank. As Frank, Elad quickly became known in Cairo's German colony as a dashing businessman. His actual duties were to track down former Nazis who had escaped to Egypt.

Elad's operation was activated by a message broadcast on July 9, 1954, over the Voice of Israel radio show "For the Housewife." The signal was a recipe for English cake and it meant that the time was ripe for Elad to launch his agents against American and British targets. Within five days, Elad's cell of four agents firebombed U.S. cultural and information centers in Cairo and Alexandria. Damage was slight and there were no injuries, but the attacks were numerous enough to draw the attention of the news media and Egyptian security authorities.

Elad, pleased with the attacks, ordered a new round on July 23, the start of a long holiday weekend celebrating the second anniversary of the Nasser revolution. Police and firemen patrolled the streets, alert for trouble from the religious fanatics of the Moslem Brotherhood, the Communists and other foes of the regime. Incendiary devices were successfully planted by the Israeli saboteurs in Cairo's main railway station and at the entrances of two cinemas. Two other cinemas, both British-owned, were targeted for Alexandria. As one of the agents, Philippe Nathanson, twenty-one, approached the Rio Cinema, the phosphorus bomb hidden in his spectacles case ignited prematurely and set his clothes afire. A police captain smothered the fire and soon discovered its cause: the remains of charred chemicals inside the blackened eyeglass case. Nathanson was briefly treated at a hospital and then taken to Atarin police station for questioning. A raid on his apartment uncovered a photo lab and hundreds of negatives, including some with instructions received when he attended an Israeli spy school in 1952–53.

The police moved quickly and arrested all four saboteurs, plus seven other alleged Israeli spies who had no direct connection with the operation.

While the spies were being questioned, Avri Elad calmly concluded his affairs, sold his convertible auto and flew out of Egypt on August 6. His leisurely departure raised suspicions in Tel Aviv, but for the moment he remained free.

• •

In Israel, Prime Minister Sharett, unaware of the sabotage operation, had watched the progress of the withdrawal talks with trepidation. He shared the concerns about the negative implications of such an agreement for Israel's security. But he was especially distraught that the talks were proceeding without apparent concern for Israeli interests. He thought that at the least Israel might be able to salvage some advantage out of the talks by getting Egypt to agree to open the Suez Canal to Israeli shipping.

Egypt's action was economically damaging to Israel, and its additional closure of the Straits of Tiran on the Red Sea compounded the injury. The straits controlled traffic to Elath, the only Israeli opening to the Indian Ocean and Asia. As Moshe Dayan, already Israel's most glorified soldier and who in 1954 was appointed chief of staff of the Army at the age of thirty-eight, noted in his diary: "The closure of the waterways amounted to a blockade which was not only a front political issue for Israel but also a grave blow to her economy and a brake on her development."

The blockade meant that there was no direct sea route to the Orient, yet Asia was the natural importer of Israeli manufactured goods and some of the few natural resources Israel possessed, potash and phosphates. These minerals were harvested from the Dead Sea, near Elath, but with the Straits of Tiran and the Suez Canal closed, the only way to ship them to Asia was at excessive expense overland to Israel's Mediterranean ports and then out to the Atlantic and the whole way around Africa into the Indian Ocean.

Sharett believed that Egypt should be made to make a concession to Israel as a condition of the evacuation agreement. To force the issue, he ordered an Israeli flag ship to test the Egyptian prohibition against canal usage. Sharett calculated the incident would create such publicity that there would be a fair chance of getting incorporated into the withdrawal treaty a provision opening the canal to Israel's ships.

As expected, the Egyptians stopped the small freighter *Bat Galim,* defiantly flying the Star of David, as it tried to enter the southern end of the canal at Port Suez on September 28. The Egyptians immediately arrested the captain and the crew on trumped-up charges that they had killed two fishermen on their way into Suez.

The whole exercise demonstrated, General Moshe Dayan bitterly noted, "only the weakness of Israel and the readiness of the U.N. institutions to swallow affronts to Israel." The Security Council briefly considered the matter but without taking action. Neither Britain nor the U.S. insisted on Egyptian compliance with previous Security Council demands to open the canal, thus reinforcing Israel's sense of isolation. In the end the *Bat Galim* crew was released to Israel after three months in an Egyptian prison. The ship and cargo were confiscated—and Israel's suspicions about the indifference of the rest of the world toward its fate were heightened.

· ·

The Aman sabotage operation, like so many intelligence operations of the time, had been astonishingly amateurish and inept. It caused no major damage, nor did it impede any more than the *Bat Galim* the talks on the evacuation of the Suez base. On the same day that the first spies were arrested, it was announced in London that Secretary of State for War Antony Head was traveling to Cairo to resume the base talks. By July 27, he and his Egyptian counterpart initialed the Heads of Agreement document that spelled out the terms of Britain's withdrawal. And during the height of the Israeli sabotage operation Eisenhower had pledged "firm commitments" by the U.S. to give aid to Egypt if the talks succeeded. Nasser and Anthony Nutting of the British Foreign Office signed the final accord on October 19, 1954, calling for total evacuation within twenty months.

. .

The withdrawal accord was no more popular among a band of fanatics in Egypt than it was in Israel. A week after Nasser signed the accord, a member of the Moslem Brotherhood, spiritual cousins of such Moslem extremists as Iran's Ayatollah Khomeini, tried to assassinate him. The Brotherhood believed that Nasser had been too compromising by allowing the British to take twenty months to depart.

While the Egyptian leader was addressing a nighttime rally in Alexandria's Liberation Square, recalling how he had missed death in that plaza during the 1936 uprisings against the British, the Brotherhood assassin fired eight shots at him. The stunned crowd watched as the bullets hit a light bulb above Nasser's head and then heard the badly shaken but uncowed leader shout: "I am still alive." Defiantly, he screamed: "Let them kill Nasser. He is one among many. You are all Gamal Abdel Nassers!" His courage under fire made an instant popular hero of Nasser. There were tumultuous demonstrations marking his return to Cairo, and the next day a recording of the dramatic episode was broadcast three times on national radio.

The assassination attempt backfired violently against the Moslem Brotherhood. With his new popularity stemming from his bravery under fire and the successful withdrawal talks, Nasser moved quickly against the radical group. More than a thousand members were arrested, including the top leaders. The Brotherhood's power was broken, if not exterminated, in Egypt for the next quarter of a century.

The new national support allowed Nasser finally to gather in his hands all the reins of power. On November 14, Major General Mohammed

Naguib, the figurehead of Nasser's junta that had overthrown King Farouk two years earlier, quietly resigned as president of the country and went into permanent retirement. Nasser had been paramount for months, though not in name: now he was unequivocally Egypt's leader.

• •

Out in his desert fastness, Ben Gurion was growing increasingly distressed. His frustration was not assuaged on October 5 when Egyptian Interior Minister Zakaria Mohyeddin called a news conference, revealed a detailed description of the aborted Israeli sabotage operation, and announced that the spies would be put on public trial. Then in November, Eisenhower made good on his pledge to give aid to Egypt for its concessions in the withdrawal negotiations and offered Cairo $13 million in economic and $27 million in military aid. (But Nasser, fresh from the trauma of the assassination attempt, refused to accept U.S. military advisers. He explained that if he accepted he would be accused of "selling his country out to another big power before the British even got out of the place.")

In December, the trial of Israel's eleven alleged spies got underway, lasting from December 11 to January 5, 1955. It caused paroxysms of anger and despair in Israel, where the press labeled the trial "a political anti-Semitic farce." Sharett called the proceedings "this fake trial, these calumnies designed solely to strike at the Jews of Egypt."

An international campaign to save the accused spies ensued. Labour M.P. Richard Crossman journeyed to Cairo to plead personally with Nasser. French Foreign Minister Edgar Faure sent a personal letter to the Egyptian leader. Roger N. Baldwin, a New York civil rights attorney and chairman of the International League for the Rights of Man, went to Cairo with official Israeli backing. Their pleas were all to no avail.

When the trial ended, two of the accused were acquitted for lack of evidence, six were sentenced to prison terms of seven years to life, and the two leaders of the cells were sentenced to death. They were hanged in the Cairo Central Prison courtyard on January 31. (The eleventh defendant committed suicide.)

The uproar in Israel was one of rage and frustrated despair. Prime Minister Sharett announced in the Knesset, Israel's parliament, on the same day as the executions that the men had "died the death of martyrs." Two Israeli cities, Beersheva and Ramat Gan, renamed streets after the men. Israel went into unofficial mourning, its anguish heightened by the fact that the international campaign to save the spies had continued up to the last moment. Anticipations had been drawn taut, and until the actual executions there was a misplaced hope that somehow the men would be spared.

There was never any chance that they would be. Only the month before, on December 7, Nasser had not intervened in the hanging of six members of the Moslem Brotherhood convicted of conspiracy in the assassination attempt on his life. He was not now disposed to save Israeli lives nor was he so strong domestically to show more compassion for Jews than for Moslems, even if he wanted to.

• •

Ben Gurion perceived that the Aman sabotage operation was more than just another spy story. Important national questions were at stake, not the least of which was Sharett's ability to control the government and its various secret activities. Ben Gurion was further upset when his protégé Moshe Dayan told him the official responsible for the scheme was bibulous Pinhas Lavon, whom Ben Gurion had appointed minister of defense. In his diary, Ben Gurion wrote, "Dayan told me about a strange order by P.L.—during his [Dayan's] absence—for an operation in Egypt which failed (they should have known it would)—criminal responsibility!"

On his sixth-eighth birthday in October, Ben Gurion spoke about the operation, now known as the Lavon Affair, with a friend, who recorded in his diary: "I talked with the Old Man on the horrifying subject named Lavon. The Old Man analyzed the Egyptian matter: 'It was not the defense minister's business to decide on this [operation]. By what right did he take it upon himself to decide and act independently in and out of the political sphere?' "

• •

In Jerusalem, Sharett was still trying to get to the bottom of the ill-conceived plot. But the abrasive Lavon, who was openly contemptuous of him, and the head of Aman, Colonel Benjamin Gibli, gave him contradictory stories and tried to shift blame onto each other. In desperation, Sharett appointed a secret commission to determine who actually approved the bizarre operation. The commission was so confused by conflicting testimony and phony documents that when it rendered its decision it had to admit that "we find it impossible to say more than that we were not convinced beyond all reasonable doubt that [Gibli] did not receive orders from the defense minister. At the same time, we are not sure that the defense minister did give the orders attributed to him.''

The crisis had clearly grown beyond the capabilities of Moshe Sharett. He was able to keep the sordid affair censored in the press and therefore hidden from most Israelis and the world, but it was causing serious damage in the highest reaches of the Army and the intelligence community where factions for and against Lavon were fighting each other furiously. After another two weeks of futilely trying to find a solution, Sharett and top Mapai Socialist leaders went off to Sdeh Boker on February 1, 1955, to seek Ben Gurion's counsel. His opinion was unequivocal: Lavon had to go. It was also obvious to the Old Man that Sharett had to go too if the Army was to be rescued from its morass of intrigue and bitter infighting. But for the moment he kept his own counsel.

• •

On February 17, Lavon handed in his letter of resignation. That same day Sharett requested Ben Gurion to give up his retirement and return to the government as the minister of defense. The aging leader had no hesitations after the past fourteen months of adversity that Israel had suffered during his desert stay. "I decided I must accept," he wrote in his diary. "Defense and the Army precede everything."

He returned in high dudgeon, determined to clean up the mess he felt Sharett had made during his absence. He removed Gibli from the command of Aman, thereby returning the Central Institute for Security and Intelligence, better known as the Mossad, Israel's equivalent of the CIA, to the center of Israel's five intelligence services (the other three were the FBI-like Shin Bet, the police special branch and the Foreign Ministry service) under his direct control. He also approved the eventual trial of Avri Elad, alias Paul Frank, and his imprisonment. Elad was convicted on a technicality of retaining secret documents to sell to the enemy. He served eight years in prison.

The Lavon Affair was never adequately resolved. Details of the shoddy operation only began leaking in public in the winter of 1959, causing an uproar. The affair struck deep into Israel's sense of itself, of its role in the world, and of the precarious balance of power between civilians and the military in a democracy. In this case the military had gotten out of hand and acted independently and dishonorably without deference to the civilian leadership. Yet for Ben Gurion, the Army stood at the center of Israel's survival.

On his return as defense minister, Ben Gurion felt that the Army had to be brought back under control and its internal bickering stopped. One way to help accomplish both goals and to divert attention away from the sorry affair was to get the Army back to its fundamental task of fighting. The raid on Gaza helped do that.

• •

Ben Gurion's fighting mood extended to his relations with Sharett. The prime minister obviously was unable to control the military or understand the Israeli Jew of Ben Gurion's dream: "A man of integrity, a daring fighter with confidence in himself, who was unapologetic about his Jewishness, at home in the terrain, knew the Arabs and knew his profession." To fulfill that vision, Ben Gurion put Sharett on notice that he planned to run the Defense Ministry his way. If the prime minister, who also served as the foreign minister, did not like it, then "you will have to take over the defense portfolio from me or appoint someone else in my place."

To the Cabinet Secretary, Ben Gurion snapped: "Sharett is cultivating a generation of cowards. I won't let him. Infiltrators are on the prowl, and we are hiding behind fences again. I won't let him. This will be a fighting generation."

Exactly eleven days after his return to government, the bloody raid against Gaza was launched with Ben Gurion's authorization. He told *The New York Times* shortly afterward: "Israeli restraint has been misinterpreted by the Egyptians as a sign of weakness." It was necessary, he added, to "teach Egypt a lesson."

• •

The battle lines were now drawn between Ben Gurion and Sharett. A national election was scheduled for July and it would be a referendum over the type of country Israel should become, a Sparta or an Athens. Despite his hard-line policies, Ben Gurion represented something in between Israel's political extremes, for he was neither an Athenian like Sharett nor as Spartan as the head of the Labor Party's chief opponent, Menachem Begin, of the nationalist Herut (Freedom) Party. Begin was a firebrand and former terrorist who openly preached preventive war and Israel's Biblical right to all of Palestine. He was the spiritual heir of Vladimir Jabotinsky, founder of the Revisionist Party, which represented an extreme form of Jewish mystical fanaticism that Begin had incorporated into the Herut Party.

Ben Gurion despised Begin, a loathing that was rooted in his opposition to Begin's terrorist activities in the 1940s. During the British mandate, Begin had been the head of the Irgun Zvai Leumi, the National Military Organization, the largest of two clandestine terrorist gangs that operated against the British before the founding of the state. The other was the Lechi,* Fighters for the Freedom of Israel, also known simply as the Stern Gang, after its unstable leader, Avraham Stern.

The two groups committed some of the worst atrocities in Palestine's long history of bloodshed. The Stern Gang earned its notorious reputation by its indiscriminate killing of Arabs, British troops and even Jews thought to be too accommodating to the British and Arabs. The gang was blamed for the assassinations of Lord Moyne of Britain and Count Bernadotte of Sweden, killed because they were suspected of being pro-Arab.

The Irgun under Begin engaged in more ambitious enterprises than merely killing individual Arabs and British soldiers, though it did those things too, including the hanging of two English troopers and the booby-trapping of their bodies. But it earned its enduring infamy by dynamiting the famous King David Hotel in Jerusalem on July 22, 1946, with the loss of ninety-one British, Arab and Jewish lives and injury to forty-five others.

The worst terrorist act of the two groups was performed jointly and is still bitterly remembered by Palestinians. On April 9, 1948, members of the Stern Gang and the Irgun, seeking to terrify Palestinians to flee the country, attacked Deir Yassin, a small Arab village near Jerusalem that had taken no part in the fighting and had turned away Arabs seeking to use the village as an anti-Zionist base. The terrorists killed most of the villagers, 240 men, women and children, and mutilated many of their bodies, throwing some down a well and piling others in grotesque stacks. A few villagers were kept alive so they could be paraded through the streets of Jersualem as captives. Much of the Jewish community was horrified, and the Jewish Agency officially apologized to King Abdullah of Transjordan, the grandfather of Jordan's present-day ruler, King Hussein.

In America, Albert Einstein and twenty-seven other prominent Jews, including Hannah Arendt and Sidney Hook, were so revolted by Begin and the tactics of his terrorists that they took the unprecedented step of

One of the Lechi leaders at the time of Moyne's assassination was Yitzhak Shamir, who in 1980, after Begin became prime minister, was appointed foreign minister, succeeding Moshe Dayan.

writing a letter to *The New York Times* protesting his visit to the U.S. at the end of 1948. The letter, printed on December 4, 1948, stated:

> Among the disturbing political phenomena of our time is the emergence in the newly created state of Israel of the "Freedom Party," a political party closely akin in its organization, methods, political philosophy, and social appeal to the Nazi and Fascist parties. It was formed out of the membership and following of the former Irgun Zvai Leumi, a terrorist, right-wing, chauvinist organization in Palestine.
>
> The public avowals of Begin's party are no guide whatsoever to its actual character. Today they speak of freedom, democracy, and anti-imperialism, whereas recently they openly preached the doctrine of the Fascist State. It is in its actions that the terrorist party betrays its real character: From its past actions we can judge what it may be expected to do in the future.
>
> A shocking example was their behavior in the Arab village of Deir Yassin. . . . The terrorists, far from being ashamed of their act, were proud of this massacre, publicized it widely, and invited all the foreign correspondents present in the country to view the heaped corpses and general havoc at Deir Yassin. The Deir Yassin incident exemplifed the character and actions of the Freedom Party.
>
> Within the Jewish community they have preached a mixture of ultranationalism, religious mysticism, and racial superiority. Like other fascist parties, they have been used to break strikes, and have themselves pressed for the destruction of trade unions. . . . Teachers were beaten up for speaking against them; adults were shot for not letting their children join them. By gangster methods, beatings, window smashing and widespread robberies, the terrorists intimidated the population and exacted a heavy tribute.

Ben Gurion also linked Begin to Nazism. "I have no doubt that Begin hates Hitler, but that hatred does not prove that he is unlike [Hitler]," he declared.

• •

Next to such extremists as Begin, Ben Gurion seemed the epitome of cool reasonableness. Thus the secret State Department study concluded in late 1953 described him as being among Israel's moderate leaders who represented Washington's best hope to keep the fanatics from launching a holy war of expansion. The pressures to expand and take more land stemmed from more than economic or social pressures, or the patchwork of indefensible borders decreed in the U.N. Partition Plan. Expansionism was part of the gospel of Begin and the Revisionists, who mystically called for Israel's expansion into what they called the "historical" borders of Eretz Yisrael, the Biblical borders of Israel, which they claimed lay on both sides of the Jordan River. That meant enlarging Israel by an area more than four times its size and uprooting still more hundreds of thousands of Arabs from their homes.

The conclusion of the State Department study found the alternatives America had in dealing with Israel severely limited. Too much economic pressure, it pointed out, might cause the moderates to be "overthrown by the firebrands." The only slim hope, it concluded, was in Washington applying a "steady pressure for a more realistic Israeli approach to their internal problems."

Unappreciated apparently by the Washington analysts was the low regard Israelis had for "reality." The establishment of the state was a miracle, and its continued existence confounded realists. "Reality" was a word not easily applicable to the Holy Land.

• •

It was one of these three men—Begin, Ben Gurion and Sharett—and his vision of reality that the country was going to have to choose in July. The choice could decide Israel's future as a peace-loving nation in the grand tradition of enlightened Judaism or as a Zionist warrior state.

CHAPTER III

Where Is Dignity?

NASSER

THE PRESSURE ON GAMAL ABDEL NASSER to acquire weapons for his Army had grown great since the Gaza raid. "Our revolution was stimulated in the Army by a lack of equipment," he explained to columnist Cyrus Sulzberger. "If our officers feel we still have no equipment, they will lose faith in the government." His predicament was made acute by Israeli warplanes that were flying over Cairo that winter of 1955, publicly demonstrating to the world his weakness. During one noisy overflight, Nasser was sitting with CIA agent Miles Copeland and complained: "I have to sit here and take this—and your government won't give me arms."

The Gaza raid had made the area extremely tense. Border incidents, minings and exchanges of gunfire were now frequent. Israeli troops were provocatively patrolling up to the edge of the frontier and taunting Egyptian soldiers. "These patrols are in the habit of shouting at the Egyptian soldiers and cursing them in Arabic," UNTSO commander Burns complained to Israeli Chief of Staff Moshe Dayan. Burns requested that "these provocative acts" be halted because they "gave rise to many incidents." But they were not halted, further aggravating Nasser's arms problem.

For Nasser, delivery of the arms promised by Eisenhower the previous November was becoming an acute matter of face. The young Egyptian leader was painfully sensitive to slights and broken promises from the West. As a *baladi*, a scorned native who had been born into the world of British colonialism, he suffered the deep humiliations of growing up in a country ruled by foreigners. In his youth in Alexandria, where his father was a postal clerk, he had joined in demonstrations against the British and during one riot was severely clubbed by policemen and thrown in jail for two nights. He carried scars on his scalp for the rest of his life.

"Who can cry halt to the imperialists?" he wrote to a friend in 1935, when he was seventeen. "Where is the man to rebuild the country so that the weak and humiliated Egyptian people can rise again and live as free and independent men? Where is dignity?"

It was dignity more than all else that Nasser sought, and it was indignities more than any threat that provoked him. His contempt for King Farouk, and his determination to rid the country of the corrupt monarch, grew from Farouk's acceptance of a public humiliation by the British in 1942. The British ambassador, Sir Miles Lampson, who exercised almost total power, made Farouk publicly submit to a British demand by surrounding his palace with tanks and troops and presenting him with a document of abdication. The pliable king submitted to the British request and kept his throne, but he lost whatever respect he had from nationalists like Nasser.

In writing to a friend about the humiliation of Farouk, Nasser reported: "I almost exploded with rage. As for the Army, it has been thoroughly shaken. Until now the officers only talked of how to enjoy themselves; now they are speaking of sacrificing their lives for their honor. It has taught them that there is something called dignity which has to be defended."

The young *baladi* joined numerous opposition groups, the Moslem Brotherhood, the communists, the socialists, in search of a power base to challenge British rule, but always he left in disillusionment. They were all too doctrinaire and rent with theoretical bickerings to suit his straightforward goal of ridding Egypt of foreign rule. He finally found his vehicle in the Army after attending the Egyptian Military Academy and becoming a second lieutenant. Following the Lampson incident he carefully formed a group of like-minded nationalists into the Free Officers' Committee, a clandestine movement dedicated to the concept that Egypt should be Egyptian.

The Free Officers felt their movement threatened by the establishment of the state of Israel in 1948, seeing it as a creation of Western imperialism at the expense of the Arabs. In their eyes, the creation of Israel meant that part of the Arab homeland was being taken away, its Arab residents dispersed and a beachhead of Western imperialism planted in the Arab heartland. Their resistance was based more on their suspicions of Western intentions than anti-Semitism, which was rare in Egypt, where a large Jewish community flourished. The Free Officers enthusiastically joined in the war against Israel in 1948, but, like all the Arab armies attacking the new state, Egypt was soundly beaten. There was only one pocket of outstanding Egyptian heroism in the war and that was at Falluja, southeast of Tel Aviv. A small unit of Egyptian soldiers was isolated there and surrounded by Israeli troops when they were relieved by 150 men who had fought their way through enemy lines led by a husky lieutenant colonel. The colonel was Nasser and under his command the unit held out until the end of the fighting. Nasser was lightly wounded twice at Falluja, but more important than torn flesh was his realization of the weakness of Egypt's armed forces and the extent of political corruption that had left the Army poorly equipped. The Army would never be able to stand up to British troops, he realized. The British would have to be gotten rid of by conspiracy and adroit political maneuvering.

• •

Nasser's time came in 1952. By then, popular discontent against the eighty thousand British troops stationed at the Suez base had reached a point of searing hatred. Egyptian terrorists were kidnapping and killing British soldiers, throwing grenades into officers' clubs, blowing up military installations, mining roads and destroying communications. There was an incessant outcry for the British to quit Egypt. The British responded by throwing a huge cordon around the entire canal zone and searching all Egyptians going in and out. It was an outrageous indignity to Egyptian nationalists: foreign troops searching Egyptians on Egyptian soil.

On January 25 came the beginning of the end. In Ismailia, the halfway point on the canal, British troops moved in to stem recurring troubles. A battalion of Egyptian auxiliary police refused to submit and the British opened fire with light arms and tanks, killing forty-one and wounding seventy-two. The next day crazed Egyptian mobs went wild in Cairo.

The mobs surged through Cairo's downtown on that Black Saturday, as it became known, attacking symbols of British power and privilege: the posh Shepheard's Hotel, Groppi's tea room, Badia's Cabaret, the St. James restaurant, the exclusive British Turf Club. It was at the Turf Club that nine British civilians were brutally killed, four of them disemboweled and another trampled to death. Shepheard's, a gathering place of British officialdom and Egyptian aristocrats, was set afire; when Egyptian police-

men tried to intervene they were turned into human torches. By midafternoon, the streets of smoke-blackened downtown Cairo were a hell of
flames and frenzied mobs looting and killing everything in their path.
More than seven hundred buildings were burned, looted or smashed during the day of rioting, and seventeen Europeans and fifty Egyptians died
in the violence.

Black Saturday vividly demonstrated to Nasser how weak was King
Farouk and how indignant and resentful Egyptians were at the continued
presence of British troops and officials. By July, he and the Free Officers
were ready to move with the support of much of the Army, where disillusionment with Farouk was greatest. On the night of the twenty-third,
the Free Officers with the help of new recruits from the Army took over
the Army headquarters, the radio station, telegraph offices, police stations and government buildings. The coup was nearly bloodless, as Nasser had planned. By 7 A.M. the next morning, Lieutenant Colonel Anwar
Sadat, one of the most passionate of the Free Officers and destined to be
Nasser's successor, proclaimed the victory on national radio. The Army
had taken power, he declared, to purge the country of the "traitors and
weaklings" who had bowed to foreign rule.

Two days later, on July 26, 1952, a day that was again to be fateful for
Nasser four years later, King Farouk abdicated and left the country
aboard the royal yacht *Mahroussa* with the accompaniment of a twenty-
one-gun salute. The king's quick collapse left Nasser and the Free Officers with a problem. They were all so young, in their mid-thirties for the
most part, and so unknown that they feared the populace would refuse to
accept any of them as Egypt's new leader. They felt they needed a figurehead to represent them, and chose General Mohammed Naguib, an affa-
ble and well-liked career officer who had been so repelled by Farouk's
submission to Miles Lampson ten years earlier that he had dramatically
tried to resign his commission. Naguib was a necessary front man; in the
background Nasser called the shots. But, though he had since gotten rid
of Naguib, Nasser's power was still not fully consolidated by the winter
of 1955, and the humiliation of the Gaza raid in February threatened his
position.

• •

Unhappily for Nasser, Dwight Eisenhower was having second thoughts
about fulfilling his promise of arms to Egypt. Opposition to the pledge
had built up greatly, not only from Israel, which had been expected, but
from the British as well. Winston Churchill wrote Ike directly about

Britain's misgivings: "You can't give them arms with which to kill British soldiers who fought shoulder to shoulder with you in the war."

When Gamal Abdel Nasser heard of this, he noted that under the withdrawal agreement all British troops would be gone before July 1956 and archly remarked: "If you give us arms, there won't be any British for us to kill."

But British feelings were no light matter to Eisenhower. He had a deep admiration for Britain growing out of his arduous wartime service. He valued his many British friendships, respected British culture and delighted in the fighting capabilities of Britons. America's special relationship with Britain was founded on a common language and common ideals, and for Eisenhower it formed the bulwark of the West's defense against Communism.

He was not inclined to ignore British objections, especially when applied to the Middle East and particularly when they so neatly coincided with his own aversion to introducing more weapons into the troubled area. Eisenhower made a fateful decision. He decided apparently about this time to stall on his promise of arms to Egypt. Under the circumstances it seemed a reasonable course. Britain was far more important to the United States than Egypt in the global competition with Communism, or so it seemed.

. .

It was by coincidence that America's new ambassador to Egypt arrived in Cairo the day before the 1955 Gaza raid. The envoy was none other than Henry A. Byroade, the outspoken assistant secretary of state who the year before had so harshly criticized Israel's aggressiveness. His remarks, though they had been balanced by condemnation of the Arabs for refusing to sign a peace treaty with Israel, had provoked such loud protests against him among Israel's supporters that his effectiveness as assistant secretary suffered. He was accused by the Jewish lobby of being prejudiced against Israel, of lacking objectiveness in the Middle East conflict and of being anti-Semitic. Byroade considered himself as being merely objective, but he finally had to admit that his usefulness as assistant secretary had been impaired by the charges and, at any rate, he was tired of the Washington rat race. Dulles kindly offered his beleaguered colleague his choice of embassies in the Middle East and Byroade eagerly chose Egypt.

Up until that time, Byroade had enjoyed about the most successful career in government of any man of his generation. He was a West

Pointer from a modest Indiana family who in nine years in the Army rose from a second lieutenant to a brigadier general at the age of thirty-two, primarily because of his success in overseeing construction of B-29 air bases in China during World War II. He served as the chief military aide for formidable General of the Armies George C. Marshall, directed with flair the State Department desk in charge of the airlift to Berlin in the dramatic confrontation with Russia in 1948, and at the age of thirty-eight, he had resigned his commission to become assistant secretary of state for Near Eastern, South Asian and African affairs in 1952.

Byroade was well suited for Cairo. As ambassador, he was certain to get on well with Gamal Abdel Nasser. Both were former military men, each big, handsome and easygoing in manner, and Byroade at forty-one years of age was only four and a half years older than the Egyptian leader. The two men met several days after Byroade's arrival and they did indeed immediately take a liking to each other. They talked well into the night, as they were to do frequently, on the region's various problems. But inevitably Nasser guided the conversation to the subject consuming him since the Gaza raid: weapons.

If the West wanted peace in the Middle East, Nasser argued, then it had to sell Egypt weapons to make it strong. Only a strong Egypt could take the risk of sitting down with Israel to talk peace. His country had to be perceived as going to the peace table under its own will, and not being forced there out of fear of more Israeli attacks. Nasser told Byroade that his emissaries had been secretly meeting with Israeli officials in Europe during the past year while Sharett was prime minister. But, he said bitterly, since Ben Gurion's return to the government and the Gaza raid, all that was over. Egypt now had to show it could deal with Israel as an equal and that could only come about with its acquisition of weapons. Beyond that, Nasser added, the Army was growing restless. If he did not soon get the weapons the Army was demanding, his hold on the government could become precarious.

Byroade was impressed with Nasser's arguments and sympathetic with his desire for U.S. weapons. He repeatedly recommended to Washington that Eisenhower's promise of $27 million worth of weapons, made the previous November, be honored. But week after week no action was taken on his recommendation, nor was he informed that the President had decided to stall.

By March, Nasser suspected that he never would get arms from Washington. "Two years ago I told you that arms and aid were expected to arrive on payment," he declared in a national radio address on the twenty-eighth. "A mission was sent to the U.S.A., but negotiations failed because of Jewish and Zionist influence. I think it would be a miracle if we ever obtained any arms from that direction."

Nasser's quandary grew out of the Tripartite Declaration of 1950 by which Britain, France and the United States had pledged to maintain a balance of power in the Middle East by restricting arms sales to both Israel and the Arab nations. Thus he could not turn to Britain or France for weapons, and efforts to buy them in Belgium, Holland and Switzerland bore meager results.

Nasser would have to do something rash soon, thought the British ambassador to Egypt, Sir Humphrey Trevelyan. The United States "did not seem to realize that the matter [of arms] was urgent and important, or perhaps, as I have heard suggested, it was realized at a late stage that the sale of arms to Egypt was politically impossible," he recalled in his memoirs. "Nasser lost patience."

Nasser's response was to strike out in a wholly different direction. It was an action that brought consternation to the Western countries and the Soviet Union to the Middle East.

CHAPTER IV

It Could Lead to War

DULLES

No ONE REALLY EXPECTED major changes when old war-horse Winston Churchill finally took his long-delayed departure as Britain's prime minister. After all, the Conservative government remained in power and replacing Sir Winston was Anthony Eden, his old understudy who had been waiting impatiently in the wings for many years. But the change in leadership on April 6, 1955, was to have far-reaching effects in the Middle East.

President Eisenhower warmly welcomed Eden to the brotherhood of world leaders. "I most earnestly hope that your premiership will be notable in the history of your country and of the world by the progress toward world peace that will be achieved," Ike wrote Eden. "I know there is no one better fitted than you to seize the opportunities inherent in your new office for helping to guide the world toward the goal we all so earnestly seek. On a more personal side, I cannot tell you how delighted I am that my old friend Winston has been succeeded by an equally valued friend in an office in which friendliness and genuine readiness to cooperate can mean so much to my own country."

Those were words that Eisenhower later had occasion to savor as ironic and misplaced. The same was true of his next personal message to Eden, this one on June 3: "My calendar reminds me that in a matter of days you will celebrate the anniversary of your birth, your first as prime minister. I hope that in the year to come you will know the utmost measure of personal accomplishment and that we all will have the satisfaction of taking a long step forward in our goal of a secure and lasting peace for all the world."

Eisenhower's belief that the bedrock of the Western alliance was the trust and faith that existed between Britain and America extended to the relationship between the leaders of those two countries. In another friendly note to Eden that spring, Eisenhower expressed his "tremendous satisfaction" at the prospect of "concerting our actions and thinking in reaching for our common goals."

Eden gave every indication of sharing those common goals. In a series of personal notes to Eisenhower, whom Eden addressed as "my dear friend," he repeatedly assured the President of the mutuality of their objectives and their friendship. "I feel that our friendship is warmer than it has ever been," Eden wrote Eisenhower. "I value that tremendously." At another time he wrote, "I look forward to the closest cooperation with you and your Administration at all times."

And Eisenhower, implicitly stressing the importance of communication between the two countries on world affairs, wrote Eden, "Please do not hesitate to get in touch with me whenever you so desire."

• •

Eden was an experienced statesman who had served Churchill as foreign secretary as far back as 1940 and now, at age fifty-eight, had every expectation of being one of the world's great leaders. His knowledge of the Middle East was encyclopedic, and it was there that he planned to shore up Britain's crumbling empire. As foreign secretary he had come under severe attack from Conservatives for agreeing to withdraw British troops from Egypt, but he was far from ready to concede that Britain's paramount role in the region was over. Eden's plan to keep Britain supreme went under the name of the Baghdad Pact.

It was a clever scheme, ostensibly aimed at containing the Soviet Union's southern flank but equally important it offered Eden a chance to retain Britain's influence in the Middle East. The strategy behind the plan was to form an anti-Communist pact of Middle Eastern nations under British leadership, thereby giving London power over the member states through its control of economic and military aid designed for the alliance. Such power, Eden calculated, would guarantee Britain's continuing influence in the Middle East.

It appeared to be a simple and highly effective strategy, but it failed to appreciate one significant fact: Nasser suspected the nature of the pact's underlying purpose and he violently opposed it. Nasser's ambitions extended far beyond simply getting the British out of Egypt. He wanted Britain and all non-Moslem powers out of the Middle East. His dream of Pan-Arabism envisioned a unity of Moslem states, free of outside influence, capable of treading independently between the superpowers. As he explained to Miles Copeland, the CIA's undercover liaison with the Egyptian leader, the reaction among Arabs to the Baghdad Pact was that the West wanted "to get [the Arabs] to unite to fight *your* enemy [Russia] while they know that if they show any intention of fighting *their* enemy [Israel] you would quickly stop all aid. Any regional military agreement which did not take this attitude into account would be a fraud."

Despite such opposition, Eden heedlessly pushed ahead with the pact and persuaded two pro-Western Moslem countries, Iraq and Turkey, to become the initial members on February 24, 1955. The timing was bad for the future of the pact. It was only four days before Israel's Gaza raid, and in Nasser's suspicious mind the two events seemed connected. He thought of Israel as the West's cat's-paw in the region, so any attack by it was in effect an attack by the West against Islam. Since he also thought the forming of the Baghdad Pact as being aimed against Islam, he rashly concluded that the two events were coordinated.

Nasser was particularly incensed at Iraq for becoming the first Arab nation to join the pact. Iraq and Egypt were traditional rivals for leadership of the Arab world, and Iraq's sudden access to Western weaponry as a pact member posed a serious threat to Nasser's ambitions. He threw down the gauntlet by openly scorning Iraq's wily old pro-Western prime minister, Nuri es-Said. "Nuri Pasha may be willing to make his decisions on a basis of whether or not they fit your world strategy," he explained to the CIA's Copeland. "But I am not. I intend to judge issues on their merits, and to make my decisions only on a basis of what's good for Egypt. Having this kind of freedom is as important an objective as economic prosperity."

Such vocal opposition to the Baghdad Pact soon began to make Nasser's name unpopular to Anthony Eden and other colonialists in Britain. Nonetheless, the new prime minister pressed forward with his plan for securing Britain's position in the Middle East, ignoring the dangerous opposition that would inevitably result.

A confrontation was developing between the West's leading colonialist and the Middle East's leading Arab nationalist.

• •

Foster Dulles was revolted by the concept of a Third World of nations steering an independent course between East and West, communism and democracy. Neutralism, he declared sternly, "is an immoral and short-sighted conception."

But for nationalists like Gamal Nasser, caught in the snare of the West's global concerns, neutralism seemed the only escape. His interests were rooted in the Arab world, neither East nor West. He identified with the newly emerging nations that shared a common suspicion of their former colonial masters and the common problems of securing their independence. Great areas of the world were now occupied by these new unaligned nations seeking their own paths between the superpowers. They decided to meet in April 1955 to share their experiences and seek strength in their numbers. Nasser, frustrated and feeling his position threatened by Israel and the West, decided to attend the initial Afro-Asian conference of nonaligned nations in Bandung, Indonesia. It was his first journey outside the Arab world, and his entry onto the world stage.

• •

Nasser left Cairo April 9 aboard an Air India plane, chartered because he did not trust regularly scheduled U.S. or British airlines since both countries were in opposition to his attendance at the neutralist conference. He stopped for two days in New Delhi for talks with India's Prime Minister Jawaharlal Nehru, one of the organizers of the gathering. Nehru was friendly but Nasser never warmed up to his abstract intellectualism. Together the two leaders flew on to Rangoon, where they were met by Burma's Prime Minister U Nu and China's legendary Chou En-lai, the other major force behind the conference.

It was Nasser's first meeting with Chou, and the two men got on like teacher and pet student. At Chou's invitation they met privately in the former governor-general's residence in Rangoon, now a government guesthouse, in an old colonial high-ceilinged room with overhead fans and half-shuttered doors. Chou, chain-smoking and wearing a simple high-collared tunic, spoke about the goals of the Bandung Conference, Indochina and his relations with the U.S. which currently were at their nadir. The Chinese Communists only that February had driven Nationalist Chinese forces out of the offshore Tachen Islands, and Senator William Knowland was calling for a blockade of the mainland while Admiral Arthur Radford was rumored to be urging the nuclear-bombing of Shanghai. The U.S. Senate was so concerned about the fate of Taiwan that on February 9 it had passed, 64 to 6, a mutual defense treaty with Nationalist China specifically aimed at repelling any attack by Red China. Additionally, Dulles was irked at the spectacle of Nasser attending a nonaligned conference with Chou, whom Dulles had snubbed a year earlier in a well-publicized incident at the Geneva Conference on Indochina by crudely refusing to shake hands with him.

In Rangoon, Chou talked about the Third World and the possibilities of cooperation between China and Egypt. He observed that there were great potentialities. For instance, Chou said, China could absorb all the cotton that Egypt grew simply by ordering every Chinese to lengthen his coat by about an inch. It was a vivid, if farfetched, illustration of the power inherent in cooperation by Third World countries and Nasser was impressed.

But it was weapons Nasser wanted to talk about. He complained to Chou that he feared attack by Israel and yet was unable to purchase arms from the West. Nasser realized that China had few weapons to spare but wondered "whether the Soviet Union would be prepared to sell us arms." It might, Chou answered, but if it did there would be severe complications with the Western nations. Nasser responded that he was ready for anything in order to obtain weapons. He asserted that after coming to power he had cut the Army's budget and had taken seventy million Egyptian pounds confiscated from King Farouk's private treasury and used the money to build hospitals, schools and roads. "But we cannot defend ourselves with hospitals or schools," Nasser said. "All we are doing is getting them ready for the Israelis to occupy."

Chou promised that he would contact the Russians and assured Nasser that the Soviet Union was feeling well disposed toward Egypt. Moscow had its doubts at first, Chou explained, believing that Nasser and the young officers of the junta were launching another "bourgeois revolution." But their stern opposition to the Baghdad Pact and their resistance to Western pressure had begun to change the Kremlin's mind.

Indeed, as Soviet Party Chairman Nikita Khrushchev observed in his memoirs, "We were inclined to think that Nasser's coup was just another one of those military take-overs which we had become so accustomed to in South America. We didn't expect much to come of it." But before long, said Khrushchev, the Russians began to "like what we saw. They started actively to put pressure on the English to pull their troops out. Now we realized that this wasn't just another in a series of new governments that seize power and then follow old policies. We wanted to help Nasser continue his struggle against the colonialists. But it was hard to be sure from Nasser's speeches whether or not he intended to create a progressive regime in Egypt. He still hadn't laid a finger on the bourgeoisie and the banks. Our desire to affect the course of the Egyptian government was the natural outgrowth of our desire to share our [revolutionary] experience with another nation."

What Khrushchev did not bother mentioning in his reminiscences about Egypt was that since czarist times a long-term strategic goal of Russia was to exert influence in the Middle East. Nasser, by asking for Soviet aid, was finally giving the new government of Khrushchev the chance to achieve that historic goal and, additionally, to vault over the Baghdad Pact's defensive tier.

After the meeting with Nasser, Chou wrote up a memorandum for Chairman Mao Zedong, who suggested that the chairman send it on to Moscow. Egyptian journalist Mohamed Heikal obtained a copy of the memorandum after the split between Russia and China when, according to him, Peking sent Cairo a copy to disprove Moscow's accusations that China opposed aid to all but Communist nations.

Chou wrote of his talk: "When Nasser talked to me about his ideas I found that there was one idea which absorbs him completely—the idea of Arab nationalism. I gained the impression that he is convinced this idea can generate new forces which will play a vital part in liberation movements in the Middle East. I think Nasser is a firm believer in the policy of nonalignment, and as a long-term strategy. If his disagreement with the West were no more than tactical it would not have reached its present pitch."

Chou reported that he could do no more than pass on to Moscow Nasser's request for arms with the observation that "the advantages likely to accrue to the socialist camp from an immediate approach should not be underestimated. . . . From my talk with Nasser I concluded that we must expect a major collision in the Middle East between what he calls the new forces of Arab nationalism and the colonialists and reactionaries who oppose it. It is impossible for the socialist camp to adopt the role of a spectator in the inevitable battle in the Middle East.

"As I see it, our position obliges us to assist the nationalist forces in this battle for two reasons—because their victory would be in the interest of the socialist camp and because it would thwart all attempts of the Western imperialists to complete the encirclement of the Eastern camp."

•　•

At the Bandung Conference, Nasser earned international recognition with his deft espousal of the Arab cause, which led the twenty-nine independent states attending to agree that the Arab-Israeli conflict should be included on the agenda. At the conference's conclusion on April 24, the final communiqué modestly called for "the implementation of the U.N. resolutions on Palestine and the achievement of the peaceful settlement of the Palestine question."

Nasser returned to Cairo a hero, the first Egyptian ruler in modern times to perform on the international stage with prestige and stature. His reputation soared as a spokesman of the Arab cause and of the newly emergent nations.

But his ability to get arms from the West did not improve. Washington, while not flatly turning down his arms request, continued to stall. Nasser decided to approach the Russians directly.

• •

On May 18, at a party at the Sudanese Embassy in Cairo, Nasser approached Soviet Ambassador Daniel Solod and discovered his request was already in motion. "I wanted to see you," said Nasser. Solod responded, "I have been instructed to ask for an audience with you, sir."

Three days later, Ambassador Solod had his audience in Nasser's Cairo office and Gamal Abdel Nasser was about to have his arms deal. Committees were formed by both sides to discuss in secret the complex details of Egypt's military requirements. They were extensive. The meetings at first took place in Cairo and in Maadi, a Cairo suburb, and later in Prague, where two Russian generals joined the discussions.

On June 9, Nasser called in Byroade and confided that he was talking with the Soviets about buying arms. Byroade cabled Washington with this stunning news, but the response was apparent indifference. In Dulles' opinion, and that of the majority of State Department officers, Nasser was playing the favorite game of the newly emergent nations: pitting one superpower against the other in order to wring concessions from both sides. Washington was not going to fall for such a gross maneuver. It all seemed "suspiciously like blackmail," recalled Eisenhower in his memoirs, adding: "Our attitude may, with the advantage of hindsight, appear to have been unrealistic." As events were to prove, the U.S. attitude was worse than that. It was self-defeating, the product of a blind refusal to see the profound implications of the rise of Arab nationalism, a new force that was neither East nor West.

The British took the news more seriously, though they acted with no more wisdom than the United States. Byroade confidentially reported the Soviet talks to the British ambassador in Egypt at that time, Sir Ralph Stevenson, the predecessor of Trevelyan, and Stevenson went to see Nasser. "Stevenson came to me and said that [if] we take arms from the Soviet Union [the British] will not supply us with arms, ammunition or spare parts," Nasser recalled. "I told him: 'You are a free country; you can do what you like. We are a free country; we can do what we like.' They thought that I was bluffing."

Trevelyan later reported that the British threat "infuriated Nasser. He described it to me later as a threat which he could not accept, and told me that from that moment he had determined to have no more conversations with the British about arms." Nasser was also upset with Byroade for telling the British, but he still had not given up a slim hope that Washington would come through with an offer. American weapons, aside from being superior to Russian arms at that time, had other advantages too. Their technical manuals were in English, a language the Egyptians were well familiar with after nearly a century of British domination; Russian was not the average Egyptian officer's second language.

Repeatedly in June Nasser pressed his case with Byroade for U.S. weapons. Finally, he was assured that Washington would consider a specific request. On June 30, Egypt submitted a detailed list of minor weapons valued at under $10 million, less than half the amount promised seven months earlier by Eisenhower. When Ike saw the list he called it "peanuts." But he did not stop stalling.

• •

Washington's attention that summer had shifted from the imperiled Chinese Nationalists on Taiwan to the historic summit meeting of America, Britain, France and the Soviet Union scheduled for July in Geneva. The Middle East and Nasser's flirtation with Russia seemed remote. When Allen Dulles, the amiable head of the CIA, called his brother on June 13 to discuss disturbing cables about the Middle East, Foster replied that his schedule was so tight that Allen should take up the matter with one of his underlings.

Yet over the next month Foster Dulles grew concerned enough about Nasser's request to Russia that when he attended the Summit Conference he privately asked Nikita Khrushchev on July 20 whether the Soviets planned to sell arms to Egypt. Khrushchev denied it and Dulles did not press the matter.

On that same day, an Egyptian military delegation flew to Prague to conclude with their Soviet counterparts the final details of the arms deal. At the Russians' suggestion, the Egyptians agreed to the fiction that Czechoslovakia was going to provide the weapons, thereby making Khrushchev's denial to Dulles technically correct.

• •

Dmitri Shepilov, editor of *Pravda* and soon to become Russia's foreign minister, arrived in Egypt on June 16 to look Nasser over and determine the dimensions of the transaction. "I discussed with him (we were at Alexandria at that time) about the delivery, about quantities, whether they would give us facilities in paying," recalled Nasser. "They agreed." There were no strings attached. The deal was struck. It was that simple.

• •

Israel held its elections on July 26 and the results were devastating for Sharett. The nation rejected Sharett's moderation and gave Begin's Herut an increase of seven seats, still not enough to take power but a significant gain. Sharett's Mapai faction lost five seats. The voters had rejected both Athens and Sparta. With support from other Labor factions, Ben Gurion would be the new prime minister.

• •

The election of Ben Gurion did nothing to assuage Nasser's fears of Israel's aggressive intents. "Fear dominates the area," he told columnist Cyrus Sulzberger in August. "What do you think I feel when I hear that the Herut Party in Israel wants expansion from the Nile to the Euphrates? This was said in Herut speeches in the recent election campaign. And they said that the Arabs must be pacified by force."

Nasser, noting Herut's election gains, said to Sulzberger: "At the next election they may have seventy [seats]—all of them for expansion. Once I thought we could live in peace. I said to my troops and officers in Palestine that we must do our best to have peace in this area. But after the bloody Gaza incident, I felt responsible for the deaths of those men. They were killed in cold blood."

The interview provided the occasion for Sulzberger to study Nasser and afterward he jotted down in his diary his impressions of the Egyptian leader. "He gives one the feeling of being energetic, brave, modest, and disinterested in wealth. However, he is clearly lacking in serious education or worldly experience. Furthermore, he tends to look beneath and behind even the most simple proposition for invidious meanings. Undoubtedly this is part of his heritage of conspiracy and of deep resentment against colonialism and imperialism. He is surely naïve and could be easily fooled."

A secret CIA profile of Nasser had come to similar conclusions, picturing him as a man of "vanity, obstinacy, suspicions, avidity for power. His strengths are complete self-confidence, great resilience, courage and nervous control, willingness to take great risks, great tactical skill and stubborn attachment to initial aims. He gets boyish pleasure out of conspiratorial doings. Has a real streak of self-pity. While a patient, subtle organizer, he can lose his head."

Both Sulzberger and the CIA underestimated the Egyptian leader. He was not easily fooled, nor did he easily lose his head. He was cool under pressure and he was extremely shrewd in deciphering the machinations of the West in the Middle East. He suspected, for instance, that despite the Tripartite Declaration's prohibition against one-sided arms sales in the Middle East, the French were secretly selling weapons to Israel as a way to oppose his support for the rebellion in Algeria. His suspicions were borne out after Israel's elections when British intelligence, fearful that his election victory might tempt Ben Gurion to launch an attack on Jordan, began leaking details of the covert Franco-Israeli relationship. Britain had a defense treaty with Jordan, and its intelligence establishment calculated that exposure of Israel's arms purchases would serve as a warning to Ben Gurion to curb his aggressiveness. British intelligence thus revealed that Israel was going to receive from France the multipurpose Mystère IV, which would be the most advanced jet fighter-bomber in the Middle East. When France and Israel denied the charge, the British replied by leaking more specifics about the active arms trade between the two countries. The revelations did nothing to impede Israeli arms purchases, but they exacerbated Nasser's suspicions and his determination to buy Soviet arms.

• •

Foster Dulles was finally alarmed by increasingly ominous reports of Soviet moves in the Middle East. In a telephone conversation with his brother, Allen, on August 17, Foster said, "Things are getting pretty bad in connection with the Arab-Israel problem." He wondered "how seriously we should take the Russian proposals about Egypt," referring to the pending arms deal.

Foster was concerned enough about the drift in the region that he was working on a major speech to try to cool off tempers. The next day, in a telephone call with Eric Johnston, a special ambassador assigned to work out a regional water plan between Israel and its Arab neighbors, Foster warned that he was about to make his speech and hoped that did not interfere with Johnston's negotiations. It was axiomatic that any statement from Washington on the Middle East was certain to anger both sides.

"To be perfectly honest," said Johnston, "I'd prefer you not to make the statement now."

Dulles replied that the reasons for making the statement now were urgent. "If the Russians begin to get into the scene, particularly in Egypt, we would have to alter our entire position from one of neutrality in the area. The situation is rapidly changing and we should do something soon. It is more or less perhaps backing Egypt against Israel. There are risks involved."

Later, in a telephone call to Walter George, a leading Senate Democrat, Dulles revealed that the Middle East "situation is getting bad. The Russians are offering armament to Egypt. We ought to make our position clear. I will make a statement that if they can settle their differences, the President would recommend we contribute to the resettlement of the Arabs and join in an international guarantee of agreed boundaries. The first reaction will probably be bad," Dulles added, "but then it may help the situation." It did not.

· ·

Before Dulles could make his speech, events swirled out of control in the Middle East. The relatively quiet interlude of the summer was shattered on August 22. After an exchange of shots between Egyptian and Israeli border guards, an Israeli motorized patrol crashed across the frontier and occupied Egyptian positions near the U.N. hut at Kilo 95 in the Gaza Strip. One Egyptian officer and two men were killed.

The next day U.N. commander General Burns visited Cairo and talked with Ambassador Byroade. "He told me that the latest incident had been taken badly by the Egyptians and deplored Israeli activism," Burns recalled. "He also told me that the Russians were offering Egypt arms and many economic advantages and the prime minister was under much political pressure to accept the Russian offers."

Several days later, Burns reported, "We heard for the first time the expression *fedayeen* applied to the Palestinian agents sent into Israel to carry out attacks on the population and destroy property." Nasser had kept his vow made after the Gaza raid the previous February and had unleashed *fedayeen* forces against Israel.

Starting August 25, *fedayeen* commandos, Palestinian refugees trained by Egypt, carried out a week-long series of mine laying, ambushes and attacks that took the lives of eleven Israeli civilians and soldiers and wounded nine. An Israeli Army spokesman described the Egyptian tactics as "something entirely new," and Sharett, still acting prime minister while Ben Gurion strove to form a coalition government, told General Burns to warn Nasser that "Israel would react if the incidents continued."

Tensions suddenly were so high that *The New York Times*'s Cairo correspondent Kennett Love, who at the time was serving temporarily in Israel, wrote a lengthy military analysis of the strength of the two countries. "Israel could mobilize 250,000 men and 100,000 women soldiers in 48 hours," he wrote, "while the total strength of all the Arab League was only 205,000 men of mixed quality, of which 100,000 were in the Egyptian Army. Israeli troops had rehearsed every military contingency they could imagine while the Arabs had neither a unified command nor even a code signal to alert their several armies." Love concluded that "despite Egyptian assertions of confidence, any friend of the Arabs would advise them to avoid hostilities with Israel."

· ·

Dulles went ahead with his speech the next day, August 26, before the Council on Foreign Relations in New York, stressing that "I speak in this matter with the authority of President Eisenhower." As he had told a friend earlier, the speech was "hot." It called for concessions from both sides. "Three problems remain that conspicuously require to be solved," Dulles said. He identified them as the plight of the 750,000 refugees, a lack of permanent boundaries for Israel, and "the pall of fear that hangs over the Arab and Israeli peoples alike. The Arab countries fear that Israel will seek by violent means to expand at their expense. The Israelis fear that the Arabs will gradually marshal superior forces to be used to drive them into the sea, and they suffer from the economic measures now taken against them."

To sweeten the proposals, Dulles offered generous U.S. economic and diplomatic aid, plus a guarantee of borders once they were fixed. "President Eisenhower has authorized me to say that . . . he would [be willing to] recommend that the U.S.A. should join in formal treaty engagements

to prevent or thwart any effort by either side to alter by force the boundaries between Israel and her Arab neighbors.''

It was an objective and fair proposal, but in the region the speech was
predictably disliked by both sides. Nasser thought it too vague and said
he was disappointed; Ben Gurion answered by yet another act of violence
in retaliation for the *fedayeen* attacks. Among the Israeli victims of the
fedayeen were four unarmed workmen slain in an orange grove. Ben
Gurion and Dayan insisted the deaths be avenged by an assault on the
Gaza Strip and ordered up an attack. But Sharett demanded at the last
moment that the assault force be recalled. The next day Dayan submitted
his written resignation to Ben Gurion, who presented it to the Cabinet
with an ultimatum: "Either the Sharett line or the Ben Gurion line, because following them both alternately causes nothing but damage.'' Then
he stalked out and went home. The Cabinet and Sharett capitulated and
that same night Israel launched the biggest attack since the Gaza raid six
months earlier.

Unit 101 penetrated three miles inside Egyptian territory along the
Gaza Strip and assaulted an Egyptian police station at Khan Yunis and,
as a diversion, terrorized the small Arab village of Abasan. The casualties
were thirty-six killed and thirteen wounded, most of them police and
military personnel but some civilians as well.

• •

Foster Dulles still did not know of the attack early September 1 when
he telephoned his brother about a cable from Sharett pledging Israel's
peaceful intentions.

"I ought to send some reply to Sharett," said Foster.

"Trouble is," said Allen, "it was answered by an attack last night."

Foster wondered how Sharett could reconcile his cable with the attack.
"I can't reconcile it," said Allen.

Then Foster noticed the timing on the cable. It was sent after the
attack. Resignedly, he told Allen "to give some thought about what I
should do—if anything."

He did the only thing he could do: nothing.

• •

By mid-September, Dulles' concern about Egypt's arms negotiations
was becoming acute. On September 20, he had a morning meeting with
Soviet Foreign Minister Vyacheslav M. Molotov in New York, where
they both were attending U.N. sessions, and asked the Russian official

directly about the deal. Molotov admitted talks were going on but insisted that "we are doing it on a commercial basis and there are no political implications and no political ambitions or policies in that area."

"Whatever the basis is or is not," replied Dulles, according to his later telephone report to Herbert Hoover, Jr., the son of President Hoover and now the under secretary of state, "the fact is that if the military balance there is appreciably changed and if the situation were created where the Arabs felt they could destroy Israel and vice versa, it would probably lead to a war. It would be difficult for the U.S. to be wholly disinterested."

Molotov had replied that he did not think anything like that was going to happen. Nothing, he asserted, is likely to "develop there that will have serious repercussions."

Said Dulles to Hoover: "Molotov was a bit evasive." But, he added, "probably it was useful if things have not gone too far."

Hoover noted that reports from the area indicated that the deal had already gone quite far. But he suggested making "one further, final try —if it is not too late."

Hoover wanted to send to Cairo Kermit Roosevelt, a grandson of President Theodore Roosevelt and the CIA's specialist on the Middle East. Roosevelt was thirty-nine, roughly Nasser's age, a slim, short man with an infectious sense of humor and a winning smile who had known Nasser since early 1953. He had become extremely close to the Egyptian leader before Hank Byroade had arrived as ambassador, largely because Nasser had been uncomfortable with the previous ambassador, Jefferson Caffery, a gentleman of the old school who was in his advanced age and about to retire. Nasser could not identify with Caffery and finally complained, "I need an American I can talk to." He got the CIA's Roosevelt, who not only shared Nasser's youthful enthusiasms but also his fascination with intrigue. Roosevelt almost single-handedly had engineered the overthrow of Mohammed Mossadegh and the return of the Shah to the throne in Iran in 1953 and he was active with CIA plots throughout the Middle East. But he almost went too far in his early relations with Nasser.

At the suggestion of his undercover agent in Cairo, voluble Miles Copeland, he tried to put the new Egyptian leader on the CIA's payroll with a $3 million bribe. Copeland delivered the money to one of Nasser's aides late in 1953, but Nasser was offended and at first angrily thought of returning it. Then he had a better idea. He ordered the money spent on the construction of an ostentatious tower on Gezira Island in the Nile across from the future Hilton Hotel. Nasser's aides called the useless tower *el wa'ef rusfel,* Roosevelt's erection. Nasser had his laugh and forgave Roosevelt.

Despite Roosevelt's close relations with Nasser, there was a problem about sending him to see the Egyptian leader in the fall of 1955. Ambassador Byroade had also gotten close to Nasser by then and he was certain to resent Roosevelt's arrival as interference in his domain. Such considerations did not deter the gruff Herb Hoover. So far as he was concerned, Byroade had largely lost his usefulness in Cairo because his cables over the past months had become increasingly shrill about the dangers of not countering the arms offer by the Soviet Union. In typical bureaucratic fashion, the State Department began discounting Byroade's professionalism because his recommendations were at odds with official policy.

Dulles and Hoover devoted some time to the touchy question of Byroade's reaction to Roosevelt's arrival. It would, admitted Hoover, cause "an explosion, but enough is involved that we should not let it stand in our way. I would not feel satisfied we have done everything in our power unless Kim could go himself and talk with [Nasser]."

Dulles suggested that Byroade's feelings could be salved if they told him that the "CIA wants to see [Roosevelt] out, and we are not disposed to say no."

"That's a good idea," replied Hoover.

Dulles summoned Roosevelt and told him: "I want you to go to Cairo, Kim, and tell your friend Nasser that this [arms deal with Russia] would be a foolish thing to do."

While Roosevelt prepared for his unannounced trip, Dulles and Hoover continued to worry about the consequences of the arms deal. "I fear," Dulles said with prescience, "that the Israelis might start a war with Egypt. You could not expect the Israelis to sit idly by while Egypt was being fully equipped with massive armament by the Soviet Union."

"Nasser is under extreme pressure within his own group" to acquire weapons, said Hoover. He added that the Egyptian leader "was doing a lot of things to stave off being thrown out."

"Perhaps that is so," replied Dulles, "but on the other hand if the Soviets are going to send arms to Egypt we are almost forced to give arms to Israel. We will have to have some sort of agreement whereby we can do this. Otherwise things will develop in a very dangerous way."

. .

On September 21 Nasser privately informed Ambassador Byroade that he had definitely made up his mind to accept Soviet weaponry, and Byroade cabled that information to Washington. Yet on September 24, Foster Dulles still seemed confused about the matter, even after his conversation with Molotov, who had admitted to a commercial deal. In a telephone conversation with his brother, Foster said, "I don't know how reliable our facts are."

"The facts seem pretty firm," replied Allen.

"I talked with Molotov and he didn't deny it," admitted Foster, "so I think there is something to it. The magnitude [of the deal] is the important thing."

"I don't think we are going to get far protesting to the Russians," said Allen. "They will say you send arms to Iran and Turkey."

Of course, said Foster, "they have the legal right to [sell weapons to Egypt], but it may lead to war."

"Maybe that is what they want," said Allen.

"I don't think we'll get very far talking with Egypt," said Foster. "I really want to know how solid the facts are."

Allen assured the secretary of state that he would "check around and also find out what the British know. Wait until Kim gets back—a couple of days."

Foster Dulles, harassed by the rush of events, was incapable of recognizing how firm his facts already were. He had the confirmation of Molotov, Byroade's reports, and months of hints and rumors about the negotiations. Yet he was still not sure. He seemed unable to apprehend the reality that was there for all to see. The Soviet Union was about to make its historic move into the Middle East.

• •

Kim Roosevelt suffered no illusions about stopping Nasser. He was convinced that the process had already gone too far to be reversed, and he decided that the best he could do was to try to soften the impact. Over the years the relationship between Roosevelt, Copeland and Nasser had become so close that they were on a first-name basis, and the CIA agents felt quite comfortable in advising Nasser on everything from how to deal with the U.S. government to the finer points of diplomatic protocol, about which Nasser in the early years knew little. This became clear when Byroade first arrived in the country and weeks went by without Nasser officially receiving him, though they were meeting almost daily well into the night. Byroade began to suspect that Nasser was up to some kind of convoluted diplomatic game and complained to one of the leader's aides, only to discover that Nasser simply had not realized the importance of formally accepting Byroade's credentials as a new ambassador. The first thing the next day Nasser summoned Byroade to the presidential offices and officially welcomed him. "In those days Nasser and the colonels just didn't know anything about protocol," observed Byroade.

Roosevelt and Copeland, who by now had been reassigned to Washington, flew out to Cairo on September 23 and went directly to Nasser's apartment atop the Revolutionary Command Council building. "Nasser was in a teasing, 'I told you so' mood," recalled Copeland, "very cheerful and all set to enjoy hearing the famous Roosevelt persuasion grapple with his own unanswerable arguments. But Roosevelt surprised him."

Roosevelt suggested that Nasser couple the arms announcement with a peace gesture to Israel. "If the deal is as big as we hear it is," Roosevelt explained, "it will worry some people but in general it will make you a big hero. Why don't you take advantage of the sudden popularity to do something really statesmanlike?"

Nasser liked the idea and Copeland was assigned the task of writing up a conciliatory section toward Israel for the Egyptian leader's address. The night before Nasser planned to announce the deal, Copeland and Roosevelt went to his apartment with the moderating passage. "Nasser liked it and said he could easily work it into his speech—the only alteration being that he couldn't bring himself to mention explicitly 'peace with Israel,' " recalled Copeland. "Instead, he would say 'reduce the tensions between the Arabs and Israel.' "

While the three men sat talking, the duty officer called Nasser and said British Ambassador Trevelyan had urgently requested a meeting. "What could he want?" asked Nasser.

"Obviously, he wants to talk to you about the Soviet arms deal," replied Roosevelt. "Even if your own people haven't leaked it, the Soviets would have. It's not in their interests to keep it secret."

The British Embassy was across the Nile River from Nasser's second-story apartment, and the three men could see Sir Humphrey Trevelyan's Bentley pull out of the courtyard and work its way through traffic to the bridge. The two spies experienced a certain self-satisfied amusement in being in Nasser's private quarters while the British ambassador was formally received downstairs. The meeting lasted only a few minutes, during which Nasser admitted that the arms deal was set, saying it was not with the Soviet Union but with Prague.

The spies upstairs were a bit giddy under the unusual circumstances. "It was all very cheerful," recalled Copeland, with "jokes about what would have been the look on the British ambassador's face had Kim or I interrupted his meeting with Nasser to ask, 'Excuse me, Gamal, but we're out of soda.' " In high spirits, Nasser and the Americans, along with two other Egyptian officials, went off to the home of Ambassador Ahmed Hussein, the Egyptian envoy to Washington who was on home leave.

They were more than an hour late in arriving at Hussein's. Already there were Hank Byroade, unaware that the two Americans were even in the country, and Eric Johnston. The State Department had failed to inform the embassy of the CIA agents' arrival, presumably to avoid hurting Byroade's feelings, though Copeland suspected that Dulles and Hoover were simply too insensitive to think of it. "Ambassador Byroade is the most easygoing, unjealous, unstuffy, unbureaucratic senior official I have ever come across," wrote Copeland later. "But even he was likely to be stunned at the sudden sight of Kermit Roosevelt, of all people, walking one hour late into a dinner party arm-in-arm with the chief of state of the country and two of his top ministers, under circumstances that made it plain that they had just come from a meeting. And then there was the esoteric humor. Even under the best of circumstances it is annoying to find oneself on the fringes of a group absorbed in a private joke."

For Byroade, it was not even the best of circumstances. Several days earlier his labor attaché had been severely beaten by police in Alexandria, presumably because he was trying to promote a stronger labor union than the authoritarian regime wanted. Interrupting the jovial mood, Byroade, who was drinking Scotch, sternly said to Nasser, "Gamal, there is a matter which I would like to bring to your attention. One of my men was beaten nearly to death." In the sudden hush in the room, Nasser said he had heard of the incident and that the attaché had been suspected of being a spy. "He was no spy and yet he was beaten," snapped Byroade. He then launched into a diatribe against the Revolutionary Council members, accusing them of "acting like a lot of juvenile delinquents. I'm sorry, I thought we were in a civilized country."

Nasser furiously stubbed out his cigarette, spun on his heel and stormed out, much to the chagrin of everyone, especially the Americans.

"Roosevelt followed [Nasser] to the car and made some kind of apology," recalled Copeland. "Byroade sat rigidly, stunned not so much by Nasser's dramatic exit as because of the implications for him of Roosevelt's and Johnston's presence. Johnston waited until he heard Nasser's

Cadillac drive off, then tapped Byroade on the arm and said, 'Time to go home, Hank.' Off they went, Byroade looking like a somnambulist being led back to bed.''

Roosevelt and Johnston later went to the U.S. Embassy and sent a long cable to Foster Dulles describing the event and what Roosevelt called "Byroade's extraordinary behavior." Johnston said in the cable that he thought Byroade "needed a rest."

Byroade was beside himself the next morning when he learned that the two men had used his embassy to send the cable, taking all copies with them. He telephoned Roosevelt at his CIA safe house and demanded a copy. Roosevelt hesitated and the angry ambassador shouted: "If you don't bring that goddamn cable here I'm coming over with my Marine guard and take it." Roosevelt brought it over.

• •

Foster Dulles was angered by the British during the crisis. A story in *The New York Times,* datelined from London the same day as Byroade's disastrous dinner party with Nasser, asserted that the United States was about to sell arms to Egypt. "America is embarking on a slippery slope if it agrees to furnish arms to a country under virtual threat of blackmail," said an unnamed British official in the story. "Where does such a policy lead?"

Dulles and Hoover were upset. "It is one hundred and eighty degrees from the truth," protested Hoover in a telephone conversation with Dulles. Dulles concurred, adding: "[British Foreign Secretary Harold] Macmillan urged us to give more arms to Egypt."

"We can romp all over the British on this," declared Hoover.

"We can say categorically we have not discussed it for a couple of months or several weeks," added Dulles.

Cables arriving at the State Department estimated that the size of the Czech arms deal with Egypt was as great as $80 million. "If it is that large," said Hoover, "the Egyptians will be using a large proportion of their total exportable surpluses and will get in debt to the Russians, who will have a stranglehold." The two officials agreed that such a situation would make it difficult for America to continue to provide economic aid to Egypt since it "would help them pay for the arms."

Frustrated and at a loss about how to counter the Soviets in Egypt, Dulles became vengeful. He called Hoover again that day, September 27, and proposed some highly irregular actions against Nasser. "We have a lot of cards to play with Nasser—although they are mostly negative. The waters of the Upper Nile: we can strangle him if we want to. We can develop the Baghdad group and [we can] ruin the cotton market. We can switch this year's economic aid from Egypt to Iraq.''

Hoover had his doubts about the effectiveness of these procrustean schemes and reminded Dulles that the central issue was the great gain the Soviet Union was making in the region, not how to punish Nasser.

"We ought also to think about the stranglehold the Russians will have," said Hoover.

Dulles agreed. "The Russians will be the creditor and they can exploit it."

As indeed they did.

•   •

That same evening Nasser publicly announced that Egypt had completed an arms deal with Czechoslovakia after futilely seeking weapons from the West. "Heavy arms are controlled by the big powers and these agreed to provide Egypt's armed forces with arms, but on certain conditions," he said to the Egyptian people. "France bargained with us, saying that she would only supply us with arms if we refrained from criticizing her attitude in North Africa, which was another way of saying that we should abandon our Arabism . . . shut our eyes to massacres. The United States only gave us promises, making it a condition that we should sign a mutual defense agreement or pact. The United Kingdom said she would readily supply us with arms, but she has only sent us very small shipments."

Nasser said the arms transaction was a straight barter deal "on a purely commercial basis" by which Egyptian cotton and rice would be swapped for guns and ammunition.

Egyptians were jubilant about the historic deal and Arabs throughout the Middle East extolled the *baladi* from Upper Egypt who had finally broken the West's monopoly in the region. Nasser was the man of the hour in the Arab world.

•   •

Nasser's announcement on September 27 and the cable about Byroade hit Foggy Bottom like a bomb. "It is impossible to have a crisis and no recourse to the head of government," groaned Dulles to Assistant Secretary of State George V. Allen. He ordered Allen to fly to Cairo and "find out about the relationship between Byroade and Nasser." Then he made a grave mistake. He gave Allen the original of a cable he had sent

93

earlier to the embassy for Byroade to present to Nasser, insisting that Nasser not go through with the arms deal. He told Allen to deliver the cable personally to Nasser. It was, in effect, an ultimatum. But Dulles did not want to give the appearance of publicly threatening Nasser with cooler relations or a suspension of aid, so Hoover suggested that they explain Allen's trip by saying that he had been in Byroade's old job of head of Near Eastern affairs for several months now and had thought it was about time to visit the area of his responsibility. He could also go to Athens, Beirut and Tel Aviv to make it look like a swing through the region, suggested Hoover.

Allen wondered how he should explain to the press the purpose of the trip. Just say, advised Dulles airily, "to discuss et cetera current matters in the area."

Dulles wanted to pull Byroade out of Cairo for a personal explanation of what happened. But, he noted, "we are in a dilemma. If we pull him back, it looks like we are breaking relations." It was decided to let him stay temporarily.

Allen Dulles called Foster and relayed a message from Roosevelt. "Kim strongly urges there be no leaks to the press about the message Allen is bringing to Nasser. It is most important not to put him on the public spot."

Dulles assured him that there would be no statement. But before Allen even boarded the plane, the news leaked that a top State Department official was heading toward Cairo with an ultimatum for Nasser. The sensitive Egyptian leader was furious at the prospect of Washington treating him like a colonial lackey.

· ·

Kim Roosevelt met privately with Nasser to try to calm him before George Allen's arrival. He evasively told Nasser he doubted there was an ultimatum, but, he added, if there was one, why "don't you get the ultimatum first and raise a row later, rather than vice versa? If Allen gives you an ultimatum, react to it the way you think you should. But I don't think Secretary Dulles would be sending you an ultimatum without telling *me* about it." But Nasser pointed out that the Associated Press was telling the world that Allen was arriving with an ultimatum. "Associated Press is occasionally wrong, you know," Roosevelt insisted, knowing it was not in this case.

Nasser was somewhat assuaged, but he warned Roosevelt that if Allen delivered an ultimatum "I will throw him out."

Roosevelt and Byroade were distraught. They knew that if Nasser was given the ultimatum it would backfire against American interests. Yet Allen was on his way and they were unable to stop him.

• •

Allen arrived conspicuously as the only passenger aboard a special air force plane at 9:40 A.M. September 30 at Cairo airport. Jostling reporters and photographers were waiting for him and so was an anxious Ambassador Byroade. He bounded into the plane to warn Allen that the papers were filled with stories that he was bringing an ultimatum. It had "created a hell of a situation," he told Allen, and he urged him to be very careful in his remarks because tensions had propelled the Egyptians to the point of breaking diplomatic relations with Washington. "If you say anything about an ultimatum," warned Byroade, "your ass is out of here right now."

Before they could join the newsmen, an Egyptian messenger ran up to them with an envelope marked "Personal. To be opened on the plane." Inside was a message from Kim Roosevelt also warning Allen not to make any mention of the ultimatum. The emissary from Washington was getting the message.

The first question from the reporters, of course, was whether he carried an ultimatum. No, replied the courtly Allen. In fact, he added, he did not even have an appointment with Nasser.

For a while it looked as though he might not get one either. When the U.S. officials arrived at the embassy, Allen had an aide telephone for a meeting with Nasser but was told that the Egyptian leader was not available that day.

Allen, Byroade, Johnston and Roosevelt discussed what to do with the ultimatum. "If your ultimatum has any threats in it we can carry out, by all means present it," said Johnston. But it was obvious that it did not. Then, asked Johnston, "I don't suppose it would do any good to tell you just to tear it up and throw it away?"

Allen could not do that. An order from the secretary of state was binding. Perhaps he could mumble when he read it, someone suggested only half facetiously. About this time Kim Roosevelt became so impatient with the futile talk that he left to play tennis. In the end, the officials agreed that Allen should read the ultimatum but under no circumstances should he leave it with Nasser, who might be tempted to publish it in order to embarrass Washington.

After the others had gone, Byroade said to Allen, "George, your coming here was a goddamn mistake." "I know," replied Allen, "but I have my orders." It was obvious that those orders were turning the whole affair into a major international flap, a flap that could have been avoided if Byroade had been allowed to deliver the message in the normal course of his duties. Instead, the whole affair was now being played out in headlines. Allen explained to Byroade that Hoover had insisted on his trip because of the ambassador's quarrel with Nasser. But what Washington had not known was that Byroade and Nasser, by now close friends, occasionally had such disagreements in the past and had quickly forgotten them.

Miles Copeland discovered this the morning after Nasser's brusque exit from the dinner party when Byroade asked him to deliver a note of apology to the Egyptian. Arriving at Nasser's office, Copeland handed over the note and then waited for his comment. "I'll just file it with the others," Nasser casually remarked.

"The *others?*" asked a stupefied Copeland.

"Oh, Hank's always blowing up like that," he said. "I hope Kim and Eric didn't make too much of it."

"Make too much of it?" Copeland later wrote. "They had just sent a cable which would probably get Byroade transferred to Fernando Poo. Clearly, Byroade had established a relationship with Nasser which enabled him to speak up frankly about any of Nasser's actions he did not like; and Nasser obviously took it seriously or let Byroade's remarks go in one ear and out of the other depending on his mood of the moment, with no offense. One thing was certain: he did not want Byroade's angry remarks of the evening before to get him into trouble." But it was too late.

• •

The morning after Allen's arrival, Nasser consented to meet with him and Byroade. After keeping them waiting for more than an hour and a half in the anteroom of the ornate old Presidency of the Council of Ministers Palace, the Egyptian received them by giving Byroade a friendly smile—the flap that had sent Allen winging to Cairo no longer existed. Now there was one even worse.

Allen was forthright, declaring immediately that there was no point in denying that he was there because of the Czech arms deal. He spoke in generalities about the U.S. position against introducing weapons into the region, then he read parts of the ultimatum, changing Dulles' "I" to "we" and keeping his hand over Dulles' signature so Nasser could not see that it was a personal letter to him.

Nasser complained about his inability to get weapons from the U.S. and cited Kennett Love's story about Israel's superiority in military strength. The United States obviously wanted to keep it that way, accused Nasser, patting a pile of American newspaper clippings, or else the press would not be making such a fuss about the Czech arms deal. "This is what is wrong with your policy," said Nasser.

He expanded his remarks the next day in a public speech. "Since [the Gaza raid] we have begun to examine what is really meant by peace and balance of power in this region and what we have found was that they [the West] meant only partiality to Israel. They know that, without arms, we cannot but stay under their influence. And now that we have been able to get arms—unconditionally—we have become truly liberated." His remarks were greeted by ecstatic applause by the Egyptian people.

• •

Nasser a few days later returned to the theme of the West's partiality toward Israel in a speech to newly commissioned officers at the military academy. He charged that Israel was stronger than Egypt because the West had been secretly selling its weapons while denying them to Egypt. "I will tell you about this great deception," he declared, taking a paper from an aide. "This is a French document intercepted by the Egyptian intelligence. It lists Israeli purchases of heavy arms from the United States and Britain." He said it showed that Israel had bought ninety-seven aircraft, hundreds of Sherman tanks, armored cars and artillery pieces.

"United States newspapers say Israel can raise an army of 250,000 men, more than all the Arabs put together," he declared. "This is peace —this is the balance of power they keep talking about."

In another speech, Nasser also revealed that he had informed the United States as early as June about his talks with the Soviet Union, "but it seems they did not believe me. I suppose they thought it was a bluff. I needed the arms and I had no alternative but to supply myself from the East."

Washington officials baldly denied having advance knowledge about the deal, though of course they had. "Officials voiced incredulity at Premier Nasser's statement," reported *The New York Times*. "There was no hint in United States-Egyptian talks in June that the alternative to arms from the West was arms from the Soviet bloc, it was said.''

With such prevarications, there was little wonder that Nasser felt suspicious of the intentions of the United States and the West.

• •

Nasser had one other meeting with Allen, which, like the first one, was friendly since the ultimatum was completely ignored. But the meeting was unproductive in breaking the impasse. Nasser was going ahead with the Czech arms deal. On October 4, five days after his arrival, George Allen left Cairo without any agreement to stem the Soviet Union's entry into the Middle East. He did not even bother stopping in Athens to keep up the pretense that he was in the region on a routine trip. It had all been in vain, and Nasser had clearly won. He was becoming modern Arabia's greatest hero. But in the West, questions were being raised. Nasser, it began to appear, might be a greater danger to Western interests than had been realized.

CHAPTER V

Reduced to Derision

EBAN

IT WAS 5 A.M. when Dwight Eisenhower rose from his bed and began frying bacon and eggs for himself and his five friends, a morning chore he enjoyed performing in the coolness of the Rocky Mountains. The President was at the end of an unusually long vacation, six weeks, and had just spent four happy days fishing in St. Louis Creek, which flowed through the ranch on the edge of Fraser, Colorado. In a few hours that Friday morning of September 23, Ike was returning to Denver to catch up on some presidential paper work, then have a last round of golf before flying back to Washington.

When he walked into his Denver office, tanned and fresh-faced, his secretary, Ann Whitman, observed that "I have never seen him look or act better. He was delightful, patient with a pile of work, handed me a letter from Dr. Milton [Eisenhower] and said, 'See what a wonderful brother I have.' He sat and talked for a little while after he got through the work before he went to the golf course."

At the Cherry Hills Country Club, Ike and his party had barely started playing when he was called off the course by a telephone call from Foster Dulles. But by the time he arrived at the clubhouse telephone, Dulles had gone, off to an urgent appointment. He left word that he would call back in one hour. Ike went back to the links and an hour later interrupted his game again and returned to the clubhouse. There was trouble on the line and the two high officials could not hear each other. Again Eisenhower went back to his game and again he was interrupted, this time finally talking with his secretary of state. By this time, as Eisenhower recalled, he and his friends decided to break off their game and have lunch "because the morning's golf had been so badly broken up." After a lunch of a "huge hamburger sandwich generously garnished with slices of Bermuda onion and accompanied by a pot of coffee," he returned to the golf course—only to be called off again at the first hole.

The President drove his little golf cart back to the clubhouse to discover that the summons was a mistake. An operator had not realized that he had already completed his call with Dulles. "My disposition deteriorated rapidly," Ike mildly noted in his memoirs. Actually, said his physician, General Howard McCrum Snyder, the President was in a towering rage, worse than any he had ever seen, and he had seen much of the famous Ike temper.

After completing nine holes of golf in the afternoon, Eisenhower and his good friend George E. Allen, a jolly Mississippian, went to the home of the President's mother-in-law in Denver, a city he always remembered affectionately because it was there he and Mamie had been married thirty-nine years earlier. He and Allen played billiards and, following a dinner of roast lamb, Ike retired at 10 P.M. Three and a half hours later his wife heard him stir and asked what was bothering him. The President thought he had an upset stomach, but Mamie suspected it was more serious than that. She immediately called General Snyder, who gave Eisenhower a shot of morphine so he could sleep. Ike awoke at 11 A.M. and Snyder examined his patient again and confirmed his fears: the President had suffered a severe coronary thrombosis. Ike was rushed to Fitzsimons General Hospital, just outside of Denver, and was placed in an oxygen tent.

"Apparently the first time the President knew that he had had a heart attack was when they put him in the oxygen tent at the hospital," recalled Ann Whitman. "General Snyder said his eyes filled with tears. Of course he knew it was serious—he mentioned his wallet."

• •

The illness of Dwight Eisenhower plunged the top officials of his Administration into deep anxiety. During those first three days while the President lay under an oxygen tent, a series of urgent contingencies had to be faced by the senior members of the government. Foremost, they had to assure the continued functioning of the country both at home and abroad, yet in certain circumstances there were no clear constitutional guidelines. What if the heart attack had incapacitated Ike? There were no procedural provisions for the delegation of presidential power; the

Twenty-fifth Amendment that established the process for delegating presidential power came only twelve years later. Yet the United States could not in the nuclear age afford a replay of the anguished months of doubt and drift that had accompanied Woodrow Wilson's incapacitation by a paralytic stroke.

The dangers for the country and the Eisenhower Administration loomed large those first hectic days. But by Tuesday the oxygen tent was removed and Ike's doctors assured the White House staff that he would be strong enough to take part in conferences within two weeks. That erased the immediate fear of having a vegetable President. But it did not solve how the government should be run while he was in his Denver hospital bed.

The situation was fraught with the potential for political infighting. The election year was just months away, and it was generally believed that Ike's illness, at his age, had removed any chance that he would run again. The door to the presidency appeared wide open.

The first order of business for the Administration's senior officials was to demonstrate to the country that the government was stable and functioning normally. That could best be shown by continuing Eisenhower's habit of holding weekly meetings of the National Security Council and the Cabinet, and the senior officials quickly agreed among themselves to do that. The first Cabinet meeting took place on September 30, a week after Ike's heart attack. Every effort was made to make the meeting appear routine, but in fact its secret purpose was to thrash out how to operate the government while the President regained his strength.

In a telephone call to Foster Dulles' office, an aide to White House Chief of Staff Sherman Adams confided that "the principal subject for discussion [at the Cabinet meeting] will be the organization of the government. Every attempt is being made to make this appear as a 'normal' Cabinet meeting, and we would like to have a number of other items on the agenda which could be given to the press." Dulles was asked to talk for ten or fifteen minutes about international developments so the charade could be maintained that the meeting was just another weekly gathering of the Cabinet.

Dulles obliged, and at the Friday gathering told the Cabinet members that "the most critical problems at this time concern the Near East. The Russian armament aid jeopardizes the near settlement of affairs between Israel and Egypt, and might also be extended to create a flow of arms to other African areas." Minutes of the meeting added: "Dulles indicated existence but not the nature of U.S. plans for coping with the situation."

There was no such plan. Part of Dulles' success in gaining high office obviously included a lawyerly ability to imply that there was more than met the eye. At this time George Allen was in Cairo swallowing Dulles' ultimatum to Nasser in the wake of the fiasco over the Czech arms deal.

The meeting quickly got down to its real purpose, which as it turned out included a clever gambit encouraged by Sherman Adams and Dulles that blocked the ambitious and widely disliked vice president, Richard M. Nixon, from exploiting Ike's illness for his own political ends. The attorney general read a statement for Cabinet approval that Adams should be dispatched to Denver to act as "the channel for presentation of matters to the President." Such a move would effectively eclipse Nixon from any direct involvement in presidential matters, and the vice president questioned the arrangement. But, recalled Adams, "Dulles came out firmly and emphatically for stationing me with Eisenhower in Denver as the liaison officer who would handle all matters concerning government business coming to and from the President."

As the most powerful of the Cabinet members, Dulles, by backing the proposal, assured its passage, sealed Nixon's isolation, and incidentally saved his own position as the President's vicar of foreign policy. "He wanted to make sure that nobody would get between the President and himself," observed Adams. "I had worked with Dulles long enough so that he felt that with me in Denver he had less to worry about on that score."

After the meeting, a press release spelled out Adams' position and pointedly noted that the Cabinet had rejected any further delegation of presidential powers. Throughout Eisenhower's nearly two-month hospitalization in Denver, Nixon was confined to presiding over the regular meetings of the National Security Council and the Cabinet. He played no substantive part in the daily operation of the government, and to his credit he made no effort to subvert Adams' role.

Oddly, when Sherman Adams later looked back at that period, he counted it "good fortune" that the U.S. was spared any crisis during that last week of September 1955 while Ike lay gravely ill. Others since then have repeated the refrain, counting the country lucky that there was a "lull in international relations," as historian Herbert S. Parmet wrote.

Nothing could be farther from the truth. While the President was bedridden and the highest officials of the government struggled with the constitutional complexities of exercising presidential power, the Soviets irretrievably entered the Middle East and the region was set on the path to war.

. .

In the Middle East, Egypt had retaliated on September 11 for Israel's August raids by tightening its blockade of the Straits of Tiran at the mouth of the Gulf of Aqaba. Cairo declared the straits Egyptian territory and warned all shipping and air companies that passage through the straits, whether by sea or by air, required Egyptian approval. The move completely blocked Israel's Negev port of Elath from trade with Africa and Asia, and brought a sharp reaction from Tel Aviv. Israel contended that the straits were an international waterway through which, under international law, all countries enjoyed free passage. The Egyptian action, Tel Aviv charged, was illegal and would "aggravate the danger of incidents prejudicial to peace and security in the area." Egypt maintained that since the countries were at war, the blockade was legal.

Privately, General Moshe Dayan declared the action "the last straw."

But Dayan was wrong. There were even graver developments in store for Israel. On September 27 came the announcement of Egypt's Czech arms deal. The shock to the Israeli public was traumatic. Though no weapons had arrived yet and it would take at least another two years for the poorly trained Egyptian troops to learn to employ them, the public perception in Israel was, in the words of historian Michael Bar-Zohar, that "suddenly, the danger of Israel's destruction by the Arab states had become very real."

Thousands of worried and frightened Israelis donated jewelry and other valuables to the government for the purchase of arms, unaware of Israel's secret purchases of superior French weapons. Nasser, who in Arab eyes was now the great hero of modern Islam, became for Israelis the devil who was threatening their existence. Such perceptions at this point were exaggerated. What the Egyptian Army needed "more than modern weapons," observed the U.N.'s chief of staff, General Burns, "was better morale, better discipline, better training." As for Israeli charges that Egypt was arming to go to war against the Jewish state, Burns noted: "No Israeli ever so much as suggested that it was the tough Ben Gurion-Dayan policy that had practically forced Nasser to accept the Russo-Czech arms proposals. What other enemy threatened Egypt?"

However hyperbolic Israeli fears, the country's trepidation was heightened further on October 4 when Dulles coolly said at a press conference that Egypt could hardly be blamed for buying weapons. It is "difficult to be critical of countries which, feeling themselves endangered, seek the arms which they sincerely need for defense," Dulles said in Washington. The U.S. was obviously still courting Nasser, whom Ben Gurion began to loathe.

Nasser at first had seemed a pretty decent fellow, Ben Gurion confided to *The New York Times*'s Cyrus Sulzberger that autumn, but now he found Nasser to be "a crafty, deceitful, Arab type."

• •

It was a difficult and frustrating period for Ben Gurion and his struggling country. Attempts to draw Israel closer to the United States were continually rebuffed by Washington. Israel wanted American weapons and American guarantees of its existence, but Washington was leery. Ben Gurion went so far as to promise that "if the United States built up airfields, roads and ports and industrial backup [inside Israel, then] all Israel was a base for the United States in the event of trouble." Dulles and Eisenhower rejected the offer, realizing that such a close association would make Israel more of a U.S. dependency than it already was and would alienate even further the Arab world.

Dulles also put off repeated importunities by Israel's ambassador, Abba Eban, for a U.S. guarantee of Israel's security by pointedly observing that America could not "guarantee temporary armistice lines." Israel must first define its borders, insisted Dulles, before America could guarantee them. That, of course, Israel had no intention of doing. Set borders would mean limiting future expansion, and no Israeli politician was strong enough to defy the powerful Zionist expansionist elements in the country by precluding territorial growth. Ben Gurion himself had always been careful never to set limits on the size of the country, as his biographer, Bar-Zohar, related. "Ben Gurion certainly did not want to issue a specific declaration that would curtail his aspirations to extend the boundaries of the state," Bar-Zohar wrote. "He proceeded to reveal [in 1948] some of his ideas to his colleagues: 'If the U.N. does not come into account in this matter and [the Arab states] make war against us and we defeat them . . . why should we bind ourselves?' The state's boundaries would not be mentioned in the Proclamation of Independence." Indeed, Israel had expanded its boundaries in the 1948 war from 5,893 square miles, 56.47 percent of the land of Palestine, granted it under the U.N. Partition Plan of November 29, 1947, to about 8,000 square miles, equal to 77.4 percent, an increase in total acreage of nearly 40 percent.

Eban, in his discussions with Dulles, contended that a security pact between Israel and America should not depend on set borders. He claimed that "the entire principle of a defense agreement with the United

States was reduced to derision when it was made dependent on impossible conditions. All the Arabs had to do to prevent an American guarantee to Israel was to refuse to reach agreement on a permanent boundary." But Dulles did not buy that argument. If Israel wanted U.S. guarantees, it had to define its boundaries unilaterally; agreement with the Arabs could come later. But this Israel refused to do.

Nor was Eban any more successful in acquiring arms from the U.S. Dulles and other officials rebuffed Eban's persistent demands for American weapons with the rejoinder that "Israel would win a crushing victory" in any war, Eban recalled. "There was a total refusal to believe that there was any limit to Israel's nervous strength and that in the absence of any military aid or political commitment, desperation would come to inspire our policy.

"The fear that Israel's security was being compromised [by the Czech arms deal] to a horrifying degree was not merely a subjective 'complex' of Israelis," insisted Eban. But to a large extent that was exactly what it was. The CIA knew that Israel was secretly buying French arms, and when the time for battle came, Israeli strength proved to be, as U.S. analysts had predicted, overwhelmingly superior. The groans about Israel's supposed weakness were more a reflection of a "complex" than of reality. But the fears were real enough, and they influenced Israeli policy just as profoundly as if they were grounded in fact.

• •

Within six days after his attack, President Eisenhower was able to sign his first official document. It was a list of foreign service appointments, and he had only to initial it but he insisted on signing his full name. Sherman Adams had flown to Denver the same day as the September 30 Cabinet meeting, and he found Ike "weak but cheerful and relaxed." The Middle East and its endemic troubles were far from Eisenhower's mind, though the Czech arms deal had just been announced. He was more concerned about the future of America and what today is called ecology. "We previously considered that every man's land, as well as his home, was his castle," Ike remarked to Sherman Adams. "[The owner] was permitted to ruin it. But a nation cannot divest itself of interest in its own soil." Soil is permanent and lasting, the President observed, and he wanted to launch a program that would turn over to "coming generations an enriched soil rather than a depleted soil."

Each week Adams flew to Washington for the Friday Cabinet meeting and returned to the Denver hospital with reports on the Cabinet's actions.

For the October 14 meeting, Adams brought to the Cabinet Eisenhower's orders that 100,000 employees be cut from the federal payroll. Economy was a constant concern of Ike's. He told Adams that he suspected that "unnecessary personnel could be found in dark corners" to make the cut without affecting the government's efficiency.

During his slow convalescence, Eisenhower repeatedly returned to his enduring concern about the nation's natural resources. To his agriculture secretary, Ezra Taft Benson, Ike said, "As far as I am concerned, there is no indestructible metal in the world I would not trade for perishable items. Some day the world is going to be out of exhaustible resources. If we can trade perishable items for durable items, we are enriching our country." He urged Benson to see what kind of trade for surplus food might be established with the Soviet Union. As the President had earlier told Adams, "We would be better off if we bartered surplus agricultural products with the Russians for magnesium and titanium. Such stockpiles would not deteriorate and would be a wonderful investment."

• •

While the President spent his hospital days pondering the higher priorities of the nation, Foster Dulles remained in Washington grappling with the political realities. Ever cautious, Dulles was careful not to go beyond policies laid down by the President before his illness. Yet he was acutely sensitive to the political fallout of foreign affairs, especially in the Middle East, and he tried to protect his flank by keeping Democratic leaders informed of his policies. Now, with an election year coming up, his thoughts were on a scheme to neutralize criticism of the Administration's Middle East policies.

Dulles called Nixon on October 17 and explained that the Middle East had become so "filled with danger that we could lose the whole Arab world if we play this on a partisan basis." He wondered if it were possible to convince the Democrats "to designate someone who could work with us on this problem. The person would be in a consultative position and in close touch with leaders in Congress."

Nixon quickly got the point, noting that otherwise "both sides might make political capital out of this thing."

"The tendency here is going to be to take an anti-Arab policy," said Dulles. "It is a very difficult and complicated problem and one which I am quite sure we won't solve if both sides are looking over their shoulder at political consequences here at home."

Nixon noted that the Democrats might not want to cooperate, but he agreed to attend a meeting the next day in Dulles' office.

Dulles and Nixon were joined on Tuesday by other senior members of the government: Treasury Secretary George Humphrey, Defense Secretary Charles Wilson, Attorney General Herbert Brownell and Under Secretary of State Herbert Hoover, Jr. Dulles opened the discussion by explaining that "we are in the present jam because the past Administration had always dealt with the Middle East from a political standpoint and had tried to meet the wishes of the Zionists in this country. That had created a basic antagonism with the Arabs. That was what the Russians were capitalizing on. It is of the utmost importance for the welfare of the United States that we get away from a political basis and try to develop a national nonpartisan policy. Otherwise, we may be apt to lose the whole area and possibly Africa. This would be a major disaster for Western Europe as well as the United States."

What Dulles was really worried about, he said with stunning prescience, was that during the presidential campaign "the Israelis will make some moves which for political reasons it might seem to the advantage of some to back, but with disastrous consequences."

Nixon agreed, but he cautioned that an attempt to be nonpartisan in the Middle East "might alienate much of the Jewish vote." Others joined Nixon in expressing doubt about whether a suitable Democrat could actually be found. In the end, the meeting was inconclusive and the Republicans entered the campaign vulnerable to partisan attacks on their dealings with Israel.

• •

In Tel Aviv, Ben Gurion was not prepared to wait for any election in the United States before wresting the area back from what he considered a progressively dangerous pro-Nasser drift. His apprehensions were heightened by the fact that the United States was considering making a spectacular offer to Egypt: loans to build Nasser's dream, the Aswan High Dam, a project greater than the construction of the largest pyramid. It would be a mammoth undertaking that could only bring more glory to the soaring star of the Egyptian leader, and closer ties between Egypt and America. It was not in Israel's interests to see any of this occur.

To Ben Gurion's distress, Nasser seemed to be succeeding everywhere. On October 20, Egypt and Syria joined in a military pact that established a supreme council, a war council and a joint command under

107

an Egyptian general. The pact was aimed mainly at countering the British-sponsored Baghdad Pact, whose members included two of Syria's bordering neighbors, Turkey and Iraq, where Britain retained two air bases and enormous influence. Nasser saw association with the highly unstable government of Syria as a way of strengthening anti-British factions in the country and combating Western attempts at isolating him in the region. He was feeling outflanked and smothered by a hostile Israel on the east, a British-dominated Sudan on the south, an American-dominated Libya to the west, and the Baghdad Pact to the north. Everywhere Nasser looked he saw Western-dominated countries closing a noose around Egypt.

The alliance with Syria gave him breathing space. It interposed a fellow neutralist country between Turkey and Iraq, both totally co-opted by the West, and displayed his independence and virility to those die-hard colonialists in Britain and France who still thought of the Middle East as their exclusive economic milk cow.

The alliance was formally described as a military pact, but that was more Arabic fantasizing than reality. British intelligence estimated Syria's Army had only twenty-five thousand men and eight jets. Syria was in the throes of upheaval, assaulted both internally and externally, especially by Iraq, which with Britain's active encouragement was seeking to take over the dazed country as an extension of pro-Western power. It was not a reliable military ally, and in fact most of the military provisions of the alliance went unrealized. Nasser was so wary of Syrian factiousness that he declined to proceed with even the most rudimentary cooperative measures in the military field. It was reported, wrote the London *Observer*'s Middle East correspondent, Patrick Seale, that Nasser was "reluctant even to agree to the minimum cooperation required to group operational forces on the Palestine front under a single command." The importance of the disorganized Syrians for Nasser was diplomatic and symbolic, not as a military partner.

But in Israel, the military alliance was seen by Ben Gurion as a direct threat to his country. The only thing more threatening than friendly U.S.-Egyptian ties, in Ben Gurion's eyes, was unity among Israel's Arab neighbors. Nasser's alliance with Syria looked like a dangerous step toward that unity. His fears were now in full bloom, and his patience at an end. Ben Gurion, still trying to form his own government, decided that war was the only answer.

On October 22, he sent Moshe Dayan, then vacationing in Paris, an urgent message to return immediately. "Next day I met Ben Gurion in his room at the President Hotel in Jerusalem," Dayan recorded in his diary. "I reviewed the security situation and the current problems we faced. At the end of the talk, he, as minister of defense, instructed me, among other things, to be prepared to capture the Straits of Tiran."

Among the other things Ben Gurion gave Dayan were orders to prepare contingency plans for the occupation of the Gaza Strip and an offensive into northern Sinai. In a word, it was war.

• •

For President Eisenhower and his secretary of state, the Middle East had little importance in their thoughts in the second half of October. Ike had observed his sixty-fifth birthday in the Denver hospital on October 14, and five days later he met with Foster Dulles to discuss the approaching foreign ministers' meeting at Geneva that had been scheduled as a consequence of the highly popular Summit Conference three months earlier. The Soviet Union and the West had seemed to achieve a new trust in their relations at the Summit and the friendly echoes of the Spirit of Geneva were still resounding around the world. But privately both Eisenhower and Dulles had retained their reservations about the sincerity of the post-Stalin leadership of Nikita Khrushchev and Nikolai Bulganin. Following the summit, the U.S. news media had quickly expressed doubt about Soviet intentions (columnist James Reston opined that the "Russians are waiting it out . . . counting on our impatience and on Europe's weariness and divisions") and within three weeks Foster Dulles sent all mission chiefs a gloomy appraisal of U.S.-U.S.S.R. relations.

In Dulles' opinion, the new Soviet leadership had sought the conference because Russia needed time to catch up to American strength. The Summit was a strategic respite for the Soviets while they consolidated their economic base, he explained. Their need to buy time also explained, he contended, why the Soviets were suddenly willing to make such concessions as agreeing to the Austrian State Treaty that on May 14 had brought about Russia's willingness to withdraw its World War II occupation troops from that country.

Dulles seemed to miss, or preferred to ignore, an alternate explanation: that the Soviet Union had just changed leadership, that paranoiac old Joe Stalin was a bad memory of the past, and that a new generation might be trying to find a more conciliatory way in the world. Instead, he advised U.S. missions around the world that the Spirit of Geneva was probably a Communist ploy. Certainly the Summit had created problems for the Western allies, he noted. "For eight years they have been held together largely by a cement compounded of fear and a sense of moral superiority. Now the fear is diminished and the moral demarcation is somewhat blurred. There is some bewilderment . . . as to how to adjust to the new situation.''

He warned that no euphoric sense of the Spirit of Geneva could justify ''the free world relaxing its vigilance or substantially altering its programs for collective security. We must assume that the Soviet leaders consider their recent change of policy to be an application of the classic Communist maneuver known as 'zig-zag'—i.e., resort to the tactics of retreat . . . 'to buy off a powerful enemy and gain a respite' (Stalin). We must not be caught by any such maneuver.''

Eisenhower shared such suspicions. He was particularly worried that the Geneva thaw would lessen European resolve to keep NATO a strong defensive force. On October 19, the same day he saw Dulles in the Denver hospital, Ike remarked to his private secretary, Ann Whitman, that ''the United States did not claim we had made great accomplishments alone. We have staunch allies, we are standing together economically, militarily and morally—especially the latter—and that is why the whole world is having something approaching a rejuvenation. Collective security is our only defense against the Russians.''

Eisenhower also wrote a letter to Nixon to make it clear that the secretary of state was going to Geneva with the President's full support. The letter was vintage Ike, diplomatic and considerate, yet forcefully conveying his wishes. Dulles was going to Geneva, Ike wrote, ''not only as secretary of state, but as my personal representative having my complete confidence and with whom I have continuous close understanding . . . He must be the one who both at the conference table and before the world speaks with authority for our country.'' It was a not-so-gentle warning to Nixon and the other Cabinet members that Dulles retained the President's favor and was to be the sole spokesman on foreign affairs while Eisenhower remained hospitalized. By such sapient stratagems the President kept his Cabinet under control and spared the country the confusion of conflicting voices purporting to speak in his name.

Despite the trust expressed in him by the President's letter, Dulles had reason to be extremely cautious in his actions during Eisenhower's confinement. Whatever else he did, he did not want to follow in the footsteps of his uncle, Robert Lansing, who was dismissed as secretary of state after he tried to transform the Cabinet into a ruling body during the long illness of Woodrow Wilson. The parallels of his predicament with his uncle's were not lost on Dulles. Throughout the President's illness, he was careful to consult and stay within guidelines laid down by Eisenhower.

Because of Eisenhower's illness, Dulles was less aggressive than he might normally have been at the foreign ministers' meeting at Geneva. White House staffers had already noted how cautious the secretary of state was acting in the wake of Ike's hospitalization. "Foster seems lost without the Boss," commented Sherman Adams. At Geneva, Dulles looked tired and haggard and had a painful scab on his lip. When Britain's Foreign Secretary Harold Macmillan urged Dulles to confront the Soviets over the Czech arms deal, he declined on grounds that he did not want to seem to be exceeding the ailing President's instructions. "He wanted no accusation that he was moving without guidance, abandoning Eisenhower's pacific purposes," noted biographer Louis L. Gerson.

Two days after the conference started it was obvious that the Spirit of Geneva had evaporated. Dulles kept Eisenhower closely informed of the conference activities, and by October 29 the President told chief of staff Adams that "it finally becomes clear that the Russians are going to make no concessions. They are playing a game to make inroads on French and Italian public opinion at the same time that they double-cross us in the Middle East."

The President ordered Adams to send a cable to Dulles telling him to put on the record that the U.S. "must not be a party to a false peace or to prolongation of any kind of any conference when obviously the other side is acting in bad faith and is not concerned with the objectives of the conference." If Dulles had any hesitation about making such a tough statement, Eisenhower added, he would send him "direct instructions, unequivocal and in accordance with what I want."

The conference ended in acerbic deadlock, but not before the Middle East intruded. Though the region's problems were not on the agenda, they popped up in the form of Israeli Prime Minister Moshe Sharett and Ambassador Abba Eban. Just before he was to turn over his premiership to Ben Gurion, Sharett had impetuously decided to travel to Geneva to make a dramatic bid for weapons for Israel in private meetings with the Western foreign ministers. He even met with Vyacheslav Molotov, the Soviet foreign minister, in an attempt to persuade him to limit the Czech arms sales to Egypt. "Molotov was unresponsive to the point of rudeness," commented Eban. "He obviously regarded Israel's intrusion in Geneva as irrelevant. The issue was not Israel and the Arab states, but America and Russia."

The Israelis had better luck with French Prime Minister Edgar Faure,

III

who promised quick delivery of advanced Mystère IV jets. The United States and Britain were less forthcoming, and Sharett finally gave up his lonely pursuit.

• •

Ben Gurion had entertained no hope that Sharett's quixotic quest would succeed, nor did he believe that begging for weaponry was the principal course that Israel should pursue. He was determined to smash the pattern of events favoring the Arabs and forcefully establish Israel's paramountcy and permanence. While Sharett journeyed hat in hand in Europe, Ben Gurion orchestrated a war strategy against Egypt in the Middle East.

The focus of Israeli moves was the strategic demilitarized zone of El Auja on the Egyptian border southeast of the Mediterranean coastal town of El Arish. Control of the 145-square-kilometer zone of El Auja, called Nitzana in Hebrew, was imperative for an attack across the sandy wastes of north-central Sinai. The zone centered on an important road junction, with roads leading north to the coast and west to the Suez Canal, the only paved road directly connecting Palestine and Egypt at the time.

Israel had been quietly trying to absorb the zone for years. In 1950 it had expelled 7,000 Bedouins from part of it, and in September 1953 its armed forces invaded the zone, killed the remaining Bedouins and their livestock, and established a kibbutz called Ketsiot. Though Egypt protested the settlement in the demilitarized zone, Israel insisted that the General Armistice Agreement stated only that "armed forces" were excluded from the zone. The kibbutz was a civilian one, Israel claimed. Actually, it was made up of regular and paramilitary forces; their only distinction from being an armed force was that they did not wear uniforms. Nonetheless, Israel insisted on its civilian status and refused to abandon the settlement. Egypt did not press its claims nor did the U.N. at the time condemn Tel Aviv. Explained General Burns: "Owing to newness in the job, I did not understand the character of the settlement."

The presence of the armed kibbutzniks was a constant irritant. They did little farming, the purported reason for their presence in the zone, and instead spent much of their time roaming over the area. Like the Regular Army, they provocatively patrolled right up to the Egyptian frontier, taunting the Arab soldiers on the other side, and at times exchanged fire with Egyptian positions. On May 11, 1955, four armed Israelis emerged from the zone into Egyptian territory, attacked an Egyptian patrol and killed two of the soldiers. A month later, on June 14, kibbutzniks forcefully took away the jeep of the Egyptian member of the armistice commission despite protests of a U.N. observer and the Egyptian's special status as a neutral.

The ensuing summer months were filled with squabbling by both sides over demarcation of the international frontier of the rectangular zone in the sandy wastes of the Sinai. The Egyptians at first agreed, and then refused, to have joint Egyptian-Israeli surveyor teams mark the western frontier. They apparently feared that demarcating only the western frontier closest to Egypt would be a tacit admission that the zone was in Israeli territory, as Jewish officials were routinely referring to it. Israel then proceeded on its own, against U.N. advice, and set up a number of demarcation pillars on the western side of the zone. The Egyptians imprudently retaliated in mid-September by stealthily pulling down and destroying twenty-one of them.

The inevitable response came on September 21 when Israel openly sent two companies of soldiers into the zone, occupying the buildings used by the armistice commission and wounding two Egyptian soldiers attached to the commission as neutral observers. In negotiating the withdrawal of the Israeli troops, General Burns made a careless mistake. He agreed that Israel could place "civilian" police inside the zone to protect the "civilian" settlers at Ketsiot.

The Egyptians were outraged, and Burns soon began to realize that he had been taken in by a common Israeli ruse. Now Israel had two armed groups within the zone under U.N. auspices. Burns later admitted that he should have known better because "the Israelis played this trick of camouflaging soldiers as civil police on other occasions. Although I had been over a year in Palestine, I was still sufficiently naïve to believe that statements of senior officials of the Ministry of Foreign Affairs could be relied upon to represent the intentions of the real directors of Israel's foreign and defense policies." He meant Ben Gurion and Dayan, who had a disconcerting way of following their own hawkish policies without informing Sharett and the Foreign Ministry of their real purposes.

Egypt snapped back on October 26 by attacking the Bir Ain "police" checkpoint two hundred meters inside the zone and killing one Israeli, wounding four and capturing two. The taking of prisoners had been the purpose of the attack, for soon afterward the prisoners admitted that they were not civil police at all but members of the regular Israeli armed forces. Their admissions convinced Burns that the only hope for peace in the zone was the withdrawal of the Israeli settlers and "police," but as usual, events proved faster than pacific plans.

Two days later, on October 28, Israeli attackers retaliated for the Bir Ain raid by hitting an Egyptian Army camp in the southern Negev at Kuntilla, killing five and capturing thirty. Tensions were now so great in the area, reported the U.N. observer team, that "it only seems a question of which party will attack first."

The answer came in less than a week. Just hours after Ben Gurion presented his coalition government and took over from Sharett as prime minister and minister of defense on November 2, a large Israeli force smashed new Egyptian armed positions just across the Egyptian side of the demilitarized zone at El Sabha. Fifty Egyptians were killed and forty taken prisoner. Movement of the U.N. observers in the region was prevented by Israeli troops during the raid, though both sides were committed to allowing the observers free access to the area. Just hours before the attack was launched, Ben Gurion had assured the one hundred twenty members of the Knesset that "Israel has never initiated war and never will. This is our policy."

U.N. Secretary-General Dag Hammarskjold sent off a protest note to Israel the day after the attack, calling the Israeli action "unwarranted" and a breach of an Israeli pledge "to abstain from actions that might aggravate the situation. The possibilities of achieving stability in the area are considerably reduced by such military action as that of yesterday."

Burns called on Ben Gurion six days later and also condemned the attack, but the prime minister vigorously defended it on grounds that Egyptian troops had moved into a restricted area near the demilitarized zone shortly before. "The flaw with this argument," retorted Burns, "lay in the fact that there was a special status, internationally recognized, for the El Auja demilitarized zone, which admittedly the Egyptians had been violating, but because the Israelis had previously violated it also."

The arguments and protestations were moot. The fact now was that Israel controlled the vitally important demilitarized zone. That was what Ben Gurion most desired. The way was now open along the strategic El Auja routes for war against Egypt.

· ·

The Israeli occupation set off danger signals in London and Washington. In a statement released November 9 under his name by the State Department, Eisenhower reiterated the offer made August 26 by Dulles of a formal U.S. treaty to guarantee the frontiers of Israel and its Arab neighbors. The next day the State Department pointedly released another statement that emphasized U.S. determination to be evenhanded and favor neither side. "We will be strongly opposed to the side which starts a war in the Middle East and very favorably disposed" to the victim.

At the same time, on November 9, Britain's Anthony Eden also called for Israel and its Arab neighbors to settle their border disputes and offered in return a British guarantee. During the annual Guildhall speech in London, Eden suggested that the two sides compromise between the borders established by the 1947 U.N. Partition Plan and the larger boundary claimed by right of conquest by Israel in the 1949 armistices. On the surface, Eden's proposal was a balanced and fair suggestion for finding a middle ground between the Arab demand for a return to the 1947 borders and the Israeli insistence on maintaining the 1949 boundaries.

Nasser reacted positively, describing the Eden proposal as a "constructive attitude," thus becoming the first Arab leader to publicly indicate a willingness to compromise on something less than the 1947 frontiers.

But Ben Gurion was sharply negative. He charged that Eden's suggestion would "enlarge the territory of the neighboring" Arab states. A compromise over the boundaries could only come about with the surrender of some territory now controlled by Israel, since only Israel had enlarged its territory beyond the U.N. Partition Plan. But Ben Gurion had no intention of giving up even barren snippets of his tiny country; quite the reverse. He believed Israel's security rested with retention of the land.

The overriding reason for the existence of the state of Israel meant that never would the Jews walk lamblike in alien lands. Israel to its inhabitants and before the world stood for justice and humanity. Yet Israel was founded largely on the land of other people, Palestinians who shared no guilt in the holocaust or the suffering of the Jews, and who now had been forced into their own Diaspora. Two competing injustices were demanding redress at each other's expense. Nothing short of a miracle could solve that ferocious conundrum, yet that was what Eisenhower and Eden were trying to accomplish.

The coincidence in timing of the Eisenhower and Eden statements seemed suspiciously like a joint Anglo-American effort to impose a solution on the Middle East, though it was not. However much Israel desired peace, Ben Gurion and others believed it needed land more. Peace was for the secure; only land could provide security. The trauma of the holocaust was pervasive. Peace was as illusory and as dangerous as the security European Jews felt before Hitler. A land of the Jews was the only security; security, above all else, was the warp and the woof of Israel. Never again another holocaust.

The November statements by Eisenhower and Eden jolted Israel into an emotional reaction far exceeding anything the Western leaders had expected. What was not adequately appreciated was that Israel could not tolerate indifference from the West, and thereby lack of aid and support; yet neither could Israel accept an active attempt by the major powers to impose a settlement. Inevitably, a settlement would mean a smaller, less secure Israel.

Ben Gurion's dilemma was acute. He felt it necessary to prove once again to the Western powers Israel's independence and ability to resist pressure; but he also wanted to retain the sympathy and support of the West for the country's determination to hang on to the land it possessed, no matter how questionable its claims. His solution was an elegant one. He pressed forward with his plan to capture the Straits of Tiran, thereby emphasizing the harmful nature of the Egyptian blockade, and at the same time proving to the Western powers Israel's resolve and autonomy.

Soon after the capture of El Auja, Ben Gurion took his proposal for attacking the straits to the Cabinet and argued strongly for launching the raid in late December. The Cabinet turned him down, but it left open the door for war. "Israel will take action at the place and at the time that she deems appropriate," declared the Cabinet. It concluded, however, that the time for action had not yet arrived.

But Ben Gurion was not to be denied. He was determined to make the Arabs feel Israel's strength and the futility of their continued opposition to the state's existence. On December 11, without bothering to consult the Cabinet, Ben Gurion gave the final order for a harsh attack against Syria. That evening Israeli troops struck Syrian military outposts and civilian homes at Buteiha Farm and Koursi, on the slopes of Mount Hermon, north of the Sea of Galilee. The Israeli troopers withdrew before dawn, leaving behind fifty-six Arabs killed, including three women and five civilian men, nine others wounded, and thirty-two missing; thirty of them later turned up as Israeli prisoners. Despite official claims from Tel Aviv that the attack was in retaliation for a Syrian attack the day before on an Israeli fishing boat in the Sea of Galilee, the U.N.'s General Burns was skeptical.

After a year on the job, a change was occurring in Burns. He was less ready to accept Israel's official explanations. In his report to the Security

Council, Burns noted that the raid by several companies of troops was too large to have been planned on a day's notice. Further, he noted, "No firing at Israeli fishing boats had taken place since the beginning of the fishing season." The boat shot at on December 10 had suffered no casualties and was not a fishing boat at all but a police craft sailing provocatively close to the Syrian side of the sea. Burns concluded that it was probably sent there to "deliberately provoke an incident which should serve as an excuse for launching the attack."

Once again, Burns felt the Israelis—and this time Ben Gurion personally—had tried to dupe the United Nations. He had good reason. Only five hours before the attack, Ben Gurion had unexpectedly summoned Burns to the prime minister's office. "It was unusual," Burns observed, "for the Israeli government to do business with UNTSO on a Sunday, unless there was an emergency." But when Burns arrived, there appeared to be none. Ben Gurion simply asked about negotiations that were still dragging on fruitlessly over Israeli occupation of El Auja. Ben Gurion wanted to know about Egypt's attitude toward the talks. "Syria was not mentioned in the conversation," Burns noted. But writing in his diary later that night he wondered if "maybe Israel is preparing something."

The attack left Burns disturbed about Ben Gurion's motives in summoning him for the unusual Sunday talk. "Ben Gurion must have been well aware that the attack was mounted, and what the zero hour was," said Burns. "There was time to stop it right after I had left his office. Presumably the reply I had brought, the answers I was able to give him about Egyptian attitude, were not satisfactory.

"No one with any knowledge of military affairs would believe that such an elaborate, coordinated attack had not been planned well before, and probably rehearsed," observed Burns. "Certainly it was not improvised in a few hours."

Yet so forceful was Ben Gurion's personality that Burns thought of him, even after such an example of duplicity, as "one of the few great men" of his time. "By his own will and acts he has affected the course of world events—made history, in short." But old soldier Burns added: "There is no doubt at all that he was the person responsible for Israel's policies. When one acclaims a man as great, that does not mean that he is not capable of making mistakes; and they may be mistakes on the scale of his greatness. It is possible to be too brave, too determined, too inflexible in pursuing what one regards as the good. His frequent refusals to compromise or yield seemed to be based on a conviction that right and justice were always on the side of Israel."

• •

The Syrian raid again caused the United Nations Security Council to condemn Israel in a resolution supported by the United States and characterized by French Ambassador Hervé Alphand as "the strongest ever passed by the Council." But in Burns's opinion, it was not strong enough to "restrain the aggressive Israeli policy, which seemed to me to constitute the greatest danger to peace at that time." Burns believed that economic sanctions should have been imposed on Israel to dampen its aggressiveness, but the Security Council declined to go that far.

By hitting Syria, Ben Gurion had delivered a forceful warning to that country and Egypt not to overestimate the strength of their new military alliance. More than that, the raid focused attention on Syria's recent flirtation with Russia, which after Moscow's success with Egypt was now talking about selling arms to Syria. When he heard of the Israeli raid, the U.S. ambassador to Syria, James Sayle Moose, Jr., who displayed little bias for either side in the Middle East, craftily observed that now "Israel can justify its requests for Western arms as anti-Communist rather than anti-Arab." The attack had the effect of pushing the Syrians and the Egyptians closer to the Soviets, and transforming the character of an essentially local feud into an East-West confrontation.

• •

The immediate reaction in Washington was to lose patience with Israel. Moshe Sharett, now only foreign minister again, was in the United States for a prolonged tour for the United Jewish Appeal and Israel Bonds, as well as seeking weapons from Washington. He had seemed to be succeeding in his arms quest when the violent Syrian attack occurred. The talks were immediately suspended. "Not even the devil could have chosen a worse time or a worse context for such action," Sharett muttered about Ben Gurion's attack. Abba Eban complained too, charging that the raid was a "shocking spectacle of carnage with very little attempt to give world opinion any warning of its necessity or dimensions."

Eban reported that "Sharett thought that, at best, Ben Gurion's timing had shown indifference to his own diplomatic efforts. At worst, Sharett seemed to believe that there was something subconsciously deliberate in an action which deprived him of a slender hope of a personal diplomatic triumph. I, too, found it impossible to understand how Ben Gurion could reconcile two such lines of action. On the one hand, he had asked Sharett to make a big effort to secure a breakthrough on our arms request. On the other hand, he had authorized a military operation of such strong repercussion as to make an affirmative answer inconceivable."

Eban was so aroused by the attack that he sent Ben Gurion a long note protesting it—at the same time that he was leading Israel's defense of the raid before the Security Council. Ben Gurion replied with one of his few puckishly irreverent communications. "I fully understand your concern about the Kinneret [Sea of Galilee] operation," answered Ben Gurion. "I must confess that I, too, began to have my doubts about the wisdom of it. But when I read the full text of your brilliant defense of our action in the Security Council, all my doubts were set at rest. You have convinced me that we were right, after all." Eban never did receive a serious answer.

• •

The Middle East once again was on the verge of war. "If a conscious choice between war and peace is to be made within the next few months, that choice will be made first by the Government of Israel or to be even more specific by Mr. Ben Gurion, his top army commanders and a few other key figures in the country," reported Alexis Ladas, the perceptive U.N. political officer in the Jerusalem mission, to U.N. headquarters. There were several factors that were pushing Israel toward war, he wrote. Egypt's purchase of Czech arms would inevitably make that country stronger; Israel felt frustrated by Washington's continued refusal to sell it arms; and Israel regarded Egyptian troops stationed in the Gaza Strip, less than an hour's drive from Tel Aviv, as a serious threat to its security. "It follows naturally," reported Ladas, "that something has to be done to protect Israel from this deadly threat, and if the West will not provide the shield then Israel will have to cut the hand which wields the weapons.

"If then the West steps in to freeze the situation, Israel may be unpopular but she will be in actual possession of the ground and that counts for much. If the blow is strong enough to prove fatal to the present Egyptian regime so much the better. That might put a stop to the Czechoslovak arms deliveries once and for all. Even if the Israeli Army failed to dislodge the Egyptians from the Gaza Strip before the powers intervened—and this seems highly improbable—something would have been achieved: the West would have been given concrete proof that a Middle Eastern structure [such as the Baghdad Pact] which leaves Israel out in the cold to fend for herself is going to be a pretty difficult undertaking."

Like most foreign observers living in Israel, Ladas was struck by the excitable mood of the populace, that exaggeration of fear and aggressiveness that has variously been labeled the Samson Complex, the Masada Complex and the Holocaust Syndrome. "A state of mind has developed in Israel which at times approaches hysteria and which permeates the population from top to bottom," he wrote. "It affects not only the whispering in the market place but also the councils of the mighty. It is a conviction that Israel, a peace-loving nation of fugitives from persecution desiring nothing but to live in concord with her neighbors, is surrounded by increasingly powerful and savage enemies whose only purpose is to crush her out of existence. The prime minister himself is convinced that if Israel let her guard down for a moment the Egyptians first and then the other Arab states would attack her.

"Once given the fact that this fear exists, everything else follows quite logically. It is quite understandable that the supply of arms to Egypt should put the fear of God into the Israelis. It is quite understandable that Gaza should be viewed by them not as what it is in fact: a death trap for the Egyptian Army and a concentration camp for a quarter of a million refugees; but as what it might become in the future: a dagger pointed at the heart of Israel."

On December 13 General Burns wrote Secretary-General Dag Hammarskjold a "confidential and strictly personal" message. "I am very uneasy in regard to the possible intention of the Government of Israel to take military action against Egypt." In another message four days later, he advised Hammarskjold that the "Tiberias [Sea of Galilee] incident has hardened Egypt's attitude and any change of position unlikely." And again three days later he reported that "there is a striking disparity between the scale of the retaliation [in the Syrian raid] and the provocation which was cited by the Israeli government."

• •

The Middle East was at flash point. The raid into Syria was a lighted match to the explosive emotions in the region. Anger and resentment were at fever pitch throughout the Arab world, and in Israel there was a perceptible girding of determination to prove its superior strength and the permanency of its sovereignty over the land. No one could doubt that war was possible at any moment.

PART TWO
THE SPARK

December 16, 1955, to July 26, 1956

CHAPTER VI

Let Us Compete

KHRUSHCHEV

THE TIME FOR IGNORING the Middle East had passed. However much Eisenhower desired to devote his time to the larger strategic questions of war and peace and democracy's struggle with communism, the growing dangers of the Middle East would not allow him. The Soviets were now in the region, Israel and its powerful supporters were clamoring for arms, and tensions were so great that war of uncharted dimensions could erupt at any time. The President decided to take a bold gamble and try to win peace in one dramatic stroke.

The plan, the details of which have remained secret until now, involved two parallel efforts that amounted to the most ambitious peace effort ever launched by America in the Middle East up to that period. One part was totally secret. The other part consisted of a public offer to Egypt to finance the building of its Aswan High Dam to control the fluctuating waters of the Nile. The dam would be the biggest in the world and its construction would bring needed irrigated farmland to Egypt.

Covertly linked to the dam project was to be a secret effort to convince Egypt and Israel to come to terms with each other and live in peace. In return, the United States would offer the two countries all the economic aid, diplomatic support, guarantees and objective mediation that it could muster.

It was a generous, even munificent plan, conceived in the best tradition of American idealism and sense of fairness; and it was an embarrassingly simpleminded conception that completely overlooked the realities of the region. It was another of those innocent American ideas which naïvely assumed that the United States was the custodian of rationality and equity and all the world needed was the spiritual guidance and material help of the great U.S. democracy to live in prosperous peace.

The proposed peace plan failed to appreciate the profound sense of outraged injustice that both sides in the Middle East suffered, and the irrational hatred that suffused the inhabitants. For Arabs and Jews, peace was less important than the survival of their theocracies. This was as true for Israel, the first Jewish state for two millennia, as for Egypt. Survival took precedence above peace, and to survive in the Moslem Middle East, the Jewish leaders passionately believed that land equaled security and the fulfillment of an ancient dream. On their side, the Arabs had been humiliated by their crushing defeat in the 1948 war, shorn of part of their age-old land and scorned by the world. Their smarting pride demanded justice, and that could come only with the return of their land.

In the final analysis, land was perceived as more important by these two ancient Semitic peoples than peace or even life itself. The Eisenhower Administration did not understand this unyielding attitude on both sides any more than later Administrations did.

• •

The projected Aswan High Dam was the most gigantic undertaking in the land of the Nile since the days of the pharaohs. The dam was designed to be seventeen times the size of the Great Pyramid of Cheops and its purpose was to help feed the people of Egypt, not the vanity of a lone ruler. It was the most cherished project of Gamal Abdel Nasser and his Revolutionary Council of young army officers. Within three months of overthrowing King Farouk in July 1952, Nasser and the council adopted construction of the dam as a national goal and contracted with the German combine of Hochtief and Dortmund to conduct feasibility studies.

Only by controlling the highly variable flow of the mighty Nile could Egypt hope to cultivate enough of its land to feed its people. The first Aswan Dam had been completed by the British in 1902 and heightened in 1912 and 1933 to obtain more irrigation water. Yet the pace of Egypt's population growth was greater than the amount of cultivable land added by the dam enlargements.

The year before the British started the original Aswan Dam, in 1897, crop acreage per capita in Egypt equaled .70; by 1952, when Nasser came to power, it had dropped to .42—despite the fact that nearly twice as much land was under cultivation. The difference lay in the rapid population growth: seven million Egyptians in the 1870s and twenty-one million at Nasser's take-over. The country was in a race between people and hunger. It was not more land area that Egypt needed. It had more than enough of that, 386,000 square miles, almost all of it arid, sandy wastes. Only the fertile delta and the narrow strip of land bordering the Nile were green and under irrigation, equal to a mere 3 percent of Egypt's land; beyond lay the sere Sahara. "Egypt is the gift of the Nile," Herodotus wrote in the fifth century B.C., and that remained true in the fall of 1955. The waters of the Nile had to be captured and then carefully distributed to more acreage to allow Egypt even to begin to catch up with its agricultural wealth of a century earlier.

To accomplish that, the proportions of the High Dam had to be monumental. The Hochtief and Dortmund plan located the dam four miles up the Nile from the original Aswan Dam. It envisioned a structure 365 feet high, two-thirds of a mile thick at the base, and two and a quarter miles long athwart the Aswan reservoir. When finished, it would create its own huge reservoir, a 350-mile-long lake, give to Egypt 1.3 million acres of newly irrigated land, offer needed flood control, and produce enough electricity for more than half of the country's power needs, including those of all of Cairo, 560 miles to the north.

Its symbolic value was of transcendent importance for Egypt and the Arab world, representing a major stride into the twentieth century. It stood as the greatest inspiration of the Nasser regime, proof of Egypt's independence and sovereignty, a monument of modern Islam.

. .

The entry of Russia into the region through the Czech arms deal was the act that finally galvanized Washington into backing the Aswan High Dam and launching its secret peace plan. Talks about financing the mammoth project had been going on desultorily from the time that Eisenhower took office. But in the end the predictable opposition—from supporters of Israel opposed to anything that would help the Arabs; from cotton interests in the South, fearful of competition from Egyptian cotton, Egypt's major crop; and from conservative Republicans like Senate Minority Leader William Knowland, who saw little difference between neutralism and Communism—had prevented the Administration from pushing forward with a firm offer to Egypt. Now Israel's increasing aggressiveness under Ben Gurion and the growing Soviet influence in Egypt, which was dangerously spreading to Syria, convinced Dulles and Herbert Hoover, Jr., that they had to act before war broke out or the West's position in the region was totally eroded.

The urgency of the situation was emphasized on October 10, 1955, when Soviet Ambassador Daniel Solod, the same envoy who had first broached the Czech arms deal with Nasser, publicly announced in Cairo that the new Russian leadership of Khrushchev and Bulganin was willing to share Communism's wealth with all the underdeveloped nations of Asia and the Middle East. "We will send economic missions, scientific missions, agricultural missions, meteorological missions and any other kind of mission you can imagine that will help these countries," boasted Solod. The next day, Solod told Nasser that Russia would be willing to finance construction of the new High Dam.

Dulles, at the urging of Hoover, decided to join the British and the World Bank in financing the dam and to link the offer to the covert attempt at finding a final solution to the explosive Arab-Israel conflict.

The peace plan was the brainchild of Herbert Hoover, a gruff and dour conservative who had been brought into the department as the Number Two man at the age of fifty-one as a gesture to the Republican Party's right wing. Like his father, he had spent his career as an engineer, and was generally disliked by professionals of the department. They questioned his grasp of foreign affairs and, perhaps partly because he had a hearing problem that made him seem withdrawn, they found him cold and aloof. But Hoover had access to both Foster Dulles and the President, and his enthusiasm for the secret plan earned their endorsement. Though Hoover has since denied that there was any linkage between the two initiatives, there can be no doubt that the dam offer was meant as bait for Nasser to make peace with Israel. "Hoover tried to buy peace with the dam," said the CIA's Kermit Roosevelt, who was deeply involved in the planning and execution of the secret plan.

All that was left to be done was to find some respected civilian outside of government with the stature to deal face-to-face with Nasser and Ben Gurion as the U.S. mediator. He had to be someone who had the trust of the President and the secretary of state, and he had to be able to keep a secret.

• •

During the early planning for the U.S. peace initiative, Eisenhower remained in Fitzsimons Hospital in Denver recuperating from his coronary. It was not until the end of his sixth week there that he was finally able to walk out and board a plane to Washington, an apparently happy and hale President.

Television recorded his warm welcome on November 11 at National

Airport by Vice President Nixon, former President Herbert Hoover, the Cabinet, members of the diplomatic corps and others. Crowds lined the route to the White House and cheered the returning Chief Executive; some told jokes. A favorite of the time, since Nixon's ambitious nature was widely recognized, had the vice president greet Ike at the foot of the Capitol and say, "Welcome back, Mr. President. I'll race you to the top of the steps."

Though he looked well, Eisenhower was deeply troubled that fall. He was worried about how badly his health had been impaired and whether he should take the risk of running for re-election the following year. The question of a second term, he wrote to a friend, "swirls daily around my mind and keeps me awake at nights."

There were also other problems pressing in on him, particularly the level of increased activity by the Soviets in the Middle East and elsewhere in the Third World. Eisenhower's concern was heightened by the new diplomatic offensive being waged by Khrushchev and Bulganin. It was obvious now that the new Soviet leaders had turned sharply from Stalin's hard-line policies and were competing directly with the West for influence among the newly emerging nations. With exuberance and boastfulness, Khrushchev and Bulganin were extolling the productiveness of Communism and offering aid to any taker. In a highly publicized visit to India, Afghanistan and Burma that autumn, the two leaders loudly sounded Russia's new openhandedness.

"We are ready to share with you our economic and scientific and technical experience," Bulganin said in a speech before the Indian parliament. Khrushchev sounded the same theme more colorfully in a speech at Bhakra on November 22, where he told a wildly applauding crowd that Western charges of Soviet duplicity were false. "To those who write this, we say: Perhaps you would like to compete with us in establishing friendship with the Indians? Let us compete. Why have we come here? We come with an open heart and with honest intentions. You want to build factories? Perhaps you have not sufficient experience? Then apply to us and we shall help you. You want to build electric power stations? If you have not the necessary know-how, if you need technical assistance, apply to us and we shall help. You want to send your students, your engineers to our country for training? Please do so."

Dulles, who was becoming known as a "brinksman" for his confrontational policies, publicly cast doubt on the seriousness of the Soviet offers, but privately he and other officials worried about the strategy of generosity. Eisenhower was particularly concerned and sent Dulles an anxious letter on December 5 from his Gettysburg farm where he had gone to recuperate.

"So long as [the Soviets] used force and the threat of force, we had the world's natural reaction of fear to aid us in building consolidations of power and strength in order to resist Soviet advances," Eisenhower wrote. "More recently, they seemed to have determined to challenge with economic weapons. Now we have always boasted that the productivity of free men in a free society would overwhelmingly excel the productivity of regimented labor. So at first glance, it would appear that we are being challenged in the area of our greatest strength."

But Ike wondered. After all, he pointed out, "dictatorships can move secretly and selectively." But democracies must debate policy and announce it before any action is even taken. This gives the Soviets "the advantage of the initiative. Thus, while we are busy rescuing Guatemala or assisting Korea and Indochina, they make great inroads in Burma, Afghanistan and Egypt."

The President thought that what was needed was a collective of free world nations that would join in making long-term economic commitments to counter the Soviets. "I think that the promotion of economic associations, somewhat as we have done in the military area, would be helpful," he wrote. "If we cannot organize to protect and advance our own interests and those of our friends in the world, then I must say it becomes time to begin thinking of 'despairing of the Republic.' "

He suggested that Dulles and Treasury Secretary George Humphrey meet with him soon to chat about the subject very informally without "agenda, procedural customs, and an audience." He added optimistically: "I believe if we plan and organize properly, we can [compete with the Soviets] without going broke, and that we can . . . largely rob the Soviets of the initiative."

• •

There was considerable skepticism in the higher reaches of the Eisenhower Administration about the sincerity of the Soviet offer to build Egypt's High Dam, but the pressing need to halt the drift to war spurred Washington to move more swiftly than usual in putting together a deal to finance the dam. Within ten days of Eisenhower's return to Washington from Denver, Egyptian Finance Minister Abdel Moneim Kaissouny arrived to begin talks with officials of the World Bank. Herbert Hoover, Jr., and British Ambassador Roger Makins soon joined the negotiations aimed at resolving the myriad details of financing the Aswan project.

1

The opening of the Suez Canal on Nov. 17, 1869 (1); and traffic passing through the canal in the 1950s (2).

2

3

Shepheard's Hotel, a casualty of Black Saturday on Jan. 26, 1952, when Egyptian mobs ran riot through Cairo, killing 17 Europeans and 50 Egyptians and burning and looting more than 700 buildings in protest against the continued presence of British troops in the canal zone (3).

4

Eden protégé Anthony Nutting (4).

5

Representatives of Britain and Egypt meet in Cairo on April 29, 1953, to discuss withdrawal of British troops from the canal zone. At the head of the table is President Mohammed Naguib; to his right are Ambassador Ralph Stevenson and General Sir Brian Robertson (5).

6

Gamal Abdel Nasser and Anthony Eden in Cairo in their only meeting, Feb. 20, 1955 (6).

7   David Ben Gurion inspects a new road in the Dead Sea area shortly before his first retirement on Dec. 14, 1953 (7).

8

Foreign Minister Moshe Sharett (8).

9

BEGIN, Menachem, Polish, b. Poland 1906, 5ft. 9in., medium build, long hooked nose, bad teeth, wears horn-rimmed spectacles.
Frequents : Geula Qtr., Jerusalem ; Kafr Saba Colony and Tel Mont Colony.
Associates : Secretary of Kafr Saba Colony. I.Z.L. leader   Photo. No. 12.

"Wanted" poster issued by British authorities (9).

10

Damage to the King David Hotel caused by Irgun terrorists, August 1946 (10).

11

Secret listening device found among the belongings of one of the Israeli Lavon Affair spies in Cairo (11).

12

East and West meet separately. On the way to the Bandung Conference of nonaligned nations, Gamal Abdel Nasser, seated in the center, laughs at remark by Jawaharlal Nehru of India, on Nasser's left (12); the Big Four Geneva Conference of July 1955 (13).

13

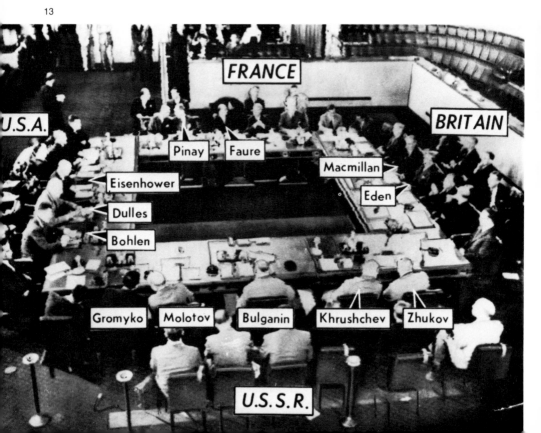

FRANCE

U.S.A.

BRITAIN

Pinay   Faure

Macmillan

Eisenhower

Eden

Dulles

Bohlen

Gromyko   Molotov   Bulganin   Khrushchev   Zhukov

U.S.S.R.

14

Time out from the Anglo-American Conference in Washington in January 1956. From left, Foreign Minister Selwyn Lloyd, Prime Minister Anthony Eden, Secretary of State John Foster Dulles and President Eisenhower (14).

Assistant Secretary of State George V. Allen, Gamal Abdel Nasser and Ambassador Henry A. Byroade in Cairo during the crisis over the Czech arms deal, Oct. 1, 1955 (16).

15

Winston Churchill (15).

16

17

French Prime Minister Guy Mollet (17).

18

Nikolai Bulganin and Nikita Khrushchev during their April 1956 visit to London (18).

19

In an emergency meeting caused by Nasser's nationalization of the Suez Canal Company, representatives of the Big Three meeting in London. From left, Anthony Eden, Selwyn Lloyd, Christian Pineau and John Foster Dulles, Aug. 2, 1956 (19).

King Hussein of Jordan and Glubb Pasha, commander of the Arab League (20).

20

21

In June 1956, the Egyptian flag finally replaced the British Union Jack on Egyptian soil for the first time since 1882 (21).

The new director of the Suez Canal, Mahmoud Yunis (22); Nasser's announcement of the nationalization of the Suez Canal (23); and the crowd in Alexandria's Liberation Square listening to Nasser's dramatic speech on July 26, 1956 (24).

The villa Bonnier de la Chapelle in Sèvres, just outside Paris, where Britain, France and Israel colluded in secrecy during October 1956 to attack Egypt (26).

Arab leaders displaying unity during the Suez crisis. From left, President Shukri al-Kuwatly of Syria, King Saud of Saudi Arabia and Gamal Abdel Nasser of Egypt (27).

27

Dulles arrives in London at the beginning of the Suez crisis Aug. 1, 1956. From left, Robert Murphy; Arthur Douglas Dodds-Parker, British Under Secretary of Foreign Affairs; Dulles; and Winthrop Aldrich (28).

Anthony Eden welcomes delegates to the 22-nation Suez Conference in Lancaster House in London on Aug. 16, 1956 (29).

Ahmed Hussein (30), Prime Minister Robert G. Menzies of Australia (31) and Ambassador Raymond Hare with Nasser (32).

Eisenhower vows during a television broadcast on the Suez crisis on Oct. 31, 1956, that there will be "no United States involvement" (33); Herbert Hoover, Jr. (34); handwritten note from President Eisenhower to Secretary of State Dulles discussing "weakening Nasser" (35).

CONSERVATION OF HUMAN RESOURCES
COLUMBIA UNIVERSITY
NEW YORK 27, N. Y.

ELI GINZBERG, DIRECTOR

July 17, 1956

President Dwight D. Eisenhower
The White House
Washington, D.C.

Dear President Eisenhower:

I have tried to put down on the attached memorandum, in as brief a form as possible, my sense of what the United States can do in the Middle East to protect its major objectives in a manner consistent with its general principles of international cooperation.

I hope that these notes will be of some help to you, and I look forward very much to the opportunity of talking with you about my trip.

Sincerely yours,

Eli Ginzberg

Dear Foster — One thing developed herein is one which the plan spoken to you — weakening Nasser.
Please return to my file
(Record of conversation will Continue I reserved attached.).

DE

36

Ambassador Abba Eban and Foreign Minister Golda Meir of Israel at the opening of the eleventh annual meeting of the United Nations in November 1956 (36). In the Security Council, foreign ministers discuss the Suez crisis on Oct. 5, 1956. From left, Dmitri Shepilov of the Soviet Union, Selwyn Lloyd of Britain, John Foster Dulles of the United States and Mahmoud Fawzi of Egypt (37).

37

Britain actively supported the idea. Prime Minister Anthony Eden had been shocked by Russia's penetration of the Middle East, and felt that involvement in building the dam was one way for his country to retain its dwindling influence in the area. "On no account," Eden told an aide, "must we let the Russians into the Nile Valley." He emphasized the urgency he felt in a personal message to Eisenhower at the beginning of December, pointing out that if the U.S. failed to act in concert with Britain the Soviets would almost certainly replace Western influence in the Middle East.

Goaded by such pressures, the negotiations moved quickly and agreement was announced on December 16, five days after Israel's heavy attack on Syria. Under the tentative agreement, the World Bank, the United Kingdom and the United States would jointly finance Egypt's dam at an estimated cost of $1.3 billion. The bank would provide $200 million, Britain and America $200 million between them, and Egypt the rest in local currency.

Predictably the loan immediately ran into criticism from southern cotton interests, the extreme right and Israel's supporters. Much of it was of a type that was damaging and difficult to dispel. It took the form of a suspicion that Nasser—and other nonaligned leaders—was "blackmailing" the West into backing expensive aid projects by playing off Soviet offers. It was a suspicion all but impossible to refute because it contained an element of truth. The appearance of the Russians on the Egyptian scene was like the arrival of a competing bidder at an auction.

Despite such suspicions, Nasser, in fact, did not excessively exploit his powerful position. The Egyptian leader publicly stated that he preferred a Western loan over a Soviet one, and his reasons were sound. The Czech arms deal had already placed Egypt's Army under Soviet influence; he did not want to further put his economy at the mercy of Moscow by accepting a large Russian loan for the dam. He repeatedly told the U.S. and British ambassadors in Cairo that his preference for financing the dam was first, the World Bank; second, the West; third, Egypt alone, though it did not have the resources. But, he added meaningfully, he was so determined to have the dam that he would go to the Russians, his last choice, if necessary.

There was an implied threat in such statements, no matter how sincerely they were uttered, and even observers sympathetic to Egypt could not help noticing the implication. "There was a bit of blackmail in this," noted British Ambassador Sir Humphrey Trevelyan about Nasser's reminders of the Soviet offer. Yet it is difficult to see how Nasser could have avoided mentioning the Soviets. He did, after all, have an offer, and by all accounts he did not abuse the strong bargaining position it gave him. In fact, when the time came to agree on the financial arrangements for the loans, he accepted terms that were not as advantageous for Egypt as the terms later given by the Russians. Nonetheless, the charge of blackmail was one that dogged the negotiations until their explosively abrupt termination.

• •

Parallel with the dam talks, the covert effort to find the right man to serve as the U.S. peacemaker proceeded. He was finally located in early December, and Dulles explained the whole plan and received Eisenhower's approval of it on December 8 during a half-hour walk in the woods of Camp David. The man selected to carry out the key part of the ambitious U.S. peace drive was one of the young Republicans Ike most admired in the country, Robert Bernerd Anderson. He was tall and lanky, at forty-five a self-made Texas businessman who at Ike's urging had already served the Administration as the secretary of the navy and then as the deputy secretary of defense, the second top official in the Pentagon. He had returned to private life in mid-1955 to become the president of Ventures, Ltd., a Canadian holding company with international mining interests.

Anderson dressed in somber three-piece blue suits and was mild-mannered and soft-spoken with something of an old-fashioned aura about him. His colleagues usually described him as being prudent, disciplined, hardworking, conservative and God-fearing. The President had unrestrained, if misplaced, admiration of him. "He is one of the most capable men I know," the President wrote in his diary after Anderson embarked on his mission. "My confidence in him is such that at the moment I feel that nothing could give me greater satisfaction than to believe that next January 20th I could turn over this office to his hands. His capacity is unlimited and his dedication to this country is complete."

Beyond Ike's exaggerated trust, Anderson seemed a perfect choice for the unorthodox mission because he knew how to keep a secret. That he personally knew little about the intricacies of the Middle East dispute did not worry Eisenhower or Dulles. It had already been agreed that expert support for Anderson would come from the CIA; the State Department, except at the level of Hoover and Dulles and a few trusted aides, was not involved.

The plan appeared deceptively simple; it used as its objectives the substance of Dulles' August 26 speech (settlement of the refugee problem, fixed boundaries and a peace treaty). The President authorized Anderson to promise in return that the United States would offer, in addition to financing the dam for Egypt, a formal U.S. guarantee of borders to both sides, substantial economic aid to help Israel pay reparations to dispossessed Palestinians, and American assistance at finding solutions to any remaining problems. It was a bountiful offer.

Eisenhower met with Dulles and Anderson for seventy-five minutes in his White House office shortly after the turn of the year, on January 11, to discuss details of the mission. The President declared the meeting off the record and no notes or reports of the talk were apparently made. But one thing was certain: the plan was going forward under the personal auspices of the President of the United States, much in the politically unfettered way he admired about Soviet diplomacy. Anderson was instructed to leave on his secret mission within four days.

• •

The afternoon before the meeting with Anderson, Eisenhower had spent an hour and a half listening to Foster Dulles discuss two other issues that were uppermost on both their minds: Russia and the election. "The secretary and I discussed the whole story of our foreign operations since 1953," Eisenhower recorded in his diary. "We have tried to keep constantly before us the purpose of promoting peace with accompanying step-by-step disarmament. As a preliminary, of course, we have to induce the Soviets to agree to some form of inspection, in order that both sides may be confident that treaties are being executed faithfully. In the meantime, and pending some advance in this direction, we must stay strong, particularly in that type of power that the Russians are compelled to respect—namely, destructive power that can be carried suddenly and en masse directly against the Russian economic structure.

"We had likewise to deal with a number of specific problems. In most of them a measurable degree of success was scored, but there have been other unsolved problems that have likewise engaged our attentions, efforts and money. One of these has been the Israel-Arab situation. This particular problem has been aggravated by the fact that Britain and ourselves have not seen eye-to-eye in a number of instances. We tried to make Britain see the danger of inducing or pressuring Jordan to join the 'Northern Tier' [Baghdad] Pact. They went blindly ahead and only recently have been suffering one of the most severe diplomatic defeats Britain has taken in many years. The Arabs apparently take the assumption that Britain does nothing in the area without our approval. Nothing could be further from the truth.''

As for the coming election, Ike was displaying doubt about whether he would run for a second term. Dulles spent a considerable amount of his unusually long conference with the President making a not-too-subtle pitch to convince Eisenhower to run again. He told Ike that ''no man of our times has had the standing throughout the world'' as Eisenhower had, the President wrote in his diary. ''There are two or three conclusions to be drawn that are not too pleasant to contemplate. The first is that if this country, with all of its riches and might, and with its foreign relations directed by people so respected throughout the world as Foster and myself, cannot point to a single conclusive sign that the world is actually moving toward universal peace and disarmament, then indeed it would appear that the world is on the verge of an abyss. Second, to an individual who so earnestly wants to lay aside the cares of public office (a sentiment that I am sure Foster shares), this estimate brings the unhappy suggestion that he must try to carry on regardless of any other factor. Certainly if, with our standing in the world . . . we are to be succeeded by individuals of less experience, lesser prestige and without the ties of acquaintance-ships and even friendships that Foster and I have with many of the world leaders in many parts of the globe, then the question arises, 'What will happen?' ''

Dulles performed his persuasion well; Eisenhower was obviously having doubts about standing down from the presidency.

Two days later Eisenhower confided to Ann Whitman that before he had his heart attack in September, he was, as she recorded, ''more deter-mined to quit than he is now.'' The confession came after a morning examination by his physicians, who reported he was responding well but advised him not to work too hard. ''He should lie down for half hour before lunch,'' his secretary reported, ''and spend an hour after lunch in nonaggravating things like talking with personal friends about noncon-troversial subjects, or light paper work. No tough conference such as Cabinet, NSC, should go more than an hour without a ten-minute rest period. If the President has any kind of social engagement at night, his day's work should be cut down correspondingly. The doctors told him it is not the really big problems that upset him, it is the little silly annoy-ances.''

In a long letter to his old Abilene boyhood friend, Swede Hazlett, now a retired navy captain living in Chapel Hill, North Carolina, the President on January 23 tried to work out his concerns about his health and a second term. To the sympathetic Hazlett he had earlier confided that he was having trouble sleeping, and now in answer to a concerned letter from him, Eisenhower wrote: "Ever since the hectic days of the North African campaign, I find that when I have weighty matters on my mind I wake up extremely early, apparently because a rested mind is anxious to begin grappling with knotty questions. So I think it is fair to say that it is not worry or useless anxiety about the past, but a desire to attack the future that gets me into this annoying habit. Incidentally," he added, "I never worry about what I did the day before. Likewise, I spend no time fretting about what enemies or critics have said about me. I have never indulged in useless regrets. Always I find, when I have come awake sufficiently to figure out what may be then engaging my attention, that I am pondering some question that is still unanswered."

Ike shared with his friend, who had earlier suffered several heart attacks, some advice he had received from famed heart surgeon Dr. Paul Dudley White, then wryly added that he had been told to "avoid all situations that tend to bring about such reactions as irritation, frustration, anxiety, fear and, above all, anger. I say to them, 'Just what do you think the presidency is?' Still only four months after the first heart attack that ever hit the Eisenhower family, I have soon to decide what is my answer with respect to the *next five years*. It is all very complicated, and I could fill any number of pages with the various considerations pro and con that I think have some bearing on the matter."

With that, Ike abruptly ended the letter with his usual warm salutations to Swede and his family. The President was obviously a man grappling with a very knotty problem.

• •

Shortly before Bob Anderson left on his peace mission, Eisenhower sat down and wrote a letter for him to give to Ben Gurion and Nasser. "This is to introduce my good and trusted friend, Robert B. Anderson, a very distinguished American and my former Deputy Secretary of Defense, whom I have asked to go over with you and others some of the various serious problems of the area which confront you, your neighbors and the free world generally," said the presidential letter. "Mr. Anderson fully understands my personal concern and hopes in this area, which I am sure you and he will want to explore completely. I am hopeful that you and he may be able to render to each other and to our countries valuable assistance in working toward settlement of these problems."

In his diary, Eisenhower observed that he and Dulles "feel certain that

if a practicable peace treaty could be arranged between these two nations, that our people and our Congress would authorize almost any kind
of material aid for the two of them that they could effectively use. But
we are convinced that the interests of this country will not be served by
attempting to arm one against the other, and we would regard it as tragic
if the U.S.S.R. began to arm one while we undertook to defend the other
with weapons and financial support. Consequently, we are ready to do
anything within reason to bring them closer together and to start between
them the cooperative process, particularly in economic matters.''

The United States, in other words, was ready to give everything to
Israel except the thing Ben Gurion wanted most: U.S. weapons. In turn,
no one could give Gamal Nasser what he wanted most—Israeli withdrawal and repatriation of the refugees—except Israel.

It was into this distorting hall of mirrors that on January 15 devout
Methodist Bob Anderson plunged, full of optimism and confidence that
at last American largess and goodwill would bring peace to the mystical
Holy Land. Flying secretly in military planes and hiding out in CIA safe
houses, Anderson shuttled in mid-January between Cairo and Tel Aviv
meeting clandestinely with Nasser and Ben Gurion. He did not visit the
U.S. Embassy in either country nor consult with the local American
ambassadors or officials. His contacts were with the CIA's top two Middle East specialists, Kim Roosevelt, the expert on the Arabs, and James
Jesus Angleton, who had such close ties with Israeli intelligence that
some of his colleagues wondered about his ability to be objective. Between them, Roosevelt and Angleton controlled the CIA's activities in
the Middle East, but in a most peculiar way. Their departments were
strictly separate, meaning that only Angleton had access to intelligence
about Israel on an operational basis and only Roosevelt received intelligence from the Arab states. There was no routine sharing of information,
merely an informal arrangement between these two bureaucratic infight-
ers to alert each other to anything they thought the other had a need to
know. The result was a predictable loss of coherence in America's overall
view of what was going on in the region.

Angleton was an intense, lean, chain-smoking man whose tastes ran to
poetry when he was at Yale in the 1930s but who spent his career in
intelligence and for twenty-five years was one of the men who dominated
the CIA. During that time he personally maintained control of the Israeli
Desk even though his major function was as head of the agency's Counterintelligence Staff, a unit charged with preventing other intelligence

services from penetrating the agency. The position was uniquely suited to Angleton's suspicious and secretive nature.

He and Roosevelt quickly realized that Anderson's mission was unlikely to succeed. The region's conflict was too intractable and Anderson had trouble understanding the complex nature of the problems—and of making himself understood. "He was the weirdest possible choice for the mission," said Roosevelt. "His Texas drawl was so thick that Nasser couldn't understand a thing he said." Nasser's English was far from perfect, and having grown up hearing clipped British tones, he frequently had difficulty following an American accent.

The first meeting was late at night in Cairo. Anderson solemnly put forward the bounties of aid and support that America was willing to grant Egypt if Nasser would make a few small concessions to Israel and lead the Arab nations into a peace treaty with the Jewish state. Roosevelt could see Nasser's eyes glaze over. "In his amiable way, Nasser was nodding at everything Anderson said and Anderson thought he was making historic advances," recalled Roosevelt.

Well satisfied with his night's work, Anderson left about 1:30 A.M. while Roosevelt stayed behind at Nasser's request. When they were finally alone, Nasser turned to Roosevelt and said, "Kim, what did he say?"

To Nasser's growing amazement, Roosevelt explained to the Egyptian leader how Anderson had proposed that Egypt accept as permanent Israel's current boundaries and how Nasser should lead the drive among the Arab states to sign a peace treaty with Israel. Nasser was dumbfounded. Arab tempers were still sizzling with rage at the massive Israeli attack against Syria, which currently was being debated daily in the U.N. Security Council. There was no way Nasser could advocate peace in such a charged atmosphere. "You know I couldn't agree to anything like that," said Nasser.

Roosevelt of course did know and he went to the CIA safe house in Cairo where Anderson was staying to tell him. There he found Anderson ecstatic. He thought he had brought peace to the Holy Land. Anderson was dictating a wildly optimistic cable to Foster Dulles reporting his phenomenal success.

"I told him that Nasser couldn't possibly agree to his proposals and that Nasser had just told me so."

"You're crazy," said Anderson. "I know what I said and I know what Nasser said."

135

The two Americans argued with some heat; in the end Anderson agreed not to send his cable report until checking out his impressions in another meeting with Nasser. The next night Nasser told Anderson at the start: "You speak English to Kim and he will speak English to me." Then, through Roosevelt, Nasser told a disappointed Anderson that it was impossible to accept his proposals.

The conferences went no better with Ben Gurion. He refused to discuss the possibility of Israel surrendering any territory and instead insisted on a face-to-face meeting with Nasser, which was impossible since it would open Nasser to fierce criticism domestically and from the other Arab states. He also insisted that the real subject of the talks with Anderson should be the supply of weapons by the United States to Israel.

With mounting despair, Anderson shuttled between the two countries for several weeks before returning to Washington to report on the dismal prospects for his mission. The Eisenhower Administration's major peace offensive in the Middle East was about to collapse, and with it the region took one more step toward war.

CHAPTER VII

Without the United States, Britain Is Alone

CHURCHILL

No WORLD LEADER in 1956 so embodied the spirit and the style of empire as British Prime Minister Sir Anthony Eden. Impeccably tailored and with a smartly clipped silvery mustache, Eden had decided it was time to visit Washington and his old acquaintance Ike Eisenhower to harmonize as best they could their two countries' varying perceptions of global policy, particularly the pace of decolonization and the growing instability in the Middle East. Though Eisenhower was still recuperating from his heart attack, he was always ready to greet his wartime colleague. They agreed that the visit would take place over three days and would be a candid and, it was hoped, a friendly full-scale tour d'horizon between themselves, their foreign ministers, and senior aides.

A Washington meeting had considerable allure for Eden that dreary London winter. He was in profound political trouble. Though he had been in power only since the previous April, there was already widespread dissatisfaction with him because of a worsening economy, higher taxes, climbing inflation, angry strikes and the general malaise that Britons were suffering from the depressing spectacle of their empire's rapid disintegration.

By January, the British press had become strident, culminating in what *The New York Times* characterized as the "most unbridled outburst of criticism any prime minister has suffered since Neville Chamberlain." From the stately London *Times* to the raucous *Mirror,* Fleet Street attacked Eden with such hot-blooded headlines as "Eden Is a Flop," "Eden Must Go," and "Ditherer," accusing him of "indecision,"

137

"timidity," "fumbling," and a "terrifying lack of authority." The *Observer* reported that "a formidable body of Conservative M.P.s is determined to try to remove Sir Anthony as head of government." The cruelest cut came from the *Daily Telegraph,* the unofficial voice of Eden's own Tory Party. Referring to the prime minister's habit of emphasizing a point by smacking his fist into the palm of his hand, the newspaper harshly observed that the "smack is seldom heard." When Eden read that, recalled his colleague R. A. Butler, Leader of the House, he uttered a "pained and pungent oath." Butler was so moved that he expressed his "warm sympathy" to his badly shaken prime minister. But the damage had been done. Eden was widely being perceived as a weak leader.

Washington represented a respite from such harsh personal attacks, and a chance for Eden to shore up his tattered reputation by emphasizing his long relationship with popular Ike Eisenhower. Though they had known each other since the tense days of World War II and routinely exchanged pleasantries, there was not the sense of intimacy between Ike and Eden that existed between Ike and Eden's mentor, Churchill. But Eisenhower always cherished the special relationship with Britain and respected Eden, granting him and his country whatever the presidency could decently offer. In planning sessions before the summit meetings, set for January 30 through February 1, Ike's generosity was obvious. His feeling about sharing atomic information with Britain was "the more we can give, the better." He was equally generous in other areas, and planned during the visit to go out of his way to help the faltering British prime minister refurbish his tarnished image.

• •

The timing of the visit was also fortuitous for Ike's embattled secretary of state. Foster Dulles that winter of 1956 was under fierce attack by foreign capitals and critics at home for his macho remarks published in the January 16 issue of *Life* magazine under the title "How Dulles Averted War." In self-satisfied tones, Dulles had bragged to interviewer James Shepley that the Eisenhower Administration had taken the nation to the brink of war three times in the past three years.

"If you are scared to go to the brink, you are lost," Dulles declared. "We've had to look it square in the face—on the question of enlarging the Korean War, on the question of getting into the Indochina War, on the question of Formosa. We walked to the brink and we looked it in the face. We took strong action."

Dulles concluded that "the ability to get to the verge without getting into the war is the necessary art."

Dulles' interview produced a fire storm of criticism. Adlai Stevenson charged that Dulles was "playing Russian Roulette with the life of our nation." *New York Times* columnist James Reston wrote that the interview proved Dulles "had added something new to the art of diplomatic blundering. This is the planned mistake. He doesn't stumble into booby traps; he digs them to size, studies them carefully and then jumps." (When Dulles was asked sometime later about his press relations, he tersely replied: "I don't meet with Reston.")

Officials in Britain and France questioned Dulles' peculiar version of history, complaining that he was being overly dramatic in referring to the brink of war, and from Moscow came a blast from *Izvestia* denouncing Dulles for "encouragement of bellicose statements by American generals and admirals." The brouhaha caused acute embarrassment for the President. At his first press conference since his heart attack, Ike was asked on January 19 why he had not gone to Congress if America had been so close to war. He replied weakly that some past crises could be interpreted "as being at the brink of something because the other fellow can react." But "when it comes to the matter of war," he declared, he would go to "only one place [Congress] and tell them what I believe." The President defended Dulles as being "devoted to peace," and said that he was "to my mind the best secretary of state I have ever known." It was about as strong an endorsement as Ike could make under the awkward circumstances.

At his own press conference, the embattled Dulles explained that "I did not write the article, I did not review or censor the article and, in fact, I did not read the article until after it was released for publication." He admitted that he had been correctly quoted, but, always quick on his feet and reluctant to admit an error, he argued that "the surest way to avoid war is to let it be known in advance that we are prepared to defend these principles, if need be by life itself. We have learned by hard experience that failure to make our position known in advance makes war more likely because then an aggressor may miscalculate."

Before the furor died down with the approach of Eden's visit, Henry R. Luce, editor in chief of *Life,* had to issue a statement explaining that headlines in the article referring to "verge of war" and "brink" "did not fully reflect the main emphasis [on Dulles'] pursuit of peace." The storm was abating, but it never completely ended. The image of brinkmanship plagued Dulles to his death.

. .

Two major topics on the agenda of the Anglo-American summit were the policies of the Soviet Union under Party Chairman Nikita Khrushchev and the Middle East. Both subjects, Eisenhower wrote a friend, "occupy my attention for part of every waking hour I have. The Arab-Israel struggle provides one of our greatest obstacles to progress in that region. Another factor that causes a great deal of trouble now is the economic challenge posed by Russia's new policy—or what appears to be a new policy. It is idle to suppose that Russia has any friendly interest in the countries that she proposes to help; her purpose is, of course, to damage our relationships with those countries and use her own economic penetration to accomplish political domination."

Eisenhower's suspicions of Russia's intentions were not mollified by a stunning Soviet initiative launched just before Eden's visit. It was a surprise request by the Soviets for a bilateral treaty of friendship. The proposal came in the form of a letter, signed by Premier Nikolai A. Bulganin, that was personally delivered to the President by Soviet Ambassador Georgi N. Zaroubin on January 25, five days before Eden's scheduled arrival. Both the nature of the delivery and its timing caused deep suspicions in Washington.

The press immediately began speculating about why the Soviet ambassador had made a highly unusual personal call on the President, and so too did officials in Britain. Was there some superpower deal afoot? Secretary of State John Foster Dulles quickly tried to calm British apprehensions by telephoning British ambassador Makins and saying that he thought the Russian gambit was "designed primarily to throw a spoke in the forthcoming talks" with Eden. He assured Makins that there was nothing in the Soviet message that was "sensational" or of an "unusual character. It is nothing we have not heard many times before."

The message was still secret, but speculation about its contents in the press was feverish. In a telephone call to his brother at the Central Intelligence Agency, Dulles said he had the "feeling that keeping it secret is not desirable." Allen concurred, predicting that "they will publish it when they think the appropriate moment is at hand." Both brothers said they took a "dim view" of the offer.

To one of his aides, Foster Dulles explained that he thought the whole thing was "for propaganda." In a telephone call to Democratic Senator Walter George, Dulles explained he wanted to "get this done before

Eden got here. If it got interjected into the talks, the French would want to be present."

Within a day after receiving the Soviet proposal, which ran to seventeen paragraphs and included a four-part draft of the proposed treaty, Dulles had drafted a letter for Ike to send to Eden to assuage any lingering suspicions. "I have not had a chance to study [the Soviet offer] carefully," the letter explained, "but it appears to be a recapitulation of the Soviet position on peace, disarmament and relaxation of tensions." The Soviets said they wanted a friendship treaty, but "I surmise that its delivery was timed with an eye to our meeting and for that reason the manner of delivery was done to promote wide speculation as to its contents. I will show you the letter when you reach Washington."

Eisenhower approved the Dulles draft and on January 26, it was dispatched to Eden, who at that moment was aboard the ocean liner *Queen Elizabeth* sailing to America for the summit meeting. As Eden must have known, there was no question of Eisenhower accepting the unexpected Soviet offer of a friendship treaty. The U.S. was simply too suspicious of Soviet intentions to believe that the proffered treaty was a sincere one and too rushed by Eden's imminent arrival to give the lengthy proposal serious reflection.

Certainly the timing of the offer did make it suspect. Though the new leaders of the Kremlin were speaking with a softer voice than had Josef Stalin, they nonetheless had proved to the satisfaction of Eisenhower and Dulles that they were still mortal enemies. The evidence seemed ample enough to them. Russia was building up its military might, rapidly advancing its technology, actively competing for the loyalties of the emerging nations, expanding its economic aid and influence, and had finally penetrated the Middle East. Such a program of national self-aggrandizement was not too different from America's, of course, but Ike and Dulles did not see it that way. Each Communist gain, in their judgment, was a Western loss.

Within three days of the Soviet offer, American Ambassador Charles E. Bohlen delivered Eisenhower's reply in Moscow. A bilateral friendship treaty, said Eisenhower's legalistic letter, was unnecessary because the Soviet proposals were "already covered by the explicit" provisions for a peaceful world spelled out in the Charter of the United Nations. As U.N. members, both countries were supposed to be abiding by such ideals anyway, Eisenhower concluded.

Though their suspicions were perhaps sound enough, Eisenhower and

Dulles reacted with unseemly haste. Nikita Khrushchev and Bulganin had taken over the reins of the Soviet government only the previous year, on February 8, and they repeatedly claimed they were actively seeking a relaxation with the West. Eisenhower might have profited by listening to the two Soviet leaders a bit more closely.

. .

It was Eden's first visit to the United States since he had succeeded Churchill. With his usual thoughtfulness, Ike sent his plane, *Columbine III,* to New York to pick up the English party. It was shortly before noon on January 30 when they arrived at Washington National Airport. Dulles was there in place of the recuperating President and greeted Eden and Foreign Secretary Selwyn Lloyd with a warm welcome. The three high officials walked out of the gloomy fog and drizzle ("weather to make a Londoner feel at home," reported *The New York Times*) into the military lounge to deliver brief arrival statements.

The special relationship and the importance of continued unity between the two countries was the theme sounded. "It is absolutely clear in my belief that the hopes for a peaceful world depend upon the friendship of our two countries," Lloyd told waiting newsmen. "If we stand together, there is almost anything we can do together." It was only later that Lloyd's prosaic remark would acquire something of the force of a dark portent.

Dulles voiced the same theme. "We meet here with a background, a tradition, of having worked together for freedom and a just peace," he said. Sir Anthony smiled, replying, "I am deeply grateful, Foster, if I may call you that." Despite the outward cordiality of Dulles' greeting, Eden may well have wondered.

The contrast between the two men could not have been greater. Eden, at fifty-nine, was worldly and elegant, a master of the style and the subtleties of statesmanship. Dulles was nine years his senior, and he looked it, his face fleshy, his hair receding, his blue eyes suspiciously peering out at an evilly inclined world. His chunky body was clad in its usual well-cut three-piece Brooks Brothers suit that somehow always looked ill-fitting. Unlike Eden, who was known for his finesse, Dulles was regarded in the chancelleries of Europe as heavy-handed and doctrinaire. Eden shared that opinion.

The press was filled with references to how the two men did not get along, and the stories were correct. They had known each other for years and it always seemed that Eden, though younger, was in a superior station to Dulles. At their first meeting in July 1942, Eden was decidedly unimpressed. Eden was already on his second tour as foreign secretary while Dulles was traveling as chairman of the Federal Council of Churches' Commission on a Just and Durable Peace, not the most pressing concern of the British at a time when they were fighting for their survival. The men had lunch in Eden's London flat and afterward Eden confided to his diary: "[Americans] know very little of Europe and it would be unfortunate for the future of the world if U.S. uninstructed views were to decide the future of the European continent. Our diplomacy should be equal to this task."

A third guest at the luncheon, Sir Alexander Cadogan, who was later to be Britain's ambassador to the United Nations, was more outspoken. He noted in his diary: "Lunched with A in his flat. J.F. Dulles there . . . J.F.D. the wooliest type of useless pontificating American. Heaven help us!"

The paths of Eden and Dulles crossed again, but not very closely, at the San Francisco meeting in 1945 at which the United Nations was created. Eden attended as one of the select foreign ministers; Dulles was there as one of the many delegates in the U.S. mission headed by Democratic Secretary of State Edward Stettinius.

Eden's aversion to Dulles bloomed in 1952 over a dispute about the Japanese Peace Treaty, which was finally concluded only that year. One of the reasons for the long delay in signing the treaty was heavy political pressure in Britain and America to obtain a prior commitment from Tokyo about its future relations with Communist China. It was a controversial political issue, exacerbated by the opposite views held in London and Washington. London wanted Japan to trade with China in order to enhance its own trading relations with the region, while Washington was violently against Japan even recognizing the Communist regime, much less trading with it. Dulles had been chosen by President Harry S. Truman as the American negotiator, a token to bipartisanship in foreign relations.

Dulles soon discovered that passions were so aroused on both sides of the Atlantic that he agreed with his British counterpart, Herbert Morrison, that the only way they could conclude an accord acceptable to their two countries was to promise that neither side would press the Japanese on the Chinese issue before the signing of the treaty. Growing pressure in the U.S. Senate, however, convinced Dulles that without a prior declaration of intent from the Japanese the Senate would not approve the treaty. To gain the treaty Dulles allowed publication of the famous Yoshida letter on January 16, 1952, at the start of the Senate debate on the subject. The letter endorsed the U.S. position, and won passage of the treaty.

Morrison and the Foreign Office were furious, feeling they had been betrayed by Dulles and unmercifully left exposed before angry members of Parliament who objected to Japan's decision. Morrison was especially incensed because he and others suspected that Dulles himself had written the letter and presented it as an ultimatum to Japanese Prime Minister Shigeru Yoshida for his signature. Morrison later wrote in his autobiography that "I may be forgiven if I resolved there and then not fully to trust Dulles again." There were others in Britain who felt the same way.

Eden was one of them. Shortly after publication of the Yoshida letter, Eden saw Dwight Eisenhower in London. Ike had just resigned his command of NATO and was on his way to America to become the Republican candidate for the presidency. Who, Eden wondered, would be Ike's choice as his secretary of state? It was not the kind of question to ask a candidate, certainly not when the answer was likely to carry so many domestic political repercussions. Ike, with his shrewd political instincts, naturally ducked the issue but Eden insensitively pressed on. He volunteered to Eisenhower that he hoped it would not be Dulles because he felt he could not work with him.

Aside from the arrogance of the remark, Eden had committed an extraordinary diplomatic faux pas. Eisenhower was surprised by the blunder, but in his memoirs he said he forgave it as an "understandable" intimacy because of "my long association and friendship with him during war and peace, involving the frankest kinds of exchanges." Still, it is notable that the scene made such an impression on him that he bothered mentioning it in his memoirs. Ike's finely tuned sense of people was already detecting a certain flakiness in Eden.

Relations between Eden and Dulles got progressively worse after Ike chose Dulles for secretary of state, a choice that should have warned Eden that Eisenhower believed only so far in the special relationship. It did not extend to Britain appointing American Cabinet members, or, as Eden was later to learn in 1956, of going against American national interests.

Eden and his aides liked to believe that Dulles was jealous of the Briton. Actually the truth was that Dulles, unlike Eisenhower, considered Eden ineffectual and the British empire impotent, nuisances that tended to get in the way of the American crusade against Communism and colonialism. John W. Hanes, Jr., a CIA employee who became one of Dulles' young executive assistants, found the secretary of state's attitude to be that "you could not count on the British to carry on in any responsible way. The secretary had some extremely close British friends and by and large liked the British, but he had absolutely no regard for them internationally. He felt they were clumsy and inept, as opposed to their carefully nurtured reputation of being the opposite, and he really, literally had no admiration for them."

His other executive assistant, Roderic L. O'Connor, also a CIA agent, recalled that Dulles and Eden "just weren't on the same beam. Every time I saw Eden I always felt an overwhelming sense of personal vanity, and Dulles was just the opposite. Dulles may have had intellectual vanity but not personal vanity at all. Just personality-wise, they weren't destined to work together: you know, [Eden's] homburg and all the rest, and his rather languid air—a calculated old English aristocracy. It wasn't Dulles' dish of tea."

Their mutual suspicions and bad chemistry showed up clearly at a meeting in London in February 1953, their first since Dulles had become secretary of state. O'Connor, who attended, recalled that Eden's speech was "all flowing rose petals" while Dulles in his lawyerly way presented the U.S. position in a droning monologue, "weighing every word and putting it down on the table exactly next to the last word." Eden appeared bored and uninterested in following closely Dulles' labored logic.

The main subject was Britain's withdrawal of its troops from the huge military base at Suez, and Eden mentioned the 1936 treaty which gave Britain its legal basis to keep military forces there. Dulles asked to see the treaty. It took an awkward half hour's search to find the document. Dulles pored over it, then subjected Eden to a close interrogation about its details. Eden was fuzzy about a number of items, not surprisingly, since the treaty had been drawn up more than sixteen years earlier. Yet it had been Eden himself who had negotiated it. "Dulles was appalled," recalled O'Connor. "The British did not know what they were talking about. I think this impression of Eden became the dominating impression in Dulles' mind. Eden wasn't doing his homework." On his part, Eden resented Dulles' brusque legal manner and found his concentration on details petty and irrelevant.

The irony was that both men ended up forming images of each other that were the exact opposite of their public demeanors. Eden was known as the subtle and suave diplomatic technician; Dulles as the crusading brinksman.

Other encounters between them did nothing to improve their relations.

145

With the end of the Korean War in July 1953, Dulles' attention focused on the perilous position of the French in Indochina, where they were being beaten by the Communist-backed Viet Minh. Dulles was not interested in supporting French colonialism. But he did fear that France's defeat would cause pro-Western regimes in the region to fall like dominoes to Communist domination. The French situation was grave. By late winter in 1954, the French garrison at Dien Bien Phu was under daily heavy artillery bombardment by Ho Chi Minh's guerrillas from the camp's surrounding mountains. A noose was slowly strangling the French troops, cutting off their supplies, reinforcements and hope. The war was unpopular in Paris and the fall of Dien Bien Phu, with its daily agonies being reported around the world, would undoubtedly mean the end of French colonial rule and the emergence of Communism in Indochina.

Dulles and Admiral Arthur W. Radford, chairman of the Joint Chiefs of Staff, concocted a plan dubbed Operation Vulture to save Dien Bien Phu. They concluded it could be accomplished by air strikes launched from U.S. aircraft carriers cruising in the Gulf of Tonkin. Dulles and Radford left for London and Paris on April 10, 1954, to discuss the plan. During talks with Eden, Radford startled the foreign secretary by hinting that a small atomic bomb dropped on the Viet Minh would lift the siege and save the French garrison.

Dulles then urged Eden to join the U.S. in a "united action" against Communism in Indochina. That was a condition imposed by Eisenhower, who was cool to the idea of U.S. involvement in Indochina. He told Dulles that he would support U.S. bombing strikes only if America entered the fray united with Britain and the Commonwealth, particularly Australia and New Zealand, and with congressional approval.

The meeting ended in a misunderstanding, not the last one that would plague relations between Dulles and Eden. Dulles thought he had received Eden's endorsement of the plan. "I did no such thing," Eden said later. "In no way did I give him any promise or hint of a promise that we would support him in his rash adventure." But, back in Washington, Dulles acted as though he had the cooperation of Britain. He grandly called a meeting of all British Commonwealth, French and several Southeast Asian ambassadors for late April in Washington to discuss "united action" in Indochina. Eden was aghast and immediately instructed Ambassador Makins to stay away under all conditions.

"Dulles was trying to bulldoze me," Eden complained. "It was an outrageous ploy—trying to exploit Anglo-American friendship to get the war he wanted in Indochina. I made it crystal clear that we wanted no part of his dangerous enterprise."

Makins telephoned Dulles at his Georgetown home on Easter Sunday to inform him of Eden's instructions to boycott the conference. Dulles answered while his sister, Eleanor, was at his side. "He looked at me," recalled Eleanor, "and he pounded the table and he said: 'Eden has double-crossed me. He lied to me.' I think this was one of his great disappointments."

Radford's memory of the London meeting with Eden was that the foreign secretary had promised to join Dulles in united action. But he admitted: "President Eisenhower said I frightened the British by my hard words or something."

Dien Bien Phu, its bunkers filled with the stench of rotting corpses and the screams of the wounded, fell on May 7, soon followed by the collapse of the French in Indochina. It marked a significant victory by an Asian army over the forces of a European power. Dulles would always blame the loss on Eden's refusal to join in united action—though the French themselves had no appetite to continue the war, and Britain believed that the conflict would be better dealt with at an international conference.

"I think Eden was rather a weak sister," recalled Radford. "My feeling is that Mr. Dulles did everything in 1954 to help the French. He was blocked largely by the British. He might likely have been blocked later . . . by the French themselves. We didn't really get to the stage where we discussed the arrangements they would have insisted on."

In Dulles' eyes there were no such ambiguities. It was the British, specifically Eden, who were at fault. Epithets started circulating in the halls of the State Department saying Eden was slipping and lacking in moral stature. In the Senate, William Knowland labeled Britain as our "undependable ally" while Democrats charged that Dulles' Indochina policy had been a "diplomatic disaster." Dulles was not likely soon to forget the grief that he felt Eden had caused him. During a meeting with American reporters in late June, Dulles observed that U.S. foreign policy had suffered because it tended to support the "colonialist" policies of Britain and France. He indicated that would change.

Relations between Eden and Dulles were further lacerated at the Summit Conference in Geneva in 1955. Ever since the death of Josef Stalin, the European powers had been calling for a meeting of the world's four ruling nations to discuss the post-Stalinist era, but Dulles was reluctant. His policy of containment of Communism was one of isolation, not ventilation, and he resisted meeting with the Russians. To accept the Soviets as equals of Britain, France and the U.S., in Dulles' view, was to grant them not only political equality but moral equality too. Dulles also had a keen appreciation for the mood of Congress, and among a powerful coterie of conservative Republicans there was a strong suspicion of all international conferences. They still believed that the Democrats had "sold out" Eastern Europe at Yalta and Potsdam during World War II. Yet continuing promises of "peaceful coexistence" by Stalin's successor, Georgi Malenkov, and then by his successors, Khrushchev and Bulganin, added force to British and French demands for a summit meeting. Reluctantly, Eisenhower and Dulles finally agreed.

The five-day meeting began in Geneva on July 18, and Eden, who had just become prime minister, had every expectation that he would dominate it. Of the four world leaders attending, Khrushchev, Eisenhower, Edgar Faure of France and himself, he was by far the most experienced in international meetings. It was the first East-West Summit for the other three, but in his long career as foreign secretary Eden had met and negotiated with Roosevelt, Hitler, Mussolini, Stalin and many other heads of state and government. Eden had the background, he knew the diplomatic game, and it was natural, if not very realistic, for him to expect that he would be the West's leading spokesman.

It turned out that Eisenhower was the star, both because of his stature as a world leader and because of his hopeful message. In his Summit address, he called for a "spirit of Geneva," a general relaxation in tension between East and West, later known as détente. The address caused a resurgence of hope that the frigid days of the Cold War were finally over. "There ain't gonna be no war," happily chirped the new British foreign secretary, Harold Macmillan.

"The Russians paid absolutely no attention to Eden," recalled Roderic O'Connor. "In the coffee break Eden would be by himself with his group, and the Russians were surrounding Eisenhower. I came away with the strong impression that Eden was very disappointed."

O'Connor suspected that much of Eden's concern was about his young mate, Clarissa, who was twenty-three years his junior and the niece of Churchill. They had married three years earlier. "She was coming into the meetings on the arms of a couple of attachés," he recalled. "There was quite a bit of polish and spit. Mr. Eden, I think, was quite interested in keeping this impression of glamour, as much to her as to the public. He was obviously taking sunbaths or a sunlamp every day, because throughout the entire conference he had a blooming vigorous tan. He was quite chagrined, I think, because he didn't come out of the conference as the outstanding diplomat.''

• •

Eden and Dulles began their working sessions the same afternoon that the British party arrived in Washington. The two areas of disagreement were, as expected, China and the Middle East. With considerable hyperbole, Dulles explained to the British side U.S. policy on China. It was important, he said, for the West to continue its support of Formosa and keep its Asian bases in such countries as Japan and the Philippines. "If we lose the chain of positions in the Western Pacific stretching from the Aleutians to Australia and New Zealand,'' Dulles explained, "it would be almost as bad as if we lost the Atlantic positions. From a physical defense standpoint it would be about equally disastrous. We would have to fall back to the continental U.S., possibly being able to keep the Hawaiian Islands. The western rim of the Pacific,'' Dulles emphasized, "was extremely vital to the U.S. from a defense standpoint.''

Disagreement between the two countries centered on the question of recognition of the Communist regime in China. The United Kingdom had been among the first to recognize the Peking government, thereby displaying its usual clear-eyed appreciation for the vagaries of history and its own economic need to trade with friend and foe. The United States remained committed to Chiang Kai-shek, a vest-pocket dictator who had deftly managed by propaganda and an open pocketbook to have himself portrayed in America as a freedom fighter.

In America, Communist China had become the incarnation of the frightful yellow horde when its troops had intervened massively against U.S. forces in Korea in 1950. Out of such imaginings had emerged a China lobby in Congress that at the time was as potent in its ways as the Israeli lobby. Both groups exerted inordinate influence on the conduct of American foreign relations. Dulles, however, needed no prompting from the China lobby to raise his suspicions about the ungodliness of Communist China; he ardently opposed the regime, refused to treat with it, and suspected the morality of any country that did. Dulles was determined that Mao Zedong's China would remain ostracized by America and by the United Nations.

Eisenhower felt just as strongly. He explained to Eden, "The sentiment in the country and in Congress is overwhelmingly against admission of Red China [to the U.N.]. The Communists were still aggressors in

Korea, they had tortured our prisoners, had thrown our nationals into jail without trial and were still holding Americans in prison in violation of their commitment to release them. They had violated all the decencies supposed to exist between civilized nations." As long as they remained as they are, said Ike, he would be "opposed to their admission" to the U.N. In fact, Eisenhower added, feelings were so strong in the country that the U.N. might have to leave America if Red China was admitted to the world organization. "It would not be thirty minutes before a resolution would be introduced upon the floor of the Senate for the U.S. to get out" of the U.N., Ike warned.

Eden pointed out that the U.N. after all was a "universal organization in which one must expect to have unpleasant people," but Ike and Dulles would not relent.

There was more agreement on the issue of neutralism. Neither side liked the spreading movement among emerging nations to remain neutral between Communism and the West. "We must be more vigorous than we have been in combating the idea of neutralism," said Dulles. He added that the new countries should "develop a crusading spirit against the evil forces of Communism. It is plain that the Communist intention is to squeeze everything they can use out of each country one by one and then move on. This is characteristic of expanding despotism which needs conquest in order to survive. These neutral governments do not seem to realize that the Communist intentions are so diabolical and so hostile to their freedom and independence."

Lloyd added that the West simply could not ignore the neutral nations, since that would throw them into Soviet arms. Dulles agreed. "We do favor countries that are lining up with us," he said, "and we should not treat neutrals better than these. But that is quite a different thing from doing nothing at all."

The most serious difference centered on the Middle East, which, as it turned out, was a far more significant disagreement than that over China. The Middle East, Dulles noted, might "flare up at any moment."

The Israeli-Egyptian conflict, Dulles explained, "posed grave difficulties for us. Israel and many supporters of that country in the United States would like for the U.S. to enter into a treaty which would protect Israel against an attack." But Dulles said he did not think that was a prudent idea because such a treaty might alienate the Arabs by causing them "to fear that we were preparing to protect Israel alone." On the contrary, Dulles thought the Western countries should be objective in the conflict and aid whichever side was attacked. This was in line with his belief that U.S. policy should be evenhanded.

Evenhandedness, of course, was the spirit of the Tripartite Declaration of 1950, under which Britain and America as well as France committed themselves not to disturb the status quo in the Middle East by introducing major new supplies of arms to either side. But since Russia had broken that embargo the previous September, Eden now proposed that the three Western powers "put teeth" into the declaration by turning it into a military alliance aimed at enforcing the arms embargo. Eden thought that would be an effective way of maintaining Western influence and reining in Nasser's ambitions. But Eisenhower and Dulles had doubts. A military alliance, they pointed out, would need congressional approval, and they believed it unlikely that Congress would approve in an election year the potential deployment of American forces to the Middle East so soon after Korea.

Dulles noted that the Administration had "a difficult public relations problem" in strengthening the declaration because "the American people were not accustomed to looking upon the Middle East as a vital area. The United Kingdom had always played an important part in that area and security matters were usually identified as a British responsibility. There might be some suspicion that any military plans developed might be related to Zionists' efforts to involve the United States in fighting to support Israel, and there is substantial opposition to the U.S. being drawn into such an affair."

Dulles also noted, "We have always played down American oil interests, and it would certainly not be popular if the impression should be given that we were risking military action to protect investments of American oil companies."

Dulles prevailed. No teeth were put in the Tripartite Declaration, though Dulles' use of the argument that Congress would probably not approve such action peeved Eden. He bitterly recalled the occasion in his memoirs, saying that the U.S. position reminded him of an incident at the 1943 Teheran Conference between Churchill, Stalin and Franklin D. Roosevelt.

"One evening," Eden wrote, "Harry Hopkins [Roosevelt's confidant] teased Mr. Churchill and myself about British constitutional practices. 'We have a little more experience of the British than you have, Marshal Stalin. Would you like to know how the constitution works?' 'I would,' said Stalin. 'It depends,' said Mr. Hopkins, 'rather on the result they want to get. If the British want to agree quickly, they manage it all right. If, however, they are not so sure, or they want to delay, they will tell you they have to consult the dominions and that until they have answers from all of them, they cannot give you a clear reply.' I wondered to myself whether Mr. Hopkins' analysis of our alleged practices might not fit that of his own country in relation to Congress just then."

Eden's ire was also raised by Dulles' defense of Saudi Arabia in its dispute with the Sultanate of Muscat and Oman, which had been under British protection since 1853. Saudi troops, traveling in ARAMCO transport, had occupied in 1952 the Buraimi Oasis claimed by Oman, and the dispute was still festering. The Saudis were claiming the area as their land and the U.S. was supporting the claim since Saudi Arabia was America's greatest oil-bearing friend in the gulf and its riches were dominated by the powerful U.S. consortium of ARAMCO. The oasis was suspected of having enormous oil deposits and ARAMCO was anxious for the Saudi claim to succeed; otherwise British oil companies under contract with the Sultan would get the exploration rights.

All efforts at arbitration failed, and Dulles now made another pitch on behalf of the Saudis. "The United States has a very large stake in Saudi Arabia," he explained. "There are massive oil resources which are extremely important, and we also have an air base under an agreement scheduled to expire this year. The United States does not want to be put in a position where those interests might be lost."

The argument found no sympathy with the British side, and the issue remained unsettled.

The final irritant between the two countries was the Baghdad Pact, and on that they could not begin to agree. Dulles had originally proposed the pact's creation as one of his series of alliances aimed at surrounding the Soviet Union, this one to extend from Pakistan through Iran, Iraq and Turkey. Eden was enthusiastic about the pact, and in April 1955 signed Britain on as a member—only to discover that the U.S. refused to join. U.S. refusal was well founded. Both Egypt and Israel were violently opposed to the pact, though for different reasons. Egypt realistically saw it as a British attempt to unite Moslem nations into an alliance that London would dominate, thus preserving its power in the area. Israel feared that if Britain's efforts succeeded in making the pact into a new Middle East condominium led by Britain, traditionally no friend of Israel's, then the Jewish state would be surrounded by a unified enemy.

The U.S. was caught in another dilemma. It saw an urgent need for the Baghdad Pact's southern bulwark against Soviet expansion into the Middle East, yet it wanted to maintain its friendly relations with Egypt and Israel. Eden inadvertently provided a simple answer for Dulles by rashly taking the lead in promoting the Baghdad Pact, thereby greatly worsening his country's shaky relations with Egypt. Since the pact now existed, Washington could see no reason to follow Britain and alienate Egypt and especially Israel by joining.

Dulles tried to explain, pointing out that it was "politically impossible for the United States to join until we were able to offer a comparable security arrangement to Israel. Without this, the United States could not get public support for undertaking the Baghdad treaty." On the Egyptian side, pointed out Dulles aide George V. Allen, "Nasser had said the Baghdad Pact was a new form of imperialism designed to imprison all of the Arab people." Either way, America could not win since both Arabs and Israelis opposed the pact.

Dulles darkly noted that "we might soon know whether our whole attitude toward Nasser would have to be changed." He was referring to the secret Anderson mission, which was currently in full swing. Dulles admitted that so far Anderson's mission "had not produced any real hopes for an early settlement. Unless there were grave issues, it was possible that Egypt would follow dilatory tactics so long as they got what they wanted. The Israelis likewise would not agree to truncate territory claimed by them unless grave issues should compel them to." Dulles thought the main sticking point to a settlement was the future of the Negev, which Israel had captured in the 1948 war and still retained. Egypt claimed the whole area from Elath to north of Beersheva.

Dulles returned to the subject of the Baghdad Pact, and repeated the U.S. position: "Since the United States could not include Israel in a security treaty, it could not join the pact." With a degree of naïveté untypical of him, Eden years later still did not seem to understand the U.S. position and thought that "the United States has sometimes failed to put its weight behind its friends, in the hope of being popular with its foes. The consequences of this uncertain diplomacy are illustrated by the United States treatment of the Baghdad Pact."

There was nothing, of course, at all uncertain about the U.S. attitude. Britain had rashly taken the lead, the U.S. had the bulwark against Russia that it wanted, and by not joining it, America had its friendly relations with Egypt and Israel too. Privately, Eisenhower had grave reservations about the pact and the British attempt to use it to maintain their Middle East position. "The British have never had any sense in the Middle

East,'' Ike had muttered the month before. The pact, he added with shrewd foresight, could cause difficulties. America never did join it.*

• •

Eden's problem throughout the Washington talks was a simple one, though insoluble. Britain needed America more than America needed Britain. The British economy was in precarious condition, as was amply demonstrated by a paper submitted by Eden during the conference. It showed that Britain had only enough gold and dollar reserves to cover the cost of its imports for a mere three months. ''The Second World War had turned us from the world's greatest creditor to the world's greatest debtor,'' Lloyd observed. ''We could not undertake any more external commitments.''

However brilliantly Eden and Lloyd argued England's cause, Eisenhower and Dulles could not be swayed by anything less than what they perceived to be in their nation's best self-interest, which in an election year was a very narrow area. Certainly it did not include ''putting teeth'' in the Tripartite Declaration, or alienating Israel by joining the Baghdad Pact, or deserting Saudi Arabia in its dispute over Buraimi Oasis. In politics and the conduct of affairs between nations, that was neither unexpected nor overly cynical, as any veteran statesman of the British empire should have appreciated. But Eden somehow could never accept viscerally the diminished state of the empire, however much he recognized it intellectually. Nor did he have the wisdom to appreciate fully Churchill's repeated warnings over the years of the absolute necessity to coordinate policy with Washington. ''Without the United States,'' Churchill told Eden more than once, ''Britain is alone.''

At the end of the conference, Eden had no cause to complain about his treatment in Washington. Ike had given him his full attention, though he was still recuperating, and had gone out of his way to help him. When the final communiqué was being drawn up, Ike called Dulles and wondered ''whether we might not help Sir Anthony a little bit by mentioning the fact that we have been warm friends since the days of World War II.'' As a climax, Eisenhower thoughtfully helped arrange for Eden to speak separately before both the Senate and the House of Representatives. That did not carry the same distinction accorded Churchill on his

* The pact came to an unmourned end under the guise of CENTO in 1979 with the overthrow of the Shah of Iran, having served no other purpose than causing anxiety in the Middle East, tension between the U.S. and Britain, bellicosity in Moscow and an unjustified contentment in Foster Dulles.

visits when he addressed the combined Houses complete with the justices of the Supreme Court and the members of the Cabinet in attendance, but it nonetheless was an honor and proof of the President's support, as well as a highly visible platform from which Eden could momentarily escape his domestic troubles.

The conclusion of his visit was celebrated with the issuance of a communiqué titled "The Declaration of Washington," in which Ike and Eden noted the "unity of purpose of our two countries." One section of the strongly anti-Soviet document vowed that "we shall never initiate violence." That was a promise that came back to haunt the hapless Eden.

The declaration received considerable attention in the press. But so too did the far more intriguing story of how Britain and America had failed to resolve any of their long-standing and irritating differences. The London *Evening Express* reported at the conclusion of Eden's visit that the "conference has failed to produce any result which could not have been procured through normal diplomatic channels."

But it was not a totally futile mission for Eden. He had sought to escape the hailstorm of criticism at home and he had done that, at least temporarily. The U.S. side had looked on benignly, perhaps a bit cynically, ready to accommodate an old wartime ally but not willing to offer anything of substance. It was as much as Eden could have expected.

Yet his visit served as a mere pause in his descent into disaster. Despite the hoopla about "The Declaration of Washington," it turned out to be only vaporous rhetoric, yet another document of empty words. In his exhaustive memoirs, Eisenhower does not mention the declaration or even Eden's visit, perhaps as much out of pique at what he considered Eden's later perfidy as his disillusionment with the conference. One reason was put forth by Ike's assistant Sherman Adams: "Eden's visit to Washington did not resolve one serious difference between the American and British positions on the Middle East question; our firm opposition to colonialism made us sympathetic to the struggle which Egypt and other Arab states were making to free themselves of the political and economic control that the British felt they had to maintain in the Middle East in their own self-interest."

The underlying conflict over colonialism that relentlessly gnawed away at the special relationship between the two countries remained unresolved, festering and ready to erupt with a vengeance later in the year.

CHAPTER VIII

I Was a Victim Myself

MOLLET

As THE NATION MOVED into the political year there oc-
curred what Foster Dulles had feared. Partisan politics started intruding
into foreign policy over the question of arms for Israel. The Democrats,
spurred by a heavy ideological commitment to Zionism by the liberal
wing of the party, went public to agitate in Israel's favor. On January 28,
a group led by Eleanor Roosevelt, widow of President Franklin D. Roosevelt, issued a statement urging that U.S. arms be sent to Israel. It was
endorsed by other political figures such as former President Harry S.
Truman (who had ignored State Department advice to delay recognition
of Israel and made Washington the first capital to do so within minutes of
Israel's proclamation of independence on May 14, 1948) and labor leader
Walter P. Reuther, vice president of the AFL-CIO.

The U.S. "must counteract every attempt by the Soviet Union to upset
the present precarious balance of power in [the Middle East]," declared
Mrs. Roosevelt's statement. "This requires that the U.S. should now
provide the defensive arms needed by Israel to protect itself against any
aggression made possible or incited by the introduction of Communist
arms." It added: "No constructive purpose could be served by gnawing
at or seeking to roll back the boundaries of Israel."

The connection between Communism and the security of Israeli borders was nonexistent, of course, but it was typical of the confusion cloud-
ing that complex region that the two issues were yoked together. The
highly distorted image that resulted was that Israeli security depended on
both getting arms and keeping its existing frontiers, and that only Israel's

156

security could provide a bulwark against Communism in the region. In fact, the reality was nearly the reverse. Israel's violent retaliatory policy and its refusal to define the limits of its state were major contributory causes of the arms race and the Soviet Union's entry into the Middle East.

With such topsy-turvy logic the tangled web that was known as the Middle East issue lurched into the presidential campaign of 1956. As the winter days passed, the clamor of arms for Israel took on the roar of a storm. Ambassador Abba Eban carried the campaign into the halls of the State Department and before the public, which was more receptive than was Foster Dulles. Eban called on Dulles on January 25 to plead unsuccessfully for weapons. After he departed, George V. Allen wryly remarked to the secretary of state: "You did a wonderful job with Eban— after his first words you didn't let him speak."

But Eban had plenty to say in public. He told the Women's National Democratic Club in Washington on January 30 that America and Britain should "rise to the level of their inescapable moral duty" and provide arms to Israel. The message was typical of many delivered by Eban around the country that winter. The cry was soon picked up by some Republican congressmen. Forty GOP House members wrote Dulles a letter on February 3 strongly recommending that Washington match Soviet-bloc arms to Egypt with U.S. arms to Israel. In his reply, which was personally edited by Eisenhower, Dulles said, "We do not exclude the possibility of arms sale to Israel." But, he added pointedly, part of the fear and tension in the area resulted from "the lack of permanent boundaries. It is our belief that the security of states in the Near East cannot rest upon arms alone but rather upon the international rule of law."

• •

Eisenhower was still struggling with the knotty question that had preoccupied him since his September heart attack. He could not make up his mind whether to seek a second term but he was increasingly leaning toward it. He called Vice President Nixon to his office on February 7 for a long, rambling chat about the kind of campaign rigors he might expect if he did run. Ike told Nixon that he had met with Republican National Committee Chairman Leonard Hall the evening before and Hall had assured him that the national committee would not put pressure on him to campaign. His efforts could be confined to three to five TV speeches, Hall had assured him. But Eisenhower said he thought Hall "is wearing rose-colored glasses. I just wonder what you think."

Nixon agreed with Hall. He told Eisenhower the way to handle the problem was to tell the national committee, "Gentlemen, here it is, this is the campaign. The President's participation is going to be limited to this extent, not because of his inability to do more but because this is the right kind of campaign."

But, argued Eisenhower, the politicians would inevitably urge him to do more, claiming that "you have to do so and so because of your health, to show that you are capable."

"I realize that the opposition will throw the pressure on," replied Nixon. "But this is what you do in a campaign—you decide at the beginning what you are going to do and then you don't deviate. My opinion is that that is the best kind of plan for you at this time. I don't say that because I am trying to give an argument to make your mind up. I honestly believe that that is the best kind of a campaign for you to put on at this time."

"I had this in 1952," protested Ike. "Everybody was saying that two Republican campaigns were lost because of lack of work," referring to the unsuccessful races by Thomas E. Dewey in 1944 and 1948. Now he added, "I have come to this point. All the way along I consented to four years only. Now I find myself almost under greater pressure than originally to continue another four years, in spite of a heart attack, and knowing that I am going to have to defend myself against certain remarks such as, 'See, he is an invalid,' and all that. It's going to be a really tough campaign this fall—not for me particularly, but the rest of the people."

Beyond that, Eisenhower added, he was distressed at the disarray within the Republican Party, which was torn between its liberal and conservative wings. "When is there going to be teamwork among the Republicans?" he asked. "I am at my wit's end to try to understand it." The meeting ended inconclusively, with the President still undecided whether to run again.

• •

The pressures on Eisenhower to resolve the question of a second term were mounting. The newspapers were filled with speculation, and his advisers and the Republican Party were pressing daily for an answer. Time was growing short. The Democrats already had an almost certain standard-bearer in Adlai Stevenson, the man Ike had beaten in 1952, and likely could beat again—if he decided to run. The question had to be answered soon.

Ike finally promised at his regular weekly press conference the day after his talk with Nixon to give his decision by the end of the month. But privately he was suffering disillusionment with aspects of the Republican Party. Why, he wondered as he sat in the Oval Office that day, should he help elect Republicans to Congress when in many cases he was just as happy to have Democrats in control? He was agitated by the furor over the Natural Gas Act, which would reduce government control of prices at the wellhead. Ike favored the act but he had decided to veto it because of charges that oilmen had greased its passage through Congress with large bribes. The selfish actions of businessmen greatly irritated him, Ike said to Gabriel Hauge, his economic aide and sometime speech writer. Of course, answered Hauge, but business must have an honorable place in American society.

"I want to give businessmen an honorable place," retorted the President, "but they make crooks out of themselves."

The next day, after extensive tests, Eisenhower's doctors pronounced him recovered from his heart attack and fit to lead an "active life satisfactorily for another five to ten years."* Now only his own hesitations stood in the way of another four years as President.

• •

The Middle East issue continued to elbow its way onto the political scene. Newspaper stories based on leaked information reported on February 16 that the United States was about to send eighteen M-41 tanks to Saudi Arabia and brought protests from Israel and its supporters. Ambassador Abba Eban declared that the shipment was "utterly beyond our comprehension. An Arab country, which is in no danger of attack from anyone, receives American arms. Israel, which is in serious danger of attack, has so far received nothing."

The protests grew so great that the State Department ordered the tank shipment suspended, provoking in turn protests from Saudi Ambassador Abdullah Khayyal. Ike had to be consulted before the flap got out of hand. With the President's consent, the State Department again switched signals and sent the tanks on their way on February 18 over the continuing vocal opposition of Israel and its supporters in the Congress and the media. The Administration stood up to the protests because in the balance was the fate of the U.S. air base in Saudi Arabia at Dhahran, whose lease was up for renegotiation with Riyadh. Both countries declared there was no linkage between the base lease and the tanks, but a new agree-

* The physicians proved too conservative: he lived until March 28, 1969.

ment was being negotiated to allow America to keep the base for the next five years and Washington was wary of angering the Saudis.

The Israeli protests failed, but the uproar had its beneficial effects for Tel Aviv by sensitizing the Administration to the issue. When a short time later, on March 5, Eisenhower was asked by Under Secretary of State Hoover whether he objected to France selling to Israel twelve advanced Mystère IV jet fighters that had been designated for NATO service, his terse reply was: "No objection."

It was through such deals with France that Israel was maintaining its military superiority, though publicly Israel claimed it was losing the arms race with Egypt. It continued to besiege Washington for U.S. weapons, at the same time warning that Nasser was growing stronger and preparing to go to war. But secretly France had become Israel's major arms supplier long before Cairo's Czech arms deal.

• •

The curious arms alliance between France and Israel began in nuclear research in the late 1940s and early 1950s. Israel had developed a cheap method of producing a vital component of nuclear research, heavy water, without using vast amounts of electrical power. In exchange for heavy water, France allowed Israeli scientists to study at the Institute of Nuclear Science and Techniques at Saclay, near Paris, and to work at the Marcoule reactor so they could develop their nuclear skills. This cooperation had profound results. It led to France's construction of the Dimona nuclear plant in the Negev where Israel eventually produced fissionable components usable in atomic bombs, and, more immediately, facilitated the intimate arms connection with France.

French transfers of conventional weapons to Israel began slowly in the early 1950s with battle tanks, cannon and surplus World War II planes. By the end of 1954, France became more generous largely as a result of the rebellion that started that year in Algeria; the Jewish state was suddenly seen as a counterbalance to the Arab rebels. There was considerable support in France for Israel, especially in the military, which admired Israel's tough tactics, and among Paris' leading politicians. Many French politicians shared socialist ideals with Israel's leaders and had fought alongside Jewish fighters in the Resistance.

Three of Israel's staunchest supporters in France were powerful men: General Pierre-Marie Koenig, Maurice Bourgès-Maunoury and Abel Thomas. Koenig was minister of defense in 1954 and his Zionist sympathies extended back to World War II when he commanded a Free French division in the Western Desert and cooperated with Palestinian Jewish troops. Bourgès and Thomas were both former Resistance fighters who admired the Jews' contribution to the Resistance and their victory in Palestine. All three men had strong ties with the French military establishment and saw Israel as a natural ally in the sense of "an enemy of my enemy is my friend."

The French military, stunned and humiliated by its defeat in World War II, shamed by its rout in Indochina, angered and frustrated by the vacillating policies of the postwar Fourth Republic governments, was determined above all else not to lose the empire's remaining great colony. In the French imagination, Algeria was more than a colony; it was a southern extension of the homeland and, indeed, had been legally integrated into metropolitan France as one of the nation's departments. France had controlled the North African nation since 1830, and, as one of its modern governors-general, Jacques Soustelle, declared: "Algeria and all its people are an integral part of France, one and indivisible, and France will no more quit Algeria than Provence or Britany. *L'Algerie c'est la France!*"

A million Frenchmen lived among Algeria's eight million Moslems, but since the rebellion that broke out on November 1, 1954—All Saints' Day —the lives of the French inhabitants were becoming increasingly endangered by the Arab guerrilla fighters of the FLN (Front de Libération Nationale). At first the FLN had been a ragtag group of leftist guerrillas with few weapons or resources but its daring raids soon attracted outside support. The French erroneously suspected that Gamal Nasser was foremost among the FLN's supporters.

In focusing their suspicions on Nasser the French made a profound mistake. They suspected that the fulminations of Radio Cairo's Voice of the Arabs broadcasts against France's presence in Algeria were only the tip of a large covert supply operation of arms and money by Egypt to the FLN. In French eyes Nasser assumed the proportions of an Arab bogeyman manipulating plots against the French across all of North Africa and in the Middle East. Soon the French were calling Nasser the dictator of the Nile, the Mussolini of the Arab world, the Moslem ogre threatening not only Western influence around the rim of the Mediterranean but also the European lifeline to the Middle East's rich oil fields.

In reality, Nasser gave little beyond rhetoric and diplomatic help to Algeria. His most notable contribution to the FLN was at the historic meeting of Third World nations at Bandung in 1955 where he sponsored a motion, unanimously passed, calling for Algeria's independence. It was at that meeting that the FLN received international recognition and massive contributions from other emerging nations to help finance the rebellion.

Long after the war, leaders of the Algerian revolution admitted to British historian Alistair Horne how little they received from Egypt and how great was their disappointment. But as Abdelkader Chanderli, who was active in FLN arms procurement, observed, "Because of the need for solidarity, we could not say so." The pretense worked, far beyond the rebels' imaginings, for it encouraged the mistaken French belief that Nasser's aid was instrumental in the success of the FLN. That error helped convince Paris eventually of the need to go to war against Egypt.

The French were encouraged in their misjudgment by several factors, not the least of them being the seductive simplicity of the idea that Nasser was the master plotter. As with many others in a similar situation, it was more satisfying to the French self-image to believe that the rebellion was guided and supplied from the outside than to contemplate the stark facts: French rule was so oppressive and exploitative that poorly armed Algerians were driven to such extremes of despair that they dared rise up against the devastating firepower of the French Army.

Israel also played on France's exaggerated apprehensions about Nasser for its own ends, as it was to do repeatedly on the road to war. Sylvia Kowitt Crosbie, a former member of the Israeli Foreign Ministry, concluded in her study of the Franco-Israeli relationship, *A Tacit Alliance,* that "there is little doubt the Israelis purposely fanned French fears of Nasser's involvement in Algeria and stressed his ambitions elsewhere in order to increase French willingness to cooperate with Israel."

• •

The secret arms deals between France and Israel became significant in 1954. In that year suave Shimon Peres, thirty-one and already the director-general of Israel's Defense Ministry, showed up in Paris to see if his country could increase its arms purchases. Peres arrived on a Friday night, called the ministry Saturday morning and was surprised to learn that Defense Minister Koenig would meet with him the very next day, a Sunday. "He listened to our arms request, asked some pertinent questions and then gave his decision on the spot with characteristic brevity," said Peres. "I agree," said Koenig. "Give me your list." Recalled Peres: "That was the start of a long and deep friendship between the general and Israel, a friendship which saw us through many critical situations."

Two months later, in early 1955, months before Egypt negotiated its

Czech arms deal, French 155mm guns began arriving in Israeli ports, soon to be followed by AMX-13 light tanks and jet planes. Within the year, Peres also met Abel Thomas, who introduced him to powerful Maurice Bourgès-Maunoury, then minister of the interior, the ministry responsible for Algerian affairs. Thomas was a Zionist Jew and the chief aide to Bourgès. Both men had no doubt that France and Israel had a common enemy in Nasser. Bourgès said he was ready to give Israel everything in his power, which was considerable (he had been a minister in nineteen of the twenty-two governments of the Fourth Republic).

"There is the same regularity in the ebb and flow of the Mediterranean tides which wash the shores of both France and Israel," Bourgès told Peres. "We must not let its troublesome waters reach our coasts. We should work together, and we can." And they did. Israel remained during the 1950s by far the best-equipped and strongest military power in the Middle East and North Africa, thanks to French arms.

• •

Nothing characterized the French Fourth Republic more than the fragility of its governments, which came and went with dizzying rapidity. The government under which Israel had achieved its closest ties with France up to that time fell at the end of 1955 and was replaced in a month by a shaky coalition of Socialists and Communists headed by Premier Guy Mollet. The change in governments, far from diluting the alliance, made the French connection even closer, for fifty-one-year-old Mollet and his foreign minister, Christian Pineau, also fifty-one, were as passionate pro-Zionists as Bourgès-Maunoury. Bourgès was appointed to the powerful post of defense minister.

Like Bourgès, Mollet had been a member of the Resistance and had witnessed German atrocities against Jews at first hand. He was the son of working-class parents who by his brilliance had worked his way through school on scholarships to become a high-school English teacher and a dedicated Socialist. Austere and slim, mild-mannered and soft-spoken almost to the point of timidity, Mollet nonetheless was tenacious in his beliefs. After the war he became secretary-general of the Socialist Party and a leading advocate of European unity. He also fervently believed that Jews should have a national homeland in Palestine.

When Shimon Peres first met him at the end of 1955 in Paris, Mollet stunned the Israeli by protesting at the start of their talk that he was not an anti-Semite. The reason for this strange declaration was that he had just defeated two Jews for the top post of the Socialist Party and stories were circulating in Paris that he disliked Jews. "The very idea that I should be termed an anti-Semite is too dreadful for words," he told Peres. "Quite the reverse. I know all about Nazi persecution. I was a victim myself. It is my warmest wish to visit Israel. I have many friends in the Labor [Socialist] group there. Israel is developing the very model of a socialist society to which we in our French party aspire."

Peres replied that he had no doubts about Mollet's "attitude, as a Frenchman, toward the Jewish people; but we had suffered many disappointments from Socialists once they reached power. Socialists were usually right on domestic matters, but they often showed a naïveté . . . in foreign affairs. You expect your enemies to behave in the same spirit of liberalism as you and your friends." Peres pointedly added that many Israelis wondered whether Mollet would be another Ernest Bevin, the foreign minister in the post-war Labour government in Britain who after reaching office became a foe of Zionism in Palestine.

"I shall never be a Bevin," declared Mollet. "You will see tangible signs of my friendship, both as a Frenchman and as a Socialist, whether in opposition or in government."

Shortly after his election, Mollet invited Peres to his official residence at the Hotel Matignon for dinner. "Now you will see that I will not be a Bevin," he said. He was as good as his word. "For the first time," noted Peres, "there was direct contact between the two defense ministries, French and Israeli, with the full blessing of the prime minister." The best of France's modern weapons began flowing in increasing numbers to Israel, and in the winter of 1956, the stage was set for the formation of a powerful secret alliance aimed directly against Gamal Abdel Nasser.

• •

The Soviet Union's Nikita Khrushchev kept the West off balance that winter with his unprecedented activism and perplexing alternations between dovish and hawkish gestures. Western leaders could not decide how seriously to take him. This was especially true in their reaction to his dramatic challenge delivered at the watershed Twentieth Communist Party Congress held February 14–25 in Moscow. In his opening seven-hour speech, Khrushchev boldly rejected Communist dogma and asserted that Communism had grown so strong that war with capitalism was no longer inevitable.

"Peaceful coexistence" is gaining "increasingly wider international recognition," declared Khrushchev. "Indeed, there are only two ways: either peaceful coexistence or the most devastating war in history. There is no third alternative. Countries with differing social systems cannot just simply exist side by side. There must be progress to better relations, to stronger confidence among them, to cooperation.''

Khrushchev boasted that with such peaceful means Communism would win out in the end. He cited as the reason a subject that had been bothering Eisenhower recently, the relative efficiency of the two systems. "Our certainty of the victory of Communism is based on the fact that the socialist mode of production possesses decisive advantages over the capitalist mode of production,'' boasted Khrushchev.

Foster Dulles reacted to Khrushchev's boasts with a self-serving analysis of the historic events occurring in Russia, completely ignoring the appeal for closer relations. In testifying before the Senate Foreign Relations Committee on February 24, he claimed that it was the strength of the free world that was causing the Soviets to "revamp their whole creed from A to Z. They have failed, and now they have to revise their whole policy. It is a tremendous process for them because they have to undo the teaching of many years. One thing that is absolutely certain is the unity and firmness and resolution of the free nations have caused the Soviet policy to fail, and today they are trying to figure out how they are going to get a better one.''

Dulles turned to the Middle East, explaining to the committee that the Administration did ''not exclude the possibility of arms sales'' to Israel. But, he added, ''Israel, due to its much smaller size and population, could not win an arms race against Arabs having access to Soviet-bloc stocks. It would seem that Israel's security could be better assured, in the long run, through measures other than the acquisition of additional arms in circumstances which might exacerbate the situation.''

America's central problem in the Middle East, Dulles admitted to the committee, ''derives very largely from the fact that the Arabs believe that the U.S., which confronts a problem which relates to Israel, is in the last analysis dominated by domestic political considerations.'' Dulles vowed that the Eisenhower Administration was determined to ''deal with the problem purely from the standpoint of the best interests of the U.S. on a basis of friendly impartiality toward both the Israelis and Arabs.''

As for the Soviets' position in the Middle East, Dulles declared: ''They made very little progress in the last few years.''

The senators were skeptical of Dulles' rosy picture of the state of international Communism, and especially its position in the Middle East, since in the past half year it had scored a series of triumphs.

On February 10, just two weeks before Dulles' optimistic appraisal,

Moscow had announced that it would supply Egypt with its first small atomic laboratory for research in the peaceful use of nuclear energy.

On February 22, a Soviet aid mission had arrived in Beirut on a tour of the Middle East, offering unprecedented technical assistance to build roads, hydroelectric dams, rail and seaport facilities. With its historic entry into Egypt with the Czech arms deal the previous autumn, its offer of help to other Moslem regimes from Algeria to Syria, and the resulting new interest in Russia being displayed by the Arabs, it was obvious to the most casual observer that the Soviets had made enormous inroads in the Middle East. Dulles' Panglossian comments seemed either deceitful or self-serving, or both, and diplomats and legislators attacked him.

Former ambassador to the Soviet Union George F. Kennan, a Democrat, quipped: "I don't recognize the world Mr. Dulles is talking about." Democratic senator from Arkansas J. William Fulbright, a prickly realist, lambasted Dulles on the Senate floor as a secretary of state who treated the American people "as children, ready to clap in delight at every fairy story, however fanciful." He wondered whether democracy was "well served when a secretary of state misleads public opinion, confuses it, feeds it pap, tells it that if it will suppress the proof of its own senses, it will see that Soviet triumphs are really Soviet defeats, and Western defeats are really triumphs."

Democratic leader Adlai E. Stevenson ridiculed Dulles' testimony with one of his aphorisms. "Surely he knows better. If he doesn't, he should; if he does, he should not mislead the country."

• •

In the Middle East, the looking-glass nature of the conflict prevailed. While Israeli public complaints made it appear that the country was fighting a desperate battle of defense, it had in fact taken the offensive by consolidating its hold on the strategic demilitarized zone of El Auja, a continuing source of tensions. Ben Gurion and Foreign Minister Moshe Sharett had promised Dag Hammarskjold during his visit to the region in January that Israeli forces would be removed from the area, but the U.N. secretary-general discovered on his return to New York in February that Israel was still stalling. In a sharp confidential letter to Sharett on February 28, Hammarskjold wrote, "On my return . . . I learned to my disappointment and great concern that for several weeks you delayed and now raise difficulties in implementing the agreements on El Auja. I fail to see that anything has happened which invalidates your unconditional acceptance of the proposals of 3 November, again confirmed when I was in Jerusalem. It is certainly needless for me to recapitulate the way in which from your side, at a stage when you had accepted the proposals 'in principle,' severe criticism was directed by you against Egypt for its delay in agreeing to the suggested arrangements.''

Hammarskjold recalled that Ben Gurion and Sharett had stressed the importance of reducing border incidents in the zone, and he warned that their intransigence was contributing to such incidents. ''With what authority could I or Burns discuss these matters with the Egyptians if you in the El Auja case may be said to have backed down from commitments to us which were part of the very background for the Egyptian acceptance of the proposals? Thus your present attitude on El Auja undermines our ability to go ahead.''

Israeli units were still patrolling provocatively up to the edge of the international border of the zone, engaging almost daily in exchanges of fire with Egyptian guards. ''A willingness on your side to adjust your patrolling policy would be a proof of your honest desire to pacify the situation along the armistice lines,'' concluded Hammarskjold. Israel ignored Hammarskjold's plea and continued sending its patrols to the edge of the zone.

As was their practice, Israeli officials maintained that in all cases of border fire fights it was always the Egyptians who started firing first. General Burns, on the same day that Hammarskjold wrote his impatient letter to Sharett, wrote an equally assertive letter to the Foreign Ministry. Citing three recent examples in which U.N. observers witnessed Israelis fire first on Egyptian positions, Burns wrote that ''in recent conversation it was asserted that it was invariably the Egyptians who opened fire. The above observed incidents prove this not to be so. It is obvious that in Israel's own interests, very strict orders should be issued and enforced prohibiting opening of fire by any individuals or units unless they are in danger of attack by Egyptians.

''I am ready to station a certain number of observers in observation posts in Israeli-controlled territory,'' Burns added. But that, the Israeli government, invoking its sovereignty, would not allow; all U.N. observers had to be kept outside of Israel and in Arab territory.

• •

Cause for the renewed urgency in the U.N.'s efforts to solve the dangerous El Auja situation was a sudden heightening of Israeli activity in the zone. In mid-February U.N. observers noted that Israel had begun training small units in the area. By the end of the month, General Burns reported to Hammarskjold that "considerable small-unit training and artillery and tank gunnery is being conducted by the Israelis. Twelve squad tents have been erected in kibbutz Ketsiot. Observation-type aircraft land almost daily at the kibbutz landing strip. Intensive patrolling noted daily within the demilitarized zone." Israeli planes were observed flying over Egyptian territory, reported Burns, and "fire was opened without provocation by both Israeli and Egyptian forces across the demarcation lines."

Far from removing its forces from the demilitarized zone, as promised to Hammarskjold, Israel was preparing them for action. Burns was openly critical of Israel's continued insistence on patrolling close to the frontier. "It often seemed that the Israelis were following a deliberately provocative policy with their patrolling," he recalled, "with the object either of overawing the Egyptians or of provoking full-scale hostilities which they were confident of turning to their advantage."

• •

Robert Anderson's first secret mission to the Middle East had been a dismal failure because David Ben Gurion had insisted on limiting the talks to what he claimed to be Israel's urgent need for U.S. arms and making fustian proposals about meeting face-to-face with Nasser; and because the Egyptian leader, for his part, wanted to hear only what Israel's borders would be if he agreed to make peace. It was the usual Middle East colloquy, uncompromising and at cross-purposes. But Eisenhower and Dulles were not ready to give up their peace effort. They were spurred by a desire to prevent the area's drift to war and a longing to have the emotional issue of Israel done with before the presidential campaign. Already it was fouling the political climate; in the campaign it would distort the issues beyond recognition.

Anderson delivered in person his pessimistic report to Eisenhower in a private evening meeting at the Mansion on February 10. A short time later Ben Gurion sent a letter to Ike which Herbert Hoover paraphrased to the President. "The prime minister outlines his views on the possibility of reaching a settlement, which he considers dim due to his lack of confidence in Nasser's intentions. He also makes a strong plea for additional arms for Israel."

Eisenhower answered the letter within a week, on February 27. "Mr.

168

Anderson's exploratory conversations in the Near East have not advanced as far toward a resolution of the issues confronting us as I had hoped, but a foundation has been laid on which we may hope to build,'' he wrote Ben Gurion. "Meanwhile, the need for a solution has become even more pressing. It is my deepest wish that the United States make whatever contribution it can in this profoundly disturbing situation. With this desire in mind, Mr. Anderson plans to return to the Near East for further discussions within the next few days.'' He sloughed off Ben Gurion's request for arms by noting that it was receiving his "sympathetic'' attention.

Bob Anderson left at the end of February for one more futile attempt at trying to cajole, with promises of U.S. aid and support, the Arabs and Israelis into drawing up a peace treaty. This time his mission was complicated by one of those little-noticed but potent political factors that plague U.S. foreign policy in election years. The cotton lobby, which enjoyed powerful support among southern congressional leaders, insisted on selling off some of its surpluses abroad. It was an act that predictably would raise the hackles of Gamal Nasser, whose country was almost totally dependent on cotton sales for its foreign exchange. The day before he left, Anderson talked about the problem with Foster Dulles. "I'm afraid Nasser will take a very emotional attitude,'' said Anderson.

Dulles, with his calculating attorney's sense of bargaining, suggested an approach to Nasser that would subtly hold out the lure that peace would stop such sales and leave the world cotton market open to Egypt, a promise that Dulles of course could not realistically expect to honor. He suggested Anderson tell Nasser that "we try to protect people as much as we can but we are in talks which may take a lot of time so we felt it would be a lot better to have a process of selling a small amount at a time over a considerable period of time rather than dump it at once. When we reach the point of partnership, we can talk things over.''

Anderson agreed that was the best approach, though both men should have realized that the proud Egyptian leader could not be bought off so easily.

• •

It was a crisp winter evening when Eisenhower walked across the lawn of the West Wing of the White House, noticing on the way the grandeur of the pale colonnades and the stark contrast between the brilliance of the lighted rooms of the national home and the sombrous darkness of the

South Grounds. In a little less than an hour, at 10 P.M., on February 29, he was going to explain to the nation why he would run for a second term.

It was only five months since he had suffered his massive heart attack, yet now he was embarking on a strenuous new course. His physicians had pronounced him fit but there was still the question of his age. At the end of a second term he would be 70 years 98 days old, older than any Chief Executive of the United States. Before him, James Buchanan had been the oldest, ending his single term at age 69 years 315 days in 1861.

As he entered the Oval Office, now bustling with TV crews and cameras, a network assistant asked Eisenhower about an inch-high plaque on his desk with the motto *Suaviter in Modo, Fortiter in Re*. The President translated it, "Gently in Manner, Strongly in Deed," then chuckled and said, "Maybe I better hide that. It proves I'm an egghead."

Going before the cameras, Eisenhower explained to the nation his medical condition, the doctors' prognosis and concluded with the pronouncement: "If the Republican Party chooses to renominate me, I shall accept." The reaction was overwhelmingly favorable in America and abroad. Typical of the enthusiastic reaction was an editorial in *The New York Times*. "This is a man with too stern a conscience to be pressured into great decision by the importunities of friends, too modest a nature to be swayed by considerations of prestige or of power. We can be certain, knowing the man, that when he says that he will run again, he does so only because he now believes that he will be capable of serving his country well."

Ike declined to discuss publicly what had made him opt for a second term or even when he had made the decision. But two days later, he was spilling out all the details in a letter to his old friend Swede Hazlett. "The whole tough business of making up my mind to bow my neck to what seemed to be the inevitable; of then deciding how and when to make my announcement as to a second term; and finally the intensive work of preparing notes from which to speak to the American people, has so occupied my mind and days that I simply had no chance of writing to you."

The decision had weighed heavily, Ike said, because "I suppose there are not two people in the world who have more than Mamie and I earnestly wanted, for a number of years, to retire to their home—a home which we did not even have until a year or so ago." His heart attack had seemed to decide his fate. "I recall that almost my first conscious thought was 'Well, at least this settles one problem for me good and all.' For five weeks I was not allowed to see a newspaper or to listen to a radio. While, within a matter of a week after I was stricken, I took up the practice of daily meetings with Governor Adams and gradually increased my contacts with other members of the staff and the Administration, the doctors still kept the newspapers away for the reason they didn't want me worried about stories and gossip concerning my illness.

"As a consequence of this hiatus in my understanding of what was going on in the world, I was astounded when I found that even as early as November a great number of people were saying that they believed I could and should run again! I had a let-down feeling that approached a sense of frustration.

"As I look back, I truly believe that could I have anticipated in early October what later public reaction was going to be, I would have probably issued a short statement to the effect that I would determine as soon as possible whether it was physically possible for me *to finish out this term, but that I would thereafter retire from public life*.

"Having missed the opportunity to do this (and again I say I cannot be so certain that I would have done it), it seemed to me that I had no recourse but patiently to wait the outcome of all the tests the doctors wanted to make on me and gradually come to a decision myself as to whether or not I could stand the pace.

"I wish I could tell you just exactly what finally made me decide as I did, but there was such a vast combination of circumstances and factors that seemed to me to have a bearing on the problem—and at times the positive and negative were delicately balanced—that I cannot say for certain which particular one was decisive.

"One—and this has been mentioned to no one else—had to do with a guilty feeling on my own part that I had failed to bring forward and establish a logical successor for myself . . . the evidence became clear that I had not been able to get any individual to be recognized as a natural or logical candidate for the presidency."

In a long passage of reminiscences, Ike recalled that he had been talked out of inserting into his inaugural address his determination to be a one-term President. "All of the people who persuaded me agreed that, at my age, one time was all that should be expected of me, or that I should attempt.

"Far more than balancing all of this is the hope that I may still be able to do something in promoting mutual confidence, and therefore, peace, among the nations. And that I can help our people understand that they

171

must avoid extremes in reaching solutions to the social, economic and political problems that are constantly with us.''

• •

About the same time that Eisenhower was writing Swede Hazlett about his hopes for peace, Russian MiGs were being uncrated in Egypt and French-supplied Mystère IV's were landing secretly in Israel.

CHAPTER IX

We Had No Interest in Old-fashioned Domination

LLOYD

SELWYN LLOYD ARRIVED IN CAIRO on March 1 for his first and only dinner with Gamal Abdel Nasser. He was determined to try to understand this young Moslem who was causing the Tory government such difficulties with his aggressive opposition to the Baghdad Pact and his espousal of Pan-Arabism.

Lloyd at fifty-one was a comparative newcomer to foreign affairs. He had spent his first forty years becoming a devout Methodist and a lawyer specializing in insurance cases, picking up on the way all the pretensions of Britain's imperial style. It was not until 1945 that he entered government service by being elected to Parliament, where he quickly caught Eden's eye by his spirited debating style. He was made Britain's ambassador to the United Nations in 1952, where he earned a reputation for beating the Russians at their own game of quoting proverbs by making up such fictions as "the more moo, the less milk." When Eden came to power in 1955, he made Lloyd his defense minister and then in December of that same year his foreign secretary, a choice that disappointed many Conservatives since Lloyd was almost totally an Eden creation. With Lloyd heading Whitehall, Eden's will was carried out without objection. Lloyd's loyalty to his patron was complete, and in the end pathetically lacking in the independent judgment that Eden so needed. In London the U.S. Embassy assessment of him was terse: "It is generally accepted that Selwyn Lloyd lacks stature."

Lloyd was destined not to get along any better with Nasser in 1956 than had Eden the year before. At that time, Eden had held his only

173

meeting with Nasser and the Egyptian leader came away irked and resentful, his sensitivities aflame. The occasion had also been a dinner, this one held at the British Embassy where Nasser had been imperially summoned with several other members of the Revolutionary Council. While they looked on, Eden with his "my dears" and fluttering hands, gestures that struck non-Britons as so arch, lectured his Egyptian guests on Arabic history and poetry. He also impressed on Nasser the importance of the nascent Baghdad Pact. After leaving the dinner, Nasser complained to Mohamed Heikal, his journalist friend and admirer, that he thought Eden had treated the Egyptians like "a prince dealing with vagabonds."

Eden was surprised when he later learned of Nasser's resentment and told Lloyd that his impression had been that the dinner was "quite friendly." There was only one time when Nasser had slightly annoyed him, he added. That was when the husky Egyptian suddenly started holding hands with him in the Arab fashion just as photographers began taking their picture.

Lloyd hoped to have a more successful dinner, and to break the ice, he expressed interest in Nasser's life and his overthrow of King Farouk. In return he received a heated litany of the insults and slights that the young Egyptian had suffered under British rule.

Lloyd was unmoved by Nasser's harangue against British colonialism, but he was struck by the conspiratorial life the Egyptian had led. "His life has been conspiracy after conspiracy and we must understand that fact," Lloyd noted darkly.

Finally the two men and their top aides got down to business, discussing the Arab-Israel conflict, about which Nasser displayed little concern, and the Western commitment to the Tripartite Declaration. Observed Lloyd: "I got the impression that he would as soon have had a scorpion in his bed as the re-entry of Western troops onto Egyptian soil, and that he would never ask for help under the declaration." It was more than an impression Nasser was trying to communicate about foreign troops; it was his granite stand.

With the inevitability of a Greek drama, the discussion moved to the Baghdad Pact. Nothing in the past year had contributed more to the growing friction between their countries than Britain's reckless determination to enlist Arab nations in the pact, and Egypt's unyielding opposition. The two countries were engaged in a tug-of-war for the allegiance of the region's Arab states. Lloyd without success tried to assure Nasser that "we had no interest in old-fashioned domination," arguing that the

174

pact "looked north, not south. It was to prevent Soviet infiltration and to protect the oil."

Lloyd's protestations were as unbelievable to Nasser as the earlier pretenses of Britain that Farouk had been a sovereign king. The Egyptian would have none of it. He had embarked on a bold course of neutralism, treading gingerly his way between the Goliaths of East and West. He was convinced that Islam's salvation lay in nonalignment, and determined to oppose Arab entry into the pact.

Iraq remained the only Arab member, an obedient vassal that Britain had wrested from the decaying Ottoman empire at the end of World War I and had installed its handpicked ruler, King Faisal, on the throne in 1921. A descendant, King Faisal II, now ruled Iraq. Though Britain had supposedly recognized the country's independence in 1932, it retained special treaty rights even broader than those foisted on Egypt in 1936. These privileges allowed London to retain a dominant influence in Baghdad even at the time that Lloyd was attempting to assure Nasser of Britain's benign intentions.

Britain enjoyed similar treaty privileges with tiny Jordan, and hoped to pull that country into the pact. The British presence in Jordan was personified by Sir John Bagot Glubb, known in legend as Glubb Pasha, the austere leader of Jordan's highly respected army, the Arab Legion. Glubb was one of those adventurous Englishmen like Lawrence of Arabia, and to a lesser extent Eden himself, who romanticized the nomadic Bedouin Arabs. In the British imagination, these were the Arabs who made up that fanciful "world of camels and childlike Bedouins with flowing cloaks," a vision that conveniently ignored the fact that the real power resided with their wilier brethren like Nasser in the cities.

Glubb had first gone to the Middle East in 1920 at the age of twenty-three as a British Army officer and became enthralled with the Bedouin. After five years among them, he said, "I made up my mind to resign my commission and devote my life to the Arabs. My decision was largely emotional. I loved them." But, as a symbol of Western colonialism, Arabs did not love him.

Glubb served in various Arab military commands in the region, and in 1939 he took over as commander of Jordan's Arab Legion. Since then, King Abdullah, who had been given the country's throne by the British, had been assassinated, and Jordan was now ruled by British-educated King Hussein, Abdullah's grandson who was born only four years before Glubb's appointment. Differences between the young king and the old commander were inevitable, even without being fanned by the winds of nationalism sweeping the region.

The catalyst for the showdown between King Hussein and Glubb Pasha was Britain's bullyboy attempt to pressure Jordan to join the Baghdad Pact at the end of 1955. The British wanted Jordan's enlistment badly enough to send a high-level delegation under General Sir Gerald Templer, chief of the Imperial General Staff, to Amman the previous December 6. Once the purpose of Templer's mission became known, it threw Egypt and Israel into conniptions. Egypt recognized with increasing clarity that England was trying to surround it with pro-British states (Jordan was not exactly on Russia's southern border); and Israel loathed the idea of an Arab state on its border joining the Western-aligned pact from which it was likely to gain military strength.

Nasser had been promised repeatedly by the British that they would stop their attempts to enlist other Arab states in the Baghdad Pact, but through paid informants in Amman he learned of Templer's daily attempt to persuade the nominally pro-Western king to join. Enraged, Nasser ordered a savage anti-British campaign broadcast hourly over Radio Cairo, inciting street crowds against Templer's presence in Amman.

Then occurred a wholly unpredictable event that doomed Templer's mission. Israel launched its ferocious raid against Syria on the night of December 11, killing fifty-six Arabs. The attack raised already hot tempers to the boiling point and evoked violent protests against the Baghdad Pact and Israel. By one of those uniquely Middle Eastern twists of logic, the Baghdad Pact and Israel had become identified as tools of Western imperialism and therefore common enemies of the Arabs, even though in reality Israel feared the pact every bit as much as Egypt. But since the pact was obviously Britain's creation to retain its dwindling influence and Israel was widely perceived as an extension of the West, it followed for the Arab in the street that the two were symptoms of the same evil.

Radio Cairo deliberately exploited this popular confusion, calling the pact a Zionist-imperialist plot aimed at dividing the Arabs, strengthening Israel and betraying the 750,000 Palestinian refugees made homeless in the 1948 war. If Jordan joined, Cairo Radio warned, Arab military secrets would become available to Israel through friends in England and elsewhere and eventually would be used against Arab states.

Aiding Nasser's fight against the pact was Saudi Arabia, which distrusted Britain and particularly Iraq, ruled by its ancient Hashemite enemies. Saudi bribes were passed lavishly among Jordanian officials to win their opposition.

On December 14, with General Templer still in Amman, Jordan's pro-pact government fell, followed in two days by an explosion of rioting throughout the country. The disturbances lasted for six days, during which mobs attacked British, American, French, Italian and Turkish consulates in East Jerusalem, Jordan's half of the ancient city. Before the violence subsided, two more Cabinets were formed and fell, and 41 persons were killed and 150 injured. Hundreds of British and American dependents and tourists had to be evacuated for their own safety.

Templer returned to London in failure, further tarnishing Prime Minister Eden's diminishing reputation. After a lifetime of achievement and prodigious praise, Eden was increasingly proving to be a fumbler, a man who could not even outwit a young "wog" like Nasser. Eden's resentment of Nasser began at this point to grow to irrational heights.

Despite his victory, Nasser too harbored resentment. He had been repeatedly assured by the British that the Templer mission's purpose was to discuss military aid with Jordan—not the Baghdad Pact. After that Nasser no longer placed any trust in Eden and, Ambassador Trevelyan noted, his suspicions hardened into the conviction that Britain was trying to surround Egypt in order to "reduce it again to dependence on the British."

• •

Still, Eden remained obsessed with the idea of enlisting Jordan in the pact. For a variety of reasons, he felt he desperately needed Jordan, especially because of his failure to persuade Eisenhower and Dulles to join. Instead, the U.S. leaders had chosen a strategy of pampering Egypt and trying to woo it away from Russia by such offers as the enticing cornucopia of aid dangled by Robert Anderson during his secret mission. One reason for the U.S. strategy was the CIA's intimate connection with Nasser. He was considered an agency asset because of Kim Roosevelt's extremely close ties with him, a leader who could be called up in the middle of the night for consultations and who at least seemed to listen to U.S. advice. The British were aware of this close relationship between the CIA and Nasser, and they resented it. Its existence helped nudge London in opting for the Baghdad Pact strategy, both as a way of maintaining an independent posture in the region and out of an undisguised pique at U.S. ascendancy in a country that not too long ago was an exclusively British domain.

This difference of strategy between Washington and London was a major undercurrent of friction between the two countries, causing resentments and misunderstandings on both sides that increased as the months passed. Both countries were out to blunt Soviet influence, but each was constrained and rendered myopic in its perceptions by domestic imperatives and the natural postwar competition for influence in the world.

Despite the Jordanian riots, Eden pushed ahead with his attempts at enlisting Jordan in the pact with Glubb Pasha and his Arab Legion playing a key role. Officers of the legion went around Jordan that winter, after Templer flew home in humiliation, still trying to convince Jordanians that their country should join the pact. They spoke of "the folly of throwing in their lot with Egypt and Saudi Arabia," reported perceptive U.N. political officer Alexis Ladas from his Jerusalem observation post. "They have in fact been distributing a pamphlet which is virulently anti-Egyptian and anti-Saudi Arabian and pokes unmerciless fun at the armies of these two countries. I understand from a reliable source that the British are determined to have their way and to use whatever pressure is needed to achieve it."

Ladas observed how fatalistic the atmosphere in the region had become. "It is as if the people were mesmerized by some monstrous snake. General Burns remarked to me the other evening that everyone seems to know where the danger lies and what its nature is but no one is prepared to do anything serious about it. In his opinion anything can happen.

"There is a sort of dreamlike quality about the whole thing. Take the case of the surplus war material sold by Britain about which such a fuss is being made. The Valentine tanks which are the main item sold to Egypt are obsolete. They were obsolete in 1941. General Burns directed their production in Canada and he ought to know. They are worse than useless against the Sherman tanks with which the Israeli Army is principally equipped."

It all seemed unreal, Ladas reported, and "the conclusion is that the situation is getting out of hand."

• •

Despite the failure of the Templer mission, the riots and the continuing opposition by influential Arab politicians to the Baghdad Pact, Selwyn Lloyd was still trying subtly to sell it to Nasser during their March dinner in Cairo. When Lloyd suggested that there remained support for the pact in Jordan, Nasser warned that London should not believe Glubb. "I know the people," said Nasser, "and they are against it. People like Glubb are out of touch and their days are numbered."

Toward the end of the dinner a British official arrived with a message, which Trevelyan went outside to take. He said nothing about it to Lloyd until they were on their way back to the embassy in their chauffeured limousine. Then he broke the shocking news: Glubb Pasha had been summarily dismissed and given twenty-four hours to leave the country he had served for more than a quarter century. The news was not made public in Jordan until 7:30 A.M. the next day.

For the British, Glubb represented more than the proud Arab Legion with its many English officers. He was the final embodiment of empire in the Middle East, the last relic of their once great dominion, and Lloyd reacted with fury.

Lloyd's anger was lacerated by his belief that Nasser had deliberately toyed with him during dinner in order to humiliate him. He was convinced that Nasser somehow conspired to have the announcement of Glubb's dismissal coincide with his visit, thereby shaming both him and his country. "It put him in a most embarrassing situation," noted Trevelyan. "He was being attacked in the British press for coming to Cairo at all. This would be interpreted as a deliberate affront which he had to swallow." Lloyd considered canceling his meeting the next morning with Nasser but finally attended with stiff upper lip and overflowing bile.

Though Lloyd believed until the end of his life that he had been deliberately insulted, King Hussein said later that Glubb's firing had nothing to do with Lloyd's presence in Cairo. The timing was purely coincidental, Hussein claimed, a step he had been considering for a year because of a number of irritants between the two men, particularly Glubb's delay in replacing British officers with Arab ones. When he pressed the issue, Hussein said, "I was gravely informed that the Royal Engineers of the Arab Legion would have an Arab commander by 1985! The British government at that time was incapable of realizing that one cannot brush aside a nation's aspirations with the words: 'We will talk about it in thirty years.' " Emboldened by his country's successful defiance of the Baghdad Pact, the king finally acted against Glubb.

Nasser did not hear the news about Glubb until shortly before his morning meeting with Lloyd, according to Mohamed Heikal. Nasser's reaction was untypically naïve. According to Heikal, Nasser assumed the British had been forced to back the move as a gesture to him since his propaganda machine had been pounding away at the indignity of a Briton leading the Arab Legion. "What an intelligent move," he said to Heikal. "So they really are sincere in their talk about starting a new page."

When Lloyd arrived, he found himself being congratulated "for Glubb's dismissal in order to improve relations between Egypt and Britain. It was very wise." But Lloyd was in no mood to believe Nasser. He felt humiliated and believed Nasser was making fun of him.

"In spite of what he had said the night before about having been a conspirator from 1942 onwards and having always thought as a conspirator, this pretense seemed to me to be outrageous and I showed and said what I thought of it," recalled Lloyd. Both he and Trevelyan later reported in identical words that "the meeting was polite but not cordial." Nonetheless, the two sides managed to agree tentatively that Britain would refrain from enlisting additional Arab states in the Baghdad Pact if Egypt would halt its anti-British propaganda.

The experience turned Lloyd into a bitter enemy of Nasser, which the Egyptian leader realized and regretted. "He thought that I misled him, which was completely untrue," Nasser said. "He became completely hostile to us."

That was completely true. Lloyd never believed that Nasser had not made sport of him, and he never forgave the Egyptian. The slights of pride pained as much for colonialists as for natives.

• •

Anthony Eden was shattered by the sacking of Glubb Pasha. He exaggerated its importance, confused its causes and lost his sense of proportion. With the humiliation of the Templer mission still fresh and smarting, he rashly concluded that both reverses had a common sponsor: Nasser.

News of Glubb's firing reached London in the afternoon of March 1, touching off a round of crisis meetings and frantic messages. Eden cabled Lloyd in Cairo with the suggestion that he fly to Amman to talk with King Hussein, but the foreign secretary prudently concluded that his success would be unlikely and failure "would have been another humiliation." Another Eden cable went to C. B. Duke, the British ambassador in Amman, instructing him to see the king. Eden sent yet another message that evening to Amman, this one personally to Hussein, urging him to reconsider his precipitate action.

Throughout the long night of conferences and cables, Eden found himself in growing disagreement with his friend and protégé Anthony Nutting, at thirty-six the brightest rising star in the Foreign Office, where he served as minister of state. Nutting was appalled at Eden's simplistic conviction that Nasser was at the root of all his woes.

He found Eden furious and insisting that "this reverse was Nasser's doing." When Nutting tried to suggest that Hussein had acted on his own, Eden would not listen. He had concluded, noted Nutting, that

"Nasser was our Enemy No. 1 in the Middle East and he would not rest until he had destroyed all our friends and eliminated the last vestiges of our influence."

Eden railed endlessly through the night, charged that Nasser's treatment of Lloyd had been shameful and vowed that the Egyptian leader "is our enemy and shall be treated as such." Eden had come to the conclusion, observed Nutting, that "if he [Nasser] succeeded, it would be the end of Eden. Nasser must therefore himself be destroyed."

As the tense days passed with Britain in an uproar and demonstrations of joy occurring in Amman, Eden's hatred of Nasser increased and his judgment ebbed. In the House of Commons, which was in full voice debating the matter, Opposition leader Hugh Gaitskell charged in a withering speech that the government's Middle East policy was "ill-formed, ill-prepared and has managed, rather remarkably, to be both weak and provocative at the same time."

Eden, always sensitive to criticism, went before the House on March 7 to defend the government, only to make what he conceded was one of the worst speeches of his career. For the first time that anyone could remember, Eden lost his temper during the debate, a grievous lapse in the unwritten code of the Parliament. *The New York Times* reported that Eden was "subjected to a storm of vituperation and abuse beyond anything heard in the Commons since the last days of Neville Chamberlain's prime ministership."

"My friends were embarrassed and my critics were exultant," Eden poignantly admitted.

British columnist Ian Waller concurred, predicting with astonishing accuracy: "If the year goes on as it has begun, it will not be Sir Anthony but Mr. Harold Macmillan who reigns in Downing Street in 1957." Randolph Churchill, the splenetic son of Eden's old mentor, acidly noted that the "debate marked the beginning of the disintegration of the personality and character that the public thought Eden to possess."

Nutting had come to the same conclusion. He observed, "From now on Eden completely lost his touch."

They had been close friends for eleven years but Nutting now began to feel that he was talking with a total stranger. "No longer did we see things the same way; a wide gulf was now between us."

Still, Nutting tried to calm and assuage his prime minister. Five days after the debate, Nutting sent Eden a memorandum containing several suggestions about how to improve Britain's position in the Middle East. That evening Nutting was dining with visiting Harold Stassen, a fellow member of the U.N. Disarmament Commission, at the Savoy Hotel when he received a telephone call.

"It's me," said Eden's voice. "What's all this poppycock you've sent me? I don't agree with a single word of it."

Nutting explained that he and the Foreign Office advisers who helped draft the memo had found nothing exceptional in it.

"But what's all this nonsense about isolating Nasser or 'neutralizing' him, as you call it?" shouted Eden. "I want him destroyed, can't you understand? I want him removed, and if you and the Foreign Office don't agree, then you'd better come to the Cabinet and explain why."

With his meal and guest waiting, Nutting patiently tried to reason with Eden, pointing out that "without an alternative leader in mind the destruction of Nasser would leave Egypt in anarchy."

"But I don't want an alternative," shouted Eden. "And I don't give a damn if there's anarchy and chaos in Egypt."

The prime minister slammed down the phone, leaving Nutting to return to his dinner with a feeling that "I had had a nightmare, only the nightmare was real."

From the time of the sacking of Glubb Pasha, Anthony Nutting observed, Eden's attitude toward the Middle East changed drastically. Now the smallest incident was "treated as a major challenge, inspired, of course, by the arch-enemy, Nasser."

• •

Unknown to most of the world, Eden was still suffering the effects of a botched gallstone operation in early 1953 by a British surgeon. A second operation in London was equally unsuccessful, and finally the ailing Eden was flown to Boston's Lahey Clinic where noted surgeon Dr. Richard Cattell unblocked the painfully obstructed bile duct. The experience was wearing on the handsome Eden; he aged visibly after the operations.

To control an incurable infection in the damaged duct, Eden thereafter had to take antibiotics. Stress and fatigue aggravated the duct, suddenly sending his temperature soaring and further debilitating his strength and his mental faculties. He bolstered his waning energies by taking amphetamines, which in those days were not widely understood by physicians to have such potent psychedelic effects.

His work habits aggravated his condition. A workaholic in even normal times, Eden under the confluent pressures buffeting him at home and abroad now began working later into the nights. His sleep was frequently interrupted because of the devilishly different time zones between Britain, America and the Middle East. The time was five hours earlier in Washington and New York, meaning that to get emergency instructions to late meetings in America they had to be sent off from London in the middle of the night. It was two hours later in the Middle East, so news of early morning crises arrived in London at the crack of dawn.

Eden soon was getting only five hours of sleep a night. Fatigue, stress, drugs and his faulty bile duct were inexorably taking their toll. Slowly, silently, his rationality was being eroded.

"I knew then," Nutting sadly noted about that March period, "that nothing about our old friendship would ever be the same again. What I did not know was how much of this metamorphosis was due to sickness and the poison from the damaged bile duct, which was eating away at his whole system."

Eden's impatience, short temper and edginess became increasingly noticeable to those around him. But no one realized how severely his normally pacific instincts and cool judgment had been afflicted. When the truth became obvious, it was too late either to save Britain's honor or Eden's own once-gallant reputation.

• •

Until his premiership, Eden had seemed to lead a charmed life. He had excelled from the time he entered the King's Royal Rifle Corps in World War I direct from Eton to become, at nineteen, the youngest adjutant in the British Army. Under heavy German fire, he crawled through the mud of Ypres to rescue a wounded sergeant and won the Military Cross. He served in the Army for four years, three of them on the Western Front, and eventually commanded his own brigade.

While at the front, he wrote his mother, "I have seen things lately that I am not likely to forget." Of the twenty-eight members in his class at Eton, nine were killed. Two of his three brothers also perished in combat.

The war, observed Eden, "saw the destruction of the world as I knew it." Afterward, he took every opportunity to condemn the horrors of war.

His age and wartime service made him one of those romantically tragic and melancholic figures of the "Lost Generation," that fated group of British schoolboys who fought, many to their last breath, in World War I and were so painfully reflected in the poetry of Wilfred Owen and Rupert Brooke. For Englishmen, it was a hauntingly special generation, and Eden's association with it helped his popularity in politics.

When he returned to civilian life, Eden enrolled in Oxford and won

honors, taking firsts in Persian and Arabic. Those years marked the beginning of his lifelong fascination with the Middle East. His classmates
found him a bit of an esthete, an admirer of French art, and reserved,
though friendly enough in small groups. He was a serious student and
applied himself diligently to his studies, as he was later to do in government.

After graduation, Eden went directly into politics, winning the Conservative House seat of Warwick and Leamington, some distance from Win-
dlestone Hall, where he was born and which for more than three
centuries had served as the Eden family seat.

On January 5, 1924, Captain R. (for Robert) A. Eden, as he then was
known, at the age of twenty-six was sworn in the House of Commons
where he retained his seat for the next thirty-three years. "The dignity,
dullness and mastery of the commonplace came to him naturally," *Time*
magazine archly observed. "Soon he was possessed of that mysterious
but vital quality which M.P.s call a 'sense of the House.' "

Eden was a lucid rather than brilliant speaker. To the end of his career
he found delivering parliamentary speeches an "ordeal." But he had a
distinguished and reserved style that was appealing, and he worked hard
and was a master of detail. Soon he caught the eye of Tory leaders and,
as he recalled, he was rapidly "propelled into the political stratosphere."

Foreign Secretary Sir Austen Chamberlain, a power in the party, chose
him as his parliamentary private secretary, a coveted post for young
M.P.s, and in that capacity he began in 1927 accompanying his minister
to meetings of the League of Nations in Geneva. He early gave voice to
the merit of cooperation between England and America, calling it "the
most important safeguard for world peace in the years that are to come."

Eden's progress in Parliament was so rapid that in 1931 a former prime
minister, Stanley Baldwin, who had adopted the young M.P. as his
protégé and soon was to become prime minister again, revealed that he
had recommended Eden be given a position in the Foreign Office. He
added that Eden showed such promise he thought he would become
prime minister within ten years.

That same year Eden got his Foreign Office appointment as parliamentary undersecretary of state, at the age of thirty-four. In four years he
became foreign secretary. Eden threw himself into frantic efforts to save
the League of Nations and to divert Europe from its ominous drift toward
another war, but in 1938 he resigned in protest against Neville Chamberlain's policy of appeasement.

When Neville Chamberlain was replaced in 1940 as prime minister by aging Winston Churchill, Eden was summoned back to the Foreign Office. Churchill, then sixty-six, told Eden that he had no intention of serving beyond the end of the war and, as Eden recorded in his diary, "The succession would be mine." To cement his promise, Churchill put it in writing in June 1942, inspiring Eden to note somewhat warily that the "era as crown prince was established, a position not necessarily enviable in politics." It looked as if Baldwin's prediction would be borne out.

But Churchill was reluctant to retire. Eden did not assume Churchill's mantle until 1955, a trying and difficult period for the aspiring foreign secretary, who was left like a bride tottering on tiptoes anxiously waiting to be kissed.

During the long period in waiting, Eden and his first wife, Beatrice, divorced in 1950 after twenty-seven years of marriage. They had had two sons, one of whom, Simon, was killed in World War II. In 1952, Eden remarried. His bride, Clarissa Churchill, was a descendant of the Duke of Marlborough and the Earls of Abingdon. Slim and crisp, she was remote, easily bored and perpetually late. She disliked sports and refused to cook, but in addition to her willowy beauty Eden admired her quick wit and her appreciation of books and art. They were an elegant couple, charming to each other in their happiness. But when the mood was on her, Clarissa could be as snappish as Eden himself.

The marriage made Eden a member of his prime minister's family, which was just as well since his relations with Churchill, while good, were more like those between father and son than Britain's two top officials. Even into Eden's own approaching old age, Churchill frustratingly insisted on maintaining that kind of filial relationship. As late as 1954, with Churchill then seventy-nine and still hanging on, his physician, Lord Moran, noted in his diary that Churchill "still regards him [Eden] as a young man." Eden was fifty-six at the time.

As Churchill grew older, his determination to hang on to power increased. Soon he was finding faults in his selected successor that helped to justify to himself his retention of the prime ministership. "It is not as if I were making way for a strong young man," he told Moran at another time in 1954. "Anthony seems to me very tired. I detect strain in his telegrams. Sometimes he sends three thousand words in one day—and there is nothing in them."

Churchill also fretted about Eden's attitude toward Washington, which he found too critical. "I hope Anthony won't upset them," he told Moran. "They are so kind and generous to their friends." He began questioning whether Eden could "distinguish between a big and a small issue," observing that "Anthony works very hard and is most conscientious, plugging away at routine.

"But that's not what is wanted at the Foreign Office, where you must take up big issues and deal with them."

When finally the ailing Churchill took his leave amid demands for fresh leadership from both Tory and Labour benches, there had already grown a gnawing misgiving about Eden's excessively long apprenticeship. Harold Macmillan, a Cabinet colleague and political rival of Eden's, expressed it to Moran. "For fifteen years Winston has harried Anthony unmercifully, lectured him and butted in on his work, until poor Anthony is afraid to make a decision of his own." Observed the physician: "Anthony apparently has taken this a good deal to heart, and had been very nervy lately."

The succession had been expected too long and Eden's apprenticeship was too loyal for it not to take place. On the same day that Churchill left No. 10 Downing Street, April 6, 1955, a subdued Eden moved in as Britain's new prime minister. He was filled with less than elation. The fifteen long years of waiting, Eden noted, had "dampened my exhilaration."

• •

Anthony Eden was fatefully slow in remolding the government in his own image. He delayed until December 22 before changing Churchill's old Cabinet with one of his own choosing. By then, the public's keen anticipation had turned to impatience and there were loud complaints about Eden's inability to take control and his indecisiveness. His cabinet choices were greeted with disappointment.

Instead of reaching out for young blood and new faces, Eden kept most of the old ministers and merely transferred them to different posts within the Cabinet. Selwyn Lloyd's appointment as foreign secretary was a rebuke for those who hoped to see a reinvigorated foreign policy under a fresh minister. Lloyd was too pliable in Eden's hands, and his selection doomed any chance that the Foreign Office would launch new policies.

The Tory's No. 2 leader, Rab Butler, at fifty-three years of age considered a possible prime minister himself, was moved from Chancellor of the Exchequer to Lord Privy Seal and Leader of the House of Commons. He did not ease Eden's burden from public attacks when he replied to a reporter's critical question about Eden with the flip retort that he was "the best prime minister we have."

With Britain's economy continuing to worsen and its foreign policy meeting reverses in the Middle East, the pro-Tory *Spectator* was reporting by the end of the year that "there is a terrifying lack of authority at the top. It becomes more and more clear that, contrary to what many Conservatives said, Sir Winston Churchill was far more important as a directing, energizing, initiating force than even his colleagues realized."

A joke going around at the time had Churchill returning from vacation and being asked how he felt. "Very fit," he replied, "Have to be. Anthony's getting old."

By the time of Glubb Pasha's humiiiating firing, the criticism had grown incessant and the thin-skinned prime minister was reeling from its enervating effects. He was determined to counteract the criticism by getting tough—with Gamal Abdel Nasser.

CHAPTER X

I Prefer Arabs to Jews

EDEN

GUY MOLLET HAD BEEN SUSPICIOUS of Nasser from the beginning. He suspected that the Egyptian leader was covertly aiding the FLN rebels and compounding to the point of agony France's difficulties in Algeria. For Mollet, this was intolerable. He had vowed when he assumed office early in 1956 "to devote my fullest personal efforts" to find a peaceful solution in Algeria. Yet by March, the rebellion wracking the French and Moslem communities had descended to a hellish nightmare. Despite Mollet's best efforts, Algeria was disintegrating into a bloodbath of untold horror.

The savagery had begun in earnest the previous summer when the FLN adopted a policy of total war on all French civilians, regardless of age or sex. The terrible meaning of that decision became clear in August when Moslem mobs went berserk in the northeastern part of the country around Constantine and the port of Philippeville. Arabs of both sexes swarmed into the port's streets, tossing hand grenades into cafés and dragging European motorists from their cars and hacking them to death with knives and razors. In one area a family of French colonialists was caught in its house. The seventy-three-year-old grandmother and eleven-year-old daughter were slain. The father was killed in his bed, his arms and legs chopped off. The mother was disemboweled, her five-day-old baby slashed to death and placed in her open womb.

French paratroopers reacted with their own savagery, shooting down every Arab they could find. Before the day was over, seventy-one Europeans had been killed. The French claimed 1,273 "insurgents" were slain; the FLN charged that as many as 12,000 Moslems were indiscriminately gunned down.

In the midst of such violence and hatred, Mollet's efforts to seek reconciliation between the Arab and French communities had no chance of success, and his call for electoral reforms to give the Moslems a greater voice in the government was met with contemptuous scorn by the *pieds noirs*. Within a week of assuming office, Mollet felt compelled to fly to Algiers to see the situation for himself.

February 6 was a frigidly cold day, and Mollet's arrival was greeted with equal coldness by the French community. Only a few officials bothered to greet him at the airport, and his route into the city was empty except for the presence of reinforced troops that had been dispatched from France to ensure his security. A general strike had closed down all businesses in the European sections of Algiers; an occasional sign pinned to a shuttered window proclaimed: "Closed on account of mourning."

As Mollet's motorcade arrived at the grassy Forum where he placed a wreath on the *monument aux morts,* he was greeted by a hostile crowd of thousands of chanting Frenchmen. "Mollet resign" and "Mollet to the stake," the *pieds noirs* screamed at the new prime minister. Their shouts were followed by volleys of tomatoes, eggs and dirt scooped out of the lawn. Mollet was hit several times. The fury of the mob propelled it through heavy lines of troops and it was only turned back by clubs and tear gas. When Mollet withdrew to the governmental residence at the Palais d'Eté, the mob broke through barriers and trampled to pieces Mollet's wreath.

The mob was protesting Mollet's appointment of General Georges Catroux as the successor to Governor-General Jacques Soustelle, who was highly popular with the French community. Catroux at seventy-nine was considered too old and too much of a *bradeur,* a capitulator, because of his part in granting to Moslem Algerians equal legal status with French nationals more than a decade earlier when he had first been governor-general of Algeria. His reappointment had ignited a fire storm of protest among the *pieds noirs,* who feared the old general might actually try to carry out in practice the reforms he began in 1943 and deprive them of their special advantages over Arabs.

The badly shaken Mollet, badgered by the shouts and gibes of the mob outside, finally picked up the telephone and talked with Catroux in Paris, requesting his resignation. The general stepped down immediately and

Mollet announced that "anxious not to add to the drama that divides Algeria, I have accepted this resignation." The mob reacted with delirious joy. *"Victoire! Victoire!"* resounded throughout the city.

Inside the government residence, Mollet muttered: "I should not have given in."

Indeed, it was a bad start for Mollet's premiership. He had acted weakly and FLN propaganda successfully exploited the incident by claiming it showed that Paris could not be trusted because it would always capitulate to the demands of a French mob. On their side, the intransigence of the *pieds noirs* was strengthened by the realization that they could cause the government to change its decisions.

Mollet's trip of reconciliation brought about exactly the opposite of what he had intended. The two sides were now irrevocably alienated. Mollet found himself under severe criticism by both Arabs and French colonialists in Algeria and the right and left at home. On his return to Paris on February 11 he was greeted by street demonstrations protesting his Algerian policy and calling into question his ability to govern.

• •

Washington's opposition to colonialism was acutely resented in Paris, where it was suspected that America's anticolonialism was based more on a hope of replacing France in North Africa than on any native idealism. Thus, as the fighting in Algeria grew more vicious and FLN gains became greater, there began building up in France a strong wave of anti-Americanism.

By early March, French anti-Americanism was approaching alarming heights, causing a flurry of worried top-secret reports to Washington. On March 3 alone, three cables flowed into Washington describing in distressing terms the danger of the situation. One cable came from Robert Murphy, a veteran observer of the European scene and now under secretary for political affairs, the No. 3 spot in the state department and the highest post held by a career diplomat. Writing directly to Herbert Hoover, who was running the State Department for traveling Foster Dulles, Murphy reported that "even though I was in Paris for only three days, I realized that there is a curious, and from our point of view a very unhappy, French attitude developing which seeks to place the onus for the French predicament in Algeria . . . on the United States. This is a psychological phenomenon which undoubtedly results from a sense of frustration and failure to develop a constructive and sound program for the area. Intelligent Frenchmen, of course, know that without American aid in World War II, French North Africa would have been lost to them. Through the postwar period, we have also consistently supported them in the United Nations on many occasions when issues relating to French North Africa were involved, sometimes to our own embarrassment, because of the issue of colonialism."

Yet, Murphy noted, anti-Americanism was on the rise. "This French sentiment is more complex than just an attitude regarding French North Africa," Murphy continued. "It includes other factors such as resentments over Indochina; general discomfort over France's weakened world position; a natural human tendency to blame a benefactor; plus insidious work by the French Communist Party with Soviet support to destroy Franco-American friendship."

That same day, the army military attaché in Paris also weighed in with an excitable cable for the army chief of staff. "I cannot adequately express to you my alarm over deteriorating trend of events Algeria. The problem is growing by leaps and bounds and I would not be surprised to see mass bloodshed therein in a matter of weeks if not days. I am becoming increasingly convinced that the French are incapable solving their problems Algeria. They face situation of enormous consequences to themselves and to free world, helpless, humiliated, resentful, and bewildered. They see coming in Algeria a state of anarchy marked by bloodshed, riot and pillage.

"They are aware that such state of affairs Algeria could result in revolution in France culminating in fascism or communism or some weird combination of both. Before this impending doom they stand idly by and whatever uncoordinated badly conceived action they are taking is either too little, too late, or in wrong direction. [General Jean] Valluy feels that when explosion comes, its consequences will spread throughout Western Europe and in his words, 'That will be the end.' "

Valluy had recently been seen speaking with General Catroux's replacement as governor-general in Algeria, Robert Lacoste, originally chosen by Mollet as economic minister. Lacoste had tears in his eyes, saying, "My friends, only recently I was like you. I thought this thing could be negotiated and could be maneuvered but now I assure you gentlemen we are on the brink of disaster."

The cable concluded: "Whatever happens, the potential consequences to us are of extreme gravity. I have impression that our government is not sufficiently aware of how much its future in Europe and throughout the free world depends on outcome of situation North Africa particularly Algeria."

A third cable that same day, this one from Ambassador to France Douglas Dillon, reported that "I am impressed by the volume of reports from all parts of France indicating a dangerously sharp rise in anti-Americanism sentiment because of what French public opinion believes our North African policy to be. Algerian crisis is largely responsible for this outburst of French feeling. Belief that we are at heart sympathetic to total ejection of France from North Africa has gradually gained currency during last few years and is now spreading like wildfire. This feeling is being positively fanned by fact that no U.S. official either in France or in U.S. has made any major public announcement sympathizing with continuance French presence in North Africa. Lack of such statements is being construed as admission of accuracy of current French thinking.

"I have frequently pointed out over past years potential seriousness of French reaction to serious reverses in Algeria particularly when coupled with feeling that United States was standing by unsympathetically while French feel they are fighting for their very lives. I must now report that this dangerous potentiality is nearing realization.

"The danger is becoming imminent, the immediate weeks and months ahead will be crucial."

Dillon volunteered to make a series of statements sympathizing with the continuance of the French presence in North Africa. "I recommend that this whole problem . . . be given prompt consideration at the highest level so as to reach a policy decision before we are overtaken by rapidly moving events."

Two days later, Eisenhower and Hoover discussed the problem. They agreed that "in view of the long association of these territories with France, it would be hoped that ties of interdependence could be established and maintained to the benefit of both groups."

It was during the same meeting that Eisenhower said he had no objection to France sending twelve Mystère IV's to Israel. It was a decision that needed little encouragement. By approving the jet sale, Eisenhower was relieving two pressures: French suspicions of U.S. goodwill and loud Israeli complaints that it was being denied weapons. But he was hardly helping the chances of peace.

• •

Under Mollet, France's involvement with Israel had reached the point of an informal secret alliance. Even before Ike gave his approval for the Mystère sale to Israel, France had decided to sell Israel many more than twelve of the jets. Israeli pilots had already been in southern France training to fly the sophisticated warplanes. They covertly began flying the planes back to Israel at the beginning of March and continued through the summer. The Mystère had limited range, and could fly to Israel only by refueling in Italy. The Israelis acquired Italian approval to make secret fuel stops at Brindisi, on the southeastern heel of Italy, for a small number of Mystères. But as the number grew from twelve to at least sixty, the Israelis became worried that the Italians would object. They then employed a clever ruse. By using the same identification numbers on later planes as those on the first Mystères, the Israelis convinced the Italian authorities at Brindisi that the planes were being returned to France because of defects. In fact, of course, they were heading straight to Israel. "The Italians even expressed their sympathy over the additional trouble we were being put to," chuckled Ezer Weizman, who was the Israeli Air Force colonel in charge of the clandestine operation and later defense minister of Israel under Begin.

At about the same time the Mystères were landing secretly in Israel, David Ben Gurion was warning in a speech on March 6 before the Israeli parliament that the chances for peace were decreasing. He vowed, however, that "this government will not start a war." The Knesset voted 66 to 13 in favor of his policies.

• •

Tensions in the Middle East were again at a high point. Four Israeli policemen had been killed on March 3 after their patrol boat ran aground less than a hundred yards from Syrian territory on the Sea of Galilee, not far from where Israeli raiders had killed fifty-six Syrians three months earlier. Israel officially complained to the United Nations, but it was noted by U.N. investigators that Syria had previously warned Israeli boats to stay well clear of its territory, that the Syrians were frightened by close approaches at night and feared another Israeli attack. No U.N. action was taken. Public opinion in Israel was outraged.

The heightened tension also extended along Israel's border with Egypt. The weekly report by U.N. observers noted on March 8 "a definite increase in the general tenseness along the [Gaza] Strip, which is evident from the heavy increase in the number of incidents involving firing across the demarcation line." Both sides were firing without apparent provocation, said the report. Casualties during the week included one Egyptian soldier killed and three Arab civilians seriously wounded; no Israelis were reported injured.

The violence along the borders was not a cause of the increased tension but a reflection of it. Far more serious than border incidents were the broader political movements in the region. The stunning blow of Glubb Pasha's humiliating removal as head of Jordan's Arab Legion was still reverberating throughout the West and the Middle East. It was clearly a reverse for the West and a new assertion of Arab independence. Worse, it was widely seen as another victory for Nasser in his unrelenting struggle against the British, a victory for Pan-Arabism against imperialism. In Israel, and among its Western supporters, that translated into a strengthening of the Moslems surrounding the Jewish state.

Western jitters and Israeli fears were not calmed when Nasser began a six-day meeting in Cairo March 6 with King Saud of Saudi Arabia and President Shukri al-Kuwatly of Syria. Nasser was showing off his alternative alignment of Arab states to the Baghdad Pact, trying to demonstrate to the West that the Arabs could unite in a common cause. But the bugaboo of unity remained more a figment of Arab wishes and Western fears than of reality.

This was shown during the conference when Egypt, Syria and Saudi Arabia offered generous aid to Jordan if King Hussein rejected British aid. Hussein wisely refused, realizing that his existence depended on the maintenance of a certain distance between both his wooers in the West and in the Middle East. Jordan was too small to survive the exclusive embrace of either side, and Hussein was too wily to succumb to such blandishments.

Nasser and his two Arab confreres were left with no more serious outcome of their conference than the issuance of another windy communiqué announcing that the three countries had drafted plans for united Arab action against the "danger of Zionist aggression" and would render "all possible support" to Jordan to help it resist "foreign pressure or Zionist aggression."

It was rhetoric without substance, more a function of pride than of purpose. Yet no one could be sure, certainly not among the increasingly besieged leaders of Britain and France. After all, there never had been anyone like Nasser before in the modern Arab world. Who knew his limits?

• •

Eisenhower, buffeted by the imperatives of a campaign year, was also developing grave doubts about Nasser. The Anderson mission was having no more success on the second go-around than on the first, though in early March the former defense official was still shuttling between Cairo and Tel Aviv vainly trying to find an area of agreement between Nasser and Ben Gurion. Not only was Anderson making no progress, but Ike was suffering increased attacks from the Democrats for denying Israel weapons. The latest one had come on March 4 from New York Governor Averell Harriman, former ambassador to Moscow and a powerful Democratic leader. In a blistering assault on the Administration's foreign policy at a political fund raiser in New York, Harriman charged that America was "unwittingly helping the Soviet campaign" for world domination. One of the vigorous steps that the United States should take, Harriman declared, was to send defensive weapons to Israel immediately.

Though the Democrats had cornered the Jewish vote, there was no political advantage in the Eisenhower Administration espousing the Arabs' cause, either in the campaign or among America's staunchest allies. Americans still supported Israel out of a combination of holocaust guilt and an instinctive cheer for the presumed underdog; and Britain and France were both increasingly ascribing all of their colonial woes to the emergence of Gamal Abdel Nasser. The Arabs had no eloquent spokesmen or meaningful constituency in America. Additionally, their cause suffered from the ancient rivalry between Christians and Moslems. It was a rivalry extending back well before the massacres of the Crusades and it fed the darkest imaginings of Christians about the cruelty and corruption of heathen Moslems. Such imaginings made it as natural for Americans and Europeans to fear the newly emerging Moslem countries as it did to support the struggles of a seemingly weak Israel.

Dwight Eisenhower was not a prisoner of these prejudices but he recognized the power of the political support that Israel enjoyed in America, and he appreciated more than most how dependent Europe was on Arab oil. America's leadership of the Western world rested on a strong and supportive Europe. Somehow he had to span these many contradictions that were building up between U.S. national goals, the aspirations of its allies, which were frequently not in America's interest, and the political realities at home.

The complexities were considerable. Eisenhower opposed Britain's and France's bald efforts to retain their colonial status in the Middle East, but felt compelled to support them in the name of the Atlantic Alliance that was forged out of a common heritage and the threat from Soviet Communism. He considered Israel's aggressive policies toward its Arab neighbors shortsighted, but he believed that for both moral and domestic political reasons America should support its existence. America's closest friend in the Arab world was Nasser, but Britain, France and Israel were now perceiving the Egyptian leader as their common enemy. Yet America needed a staunch Arab ally in that oil-rich part of the world.

Eisenhower's solution to this nexus of conflicting interests and contrary trends was at first hesitant and tentative. Trying to work through the tangle of problems in solitude, he sat down on March 8 and wrote in his diary. "If present policies fail (as they have so far) to bring some order into the chaos that is rapidly enveloping that region, then a new approach must be made."

That said, he immediately reminded himself that it was the approach that must be new; not America's basic policies. "There can be no change in our basic position, which is that we must be friends with both contestants in that region in order that we can bring them closer together. To take sides could do nothing but to destroy our influence in leading toward a peaceful settlement of one of the most explosive situations in the world today."

Eisenhower thus tried to find a course that would neither upset Israel and the European allies nor cause him too many political problems at home. The idea was still inchoate, but as the President talked to his diary it became increasingly clearer. It was true, he noted, that the Israelis had been foolishly arrogant in their treatment of the Arabs. But now, with the infusion of Soviet arms into Egypt, the Arabs "are daily growing more arrogant and disregarding the interests of Western Europe and of the United States in the Middle East region. It would begin to appear that our efforts should be directed toward separating the Saudi Arabians from the Egyptians and concentrating, for the moment at least, in making the former see that their best interests lie with us, not with the Egyptians and with the Russians."

It was obvious, he wrote, that "we have reached the point where it looks as if Egypt, under Nasser, is going to make no move whatsoever to meet the Israelites in an effort to settle outstanding differences."

Eisenhower's struggle for a new approach was leading him toward the most self-interested and simplistic answer. Instead of trying to resolve America's differences with Britain, France and Israel, he was lapsing into the easiest course by picking on the weakest of the countries in the equation, Egypt. Egypt was certainly no saint in the international arena, but then neither were Britain, France and Israel. What particularly distinguished Egypt for Eisenhower's baneful attention was the unexpected success of Gamal Nasser in sparking an Arab renaissance that was considered anti-Western, and the country's lack of political clout or popular support in America. Of the four nations, that made Egypt the odd man out.

Eisenhower concluded his diary musings that winter day on a somber note for Nasser. "I am certain of one thing," he wrote. "If Egypt finds herself thus isolated from the rest of the Arab world, and with no ally in sight except Soviet Russia, she would very quickly get sick of that prospect and would join us in the search for a just and decent peace in that region."

Like the leaders of Britain and France, Eisenhower was slowly groping his way to the mammoth miscalculation that Nasser was the common author of all their woes in the Middle East. It was not Nasser who was the sole cause of the decline of colonialism or the resurgence of Islam. But it was Nasser who was being blamed solely, an exaggerated charge that only added to his stature throughout the Arab lands and the Third World.

• •

Four days later Ike moved a step closer to concluding that Nasser was indeed the villain. Robert Anderson returned from his second and last Middle East mission late in the afternoon of March 12 and went directly to the White House. "He made no progress whatsoever," confided the President to his diary.

"Nasser proved to be a complete stumbling block. He is apparently seeking to be acknowledged as the political leader of the Arab world. Nasser has a number of fears. First of all, he fears the military junta that placed him in power, which is extremist in its position to Israel. Next he fears creating any antagonism toward himself on the part of the Egyptian people; he constantly cites the fate of King Farouk. Because he wants to be the most popular man in all the Arab world, he also has to consider public opinion in each of the other countries. The result is that he finally concludes he should take no action whatsoever [in seeking peace with Israel]—rather he should just make speeches, all of which must breathe defiance of Israel."

The failure of Anderson was not all one-sided, Eisenhower noted. "The Israel officials are anxious to talk with Egypt, but they are completely adamant in their attitude of making no concessions whatsoever in order to obtain peace. Their general slogan is 'not one inch of ground,' and their incessant demand is for arms."

Eisenhower then shrewdly observed: "Of course, they could get arms at lower prices from almost any European nation, but they want the arms from us because they feel that in this case they have made us a virtual ally in any trouble they might get into in the region."

Still, something had to be done. "Public opinion on both sides is inflamed and the chances for peaceful settlement seem remote. To both Ben Gurion and Nasser, Anderson held out every pledge of assistance and association that the United States could logically make in return for a genuine effort on the part of both to obtain a peace."

Thus came to end the highly ambitious Anderson Mission. Its only apparent result was to prove again how difficult and complex was the quest for peace in the Middle East. But it may also have helped nudge Eisenhower closer to turning against Nasser. He concluded his diary entry with a plan that involved isolating Egypt.

"It begins to look to me as though our best move is to prevent any concerted action on the part of the Arab states. Specifically I think we can hold Libya to our side through a reasonable amount of help to that impoverished nation, and we have an excellent chance of winning Saudi Arabia to our side if we can get Britain to go along with us. Britain would, of course, have to make certain territorial concessions and this she might object to violently.

"If Saudi Arabia and Libya were our staunch friends, Egypt could scarcely continue intimate association with the Soviets, and certainly Egypt would no longer be regarded as a leader of the Arab world."

Eisenhower's ideas about a new approach had still not congealed, but the outlines were becoming clear and they almost certainly would involve bad news for Gamal Abdel Nasser.

. .

While Eisenhower was toying with the fate of Nasser, Foster Dulles was traveling through Asia tending to one of his beloved pacts, this one SEATO, the Southeast Asia Treaty Organization.* In his pactomania, Dulles had spearheaded SEATO's creation in 1954 to contain Communist China, much as NATO contained Russia, and to help keep South Vietnam in the Western orbit.

The SEATO foreign ministers met in Karachi, Pakistan, for three days,

---

* The members were Australia, Britain, France, New Zealand, Pakistan, the Philippines, Thailand and the United States. Like its British counterpart, the Baghdad Pact, it was never effective: a congressional committee examining it after Dulles' death concluded that it was "not a going concern but a sham."

starting March 6, giving Dulles a unique chance to talk with both his British and French counterparts. Since Lloyd had just come from Cairo, Dulles was interested to hear his impressions of the Middle East and Nasser. Lloyd told him that he thought the region was drifting into dangerous waters and that no reliance could be placed on Nasser. Dulles replied that "some people in the United States Administration had reached the same view." Added Lloyd: "Dulles had himself not quite reached it although he was not far off. Unless Nasser did something definite soon, we would have to 'ditch' him."

Dulles was unhappy about Nasser's flirtation with Russia, uneasy with his anti-West propaganda and suspicious of the Egyptian's role in the recent sacking of Glubb Pasha. A large anti-Egypt constituency was growing in America, made up of that disparate mixture of special-interest groups including right-wing Cold Warriors alarmed by Nasser's dealing with the Soviets, southern cotton interests and supporters of Israel. Against that grouping, the championing of Egypt's cause was a losing battle. Dulles was becoming inclined, like Eisenhower, to isolate Nasser and the problems he presented to the Administration in an election year. He told Lloyd that he believed Nasser should display his goodwill to the West by stopping propaganda broadcasts against the Baghdad Pact and by taking a specific step toward finding peace with Israel.

Perhaps, Dulles suggested, Nasser would do those things if the British promised that they would not enlist any more Arab members in the pact. Though Lloyd had promised Nasser only days before to pursue such a policy, he now told Dulles that an understanding like that "would have a bad effect upon the other members," particularly Iraq, which would see British restraint as a victory for Egypt.

At another private meeting in Karachi, Dulles informed Lloyd that the U.S. soon was going to take a more active role in the Middle East. How? Lloyd asked. Dulles replied that he had not yet thought it out. Somewhat wistfully, Lloyd once again urged that one way was for the U.S. to join the Baghdad Pact.

"Quite impossible," retorted Dulles, referring vaguely to the Jewish lobby and congressional opposition.

• •

Dulles also met in Karachi with France's new foreign minister, outspoken, irrepressible Christian Pineau. He was a bundle of intriguing contradictions, a socialist who was once a banker, a practitioner of realpolitik who wrote delightful fairy tales, a Gallic skeptic and political idealist. His protean nature was a reflection of his parentage. His father was an army officer who died young; his stepfather was playwright Jean Giraudoux.

During World War II, Pineau headed a large Resistance organization and edited the influential underground newspaper *Libération*. He also acted as a liaison agent between occupied France and General Charles de Gaulle's London headquarters, which he secretly visited several times, returning to France by parachute. Twice he was picked up by the Gestapo after such trips. The first time he escaped. The second time he was thrown into Buchenwald concentration camp where he witnessed at first hand the inhuman treatment of Jews and others. He remained there for more than a year before being liberated by American forces in April 1945. Despite his grueling experiences, he spurned those seeking revenge on Germany and became an outspoken partisan for Franco-German relations. His explanation was that "I seek no form of vengeance. My only hope is that we shall never know those camps again." The experience also made him a passionate advocate of Zionism.

After the war he served in a succession of high government posts and as a leader of the Socialist Party. In 1955 he was designated to try to form a government but failed and finally took the Foreign Ministry post in the government formed by fellow Socialist Guy Mollet. Pineau wasted no time in expressing his iconoclastic views. Just before leaving for Karachi, he had caused dismay in Washington and London by heatedly criticizing the West's continuation of Cold War suspicions since the death of Josef Stalin.

"I am in deep disagreement with the policy followed by the Western nations during recent years," he said in a speech before the Anglo-American Press Association in Paris on March 2. "We have made an enormous mistake in deciding that security problems were the only international problems we had to worry about. Of course we need security. Of course we need strong armies. But need we talk of this all the time?"

Pineau lambasted Britain's promotion of the Baghdad Pact and America's unyieldingly antagonistic attitude toward the Soviet Union and Communist China. Turning to Indochina, he charged that U.S. support of the anti-French regime of Ngo Dinh Diem* was a tragic mistake. Vietnam would not now be divided and have a growing Communist insurgency in the south, he said, if the U.S. had cooperated more with France. Then he cast suspicion on America's intentions in the Middle

---

* He was assassinated seven years later with tacit U.S. approval.

East, saying, "We have the impression that . . . there lurks the desire of certain powers to swallow up the heritage of France."

Actually, he concluded, "despite alliances, despite affirmations, there is no real common French-British-American policy today."

Those were as strong words as Washington had heard in many years, and indignation swept the capital. Pineau was soon being called "Peck's Bad Boy of the Atlantic Alliance" and the "Nehru of the West." Unnamed State Department officials derisively whispered that Pineau could not tell the difference between the real world and his fairy tales, or between conciliation and appeasement.

Pineau's criticisms were still ringing in Dulles' ears, as well they should have since most of them were directed at his policies, when the two men met for the first time in Karachi. Pineau was surprised by Dulles' opening declaration: "For me, there are two types of people in the world. Those who are Christians and partisans of free enterprise—and the others."

"I quickly reminded him," recalled Pineau, "that we were in Karachi, in a Moslem country, that economic liberalism did not make much sense in an underdeveloped country."

For two hours, the two foreign secretaries sparred, trying to get a sense of each other. At one point, Dulles demanded: "Are you or aren't you for liberty?"

"For political liberty without a doubt," shot back Pineau. "But I have reservations about what you call free enterprise."

Dulles explained at length to the new French minister his ideas about combating Communism. "To him," said Pineau, "Communism was like gas compressed in a bottle. If it is not hermetically sealed, it escapes, spreads and poisons the environment. He did not want to leave a gap through which the expansionism of Soviet thoughts could pass. To prevent that, he thought it necessary to ally with those countries surrounding the Soviet Union, help them, give them arms and install military bases on their territory."

Dulles later confided to Lloyd that he had been "most unimpressed" with Pineau. "I forbore to tell him that I knew that the feeling was mutual," Lloyd noted with satisfaction.

However lowly Lloyd and Pineau regarded Dulles, they knew they were doomed to deal with him. Eisenhower, by running for a second term, had practically certified that he would be President for four more years and his secretary of state would be Dulles.

The three-day SEATO meeting ended with Dulles' apocalyptic world view prevailing over Pineau's sensible tocsin. In their concluding communiqué, the SEATO ministers declared that though post-Stalinist Russia was acting less aggressively, "This shift in tactics was unaccompanied by any convincing evidence of intent to abandon efforts to subvert, weaken and overthrow the political, economic and social systems which have been freely chosen by the peoples of the area." That being the case, the ministers declared, they "recognized the necessity of creating and maintaining powerful deterrents against aggression lest potential aggressors come to believe that aggression would not be effectively and immediately resisted."

With America's Asian flank presumably secured by such rhetoric, Dulles toured Asian nations before returning to Washington to help the President find the country's new approach in the Middle East.

•   •

If he had not completely taken leave of his reason over Glubb Pasha's firing, Anthony Eden did so in Cyprus. The strategically located island in the eastern Mediterranean had been ruled by Britain since 1878, another plum snatched from the crumbling Ottoman empire. But now the large Greek majority was demanding *enosis* (union) with Greece and control of the Turkish minority. Britain, with its troops evacuating the huge Suez base in Egypt, had several large military bases on Cyprus and it meant to keep them there, the last major British bastion in the eastern Mediterranean. As a symbol of his determination, Eden had sent a field marshal, Sir John Harding, former chief of the Imperial General Staff, as governor of the island the previous September 25.

Harding's arrival touched off a wave of terrorist actions by EOKA (National Organization of Cypriot Fighters), the Greek Cypriot underground, throughout the island. By November 27, a state of emergency was declared and Britain's ten thousand troops were placed on a war footing; in January and February reinforcements were sent in from the Highland Light Infantry and the Royal Horse Guards. But rather than stemming the atrocities, they increased in number. Britons were shot down as they walked the streets, bombs were tossed into bars and homes, British cars were ambushed on the roads. By early March, seventeen British soldiers had been killed and scores of soldiers and their families had been injured in terrorist attacks.

Despite stern warnings from Harding, Archbishop Makarios, the wily leader of the Cypriots, refused to condemn publicly EOKA's war of terror. In fact, it was discovered that one of his cousins had been shot dead the previous December 15 during an ambush of a British military vehicle. The archbishop was widely suspected of being a leader of the terror campaign, but no direct evidence could be found against him.

The challenge in Cyprus to British rule "surely contributed to the British mood of 'enough!' " recalled Eisenhower. "They had agreed in 1954 to leave their Suez base, an act of incalculable significance for the British end-of-empire feeling; they were being subjected to taunts and insults in Cairo; and now their last important bastion in that part of the world was quaking."

Eden had had enough. He was determined to show how tough he could be. On March 5, he took the highly unusual step, one that Britain had not taken even during World War II, of jamming all Greek broadcasts to Cyprus, which were openly inflaming anti-British emotions. Then he took another step that caused its own quake. He ordered the exiling of Archbishop Makarios on March 9 to the Seychelle Islands in the remote Indian Ocean without trial or legal process.

British hard liners cheered, especially the reactionary Suez Group of Conservatives in the House, whom Anthony Nutting tabbed the "whiff of grapeshot school" within Parliament. They formed a powerful coterie that advocated firm actions by the government to preserve its colonial possessions and were a constant prod for Eden to be tougher. But in reality, the exile of Makarios only exacerbated Britain's difficulties in Cyprus.* The EOKA terrorists continued shedding British blood and the Greek community was drawn together as never before in its opposition to British rule.

For the Middle East, Eden's exiling of Makarios was less interesting in its effects on the region than in what it indicated about the prime minister's state of mind. Hounded and tormented in the House and the press for months because of his dithering and dawdling, Eden had at last decided to prove that he was a worthy successor to Churchill. He could be as tough as the old wartime leader, and he apparently concluded about this time that his next move after Makarios was to take action to get rid of Nasser.

• •

Another Western leader had also irrevocably come to the same conclusion that something had to be done about Nasser. Since the publication of Nasser's book, *The Philosophy of the Revolution,* Guy Mollet had

* Cyprus received its independence in 1960; Makarios became its first president.

203

kept a copy on his desk and cited it as another *Mein Kampf*. It proved, Mollet maintained, that Nasser's ambition was to unify the Arab world from Morocco to Saudi Arabia in a coalition against the West. This was perhaps true in terms of Nasser's ambition. But it was an excessively credulous appraisal of Nasser's slim volume of reminiscences about the revolution and his youthful fancies about the future of Islam. Yet Mollet genuinely began seeing Nasser as an Arab Hitler, accepting his every boast and dreamy arabesque as a cunningly plotted scheme against the West.

Repeatedly, as the Algerian rebellion grew worse, Mollet and other French officials began invoking the image of Munich, wildly summoning up the specter of another world war. It was conciliation at Munich in 1938 that had brought about World War II, and now weakness toward Nasser would lead to another catastrophe. Though there was no parallel at all between Hitler in the 1930s and Nasser in the 1950s, Mollet and his subordinates were indelibly imbued with the tragedy of Munich, which had occurred in their youth. As the leaders of the 1950s they were passionately determined not to submit their country to similar carnage and humiliation.

This Munich complex was shared by Britain's leaders. Soon the invocation of Munich and Hitler was also being heard in the Parliament and the press on the other side of the English Channel. Stung beyond sufferance by the humiliation of the expulsion of Glubb Pasha, the British press blossomed with a vitriolic campaign against Nasser. The *Daily Express* called him a "tin-horn dictator" and the *Daily Mail*, attacking his anti-British propaganda, printed a cartoon showing him as a turbaned bazaar Arab holding a radio and hissing, "Feelthy words?" The British press portrayed Nasser as a fascist obsessed with conquering an empire—Britain's. In its chauvinism, it overlooked the fact that there really was little of the empire left.

The press and the parliaments in Britain and France from this time on, encouraged by Israel, maintained a steady drumbeat of shrill criticism against Nasser, all the way to war. It seemed to make no difference that the implicit comparisons between Germany and Egypt, and to the personalities and ambitions of Hitler and Nasser, had no basis in reality. Egypt had no industrial infrastructure, much less war-making capacity, and its military machine was without might, as it was soon dismally to prove. In no way did Egypt resemble the aggressive might of the Third Reich on the eve of World War II, nor did Nasser resemble Hitler.

Yet the insistent comparisons were leading to a historic distortion.

They were blinding Britain and France to a sensible appreciation of Nasser's weaknesses. At the same time, by their excessive enmity they were bolstering his prestige in the Middle East and the Third World, where anticolonialism still stirred deep emotions. Suddenly this peasant leader of a weak and impoverished country was being treated with the same venom and fear as a major power. The boon to Nasser's image was inestimable. He was becoming a self-fulfilling prophecy of the West: a world leader. The message was not lost on the vast multitudes of peoples emerging from the exploitation of colonialism in Africa and Asia and, especially, in the Arab world. If the West hated Nasser so much then surely he must be powerful.

• •

Though Mollet and Eden were opposites in background, style and ideology, they were unique for contemporaneous modern rulers of France and Britain: they actually admired each other's country. Eden had long appreciated things French, especially the arts, and Mollet had spent his career teaching the alluring subtleties of the English language. They both now found themselves fighting to retain some semblance of their empires and, they suspected with justification, they shared the burden of opposition to colonialism from Washington and throughout much of the world.

They also had a common repugnance to Foster Dulles' Calvinist brand of anti-Communism. While Dulles and Eisenhower seemed content to disparage or ignore the changes occurring in the Soviet Union, the countries that Mollet and Eden ruled were three thousand miles closer to Russia and they were anxious to explore any new opening with the East. Eden was going to receive in London the Soviet leaders in April and then Mollet was going to travel to Moscow in May. The visits would be the first since the Communist revolution nearly forty years earlier. Beyond that, Mollet and Eden both found themselves under severe political attack for their Middle East policies.

All this gave the two leaders a full agenda to discuss and, at the beginning of March, Eden invited Mollet to his residence at Chequers for private talks. They met March 11 and 12 with no other ministers and had a thorough airing of their mutual problems, especially in the Middle East. The meeting revealed an astonishing similarity of views.

The harmony between the two leaders was even more surprising because of their different attitudes toward Israel. While Mollet was a Zionist, Eden was an Arabist. He had studied Arabic, liked Arabs and generally sided with them in their struggle with Israel. His private secretary during World War II, Oliver Harvey, noted in his diary that "A.E. is immovable on the subject of Palestine. He loves Arabs and hates Jews." Eden himself had admitted to Harvey in 1941 while serving as foreign secretary that "if we must have preference, let me murmur in your ear that I prefer Arabs to Jews."

Eden's regard for Israelis was not enhanced during the bitter final years of Britain's mandate over Palestine when Jews waged a campaign of terror against British troops, killing 338 British subjects in the three years between the end of World War II and the time the Union Jack was finally struck at the founding of the Jewish state. The terror campaign had created considerable animosity throughout much of Britain, especially in the traditionally pro-Arab Foreign Office. Though Eden was not in the government during that period, he shared the general British revulsion against the barbarity of the Jewish terrorists.

Yet now in his meeting with Mollet Eden was suddenly displaying an untypical sympathy toward Israel. When Mollet claimed that Nasser was aiding the terrorists in Algeria and threatening Israel, Eden did not disagree. Mollet continued by asserting that Israel was in "extreme trouble. France would be failing in her duty if she did not extend all possible help."

Eden concurred. He replied that it was important for the Western powers to show that they could not be defied "by an upstart like Nasser."

For the first time in a half century, Britain and France were largely in agreement about the Middle East. The old Entente Cordiale * was being revised, not this time to share spoils but to join against a common foe named Nasser.

• •

Immediately after their meeting, Mollet and Eden each took forceful actions that significantly influenced events in the Middle East. Mollet announced on March 15 and 17 the transfer of two divisions (half of France's NATO commitment in Germany) to Algeria, where there already were 200,000 French troops. And on March 17, his Cabinet approved a range of tough measures in Algeria under a newly passed Emergency Powers Act that gave France virtually unlimited extralegal powers to put down the rebellion. Governor-General Robert Lacoste was authorized personally to exercise such powers as ordering the search of

* The original entente was signed in 1904 in recognition of British claims in Egypt and French supremacy in Morocco; the peoples of the two African countries were not consulted.

ships in Algerian harbors to the banning of individuals from either leaving or entering the country. Yet the carnage mounted. More than a hundred persons, most of them identified as rebels, were being killed daily in Algeria's tortured towns and countryside.

Eden now too displayed a new decisiveness. He ordered all British military advisers out of Jordan in retaliation for Glubb Pasha's sacking and pressed for harder measures against the terrorists in Cyprus. Though the scale was much smaller than in Algeria, the violence in Cyprus was also picking up in pace. On March 20, Governor Harding's bed was booby-trapped with a bomb. It was discovered in time between the two mattresses and was detonated harmlessly in the garden. His Cypriot man-servant was suspected since he disappeared the next day. In response, Harding dismissed all Cypriot members of his household two days later. Then on March 25 he imposed a twenty-four-hour curfew on Cyprus' thirteen major towns to prevent demonstrations on the 135th anniversary of Greece's independence of Turkish rule. But the killings went on: a British corporal was fatally injured by a bomb on March 21, and two others on March 27 in an ambush.

Reflecting Eden's animosity toward Nasser, the Foreign Office on March 23 publicly reported that two hundred Egyptian officers and men were training at a Soviet base in Poland. It also asserted that Egyptian pilots were being trained by Czechs to fly thirty Ilyushin bombers and as many as fifty-one MiGs. Soviet technical experts also were reported in Cairo discussing new arms deals. The revelations, while no doubt true, were aimed at further isolating Nasser from the West.

Eden's ire against the Egyptian leader was increased that March by interviews Nasser gave to the correspondents of the *Sunday Times* and the *Observer*. The point he wanted to make, Nasser said, was that the Baghdad Pact had been a sorry failure. The only Arab member was toadying Iraq. Since that was the case, he was extending an olive branch to Britain. He would no longer beat the dead horse that was the Baghdad Pact but instead would concentrate on strengthening the Arab League. It was a calculated insult, but also a tentative gesture of friendship since he offered publicly to stop his anti-British propaganda. Eden saw only the insult and rose to it with all the injured pride of a colonial master who discovers his subjects can be as witty as he.

Eden ordered Whitehall to respond with a blistering attack. Nasser's words of wanting friendship with the West did not correspond with his actions, charged Whitehall. The Foreign Office spokesman went further. Egypt's real aim was to eliminate British influence throughout the Arab world. It was, he claimed, absurd to equate the idea that it would be a fair exchange if Britain refrained from trying to enlist more Arab members for the Baghdad Pact in return for a halt to Egypt's anti-British propaganda. After all, said the Whitehall statement disingenuously, the terms of the pact made it open to any state that wanted to join.

"Nasser took this statement as a declaration of war," reported British Ambassador Trevelyan. Eden's protégé, Nutting, added: "I can testify that this was exactly what Eden intended it to be. Nasser certainly responded in kind, and abuse of Britain and the Baghdad Pact now poured forth from Cairo's transmitters with renewed frequency and fervor."

From this point, said Trevelyan, "The British government seemed convinced that Nasser was our enemy. Officials were asked to produce ideas how we could oppose his aims." That was not easy to do, as Trevelyan well knew. "If he had been a lesser man, interested only in his own power or the material advantages which power brings, he would have been easier to deal with," observed Trevelyan. "But he was a visionary, whose visions could not be reconciled with British interests in the Arab world and who was apt to identify his own ambitions with the will of Providence."

Nasser was aware of these strengths. One day he said to Trevelyan: "You cannot carry out a gunboat policy against me as you could against Farouk. I have no throne, no hereditary position, no fortune." Indeed, even after he had become president, Nasser continued to live in the same modest officers' quarters he and his wife and five children had lived in before.

. .

On the same day that Eden and Mollet finished their talks, General Alfred Gruenther, commander of NATO and a close personal friend of Eisenhower's, cabled the chairman of the Joint Chiefs of Staff: "There is a stronger anti-American feeling in France now than at any time in the last five years. Somehow most Frenchmen would like to blame their troubles on the United States." The top levels of the French government and Army were distraught about FLN gains in Algeria, Gruenther reported, and suspicious about the sincerity of U.S. support for their cause. "The French frame of mind is badly disorganized at this time. I will not hazard a guess as to the outcome."

Over the next few days, more warnings from official and unofficial sources poured into Washington about the near hysterical state of the French leaders. "The French public is more aroused on this issue [Algeria] than on any since the war," reported one. Another noted that France "presently faces a large-scale rebellion in Algeria which if not contained may prove dangerous because of the repercussions it could have on national as well as international affairs."

Eisenhower finally felt compelled on March 15 to write a note to Foster Dulles, who had still not returned to Washington from his tour of Asia following the SEATO foreign ministers' conference. "The Mid East and North African situations grow more and more complicated, but all of us are earnestly considering every possible line of action that occurs to us in the hope that we may have some fresh ideas to bring to bear by the time you return."

America's problems were not only with the French, but increasingly with Britain too. The exiling of Archbishop Makarios upset the large Greek lobby in the United States and so Washington expressed its "sympathetic concern" to the Greek government. U.S. Ambassador Cavendish W. Cannon also assured the Greeks that Washington had not known in advance of Britain's plans to deport Makarios.

That same day, Eisenhower noted tersely in his diary: "British are outraged by contents of message to the Greek government released by our embassy there."

There began to be an anti-American tinge to the speeches in Parliament. Earl Attlee, the former Labour prime minister, complained about America's "rather outdated anticolonialism. I sometimes feel with all friendliness to our American friends that they are a little apt to stand on the sidelines and leave us to carry the fight." Eden remarked in the House that it was "the British government and British forces which delivered Greece at the cost of British dead and wounded from the certainty of Communist rule" in 1948. He declared that "the welfare and lives of our people depend on Cyprus as a protective guard and staging post to take care of their interests—above all, oil. This is not imperialism. It should be the plain duty of any government and we intend to discharge it."

Such a vow was becoming costly to fulfill. While terrorism on Cyprus still in no way compared with the butchery being committed by both sides in Algeria, it nonetheless was becoming fierce. On the same day that Eden spoke, a British police sergeant was shot dead in Nicosia; two army trucks were stoned in Larnaca and a British soldier fired into the crowd, killing a seven-year-old Cypriot boy; and in Dhora two Cypriots were shot dead in a coffeehouse by three masked men who shouted "Death to traitors." British troops had their hands full trying to maintain order throughout the small island, much less keeping it alert as Britain's strategic outpost in the eastern Mediterranean.

• •

Algeria and Cyprus were sideshows to the Israel-Arab dispute, but now that area too was heating up dangerously again after a brief respite. "The tension along the demarcation line [between Israel and Egypt] is steadily increasing," warned General Burns on March 14. Exchanges of fire between the two sides were "almost daily events" during the past week, killing one Egyptian soldier and wounding two others. Overflights by Israeli aircraft had increased dramatically, with seventeen reported by Egypt and "a number of which were witnessed by United Nations observers. Two mine incidents were reported by the Israelis, as the result of which one Israeli soldier has been killed and two soldiers wounded."

Tensions were aggravated by the lack of meetings of the Egyptian-Israeli Mixed Armistice Commission, which was supposed to adjudicate violations of the armistice. When Burns had called a regular meeting on February 28, he explained to U.N. headquarters, Israel insisted without cause that the Egyptian representatives use the Rafah road to reach the meeting site at El Auja. Instead, they used, as was their practice, the Ismailia road and were stopped by Israeli authorities at the international frontier. No meeting was held that day and none since. "The deadlock has not yet been solved," reported Burns.

Tensions continued to mount in mid-March. On the sixteenth, Israeli troops fired on three U.N. jeeps, painted white and flying white flags, in the southeast part of the El Auja demilitarized zone. About twenty-five shots were fired but none of the U.N. observers was injured. Israel later apologized, declaring, in the words of Burns's report, "it to be due to a misunderstanding."

• •

It was in mid-March too that Eden wrote a fateful letter to Eisenhower. The letter has remained classified, but a sense of its incendiary contents can be glimpsed in Eisenhower's reply and in the actions the President took immediately afterward. The letter, written three days after Eden's portentous meeting with Mollet, apparently finally nudged Ike into viewing Nasser as the West's bête noire.

"The enclosure you sent me with your letter of March Fifteenth is a most interesting report on the intentions of the Egyptian government," wrote Eisenhower on March 20. "Assuming that the information therein contained is completely authentic, it seems to me to give a clue of how we—your government and ours—might operate with the greatest chance of frustrating Soviet designs in the region.

"Foster will return in a couple of days, and he and I will then go over this document and a good deal of other information which we have on this subject."

Eight days later, Eisenhower, Dulles, Secretary of Defense Wilson, Chairman of the Joint Chiefs of Staff Radford and three other top officials met in the late afternoon to discuss the disturbing Middle East and Eden's letter. Dulles had prepared a four-page outline of actions Washington could take "to let Colonel Nasser realize that he cannot cooperate as he is doing with the Soviet Union and at the same time enjoy most-favored-nation treatment from the United States."

Dulles' policy paper observed, "We would want for the time being to avoid any open break which would throw Nasser irrevocably into a Soviet satellite status and we would want to leave Nasser a bridge back to good relations with the West if he so desires." But the proposals that Dulles now made could hardly accomplish anything other than Nasser's alienation.

The new policies, the Dulles paper emphasized, "would in the main be coordinated with the United Kingdom."

Significantly, an item high on the list of actions to be taken against Egypt was a coordinated tactic by Washington and London to "continue to delay the conclusion of current negotiations on the High Aswan Dam." Other actions included continued refusal to sell arms to Egypt, delay in granting grains and oil, and delay or elimination of financial aid.

In the region as a whole, it was proposed that Britain should retain its treaty relationship with Jordan and "help prevent a situation in which a pro-Egyptian coup d'état would succeed." Increased support would be given by Washington to the Baghdad Pact "without actually adhering to the pact or announcing our intention of doing so. In addition to accelerated aid to the pact countries, this support . . . will also display an increased interest in the economic aspects of the pact." Pro-Western political groups in Lebanon would be given immediately grants and loans to strengthen their position.

The Dulles paper considered it "extremely important that the American position in Saudi Arabia be strengthened." Ways to accomplish this were to provide King Saud with more weapons, and to press the British to make a generous settlement with the country over the disputed Buraimi Oasis.

With Israel, "The U.S. will seek to dissuade the Israelis from under-taking . . . precipitate steps which might bring about hostilities and thus endanger the whole Western position in the Near East to the direct ad-vantage of the Soviets."

The Dulles document concluded on an ominous note, one which soon spread its venom in the Middle East cauldron. "Planning should be un-dertaken at once with a view to possibly more drastic action in the event that the above courses of action do not have the desired effect."

What that planning covered has been deleted by government censors from Dulles' memorandum and remains secret. But it is now known that on the British side it included plotting a pro-Western coup in Syria and deposing Nasser.

That evening, Eisenhower confided to his diary that he had approved all of Dulles' recommendations. He also noted that the idea he had been toying with since the beginning of the month had finally taken shape and he urged its implementation. The plan: "Begin to build up some other individual as a prospective leader of the Arab world—in the thought that mutually antagonistic personal ambitions might disrupt the aggressive plans that Nasser is evidently developing." Eisenhower had finally con-cluded, apparently on the basis of his own suspicions, Eden's letter and perhaps other evidence—though none has been declassified if it exists—that Nasser was indeed the villain.

"A fundamental factor in the problem is the growing ambition of Nas-ser," Ike wrote in his diary that night, "the sense of power he had gained out of his associations with the Soviets, his belief that he can emerge as a true leader of the entire Arab world—and because of these beliefs, his rejection of every proposition advanced as a measure of conciliation between the Arabs and Israel."

The President's personal choice as a competitor to Nasser was a bi-zarre one: King Saud. He was the son of Abdul Aziz Ibn Saud, the founder of Saudi Arabia, but hardly his match in intellect or stature and certainly not equipped to become the leader of the disputatious Arab nations. Saud also suffered a fatal political handicap. It was his family who had driven the Hashemites out of Arabia, and it was a later genera-tion of the Hashemites who were now the kings of Iraq and Jordan. The elevation of Saud almost surely would have driven Iraq and Jordan into Nasser's camp.

But Eisenhower was groping, like many others in Washington, London and Paris that winter, for an alternative to Nasser. After all, he reasoned in his diary, "Arabia is a country that contains the holy places of the

Moslem world, and the Saudi Arabians are considered to be the most deeply religious of all the Arab groups. Consequently, the king could be built up, possibly, as a spiritual leader. Once this were accomplished we might begin to urge his right to political leadership.''

But even Eisenhower, who wisely disclaimed any expertise in the convolutions of Middle East rivalries, seemed to sense the futility of his idea. In parentheses, he added: "Obviously this is just a thought, but something of the nature ought to be developed in support of the other suggestions contained in this memorandum.''

• •

Most of the policies—including Ike's quixotic notion to build up Saud —were eventually attempted, though with indifferent results.

The realities of the region had an uncomfortable way of intruding on the policies of Washington. Two days after the Administration had decided on its new course, Dulles complained to one of his Middle East assistants, Francis H. Russell, that Israel was not being cooperative. "Their only theme is arms," Dulles said. "We get no benefit of their thinking, their intelligence, et cetera. What do they think about Syria? Jordan? The problem is more complicated than just arms. If their only contribution is [asking for arms] our effort will be less successful.''

Dulles was also having second thoughts about closer cooperation with the Baghdad Pact. "The impact on Egypt will be considerable," he observed on March 31 during a conversation with another of his assistants, Douglas MacArthur II, a nephew of the general. "It will indicate that we are building up the Baghdad Pact not only as a defensive organization against the Soviet Union but an economic pact against Egypt.''

"We may want to do it," replied MacArthur, "but we must think about it.''

Yet the speed at which events began moving in the Middle East left little time for Washington or any other capital to devote to thinking.

CHAPTER XI

We Have Decided to Fight

PERES

By April, Anthony Eden's hatred of Nasser was shared by many Britons. The Parliament, the press and the public had become sensitive to the smallest slight from Egypt, and regarded each one, whether real or imaginary, as a potential casus belli. In this near hysterical atmosphere the relatively mild public attitude of Washington toward the Egyptian leader was exasperating and greatly resented by Britons, and they vented their anger on Foster Dulles unmercifully. "It is painfully clear to everybody, except Mr. Dulles, not only that the Middle East might blow up at any moment, but also that American dilatoriness and reluctance to look at the Middle East as it is impose the severest possible strain on Western unity," complained the weekly *Spectator*. When Dulles explained at a press conference in early April that he thought Nasser's actions were "actuated primarily by a desire to maintain the genuine independence of that area," a British cartoonist showed a helpless Eden being kicked by a childlike Nasser and nursemaid Dulles saying, "Don't take on so, Master Anthony, the little lad appears to be actuated by a desire to maintain genuine independence." The *Daily Mail* angrily observed: "In sermons against colonialism [the Americans] have helped preach faithful allies out of invaluable bases. But they have not preached themselves out of Okinawa, Formosa or Puerto Rico."

The anti-American tone of British press reports increased so sharply during April that Eisenhower telephoned Dulles about the matter. "I want to talk to you about constant references in the press to the effect that the British press is getting awfully sore with you and me and saying

214

we are vacillating around about the Middle East,'' said Ike. "I don't know what they are talking about. It looks like the British government is handing out some things to the papers about us.''

The President suggested that Dulles write Eden, saying, "Here, if you want policies published, we have been trying [to work] together on policy so we could make a public statement. If they want our support on the Baghdad Pact they will have to make certain concessions.''

Eisenhower's anger was understandable since the United States had toughened up its Middle East position considerably since Eden's anti-Nasser campaign had begun in March. Negotiations for financing the Aswan High Dam were being stalled, Washington was about to associate itself with the Baghdad Pact, joining its economic and countersubversive committees on April 18, and Eisenhower was still flirting with the idea of building up the inept King Saud as an alternative to Nasser. Twice in his telephone conversation with Dulles he mentioned Saud, observing that "we must find some way to be friends with King Saud. Is there any way we could flatter or compliment him?''

The Administration was also seeking other schemes to preserve the peace and the West's position in the Middle East. Robert Anderson's mission had been such a total failure that no more thought was being given to sending him back to the region, but now Anderson came up with an idea of his own. He called Dulles on April 4 and suggested that NATO, which was largely dependent on Middle East oil, work out a military plan to protect the supplies. Dulles said his thinking was leading him to believe that the West's best hope was "to develop alternative sources so that the NATO countries do not have to get oil from there. If we reduce our dependence on the area and develop alternative resources we might strike more effective terror in their hearts by threatening their oil royalties.''

"Developing alternative resources takes months," Anderson replied, demonstrating how little he or most other Americans knew of the subject. They prudently agreed to give the matter more serious thought.

• •

Out of the gaze of the media other more ominous plans were being hatched. Eden's determination to get rid of Nasser had found a receptive audience in Britain's Secret Intelligence Service. The SIS's deputy director, George Kennedy Young, called a joint meeting with the CIA in the beginning of April to discuss the effects of Britain's hardening Middle East policy. Allen Dulles' personal undercover representative in the Middle East, Wilbur Crane ("Bill") Eveland, and James Eichelberger of the Cairo CIA station flew to London for the meeting.

Young told the astonished CIA agents that as a result of Britain's new policy the SIS had decided that the governments of Egypt, Saudi Arabia and Syria had to be subverted or overthrown. All three countries threatened Britain's survival, he declared. Syria was about to become a Soviet satellite, and the fates of Jordan and Lebanon depended on the prompt overthrow of the Syrian government, declared Young. After that, King Saud and then Nasser would be removed. Young added that all of Britain's support was aimed at pro-British Iraq, with its rich oil fields and pliant royal family. "Britain is now prepared to fight its last battle," said Young.

The surprised CIA men, accustomed as they were to some fairly farfetched schemes, could not believe their ears. But they reported Young's remarks back to Washington.

• •

The Middle East and Nasser were driving England to extremes of anxiety. Columnist Joseph Alsop, who had excellent British sources, was in London that spring and found that "Middle East developments are causing gloom so deep that it all but approaches despair." Alsop was told that Eden was bombarding Washington with urgent pleas for a tougher American policy in the Middle East, and he observed that "Britain is like a man who feels an enemy's hard fingers reaching for his jugular vein (which in Britain's case is the Middle East oil source) yet can do nothing to ward off the attack."

Alsop would have been less sure of Britain's impotence had he heard of the SIS's plans for Egypt, Saudi Arabia and Syria. But the British were indeed frustrated, partly because Washington was resisting SIS's plot. It was another underlying factor in the mounting tensions between England and America. But with Eisenhower looking at King Saud as a possibly replacement of Nasser, there could be no chance that he would go along with the SIS plot to overthrow the king. Nor had Washington yet lost all of its patience with Nasser. When Foster Dulles called CIA Middle East boss Kim Roosevelt to his office to ask him about the SIS plan, Roosevelt strongly opposed taking any action against Nasser, arguing that his popularity among the Egyptian and Arab masses was so great that there was no way to depose him short of assassination. Nasser still remained extremely close to Roosevelt and the CIA, providing

Washington with a valuable window into the Arab world and unique access to its most dynamic leader.

But Syria was different, unstable and fractious, growing closer to the Soviets and Nasser, and an increasing threat to Iraq. The pressure from Britain was great for America to display its support in the Middle East, and Syria looked like a natural place to do it. The matter was placed under active study.

During a telephone call with Henry Cabot Lodge, Dulles assured the U.N. ambassador in early April that Washington was not thinking of taking any extreme measures in the Middle East, adding: "The British are making more drastic plans than we are."

• •

Nasser, still short of forty, was turning out to be one of the most adroit leaders on the world stage. He recognized the profound forces sweeping away the old colonialism. But, from his viewpoint, Washington seemed indifferent and Britain and France blind to the wave of history. In temperate and rational terms, he tried during early April to explain his world view to the West in a series of press interviews.

"You Americans, probably without even being aware of it, suddenly burst into the home and life of every Arab," he explained in an interview with *Life*. "Eight years ago you unalterably changed my life and my children's lives. You became the champions for the Jewish victims of Nazi purges. That was compassionate and commendable. But then you went one step farther. You used your fullest political strength to thrust a foreign state among us Arabs. Oh, you meant well. [But] hasn't something more been overlooked? What about us? One million Arab refugees driven from their homes!

"We looked to America for perhaps the most difficult thing of all— understanding. We felt sure that Americans would help us with our greatest problems. You were a democracy; you were still our star. At your embassy we were met with understanding and friendship. Plans were drawn, programs drafted, dreams dreamed. . . . Nothing happened.

"If we wished to do business with America we were dependent on your domestic political machinery. There were strings on practically everything offered us. Our requests for arms, even those that were obsolete, were gently discussed and then forgotten. We learned that American foreign policy today is still largely shaped by your apparent belief that survival of America depends on military pacts and overseas air bases. Sadly enough, from an American point of view, the Communists are given credit for fighting against colonialism and America is viewed as a country now opposed to the very moral principles on which you were founded.

"We learned another clear lesson while dealing with you. We learned that your Congress is subject to unrelenting pressure from highly organized, enormously wealthy Zionist groups which solicit for Israel right across the face of America as though your land were Israel itself. It is not extreme, perhaps, to think that Israeli weapons, paid for by American citizens, have killed Egyptians on the Gaza front. It would not require too broad an interpretation to consider these American contributions as an enemy act against us."

Nasser returned in other interviews to the theme of what he perceived as the erosion of America's traditional anticolonialism. "I say a third world war is going on right now," he told *The New York Times*. "We are in it. It is an invisible war. It is a war of nationalists all over the world to gain their independence. It is a psychological war and you cannot fight it with tanks.

"Do you not look at a map of the world and wonder why the Soviets are winning this war? The only way to win this war is to support the nationalist struggle along the lines of the United Nations Charter. You will upset your allies, Britain and France, but you will have the whole world with you."

Repeatedly Nasser vowed that he had no intention of using his new Soviet weapons against Israel. But, as usual, events outpaced intentions.

• •

The frontier between Egypt and Israel along the Gaza Strip, with its teeming, restless refugees living in hovels, had grown explosively tense. Both sides accused the other of repeated firings across the border, and Israel charged that between March 1 and April 4 there had been thirty-nine illegal crossings into its territory. U.N. observers determined that the crossings were "principally by Arab shepherds and farmers for the purpose of grazing or harvesting," but that did nothing to alleviate the uneasy atmosphere.

Blood began flowing again on April 4 when Israel sent a patrol of fourteen soldiers along the frontier with Egypt. During its movements there were three exchanges of fire with Egyptian outposts. Three Israelis were killed and one Egyptian. Fire also broke out later in the day, and then near dusk Israel shelled a small Arab village south of Gaza, Deir el

Belah. Structural damage was caused but there were no further injuries in the barrage.

Shortly after 9 A.M. the next day the fighting began in earnest. Firing broke out again at Deir el Belah. Soon Israel fired five mortar or artillery shells at an Egyptian outpost and seven shells at another position. By 1 P.M., three other Egyptian villages were under shellfire and four Arabs had been killed and nine wounded. Sporadic shelling by Israeli soldiers continued up and down the frontier until midafternoon when Egyptian troops retaliated by lobbing 120mm mortar shells against four Israeli settlements. Two men were wounded at the Nahal Oz settlement and buildings were damaged at two other kibbutzim.

At that point Israeli gunners aimed their heavy mortars on the civilians in the center of the crowded town of Gaza, turning it into a slaughterhouse. "The investigation team counted seventy-nine impacts of 120mm mortar shells, all of them at a distance of more than one kilometer from the nearest Egyptian military position," noted the official U.N. observers' report. "Shelling was centered on the main street of the town. The Israel allegation according to which the Egyptians had 'fortified emplacements within the confines of the city of Gaza' and 'heavy mortar fire from these emplacements was directed at Israel settlements' was without any foundation in fact. The only 'fortified emplacement' within the confines of the city of Gaza was the police station, if a building protected by barbed wire and sand bags can be called a fortified emplacement."

The bombardment of Gaza started at 4:15 P.M., and resulted in the deaths of sixty-two Arabs, including twenty-five women and children, and 107 wounded, forty-six of them women and children. Israeli casualties were no deaths and six wounded, including four civilians.

Retribution was not long in coming. Nasser unleashed the second wave of the dreaded *fedayeen* guerrillas on the Israeli countryside. Hand grenades were tossed into Jewish villages and homes, and water towers, tractors, railroad tracks and bridges were attacked with explosives. At Shafrir, just outside Tel Aviv, *fedayeen* invaded a synagogue during evening prayers and machine-gunned the worshipers, mostly young boys. Three boys and their teacher were killed, three others wounded. At Migdal, a woman was killed and two teen-agers wounded when a hand grenade was thrown into their house. A woman was wounded when shots and grenades were fired in Gal-On, southwest of Tel Aviv. All told, in five days of raiding, the *fedayeen* killed fourteen Israelis; ten *fedayeen* were killed and seven captured.

Though the overall damage and casualties caused by the *fedayeen* were slight by comparison with the Gaza attack, the raids had their intended result. They sparked a spasm of fear and anxiety throughout Israel. Nearly a thousand schoolchildren were recruited to build fortifications around settlements near the Egyptian frontier, army units scoured the countryside for *fedayeen* and emergency regulations were declared.

In New York, a band of twenty-two Jewish youths invaded the Egyptian Consulate and occupied it for more than an hour to hold memorial services for the victims of the *fedayeen*. There were no similar services for the Gaza victims. In fact, so strong was the hold of Israel's struggle on the American imagination that there was a perceptible negative shift in Washington's attitude toward Nasser as a result of the events.

"There has been a tendency here to see Colonel Nasser as a patriot who was merely working for the independence of his country after generations of Western control," wrote James Reston on April 10. "Colonel Nasser's attitudes and his propaganda, however, are now beginning to be seen here as something more menacing. He has been exploiting the Western-Soviet 'cold war' for his own advantage, and his propaganda has been ranging wider and wider throughout the Moslem world, often defending Soviet policies and vilifying the West. The British have been taking an extremely suspicious attitude toward Colonel Nasser for some time. They see him as a rising ambitious dictator. Washington is now beginning to take this thesis more seriously. It is beginning to wonder whether Colonel Nasser wants a settlement with Israel on any reasonable terms or whether he would prefer, instead, to use the Israeli issue to further his own ambitions."

Reston was reflecting a national attitude that seemed automatically to overlook or ignore transgressions by Israel but not those by Egypt, an attitude that was outraged by attacks against Israel but was indifferent to the Gaza bloodbaths that provoked them. Thus the Administration sent a message of condolence to Tel Aviv on April 10 expressing gratitude at the restraint Israel had shown in the face of the *fedayeen* attacks.

For Nasser, it was a Kafkaesque world. Only the previous September he was being hailed as a new Atatürk. "In Western capitals," wrote *Time* on September 26, "Nasser is still looked upon as Egypt's best hope for decent government, a moderate among the hotheaded many who would fight Israel even at the cost of suicide, a man who perhaps some day can grow into the dominant Middle Eastern leader he aspires to be. Even in Israel, officials say privately that they would be sorry to see Nasser fall from power. 'Without Nasser,' says a British Foreign Office diplomat, 'Egypt will be one unholy mess, another Syria.' ''

• •

It was into the Middle East's maelstrom of violence and tortured perceptions that U.N. Secretary-General Dag Hammarskjold arrived that April. Nothing in Hammarskjold's past could have quite prepared him for the convolutions of the Middle East. He was a private, serious, upright man, the former minister of state of Sweden, more at home in the salons and studios of poets and painters than the sandy wastes of the desert. But he brought to his U.N. post a high degree of dedication and commitment, and at age fifty, he also had the necessary energy for a personal mission to the region.

Under an American initiative, the Security Council had unanimously requested Hammarskjold to go to the Middle East to calm passions even before the Gaza attack and the *fedayeen* raids. Now his mission was even more urgent because Ben Gurion had privately warned that if Nasser did not withdraw his marauding *fedayeen* raiders by noon on April 10 he would retaliate. The region was at the edge of war.

Foster Dulles was concerned enough on April 9 to make a series of telephone calls about the chances of war. He asked his legal adviser to suppose "war broke out and the Soviets wanted to send supplies et cetera to Egypt, could they send them through the Straits [Dardanelles] and would anyone have the right to stop them?" Dulles was worried whether American citizens might have to be evacuated or at least protected. Chairman of the Joint Chiefs of Staff Admiral Radford said there were small arms and ammunition at the Dhahran airbase in Saudi Arabia, "illegal but they are there."

Foster's brother, Allen, cautioned that the CIA estimated the situation was tense, even grave, but "inclined to doubt the outbreak of large-scale hostilities."

"Why doesn't Ben Gurion wait?" asked Foster.

Allen thought the Israeli leader would wait to see Hammarskjold, but "if he sees no signs of satisfaction at that time, the situation will be even more critical."

A few minutes later Foster Dulles asked for the schedule of Hammarskjold's itinerary.

The outcome of war or peace now was in the hands of the Swedish economist who for the past three years had served as the head of the

United Nations. Hammarskjold had won wide acclaim for his coolness and fairness since becoming secretary-general. His technique was simple but effective. He conducted negotiations in secret, thereby avoiding embarrassment to either party, and he was forthright and direct in talks.

Hammarskjold was still in Europe, making his way slowly to the region, when the Middle East heated up to white pitch. He reacted by dispatching cables to both Ben Gurion and Nasser urging restraint until his arrival in Cairo. He got there a few hours after Ben Gurion's noon deadline on April 10. Following talks with Nasser and his foreign minister, Mahmoud Fawzi, he was able to obtain assurances that Egypt would stop the *fedayeen* attacks and observe a cease-fire along the frontier on April 11.

But that night the *fedayeen,* operating inside Israel without communications with Cairo, struck again, disrupting road traffic and killing four civilians, including three children. The next morning Israel claimed that four Egyptian jets had violated Israeli airspace and one of them was shot down in a dogfight.

Ben Gurion was furious about the *fedayeen* attacks and he sent Hammarskjold an emotional letter, demanding to know in the light of the new violations "what assurances have been obtained from Col. Nasser guaranteeing the fulfillment of his present undertaking. We should like to know whether you have the certainty that orders had been issued to all Egyptian forces, and what measures have been adopted, to maintain a complete cease-fire, not to cross the armistice line, to put an end to the activities of sabotage and murder gangs and to refrain from all other acts of aggression and violence."

To Hammarskjold's astonishment, Israel, in a bid to gain public support, released the contents of Ben Gurion's letter before it reached him. "I must express surprise at your publication in New York of your latest message before it had been received by me," he complained in a message to Ben Gurion. After expressing regret at the *fedayeen* attacks, Hammarskjold informed Ben Gurion that U.N. observers had placed the Egyptian planes not in Israeli territory but in the demilitarized zone where, he noted pointedly, "the presence of military aircraft from both sides would have been in contravention to the rules applying to that zone."

Hammarskjold went on to note that Ben Gurion had asked for assurances that Egypt had issued orders to its forces to observe the armistice and then observed: "I have asked for your assurance that you will issue orders to the same effect as promised by the government of Egypt. I regret that so far I have not received such assurances." To counterbalance the one-sided version given by the Israeli letter, Hammarskjold ordered immediate release of a similar Egyptian letter.

In a confidential cable to his executive assistant, Andrew Cordier, Hammarskjold confided that he had heard of Israel's "intense diplomatic activity" in New York. He concluded that "the purpose could only be to establish Israel's innocence in full oblivion of the bombardment of Gaza area and further to humiliate Nasser. The *fedayeen* actions, which, of course, are most reprehensible, were started after creation of an explosive situation in the Arab world by heavy casualties in Gaza and could be considered as an outlet for the very serious tension. The alternative might have been open warfare. This must have been understood on the Israeli side."

Hammarskjold observed that despite Nasser's assurances to halt the raids there was no immediate way to order the *fedayeen* to stop, since the raiders were operating without radios. "Under the circumstances, I have to note that the Israeli government used last night's serious incidents as a way to discredit the assurances given by Nasser. To my very great regret I must note that in these various ways, from Sunday onwards, the Israel government on various points has worked against my efforts. I will not give this attitude any interpretation but register the fact."

Still in Cairo, Hammarskjold cabled Ben Gurion on April 13, attempting to get his assurance that Israel would issue direct orders to its troops to desist from firing scross the frontier and stop other aggressive actions. The secretary-general said he had received such assurances from Egypt and hoped to receive similar ones soon from Ben Gurion. Since Hammarskjold had not yet visited Tel Aviv, Ben Gurion replied that he would rather talk over the issue directly with him, and he apologized for publication of his earlier letter, which he said had been released by "mistake."

Ben Gurion's message was conciliatory in tone and gave Hammarskjold hope for achieving a settlement. But then on April 15, Israel's Independence Day that year, Ben Gurion went on national radio and delivered a highly inflammatory speech calling on Israeli soldiers to deliver "two blows for one." Egypt was planning to "slaughter" Israel, he declared. "It may be that in the ninth year of our renewed independence we shall have to face a supreme test, graver and more difficult than that which we faced successfully eight years ago."

Hammarskjold suspected how little love Ben Gurion had for his mission but he doggedly plodded on, like others before and since him, hoping to accomplish the impossible. Before setting off for Tel Aviv, he decided to write a letter to Ben Gurion, man to man.

He was writing his personal message as "a man with heavy responsibility to a man with even heavier responsibility, and of great experience and courage," Hammarskjold explained. He told Ben Gurion he "felt let down by you" when Israel published the April 12 letter. "It was impossible for me to imagine that publication should have taken place by accident; the seriousness of the matter seemed to exclude any slip and the publication by a delegation, in this form, of such a communication was, in my experience, without precedent.

"For reasons of a very substantive nature, I had concluded that the forces for peace now had the upper hand in Egypt, and that, therefore, it was of vital importance not to counteract, as would be the case if promises given continued to be discredited." It was to set the record straight, he concluded, that he had ordered the text of Egypt's assurances released alongside of Ben Gurion's letter.

The prickly secretary-general also was angered by Foster Dulles. Even before Hammarskjold reached Israel, Dulles said at a press conference that the secretary-general was making good progress in defusing the situation. In a coded message to his assistant Cordier, Hammarskjold complained that such remarks "give rise to strong objections from my part. Neither publicly nor in relation to the representative of any government have I given any appraisal of the results so far. Mr. Dulles gives the impression of being specifically informed, which may strengthen false views of the character of my mission. Please find way to convey in proper form this reaction to [Henry Cabot] Lodge."

As an afterthought, Hammarskjold added: "For the Dulles attitude of finding me I guess naïvely optimistic while putting himself in the position of experienced skepticism, you will understand that I have smiling recognition. Generally speaking, it should be brought home that also on the New York-Washington side it is better the less that is said."

Hammarskjold did not end his mission until May 3, by which time his tireless, persistent efforts paid off, temporarily, in getting Israel and Egypt, Jordan, Lebanon and Syria to reaffirm their observance of the armistices, and for Israel and Egypt to issue strict orders instructing their troops to exercise caution along the frontier. But by then Ben Gurion had more interesting things to consider. He was about to get all the machines of war that he had ever dreamed of. And he intended to use them against Egypt.

• •

Throughout April the question of arms for Israel continued to be a major political headache for the Eisenhower Administration. Ben Gurion and Israel's supporters daily badgered Washington to relent on its arms embargo. Representative Kenneth B. Keating of New York, who years later became ambassador to Israel, was leader of a group of fifty GOP congressmen formed to champion arms for Israel. He warned in the beginning of April that his group planned to study ways to tack specific funds for arms for Israel onto the Administration's foreign aid bill if the Administration did not end its embargo. Adlai Stevenson kept up a tattoo of charges on the campaign trail that Eisenhower and Dulles were being unfair to Israel, as did his contender for the Democratic presidential nomination, Senator Estes Kefauver of Tennessee. In Miami on April 4, Kefauver declared that Washington should tell the world that "we will not sit idly by and see a brave little nation suffer aggression."

Ben Gurion also kept up his incessant demands for arms. On April 22, he declared in the Knesset: "Public opinion and perhaps some governments have realized that the only thing that might deter the Egyptian dictator and his allies from war against Israel is the supply to Israel of sufficient defensive arms in the air, on land and at sea, to enable her to face with confidence any act of deliberate aggression." His mention that "perhaps some governments" recognized Israel's need was a little-noted but pregnant phrase. Israel was on the eve of concluding its historic arms deal with France.

Two days later, after the secret French connection had been cemented, Ben Gurion was still complaining publicly about Israel's need for arms. Some three thousand members of the World Zionist Organization were gathered in Jerusalem to show their support for Israel and, among other things, to marshal world criticism of Washington for refusing arms to Israel. "The United States and Britain still maintain their embargo on Israel although public opinion in those countries largely shares our anxiety as to outbreak of a war deliberately started by the Arab rulers," declared Ben Gurion.

Such propagandizing had its effect. At the height of the tension caused by the Gaza raid and the *fedayeen* attacks, Dulles and Eisenhower privately approved on April 11 the sale of twelve more French Mystère IV jets to Israel. The next day, Dulles said in a telephone call with an aide, "In view of the developments in the Near East, we may want to license for early shipment to Israel some antiaircraft guns and radar which they have applied for."

But still Eisenhower was not ready to take the risks of concluding a full-scale formal arms arrangement with Israel. He feared rightly that such a relationship would inevitably make Washington a partner in Israeli actions and alienate the Arab nations. Despite the political flak from his Democratic opponents, Israel's U.S. supporters and even members of his own party, Ike refused to budge. He made that clear on April 23 when he called Herbert Hoover, Jr., about answering yet another letter from Ben Gurion pleading for arms. "The question of the sale of armaments is a straightforward one," Eisenhower said. "We are not yet persuaded that the most effective role for the U.S. in preserving peace is in shipping of arms."

Hoover observed that "soon we will be involved in negotiations for the Dhahran Airbase—then we will have to sell to the Saudis. How can we do that without getting into trouble with our Israeli friends?" The President had no answer.

Nor did Foster Dulles. He was being attacked brutally in the press for his policies toward the Middle East. During a telephone conversation with Richard Nixon, the vice president asked him how he was taking it. "I trust the articles by Reston have not got through your thick skin," said Nixon.

"Not at all," replied Dulles.

"Let me know if you want anyone attacked," concluded the vice president.

• •

Eisenhower was preoccupied with more than the Middle East that April. The major shifts in leadership and in policies of the Soviet Union continued to puzzle the President. There was by now ample proof that Khrushchev had indeed brought about major changes in the Soviet Union's foreign policy. Since his ascendance, the dramatic destalinization program had begun, the Red Army had been withdrawn from Austria, Tito and the satellites had been promised more freedom, the naval base of Porkkala had been returned to Finland, and efforts were under way to normalize relations with Japan and West Germany.

These were harbingers of a possibly new Soviet Union, but Eisenhower and Dulles were not convinced—and the Washington bureaucracy supported their skepticism. The changes in Soviet strategy were noted in a major report by the National Security Council that winter but were dismissed as merely a change in tactics: "Communist tactics against the free nations shifted in emphasis from reliance on violence and the threat of violence to division, enticement and duplicity." The report concluded that "the U.S.S.R. apparently desires a less tense relationship with the Western powers," but then added the warning that "the Communist powers will maintain, and even increase, efforts to weaken and disrupt free world strength and unity and to extend the area of Communist influence or control."

The remarks were contained in a thirty-six-page document titled "Basic National Security Policy," which outlined not only Washington's perceptions of the world but also America's policy in case of war. "A central aim of U.S. policy must be to deter the Communists from use of their military power," said the document. But if general war did occur, then the United States would unleash its most destructive weapons. "It is the policy of the United States to integrate nuclear weapons with other weapons in the arsenal of the United States," said the policy paper. "Nuclear weapons will be used in general war and in military operations short of general war as authorized by the President. The United States will be prepared to use chemical and bacteriological weapons in general war. The United States will not preclude itself from using nuclear weapons even in a local situation."

Eisenhower signed the report on March 15, making it national policy with the full comprehension of the devastation that would result if America ever had to use its nuclear arsenal. Earlier in the year he had received a report by a special military study group on the damage Russia and America would suffer in a nuclear exchange. "The United States experienced practically total economic collapse, which could not be restored to any kind of operative conditions under six months to a year," he confided to his diary. "Members of the federal government were wiped out and a new government had to be improvised by the states. Casualties were enormous. It was calculated that something on the order of 65 percent of the population would require some kind of medical care, and, in most instances, no opportunity whatsoever to get it. There would be no shipping in and out of our country except some small or improvised vessels for many months. It would literally be a business of digging ourselves out of ashes, starting again."

With that dismal prospect facing him, Eisenhower displayed little satisfaction in his diary notes at the extent of devastation the U.S. could wreak in return on the Soviet Union. "The damage inflicted by us against the Soviets was roughly three times greater," he wrote. "The picture of total destruction of the areas of lethal fall-out, of serious fall-out and of at least some damage from fall-out, was appalling. Under such an attack, it would be completely impossible for Russia to carry a war on further."

Even if the U.S. had a month's warning time, although without specifically knowing the precise date of the attack, the study showed, "there was no significant differences in the losses we would take. It was concluded that there was little we could do during the month of warning in the way of dispersal of populations, of industries, or of perfecting defenses that would cut down losses."

The President could see only one way to prevent such massive losses, and that was by a preventive U.S. attack. But that was unlikely, he concluded. "This would be not only against our traditions, but it would appear to be impossible unless the Congress would meet in a highly secret session and vote a declaration of war which would be implemented before the session was terminated. It would appear to be impossible that any such thing would occur."

• •

The staggering responsibilities to prevent a nuclear holocaust surely helped explain the excessive caution Eisenhower and Dulles displayed in interpreting the changes occurring in the Soviet Union. Thus for his April 3 press conference, Dulles' prepared remarks had a second paragraph that read: "The official repudiation of the last two decades of Stalin's rule seems to be an effort by the present rulers to allay popular dissatisfactions at home and to gain acceptability abroad."

Dulles went on in succeeding paragraphs to question whether the new Soviet leaders were actually changing Stalin's rule or simply blaming discontent inside Russia on the past. "The downgrading of Stalin does not of itself demonstrate that the Soviet regime has basically changed," he declared. In foreign affairs, "they continue predatory policies. They forcibly hold East Germany detached from Germany as a whole. They have not renounced their efforts to subvert free governments. In Asia the present Soviet rulers seek to stir up bitterness, and in the Near East, increase the danger of hostilities. These and other current actions fall far short of the accepted code of international conduct."

Dulles sent his remarks to the White House for presidential review before making them public. Eisenhower returned them with a note suggesting the elimination of the second paragraph because "that paragraph deals with motives, which are always obscure. The rest of the paper deals with facts or valid conclusions from those facts. Otherwise I don't think anyone could challenge it."

Khrushchev and Bulganin were due to arrive in London April 18 on their first journey to a NATO nation, and anticipation was high about how the plain-talking Russians would get on with the protocol-minded leaders of the Tory government. Eden had asked Ike if he had any suggestions to offer about the forthcoming talks and on April 15 Eisenhower sent him a letter cautioning about "the very grave threat in the Middle East. We are, I think, both of us fully alive to what this could do to the well-being and indeed safety of Western Europe, and most particularly the United Kingdom. I fully agree with you that we should not be acquiescent in any measure which would give the Bear's claws a grip on the production or transportation of the oil which is so vital to the defense and economy of the Western world."

Beyond that, Ike added, "I believe your thinking and mine are so close together on the matters that are likely to come up that any suggestions from me would be superfluous."

Eisenhower and Dulles could not bring themselves to believe that Khrushchev and Bulganin represented a truly more flexible and open leadership despite several conspicuous moves by the Soviet leaders apparently aimed at warmer relations with Washington. There had been the Moscow offer of a friendship treaty in January, however gauche its timing, and in March Bulganin generously offered to meet informally with Ambassador Charles Bohlen whenever Bohlen liked. In an "Eyes Only" cable to Dulles and Hoover, Bohlen said Bulganin offered "heart-to-heart talks" without publicity. "He said I could either see him alone or together with Khrushchev at his dacha or any other convenient place. He said he thought it was most important at this juncture that there should be means for informal discussion 'without commitment.' Bulganin made great effort to impress upon me the importance of U.S.-Soviet relations and of the desire of Soviet government to see some genuine improvement in this field. I told him of course the U.S. had friends and allies and I could not go in for bilateral deals, to which he replied that he had not in mind any deals behind backs or at expense of associates."

Bohlen observed that Bulganin's offer "might be an attempt to sow suspicion with our allies, but I am inclined more to believe that Bulganin recognizes need for some method of communication rather than official notes or highly publicized communications. I think it might be useful, if you agree, to bring this message to the attention of the President as I

229

believe almost for the first time since I have been here possibilities of diplomatic action are really opening up.''

The telegram did not convince Eisenhower that the Soviets had changed. He expressed his skepticism about the new Soviet leaders in a long, friendly letter to Winston Churchill on March 29. "The Soviets have gone through a bewildering series of turnabouts and somersaults ranging all the way from the sweet kindness they tried to exude at Geneva to their latest and curious effort to deny that Stalin ever was a true communist. It is amazing that so many people continue to believe, wholly or in part, the propaganda with which the Soviets cover the world.'' As for himself, Eisenhower could see no essential difference in Russia's new leadership, he wrote Churchill, concluding: "With deep and abiding affection from your old friend.''

By mid-April, Churchill answered with a letter filled with sweeping observations. He too found the attack on Stalin extraordinary. "I am sure it is a great blunder which will markedly hamper the Communist movement. It would have been easy to 'play him down' gradually without causing so great a shock to the faithful. Stalin always kept his word with me. I remember particularly saying to him when I visited Moscow in 1940, 'You keep Rumania and Bulgaria in your sphere of influence, but let me have Greece.' To this bargain he scrupulously adhered during the months of fighting with the Greek Communists. I wish I could say the same about the Greeks, whose memories are very short.''

Turning to the Middle East, Churchill expressed confidence that war between Israel and Egypt could be prevented if Washington and London acted in concert. "I am, of course, a Zionist, and have been ever since the Balfour Declaration.* I think it is a wonderful thing that this tiny colony of Jews should have become a refuge to their compatriots in all the lands where they were persecuted so cruelly, and at the same time established themselves as the most effective fighting force in the area. I am sure America would not stand by and see them overwhelmed by Russian weapons, especially if we had persuaded them to hold their hand while their chance remained.''

• •

---

* In 1917 the British government declared "it views with favor the establishment in Palestine of a national home for the Jewish people''; the declaration is a basic document in Israel's legal defense of its right to exist as a nation in Palestine. A rarely cited clause in the declaration adds: "it being clearly understood that nothing shall be done which may prejudice the civil and religious rights of existing non-Jewish communities in Palestine.''

Khrushchev and Bulganin arrived at Portsmouth aboard the cruiser *Ordzhonikidze* on April 18 to a chill and sullen welcome. British crowds booed them or turned their backs, and demonstrating groups of East European exiles were vociferous in their opposition. The Soviet leaders met with the Queen at Windsor Castle, traveled to Oxford and Birmingham, London and Leicester, and held lengthy talks with Eden during a whirlwind ten-day tour that was more notable for its barefisted contentiousness than its diplomatic etiquette.

At a speech in Birmingham, a hostile onlooker shook his fist at Khrushchev, inciting the pudgy, voluble Soviet chairman to shout, "Never shake your fist at a Russian. Is it not time we became more intelligent and stopped shaking fists at each other?" Then Khrushchev boisterously bragged that Russia was "the first to explode an H-bomb from an airplane. I am quite sure that we will have the guided missile with an H-bomb warhead which can land anywhere in the world. Do you think you can prevent us from doing anything? Restrictions of trade do not prevent us in any way making advances in our armaments." Though the theme of his speech was the need to improve relations through greater trade, he sounded threateningly bellicose to the British public in extolling Russia's advances in nuclear weapons.

His foray into the ranks of the Labour Party was even more disastrous. Khrushchev and Bulganin were the guests of party officials in a private dining room in the Houses of Parliament on April 23. Khrushchev immediately got into an embarrassing and bitter clash with feisty trade unionist George Brown, who later became foreign secretary.

"You don't always agree with your father on everything, do you?" Brown asked Khrushchev's studious twenty-two-year-old son.

Young Khrushchev said that he did.

"I have a daughter about your age in the university," bellowed Brown. "She disagrees with me all the time. That's the difference between your country and ours."

When Khrushchev was told by an interpreter the substance of Brown's rude remarks, he bellowed himself: "Interference in family affairs is even worse than interference in another country's internal affairs."

A marked strain descended on the dinner, and it got worse after Khrushchev launched into an hour-long tirade fueled by equal amounts of indignation and alcohol. He charged that France and Britain had turned Hitler eastward toward Russia and broadly implied that it was Russia alone which had defeated the Nazis.

"God forgive you," muttered Brown.

231

"What did you say?" demanded Khrushchev. There was a tense silence. "Don't be afraid. Say it again!"

"God forgive you," declared Brown.

The two red-faced officials broke into an angry exchange about Britain's role in World War II. Khrushchev then continued his speech, lambasting NATO and sneering at Eisenhower's "open skies" disarmament proposal for mutual inspection. "We don't want people walking into our bedroom," said Khrushchev.

Labour leader Hugh Gaitskell was visibly upset and indignant. He concluded the dinner by announcing that no one could imagine such a false account of history as delivered by Khrushchev. When someone proposed a "toast to our next meeting," Khrushchev merely glared. "It is far more difficult to discuss things with your Labour leaders than with the Conservative government of this country," he said.

When he met Brown the next day and the Labour leader offered his hand, Khrushchev turned his back and said, *"Nyet."*

Khrushchev's un-British combination of ebullience and offensive bluntness were guaranteed not to make him popular in Britain, even if the atmosphere had been friendlier. As it was, he and his gray companion Bulganin created more doubt than ever about their true intentions and probably set back relations with the West for years.

The Soviets' relations with the Tory Party were considerably better, a fact that amused conservatives the world over. Only on one point did Eden and Khrushchev come to an angry disagreement and that was over the Middle East. Eden told Khrushchev that "the uninterrupted supply of oil was literally vital to our economy. I must be absolutely blunt about the oil, because we would fight for it."

Khrushchev reacted angrily, noting that a war in the Middle East would be much closer to Russia than Britain. If Eden's statement was a threat, warned Khrushchev, he must reject it. But Eden, who at times displayed an iron streak, refused to back down.

"I repeated," recalled Eden, "that what I had said was that we could not live without oil and that we had no intentions of being strangled to death."

• •

Though it was not mentioned publicly at the time of the Soviets' visit, two episodes far more portentous for East-West relations than Khrushchev's tiff with Brown occurred. Both incidents involved highly risky intelligence operations, one British, one American. Without Eden being aware of it, the SIS secretly sent Royal Navy Commander Lionel ("Buster") Crabb, 46, a wartime frogman hero, into the chill waters of Stokes Bay at Portsmouth to reconnoiter the underside of the warship that had brought Khrushchev and Bulganin to England. The frogman disappeared the day after the Soviets arrived, but this was not announced until April 29, the day after they left. The Admiralty announcement said Crabb had been testing "certain underwater apparatus" when he failed to return from the dive. He was presumed dead.

The Soviet government asked for an explanation from London why secret dives were held next to its warship, and the Foreign Office replied that the trials had been conducted without "any permission whatever." Britain expressed its regret at the incident and Eden, who apparently had not been consulted about the operation, vowed disciplinary action. He took it by secretly firing "C," as the chief of SIS was known.

About a year later the headless body of a man in a frogman's suit washed ashore. The decayed remains were believed to be those of Crabb. A head thought to be his was found on the beach at Portsmouth eleven years later.

The other embarrassing incident occurred at almost the same time as Crabb's disappearance. On April 21, the Communists discovered a 1,476-foot-long tunnel, six and a half feet in diameter, leading directly from East Berlin to an American building replete with roof antennae in West Berlin. The CIA's highly prized—and highly costly: $25 million—listening tunnel into East Germany had finally been uncovered. For eleven months and eleven days the CIA had tapped into the East Berlin telephone system, picking up snippets of intelligence value. Existence of the tunnel was exposed when Communist repairmen accidentally ran across the tap.

The Soviets ballyhooed their discovery, invited the press to tour it and turned it into a tourist attraction. When Allen Dulles informed his brother about the exposure, Foster's first reaction was to suggest that Allen "say maybe some of our people overstepped a bit. Everybody knows intelligence and counterintelligence goes on."

"I told the President," said Allen, "and he was relaxed and understanding about it."

But it was unlikely the new Soviet leaders were relaxed. Within three days while they were on a putative friendship visit to Britain, two intelligence operations against their country had been exposed. It was not a good omen for East-West relations.

• •

Shimon Peres was an ardent believer that Israel's destiny lay with France. He had traveled and lived in America during the late 1940s and early 1950s, negotiating weapons deals and recruiting arms makers and scientists for Israel. But by the mid-50s he had become disillusioned with the Eisenhower Administration's reluctance to open the floodgates to U.S. arms. Ben Gurion had appointed him director-general of the Defense Ministry in 1953, making him the day-to-day arms procurer for Israel's war machine, and thus intimately knowledgeable of the close ties Israel had established with the French military. He concluded the ties could be made even closer.

For months Peres had been secretly traveling to Paris to meet with Abel Thomas to argue Israel's urgent need for increased shipments of weapons from France. On April 23 Peres arrived in Paris, while Hammarskjold was still shuttling between Cairo and Tel Aviv in search of peace, and declared to a concerned Thomas: "Things have so developed that war is inevitable within six months."

Peres quickly painted a somber picture for Thomas. Nasser was anti-French and was helping the Algerian rebels, who were causing such extreme difficulties for Mollet's government, Peres said. Only three weeks earlier Mollet, the socialist pacifist, approved the sending of yet 100,000 more troops to Algeria, bringing the total there to 330,000 at an annual cost of $600 million. New taxes would have to be found. Thomas and the members of the Mollet government hardly needed to be warned about the evils of Nasser.

But there was more, Peres continued. He claimed that Egypt had wanted to attack Israel five times in the past months but had been prevented because it had not yet absorbed its new weapons from the Soviet bloc. "They're not totally ready yet, but you can believe that when they are, Nasser will certainly start his religious war in a blitz against Israel. His Russian bombers can obliterate our towns. With an Egyptian victory, Nasser would try to create his Pan-Arab nation.

"He will be the guide, the fuehrer, the duce, the caudillo of this great nation," declared Peres. He developed his bleak picture of the world by asserting that the Eisenhower Administration, involved in an election campaign, was vulnerable to pressures from the pro-Arab oil lobby, thereby lacerating the suspicions that Thomas shared with many Frenchmen that the U.S. oil companies were financing the Algerian rebels in hopes of taking over concessions to the country's oil after a rebel victory.

Britain was too weak to oppose the Arabs or U.S. policy in the region, Peres said. The Anglo-Saxons refused Israel arms while Russia was giving mountains of weapons to Egypt.

"In short," said Peres, "we have decided not to run the risk of a defensive war, which will inevitably lead us to defeat and extermination. We are practically resigned to unleash a preventive offensive."

That might sound extreme, Peres added, but remember World War II. "Jews allowed themselves to be exterminated. If each one had killed his captor, the Jews would not have been reduced to slaughterhouse cattle.

"This time we have decided to fight."

Abel Thomas was so impressed that he went to see Defense Minister Bourgès the same day and urged him to meet with Mollet and request his permission to significantly increase France's arms sales to Israel. Bourgès agreed. He was the strong man in the Cabinet, the grand-nephew of Marshal Maunoury, had served valiantly as one of de Gaulle's representatives to the Resistance during the war and since 1945 had been a fixture in the revolving Cabinets of the Fourth Republic. At forty-two, he had a reputation for personal bravery and administrative skills, and his word carried considerable weight with Mollet. After hearing him out, the prime minister gave his blessing to Bourgès' proposal.

The next day Peres slipped unnoticed through a side door into Thomas' office and heard the good news. France's already "vast arms supply would be enlarged," Thomas promised. Israel could have practically anything in the French armory.

Peres had a list ready. It sought 110 more Mystère IV's, thirty-six other less advanced combat planes, one hundred tanks, forty self-propelled 105mm howitzers and other smaller arms. Thomas saw no difficulties in providing the armaments. The only questions left to discuss were those involving how to deliver such massive amounts of weaponry secretly.

France had previously funneled most of its arms to Israel through the offices of the Near East Arms Committee, which had been set up to monitor the arms balance in the Middle East after Britain, France and America had signed the Tripartite Declaration of 1950 to prevent an arms race in the region. Peres complained that the committee allowed Washington to monitor France's arms sales to Israel and in effect wield a veto over their shipments.

Thomas immediately recommended that they bypass the committee. He also would bypass the Quai d'Orsay. The Foreign Ministry's professional diplomats traditionally viewed France's interests as lying with the

Arabs and their oil; in the past they had opposed arms sales to Israel. Now they would be left out of the new connection. Both Mollet and Pineau gave their blessing to the arrangements.

A formal liaison office was established with Thomas and Peres at its head. A French general was put in charge of processing the Israeli orders with French manufacturers and the army quartermaster, as well as overseeing their clandestine shipment to Israel. To protect the secret, false invoices were made out assigning the shipments to such countries as Panama or Nicaragua. But in fact as soon as they were loaded aboard French military ships, another device to ensure secrecy, they were sent directly to Israeli ports.

"This was a definite turn in the policy of the French government to be rid of interference by the United States in our affairs in the Middle East," recalled Thomas.

From now until the crisis at Suez six months later—Peres' prediction for the timing of war was exact—French armaments began flowing in massive amounts to Israel and there was a constant succession of secret meetings as officials of the two countries traveled back and forth deepening their clandestine relationship. Israel and France were well on their way to one of the most extraordinary secret collusions in modern times.

CHAPTER XII

Nasser Soon Must Take Vigorous Steps

BYROADE

FORMALIZATION OF THE SECRET ARMS ALLIANCE between Israel and France brought a sudden hush to Tel Aviv's loud demands for U.S. weapons. Since the previous October the requests had been dominating every issue between America and Israel. Democrats and Republicans alike had taken up the theme, injecting it like a leitmotif into the winter campaign season. Now in May suddenly all was quiet. Though Israel's French connection remained a closely guarded secret, the subject of arms for the Jewish state had miraculously vanished.

The change was so sudden, and so welcome, that Dulles could not help noticing it. In a note to the President on May 22, the secretary of state observed, "It is, I think, significant that at my press conference today, as at my press conference a week ago, no questions were asked with reference to 'arms for Israel.' We are, of course, ourselves licensing minor items of munitions, spare parts, etc., for shipment to Israel and will probably step this up somewhat in connection with our program for arms to Saudi Arabia in connection with the negotiation of the new air base agreement." He added that Israel Ambassador Abba Eban "was satisfied with the way our policy was developing and that they were, in fact, getting from one source or another the arms which they felt they needed."

While the letup of political pressure was appreciated, Dulles could not have been happy had he known the reason why it had occurred. Certainly he had no reason to suspect the secret French connection since Paris had informed Washington of the Mystère sales—though of only some of them, but Dulles did not know that—and presumably could be counted on to give notification of sales of other armaments. Only two weeks earlier, Christian Pineau had assured him at a foreign ministers' meeting of NATO in Paris that the United States would be informed of any new French arms shipments to Israel. When Abel Thomas, concerned that Pineau was going to renege on the Israeli deal, questioned him privately later, the foreign minister grandly replied, "In reality, I will do what pleases me—that is to say, to do what we have agreed to do." The sending of massive amounts of weapons to Israel would remain France's secret.

The muting of Israel's arms demands was accompanied by a rare period of relative tranquility around the inflamed frontiers of the Jewish state. For the first time in ten months, since the vicious exchanges of fire around El Auja culminated in the massacres of Arabs at El Sabha (fifty killed), Syria (fifty-six killed) and Gaza (sixty-two killed), the Middle East was quiescent. It was the silence before the whirlwind.

• •

David Ben Gurion had been denied the war he wanted the previous December by the opposition of moderate Moshe Sharett and the foreign minister's supporters in the Cabinet. He was determined not to be denied his war again. Now things were different. The tensions of the winter and spring had turned a majority of the ruling Labor Party hawkish. Menachem Begin and his minority Herut Party were in full cry for a preventive war. The French connection gave Israel access to all the modern weaponry it needed to crush the Egyptian Army before it could absorb its new Czech arms. All that was needed now was to clean the slate of political opposition, and that meant the elimination of Sharett.

Though he had conducted the foreign affairs of Israel for a quarter of a century before and after its founding, Sharett was vulnerable. In Israel's increasing impatience and bellicosity, Sharett was being viewed as too temperate and too obsequious toward world opinion. His futile quest the previous November and December for arms from the great powers, hat in hand, in Geneva and Washington, was too close to the image of the meek and submissive victims of Hitler's crematoria that robust Israelis were determined to change. Though it was Ben Gurion's Syrian raid of December 11 that had doomed Sharett's chances of obtaining U.S. arms during his Washington visit, a vicious whisper campaign since then blamed him for failing because of ineptness and weakness.

His relations with Ben Gurion, his old colleague, had reached the point of open hostility and public comment. "Far from having grown together like partners in a marriage, they had become almost physically unable to bear the sight of each other," observed Abba Eban. "Ben Gurion thought that Sharett was verbose, pedantic, finicky and inclined to confuse the vital with the incidental, the primary with the secondary. Sharett, with all his admiration for Ben Gurion, considered him demagogic, tryannical, opinionated, devious, and on some occasions, not quite rational."

Sharett's fall from power came suddenly and in a surprising way. During a meeting in Ben Gurion's home in late May to discuss the selection of a new secretary-general of the Mapai Party, various names were being mentioned when Sharett jokingly said, "Well, perhaps I should become the secretary of the party."

"Everyone laughed," recalled Golda Meir, "except Ben Gurion, who jumped at Sharett's little joke."

"Marvelous," exclaimed Ben Gurion. "A wonderful idea. It will save Mapai."

There was absolutely no likelihood that Sharett would take the Mapai position and Ben Gurion's outburst clearly signaled his desire to be rid of Sharett. As the days passed, the idea took hold that Sharett's tenure at the Foreign Ministry was over. Almost spontaneously, his support evaporated and the unthinkable was not only thinkable but inevitable; he had to resign. Ben Gurion made that plain in a private talk with him on June 12 when the prime minister declared that one or the other of them had to go. When faced with that choice, the party leadership backed Ben Gurion.

Cairo Radio, in its regular Hebrew broadcasts, pleaded with Israelis to support Sharett. "The Arab countries and the nations of the world are interested in seeing that the person responsible for Israel's foreign policy is moderate, quiet, normal—a person who tackles matters with wisdom." By contrast, it declared, "Ben Gurion believes that what happened in 1948 is also possible today." It was a bitter commentary on his years of work that Sharett was ending his official position with an endorsement from the Arabs. In the hothouse atmosphere of Israel, where everything Arab was suspect, nothing could have been more damaging for the forlorn foreign minister.

At a Cabinet meeting on June 18, Sharett tendered his resignation. It was accepted without protest. "They all sat in silence," he recorded in his diary. "None of my colleagues raised his head to look at me. No one got up to shake my hand, despite everything. It was as if all their mental capacities were paralyzed, as if the freedom of expression was taken away from their hearts and the freedom of independent action from their consciences. They sat heavy and staring in their silence. Thus I crossed in measured steps the whole length of the meeting room, and thus I left."

Outside on the street, alone and shorn of office, Sharett waved away his official car and walked home to prepare his resignation speech for the Knesset session later that day. As usual, his speech was mild and contained only one modest revelation. He disclosed almost apologetically that he had asked Ben Gurion not to include him in the Cabinet because "I had well-founded reasons for fearing that this time cooperation between my comrade David Ben Gurion as premier and myself as foreign minister would not be successful." At age sixty-one Sharett's service to Israel was finished. Never again would he play an official role.

"The reason B-G forced my resignation was because he felt that I was an impediment to his policy in a situation in which he had decided there was going to be a war with Egypt within a very short time," Sharett later explained. "War was coming and B-G wanted me out of the way."

Ben Gurion followed Sharett in the Knesset debate the next day. "Recently the state's security situation became unusually grave. I reached the conclusion that in these circumstances the interests of the state required full coordination between the Foreign Ministry and the Ministry of Defense and that a different direction of the Foreign Ministry was now necessary.

"We shall not start a war in which it would be certain or even probable that we would have to fight British, Soviet or U.S. forces. Like all of you, I assisted in the establishment of the state of Israel. I shall not assist in its destruction. On the other hand, I shall not hesitate for a moment to mobilize the full strength of Israel's armed forces against every attacker, whether from Egypt, Jordan, Syria, Saudi Arabia or all those countries together without being afraid of the outcome of this contest. We must be prepared for attempts by great powers to dictate a settlement. We must muster all our strength so that we can say *no* to the greatest powers in the world."

In Sharett's place Ben Gurion appointed a person more attuned to his aggressive policies, Golda Meir, then known as Golda Meyerson. Born in Russia and raised in Milwaukee after the age of eight, she emigrated to Israel in 1921 at the age of twenty-three and worked as a farm laborer until she climbed her way up the ladder of the Labor Party. In 1948, she was appointed Israel's first ambassador to the Soviet Union after Russia became the second nation behind America to recognize the new Jewish state. She joined Ben Gurion's Cabinet in 1949 as minister of labor and social insurance, and since then had held various jobs, including acting foreign minister while Sharett was out of the country.

Now fifty-eight, she resembled Ben Gurion in many ways. She was fiery and dedicated, a born political infighter, a woman of ideals and vision, except when it came to Arabs. The U.N.'s General Burns dealt frequently with Golda Meir in her new position and found her to be "a dedicated Zionist, a person who seemed selflessly devoted to the cause she served. It was impossible not to respect her, even to like her, although one very much disliked the policies she was defending. One could say that she believed honestly in what she advocated, in the complete justice of the Israeli position. But, conversely, she seemed to me to suffer from a complete inability to see that there was anything to be said for the Arab case."

Ben Gurion had been wise in his choice of Sharett's successor. From Golda Meir, he could expect total commitment and all the support he needed for his plan to wage war with Egypt. He wasted no time in forging ahead.

• •

The day before Sharett had proffered his expected resignation to the Cabinet, a French Nord aircraft took off from Israel with Ben Gurion's two young fire-eating protégés, Moshe Dayan and Shimon Peres, aboard. They were flying secretly to France to strengthen Israel's relations with proposals for joint Franco-Israeli operations against the Arabs. The mission was called Diaspora II.

The Nord landed outside Paris and the Israelis, using false names for the airport authorities, traveled to a private home in Chantilly where they met with Abel Thomas and other French officials. Dayan, as chief of staff, headed the Israeli delegation. The purpose of the meeting was to formalize the agreement Peres and Thomas had come to in April, but Dayan tried to take the discussion further. After repeating Israel's determination not to follow the tragic example of World War II Jews, he suggested that in return for French arms Israel join France in special operations in the Middle East. Israel was intimately acquainted with the wadis and wastes of the region, he said, and Israeli troops could be of valuable assistance to French commandos. The French, who were at the meeting merely to sign the contract cementing the new relationship, demurred from pursuing this dangerous new course. "We had the suspicion that the Israelis wanted to draw us beyond the scope of the discussion," recalled Thomas. The French officials said, to the surprise of the Israelis, that they expected nothing in return from Israel for the weapons, neither money nor joint operations.

Colonel Louis Mangin, temperamental son of a famous general and one of Defense Minister Bourgès-Maunoury's aides, reassured Dayan after the meeting that more than the shipment of arms could be expected to result from the secret alliance between the two countries. "We will be brought to common enterprises going well beyond what we have envisioned in this conference," Mangin predicted with accuracy.

• •

Momentous events were taking place in Egypt too. For the first time since the Persian invasion in 525 B.C., Egyptian soil was finally free of foreign troops. It was an emotional, historic moment. Exuberant, celebrating crowds swarmed about Nasser, kissing and hugging him, as he made his way to Port Said's Navy House on the same day that Sharett resigned. With tears in his eyes he hoisted the green Egyptian flag where the British Union Jack had flown for the past seventy-four years. The last of Britain's eighty thousand troops had departed quietly five days earlier to beat the June 18 deadline set by the withdrawal agreement signed two years earlier. "We didn't want an Egyptian brass band seeing us off," admitted a departing British officer.

Nasser, dressed in his military uniform, was exultant. "This generation of Egyptian people has an appointment with destiny, privileged to see with its own eyes the remnants of the foreign invaders sneak out, back to where they came from. Oh, compatriots, this is the moment of a lifetime. Victory has come from God. Egypt today is no longer for the occupiers, the usurpers, or the oppressors. Today, oh, brethren, Egypt exists for its children.

"We have dreamed of this moment which had been denied our fathers, grandfathers and our brothers who have fought for years to achieve this moment and to see the Egyptian flag alone in our skies. Citizens, we pray God no other flag will ever fly over our land.

"Our policy is frank. We shall cooperate with anybody or any country ready to cooperate with us to build our country economically and in all fields. We shall not tolerate being a zone of influence for anyone. We must become strong so that all Arabism's lands from Morocco to Baghdad will be for the Arabs and not for the occupiers or the exploiters, so that we can retrieve for the people of Palestine their right to freedom and existence."

Nasser acknowledged that Britain had "fulfilled her obligations" by withdrawing as promised and vowed that Egypt had "no aggressive intentions toward her." He held out a hand of friendship to his former colonial masters in a newspaper interview with W. N. Ewer of the London *Daily Herald*. "I have told my own people that in thinking of Britain they should no longer think about the past," he said. "A new chapter has begun. But allow me to say that it takes two to make a friendship; and that there are some newspapers and some politicians in Britain who are anything but helpful." Ewer concluded his story by remarking that there could be no doubt about Nasser's sincerity in seeking friendship with Britain.

In England the mood was different. Selwyn Lloyd publicly expressed surprise that Britain's withdrawal had not brought an improvement of relations between the two countries. "There are no actual disputes or conflicts between Great Britain and Egypt which justify the present lack of confidence between the two countries," Lloyd averred. What he left unsaid was that Anthony Eden's unrelenting hatred of Nasser since Glubb Pasha's expulsion had caused England to reject every overture by Egypt for improved relations. The lack of confidence was not caused by disputes or conflicts; it was the result of Eden's enmity, which Lloyd fully shared.

But all that seemed remote in Cairo during the joyous celebrations commemorating the departure of the British troops. For three days Egyptians indulged in an orgy of celebrations. Loudspeakers blared patriotic songs, streets were bright with flowers and strings of light, and at night fireworks decorated the sky. Special coins had been struck showing a woman in the garb of ancient Egypt breaking her chains. Delirium reigned.

Nasser announced the end of martial law, which had been in effect since the 1952 coup. He abolished censorship of the press, freed two thousand political prisoners, promised dissolution of the Revolutionary Command Council, which had been running the country, and announced a new constitution.

The celebrations included a massive display of Egypt's new armaments. Rumbling through Cairo's streets were one hundred Russian armored troop carriers, thirty-two Czech antitank guns, seventy-five Russian medium tanks and twenty-eight heavy tanks, as well as British and French equipment. Overhead flew Soviet MiGs and British Vampires and Meteors.

The jubilant Egyptian people had much to celebrate, and much to thank their thirty-eight-year-old leader for. Nasser had deposed a corrupt mon-

243

arch, broken the feudal aristocracy's political dominance, squashed the fanatical Moslem Brotherhood, rid the country of foreign troops, shattered the West's monopoly stranglehold by opening trade with the Communist bloc, and given the country the arms to protect itself.

Perhaps most important, many Egyptians felt Nasser had provided them with a sense of pride after millennia of shame. He had accomplished this not only by ridding the country of foreign sway but by making Egypt a respected member of the Third World, a neutralist nation determinedly treading its independent course between the superpowers and increasingly out of reach of the old colonialists. In the process, Nasser himself had become a statesman of international stature and a respected Arab spokesman. To his friends he was becoming the greatest Arab leader of his time; to his enemies, the greatest threat.

Despite his accomplishments, much still needed to be done. Egypt remained desperately poor, among the most impoverished of the world's nations. As president, Nasser vowed that he would concentrate in the years ahead on improving the standard of living for the miserable *fellahin,* the impoverished farmers who eked out a hand-to-mouth existence along the banks of the Nile. The mighty river, more than any force in their lives, held vast numbers of hungry Egyptians captive to a precarious existence. They were dependent on its ebbs and flows for the rich soils that nourished their crops and fed their families, for the few extra pennies that meant the difference between shivering in the chill desert night or being covered by a rough blanket.

Nasser's dreams for improving their lot continued to center on the Aswan High Dam. But the negotiations were still dragging on without resolution. At first the sticking point was the World Bank's insistence on disclosure of basic economic data about the country, a standard procedure for the bank but one which Nasser in his suspicion of foreign entanglements feared might be a device for the Western powers to return to dominate his country by controlling its economy, much as the British had done in the nineteenth century.

Eugene R. Black, president of the bank, had been negotiating seriously with Nasser since December and was enthusiastic about the project. By spring he had overcome most of the Egyptian leader's suspicions. After meeting with Nasser on June 21 he reported that his organization was "fully prepared to finance [the bank's share of] the High Dam." But there was no answering echo in Washington.

Nasser was getting impatient and suspicious. Public criticism of the long delay in coming to an agreement to finance the dam was mounting and exerting heavy domestic pressure on him. "Nasser soon must take vigorous steps to meet domestic problems with the High Dam as primary effort," warned Ambassador Hank Byroade in a long cable June 16 to Dulles. He reported that Egyptian Ambassador Ahmed Hussein told him the day before that Nasser was "now convinced we would not follow through on the High Dam. He sees hesitations and delay for what he considers policy purposes. He undoubtedly connects with our disillusionment to move in manner we desired on Israeli settlement [during the Anderson mission]." Byroade concluded with a warning. "We know Nasser wishes to work with the West on this project but if there continues to be no response at all department should not be surprised if some day it reads in press that decision has been made to accept Russian assistance."

• •

As spring wore on, Washington's attention alternated between the Middle East and the Soviet Union. Truly momentous events were unequivocally sweeping the Communist world. On May 14, the Soviet Union announced it was cutting its armed forces by 1.2 million men and issued a strong call for the East and West to reach an overall disarmament accord. Dulles promptly put the worst motive on the Soviet move by noting publicly that "the obvious explanation is a need for greater manpower in industry and agriculture. There is nothing to prevent the speedy recall and equipping of large units of thoroughly trained reserves." The United States, he added, would not make any troop reductions "merely as a counterpropaganda move."

But within a few days the CIA came into possession of a document so explosive that it blew away even the dour Dulles' skepticism. It was a 26,000-word text of Khrushchev's secret speech denouncing Stalin at the Twentieth Communist Party Congress the previous February. Rumors of the anti-Stalin speech had begun circulating shortly after Khrushchev delivered it, and Allen Dulles had cabled all CIA stations that it was the agency's highest priority to obtain a copy of the speech.

The British SIS and other intelligence agencies were also frantically seeking a copy of Khrushchev's dramatic revelations. In the end it was Israel's tiny but effective Mossad that accomplished the feat. Details of the operation remain secret but the indications are that a Mossad agent managed to buy the speech from a young Polish diplomat for $5,000. It was a triumph for Mossad, and its pudgy chief, Isser Harel, a legendary spymaster, was sorely tempted to brag about his service's coup by re-

245

leasing the speech in Israel. But in the end he was deterred by the fear that Russia might react by taking revenge on its Jewish citizens. He decided on a far shrewder course. He flew to Washington where he met the trusted Jim Angleton and offered the CIA operative a highly unusual deal. In return for the coveted speech, Israel wanted not money but something more important: a formal agreement to swap intelligence between the CIA and Mossad on the Arab world.

The deal was accepted immediately by Allen Dulles, who was aware of how anxiously his brother and the president wanted the text of the speech with its damning denunciation of Stalin's rule. It was a portentous arrangement. It tied the two intelligence agencies into a formal collaboration, which could only exacerbate Arab suspicions about the sincerity of American evenhandedness in the Middle East, and it provided the Mossad with a unique opportunity to influence U.S. perceptions of the Arab-Israel conflict by giving it the ability to choose what information or disinformation to feed into the United States' most sensitive and vital intelligence center. The price may have seemed justified in the heat of the moment, but the leverage it offered Israel to mold U.S. attitudes was disquieting to many in the intelligence community. When William Colby became the director of the CIA in 1973 he finally fired Angleton, partly as a result of the unusual partiality Angleton had displayed over the years toward Israel.

The Khrushchev speech was handed over to CIA experts for authentication in late May and by June 4 the full text was released by the State Department. The extraordinary speech received headline treatment around the world, as Eisenhower and Dulles had expected. In it, Khrushchev, with obvious emotion, had denounced Stalin's tyrannical rule, accused him of self-glorification and the wanton murder of his enemies. He blamed Stalin for having deviated from the tenets of Marx and Lenin and condemned the cruelty of the secret police. He called for greater individual liberty, open debate and liberalization of the government to encourage the intellectual and artistic life.

It was a stunningly bold break with the past. Khrushchev was in effect admitting to communists the world over that Soviet leadership for the past generation had been severely tainted. It was a courageous move, but fraught with danger, as Khrushchev was well aware. During the speech he implored the delegates to keep its contents secret. "We cannot let this matter get out of the party, especially not to the press. It is for this reason that we are considering it here at a closed Congress session. We should not give ammunition to the enemy; we should not wash our dirty linen before their eyes.''

Distribution of the speech by the CIA signaled the end of Moscow's monolithic control of Communist parties outside of Russia. Italian Communist Party leader Palmiro Togliatti described the new relationship by noting that ''the Soviet model cannot and must not any longer be obligatory. The whole system becomes polycentric.'' Less than a decade earlier Marshal Tito of Yugoslavia had created shock waves by declaring himself independent of Moscow; now Khrushchev and Bulganin were traveling to Belgrade to apologize for Stalin's efforts to make him subservient. The revelation caused winds of change to sweep East Europe, creating restlessness in satellites like Poland and Hungary to share in Moscow's new liberalizing mood.

Even Eisenhower was finally becoming convinced by the gathering evidence that basic changes were occurring in the Soviet Union. In a meeting with Hoover, Allen Dulles, Radford and Air Force Chief of Staff General Nathan F. Twining on May 28, he remarked that he ''wanted to give the Soviets every chance to move in peaceful directions and to put our relations on a better basis and see how far they will go. For this reason it is particularly desirable to be wise and careful what we do.''

Twining had been invited to visit Moscow for the Soviet Aviation Day ceremonies and Eisenhower said he saw no reason why he should not attend. Radford remembered that at Geneva the previous year Khrushchev had laughingly told him that ''the Soviets might send their chiefs over to look at U.S. war plans. I told him that might be all right if it is fifty-fifty.''

The President told Twining that he could tell the Soviets that ''if they want to trade military visits and go around and really see what the other country has in a military sense, they might invite our chiefs. They would be prepared to visit the Soviet Union providing the Soviets were willing to have their chiefs visit us.''

At the end of the conference, Eisenhower reiterated his interest in discovering how much Russia's policies had changed. ''I am very anxious to see how far the Soviets are ready to go in making offers and working for relationships,'' he said.

But U.S. suspicions of Russia were too great to be easily quieted. Ike's pacifying remarks were made at a meeting that was mainly devoted to discussion of the launching of an aggressive new spy effort against the Soviet Union. The highly secret U-2 spy plane had just been developed and CIA-employed pilots had finished training to fly the slim, long-winged craft. It was the most advanced photoreconnaissance plane in existence, capable of flying at extended periods at the edge of the atmosphere and over enormous distances. In May there were four U-2's, six pilots and two hundred support personnel at a U.S. base in Wiesbaden, West Germany. They were standing by ready to inaugurate the hush-hush program over Soviet airspace.

Eisenhower gave the fateful order to proceed.

• •

Once again, in the midst of momentous events abroad, Dwight Eisenhower was stricken by sudden illness. This time his recovery was quick, but for a weekend the nation held its breath as the president went under the surgeon's knife, fueling intense speculation whether the old soldier was fit to complete his term, much less campaign for a second one.

The attack came at the end of a particularly busy day for the President. He had begun that Thursday, June 7, at 9 A.M. by presiding at the weekly meeting of the National Security Council, attended by thirty-four of the Administration's top officials, and then spent a crowded day in his office. He had fifteen appointments during the day and took out an hour and thirty-five minutes for lunch and another twenty minutes in the late afternoon for a bit of golfing practice on the South Lawn. In the evening he attended the White House News Photographers Association annual dinner at the Sheraton-Park Hotel where he sipped a couple of Scotches, ate a small filet mignon and rocked with laughter at the barbed jokes of comedian Bob Hope. By 11 P.M. he was back in the White House when the trouble began.

Shortly after midnight, his wife Mamie found him tossing and turning, unable to sleep because of a stomachache. It was frighteningly reminiscent of his heart attack eight months before, and as she did then, she telephoned presidential physician General Howard McCrum Snyder in his Connecticut Avenue apartment. The doctor advised her not to worry. Ike had a history of stomach complaints. He suggested she give the President a bit of milk of magnesia and go back to sleep.

By 1 A.M. Mamie was on the phone again. The President seemed worse and Snyder better come over. The physician spent the rest of the night sitting by Eisenhower's bed, once administering dextrose to build up his strength. The President slept only fitfully, and when he awoke in the morning he said he felt generally lousy. Several times during the morning he vomited.

News of the President's indisposition crackled across the country. Press secretary James Hagerty was at a loss at what to tell the clamoring press since no diagnosis had yet been made of Ike's ailment. But he did try to assuage the one fear shared by all. "There is nothing wrong with his heart," Hagerty assured the country. The President was suffering a digestive upset, he added. But then a digestive upset had been the first description of Ike's heart attack in Denver the previous September. The country was anxious and tense.

Shortly before noon, Snyder called in Dr. Francis Pruitt, chief of medicine at Walter Reed Hospital. The two men soon determined that Eisenhower's upset was more than a bellyache. It was an attack of ileitis; about ten inches of his small intestine was inflamed. Hagerty announced in his second of many medical bulletins that day that the President "is being taken to Walter Reed Hospital this afternoon. There is no indication of any heart trouble." Shortly after 1 P.M. the President was carried from the White House on a stretcher and taken to the hospital in an ambulance escorted by three motorcycles.

The suspense wore on. Hagerty issued regular bulletins to an expectant nation, finally announcing that at midnight the consulting doctors would meet to decide what must be done to save the President. It had been determined that the ileum was obstructed; if it was not soon unblocked gangrene could set in. "This will cause death," said physician General Leonard Heaton, the commanding officer of Walter Reed. The announcement sent a shock through the country.

It was after 2 A.M. Saturday morning when a worn and grim-faced Hagerty announced to a waiting world that the physicians had decided to undertake an "exploratory operation" immediately. The operation lasted just short of two hours. Dr. Paul Dudley White, the heart specialist who had attended Eisenhower in Denver, stood by in the operating room to monitor the functioning of the President's heart. The nation waited. Finally, at 5 A.M., the tired press secretary was able to state that the operation had removed the intestinal obstruction and the President's condition was satisfactory.

While Ike slept through the day, General Heaton, who performed the operation, briefed the press and was asked the inevitable question. Did he think that Eisenhower should decline to run for re-election because of his physical condition? "I certainly do not," snapped the surgeon. Ike felt the same way. He never gave the idea a thought, he later said. Within a day of the operation, he was out of bed and in three weeks he was out of the hospital and ensconced in his farm in Gettysburg. He and Mamie celebrated their fortieth wedding anniversary there on July 1 with a few friends.

"The first days after the operation were really uncomfortable," Ike wrote Swede Hazlett. "[But] now that I am here and can detect a daily increase in strength and vitality, I am ready to put the whole nasty business behind me. The farm has never looked better and I have been happily renewing my acquaintance with my tiny Angus herd. Official business, a small amount of 'farming,' and a strict regime of treatment, mild exercise and rest, more than occupy my days."

It was while surrounded by such bucolic serenity that Eisenhower waited for the execution of his order to begin the highly risky U-2 flights over the territory of the Soviet Union. On the day the flights started, the President toured his well-tended farm and several times stopped at his practice green for a little putting. He had no official appointments. It was a quiet, tranquil day in Gettysburg.

· ·

U-2 operations began against the Soviet Union by coincidence on July 4. None of the participants seemed to note the irony that on the birthday of what many Americans considered the West's most idealistic democracy Washington was launching the greatest spy effort in its history. Eisenhower, while approving the flights, was highly concerned since their route took the U-2's completely across western Russia, the whole way from West Germany to Norway. Flying at eighty thousand feet, the U-2's photographed 120-mile swaths of Russian territory in clear violation of that country's airspace and its sovereignty.

Eisenhower worried over what "if they were to do this to us?" He insisted that the first series of flights be limited to ten days so that their results could be evaluated against their severe risks.

Soviet radar immediately detected the flights, some of which went directly over Moscow and Leningrad, and on July 10 Russia strongly protested in a note to Washington and brought the matter before the Security Council. The Soviet note declared that the flights were endangering the cause of international peace. "It must be underscored that these gross violations of the airspace of the Soviet Union took place at a time when, as a result of the efforts of the Soviet Union and other peace-loving governments, a definite lessening of international tensions had been achieved, when relations between governments are improving, and when mutual confidence between them is growing. The Soviet Union considers this violation as an intentional act of certain circles in the

United States, planned to aggravate relations between the Soviet Union and the United States of America."

The Soviet note demanded that America "punish those guilty"—a rather futile request since it was the President himself who had approved the operations.

The contrary occurred. After a brief pause during which it was determined that the photographs returned by the initial U-2 flights were of stunning quality and judged to be of intelligence value—and that the planes could operate safely beyond the range of Soviet missiles—the flights were resumed as a highly heralded intelligence coup. In spite of the aggravation they caused the impotent Russians, the flights continued for four years, soaring high above the reach of Soviet missiles, until Russia finally shot down Gary Powers' U-2 in May 1960. The highly publicized incident soured the atmosphere of a summit meeting between Eisenhower, Harold Macmillan, Khrushchev, and Charles de Gaulle that was to have helped improve East-West relations.

To the end, the U-2 flights jinxed relations between Moscow and Washington, sowing suspicions and discord. They provided ammunition to unregenerate Stalinists in the Kremlin to challenge Khrushchev's new policies, and they diverted attention away from areas of potential cooperation between the superpowers. But so suspicious was Washington of Soviet intentions and so alluring was the demonstration of technical superiority to Washington that it seemed predestined to spy on Russia even at the cost of ruining Khrushchev's attempt to be friendly. The arrogance of technology, egged on by the schoolboy enthusiasms of the nation's burgeoning intelligence agency, prevailed over caution and a decent regard for peace.

The mischief of the spy boys took a toll far greater than any conceivable advantage their convoluted plots could provide. The Russians were no innocents in the corrupting back-street world of espionage, of course, but the exposure of this third major Western intelligence operation within a period of three months must have seemed to Moscow suspiciously like a calculated Western slap at Khrushchev.

• •

As the U-2's silently, untouchably winged their way across Soviet territory, there unfolded a more immediate and serious challenge to Khrushchev's destalinization policy. Workers in the Polish industrial city of Poznań demonstrated on June 28, tanks were called in, and soon there were riots and shooting. Before the one-day uprising was quelled, 48 persons had been killed and 270 wounded. All through July the Kremlin watched nervously as the Communist regime in Poland fired officials, instituted reforms and set about trying to pacify the workers.

To his critics, it appeared that Russia was not profiting from Khrushchev's liberalizing policies; all that the Soviets seemed to get in return were spy plots from the West and a workers' riot in the East. There had been positive gains, of course, such as Russia's penetration of the Middle East and India and its improved relations with Yugoslavia's Tito, but overall it was not a happy beginning for the Soviet leader's policy of peaceful competition with the West and relaxed relations with the satellite nations.

Khrushchev was leaving himself open to charges of being too soft, an accusation that no modern leader can long endure and survive in power. The time was fast approaching when Khrushchev would have to show that he too could play hardball.

CHAPTER XIII

Weaken Nasser

EISENHOWER

THOUGH THEY ADOPTED a highly moral tone in public, Dwight Eisenhower and his secretary of state did not lack in appreciation of the rougher aspects of diplomacy. Both were keenly aware how the Aswan High Dam negotiations could be used with devastating effect against Nasser. By stalling, as they had been doing since March when they secretly decided that Nasser should be weakened, they demonstrated that Nasser could not always have his own way. By withdrawing the dam offer, they could forcefully show his impotency in dealing with the West.

From Washington's viewpoint, Nasser had become too successful, his prestige too high and his policies too independent. He represented basic policy differences with the West. He had opened the Middle East to penetration by the Soviet Union. Then he had committed an unpardonable act. On May 16, he recognized Communist China, the nation that Washington insisted on keeping out of the assemblies of the United Nations and with which it boycotted all trade. Washington feared that Saudi Arabia, Syria and Yemen would soon follow. It was the final affront. Whatever lingering support Nasser retained in Washington now evaporated.

Foster Dulles wasted no time in protesting the Egyptian move. He summoned to his office Ambassador Hussein the day after the announcement and harshly complained. "You can appreciate the efforts of the President and myself in withstanding the extraordinarily hard pressures to support Israel against Egypt," Dulles said. "However, the only consequence of our stands seems to be that, in addition to alienating the Zionists and Israel, Egypt is turning against the United States. The latest example is the recognition of Communist China. Nasser must be aware of the tremendous pressures from Zionist groups which are increased by the Soviet shipment of arms to Egypt. Recognition of Communist China has brought about an almost impossible situation. I could hardly have found anything that would make it harder for us to continue good relations with Egypt.

"Now an American has only to be anti-Communist to condemn our policy toward Egypt. Nasser has touched a point on which the United States is most sensitive. Does Nasser really want to force the United States to support Israel?"

Dulles warned the hapless ambassador that there was little support in the country for financing the Aswan dam. "It is about as unpopular a thing as could be done. Every time I appear before Congress the matter of the dam is thrown at me. The situation in the Congress is boiling over the combination of arms for Saudi Arabia, no arms to Israel and Egyptian recognition of Communist China."

Dulles waited another five days before speaking out publicly about the sensitive matter. He was considerably milder in tone than he had been with Hussein. "It was an action that we regret," he said simply at his press conference. Asked by a reporter about the causes of Washington's "much more bearish view" toward Nasser in recent weeks, Dulles insisted that Washington was sympathetic to Nasser's actions to strengthen his country's independence. "But to the extent that he takes action which seems to promote the interests of the Soviet Union and Communist China, we do not look with favor upon such action."

Actually, Nasser's recognition of China was primarily motivated by his concern to secure a reliable arms supplier to preserve his country's independence, as Dulles privately suspected. Nasser had made his move less than three weeks after Nikita Khrushchev openly suggested during his London visit that an arms embargo be placed on the Middle East. Eden and Mollet both had also made similar public statements. It sounded as though the big powers were cooking up a plan to freeze the arms imbalance. Such a move would have cut off Egypt from reliable supplies, returning the country once again to the humiliation of begging the West for weapons while Israel profited from its secret deals with France. Though nothing eventually came of all the talk about a Soviet-supported embargo, Nasser moved with dispatch to secure a relationship with China. Even though China was hardly a match of the Soviet Union in modern weaponry, its comparatively crude weapons were better than none at all.

Typically, Dulles had a fine sense for the real reasons motivating Nasser. In a telephone conversation with C. D. Jackson, a top aide of Time Inc.'s Henry Luce, shortly after Nasser's action, Dulles said, "I think the recognition of Communist China by Nasser was some indication that the Egyptians do not feel confident that they can get arms indefinitely from the Russians." He added: "That, however, is speculation."

Dulles, ever careful to keep in touch with the molders of public opinion, asked Jackson what Luce thought about the Middle East. The magazine tycoon had recently visited Egypt, at Nasser's invitation, and Israel, and had a meeting with Hammarskjold. Luce's feeling about the Middle East, said Jackson, was "quite hopeful—cautiously hopeful. He thinks it might be possible to get things unstuck."

"We are doing a lot of hard thinking on the matter," replied Dulles.

Interestingly, Secretary-General Dag Hammarskjold shared Luce's guarded optimism, and in fact may have helped form it during their meeting. U.N. Ambassador Lodge had spent four hours with Hammarskjold and reported the substance of their talk on May 18 in a telephone conversation with Dulles. "He does not think there will be a war this year at all," said Lodge. "He has a lot of information about the parties, notably the Israelis, which they know he has and which makes them afraid and respectful of what he might make public. He thinks he is in a pretty strong position to get things carried out."

"That's encouraging," replied Dulles. "Does he have solid grounds for his views?"

"Everything that Hammarskjold says puts the Israeli performance in a bad light. He has got a much better reaction out of the Egyptians than the Israelis right along."

• •

Despite the wide circulation among top officials of such reports of Israeli obstreperousness, the general perception in the United States and elsewhere persisted that Israel sought only peace but was being rebuffed by its hostile Arab neighbors. It was Nasser, not Ben Gurion, who was pictured in the press and by Western leaders as the man wearing the black hat. The French in particular were growing more intense in their hatred of Nasser as their position in Algeria deteriorated and the slaughter mounted to horrifying proportions. In the first two weeks of June alone, the French military command reported that 951 rebels were killed and 25,250 suspects arrested; 77 soldiers and civilians were killed by the rebels. Such depressing reports were accompanied by a steady barrage of stinging propaganda from Egypt's Voice of the Arabs radio encouraging the Algerian rebels.

Colonel Mangin, Defense Minister Bourgès-Maunoury's aide, caused a further descent in France's declining relations with Egypt by openly referring to Nasser as Hitler. Officials on both sides of the Channel had been making that comparison for months, but Mangin was the first to utter the words in public on May 17. Nasser responded by posting a furious protest with France. The uproar became so intense that Bourgès even offered his resignation, admitting that Mangin's statement was "a declaration of war against Nasser." But to Abel Thomas, Bourgès confided that Mangin's remark "corresponds with what I think of the behavior of Nasser."

By the end of June Premier Mollet was angrily denouncing Nasser in public, though he still did not go so far as to compare him to Hitler. He did that only in private. "I denounce the megalomania of Colonel Nasser," Mollet declared at a rally of his Socialist Party on June 30. "He hopes to line up behind himself not only the Arab world but the entire Moslem world. Today Pan-Arabism is a threat to peace."

• •

The Communist bloc was taking full advantage of the opening provided by Nasser's estrangement from the Western powers. Through May and June the Middle East was crowded with Communist representatives of every description, from top Soviet officials to folk dancers and even a Chinese opera company. Communist publications filled the newsstands. Dmitri Shepilov, the new Soviet foreign minister, was touring the region with great fanfare, eliciting intense interest from Arab countries. As he made his way from Egypt to Syria to Lebanon between June 17 and 27, he dropped invitations to visit Moscow. Nasser accepted. So too did President Shukri al-Kuwatly of Syria and President Camille Chamoun of Lebanon. The crown prince of Yemen was already in Moscow for talks.

The Russians were enjoying a surge of popularity throughout that part of the Arab world that was aligning itself with Nasser against Britain and its Baghdad Pact. That included most of the region, with the notable exception of Iraq, which remained staunchly pro-British. Part of the reason for the Soviets' new celebrity were the generous offers Moscow was extending. In each of the three countries he visited, Shepilov left behind agreements to extend economic and technical aid and to expand relations. It was widely believed that Soviet aid was being offered without strings, unlike Western aid, which was often encumbered by political demands. The strings were there, of course, but they were not visible yet. For the Arab countries, so long captive to the West's monopoly in the region, the appearance of an alternative benefactor and perhaps protector was a heady experience. The Arabs and the Russians were on a honeymoon, and the West was not a guest.

• •

The Soviet inroads in the region were significant. The Russians were competing openly with the West and undermining further the tenuous position of the European colonialists. The cause of these events was painfully apparent to Western leaders. It was Nasser who started it all with his Czech arms deal. If Washington now sponsored the Aswan dam it would seem as if it was rewarding Nasser for his unceasing attacks on the British and the French and his blatant flirtation with Moscow and Peking. Other Arab states, notably Iraq, had already complained that to give Nasser his dam would make him stronger while the West's allies were left with no similar reward for their loyalty. His prestige would soar, and so too would his strength to defy the West.

Opposition to the dam was at a high point by July. The powerful coalition of Israel's supporters, southern cotton interests and anti-Communist hard liners succeeded in having the Senate Appropriations Committee approve a directive in its foreign aid report July 14 saying that "none of the funds provided in this act shall be used for assistance in connection with the construction of the Aswan Dam." Treasury Secretary Humphrey also opposed the loan, believing that Egypt was too poor to pay it back. Nasser was regularly being depicted in the press as a dictator and Commie lover, the mortal foe of the only democracy in the Middle East, tiny and valiant Israel. The ruler of the Nile was no longer anybody's favorite Arab.

In a campaign year, such vehement and widespread opposition was too great to ignore. Even if Eisenhower and Dulles had been disposed to go ahead with the deal, the forces against it were too strong to overcome.

Beyond domestic politics, there was an even more tempting reason for withdrawing from the deal. Denial of the loan would be a public slap at Nasser by Washington, a not-too-veiled warning that he could go too far in his dealings with the Communists and his opposition to the West. It would put him in an awkward position when he answered his invitation to visit Moscow in August. If the United States approved the dam, Nas-

257

ser would travel to Russia with his prestige at an all-time high and in a strong bargaining position. Without the dam, he would arrive there hat in hand.

Though Dwight Eisenhower was elusive to the point of misrepresentation in his memoirs about the dam incident, a private note he scrawled to Dulles clearly revealed his attitude. It was written on the bottom of a July 17 letter from an American Zionist pleading Israel's cause: "Any help by the West to Israel will also serve to pull Nasser down a peg." Wrote Ike: "Dear Foster—One thesis developed herein is one concerning which I've often spoken to you—weakening Nasser."

The Eisenhower Administration was now about to try to do that—with devastating results.

• •

The decision to move more forcefully against Nasser was apparently taken July 13 in a meeting between Eisenhower and Dulles. The President was still recovering from his ileitis operation at his Gettysburg farm when Dulles visited him for an hour and nineteen minutes during which they discussed the Aswan High Dam loan. Eisenhower euphemistically recalled that he told Dulles at the meeting to advise Egypt that America was not ready to go ahead with the dam because "our views on the merits of the matter had somewhat altered."

Within two days of the meeting it was revealed that Dulles was shaking up his Middle East team to give it a stronger anti-Nasser cast. The most important change was the removal of Ambassador Hank Byroade from Cairo. He was too close to Nasser and generally regarded as too pro-Arab in outlook. Replacing him would be Raymond Arthur Hare, 55, who had been working in the State Department on the Omega task force, a group studying ways to cooperate with Britain in its covert actions to destabilize regimes in the Middle East.

Nasser, whose antennae for detecting conspiracies were extremely sensitive, suspected something ominous the moment Byroade informed him of the changes. "His face went black," recalled Byroade. "He stared at me for a full two minutes. That's a long time of silence. He just stared. I am sure he feared that we were going to assassinate him and I was being removed because we had been so close."

As with Ben Gurion's ouster of Sharett the previous month, Dulles was clearing the decks in preparation for a new course. He was about to put into high gear the program to whittle Nasser down to size. There apparently was no serious plan to go so far as to have Nasser killed, though in the paranoiac world of spookdom anything was possible. But there was no doubt Dulles and Eisenhower were determined to lessen Nasser's stature. If that should happen to cause his fall from power, the young Egyptian would not be mourned in Washington, London, Paris or Tel Aviv.

. .

The same day that Dulles journeyed to Gettysburg to talk with the President about the Aswan High Dam, Nasser was in Yugoslavia meeting with Marshal Tito. The Yugoslavian leader was the world's most successful exponent of neutralism. He had successfully defied Stalin by purposefully steering his small country on a course independent of Moscow's directives, and he had recently been royally vindicated in Moscow where Russia's new leaders openly apologized for Stalin's past slurs. Washington, too, was wooing him by regularly giving his country aid, the only Communist state so honored.

Nasser's presence at Tito's side attested to the stature he now enjoyed as a Third World leader who, like Tito, was managing to navigate the dangerous shoals between East and West. Also at the meeting in Yugoslavia was the world's third great neutralist, Indian Prime Minister Jawaharlal Nehru, the successor of India's legendary pacifist, Mahatma Gandhi.

Before Nasser had flown off to Yugoslavia, he met with Ambassador Ahmed Hussein, who was so pro-American that Nasser once joked he should serve in Cairo as America's ambassador. Hussein was constantly explaining away Washington's actions to Nasser, and now he was busy promising that the dam would surely be approved if only Nasser accepted Washington's conditions for financial disclosure. Nasser was pessimistic but he was anxious to have an answer one way or the other before his scheduled trip to Moscow the next month.

"All right," Nasser told Hussein. "Go and tell Dulles that you have accepted all his conditions."

"You don't want to amend any of the conditions?" asked an astonished Hussein.

"No. I give you carte blanche. Go and tell him that we have accepted everything. But don't humiliate us."

Hussein was so jubilant that on his way back to Washington he revealed during a London stop that Egypt had accepted all conditions and "it hopes, depends and asks for" help in building the dam. On his arrival in Washington on July 17, he repeated Egypt's desire to reach an immediate accord. He excitedly telephoned World Bank president Black in Maine, where he was vacationing at London Ambassador Winthrop Aldrich's Dark Harbor summer home, to pass on the good news—or what he thought was good news.

• •

On the same day that Hussein returned, Dulles had a long telephone talk with Senate Minority Leader Knowland about the pending foreign aid bill. Knowland was explaining the legislative intricacies involved in the Appropriations Committee's ban against aid for Aswan. It was contained in the committee report and not the bill, but nonetheless, warned Knowland, the Administration would "proceed at its peril" if it tried to fund the dam.

"I am pretty sure we are not going ahead," said Dulles. "But I think it is a grave constitutional question as to the right of any committee to direct that nothing should be done without approval of a committee." They agreed that the President could veto a bill but not a report. "I think I should make my position clear to Congress so Congress would understand the executive did not feel bound by the report," said Dulles.

"It may well be those people would feel sufficiently strongly [about the dam] so that they would write into the bill a limitation that none of the funds may be used for this purpose," warned Knowland.

"They can do it," said Dulles, "but I hope they won't feel it necessary because we have just about made up our minds to tell the Egyptians we will not do it."

"The committee won't be taking it up till Friday."

"It might well be taken care of by then," said Dulles, "and [then] action on the bill won't be necessary."

On Thursday, July 19, Dulles spent twelve minutes in the morning with Eisenhower, who had finally returned to the capital four days earlier. Dulles showed him what was to become a historic document. It was a two-page press release announcing Washington's withdrawal from the Aswan High Dam negotiations. Eisenhower made no corrections or additions to the release and it was turned over to the State Department printing shop for reproduction as a one-page, single-spaced document, number 401, to be held until Dulles met at four o'clock that afternoon with Ahmed Hussein. Twenty minutes before Hussein's arrival, Dulles called his brother.

"I expect to tell him that we are not going ahead—definitely," said

Foster. "If I don't do it Congress will chop it off tomorrow and I'd rather do it myself."

Foster Dulles speculated that if the Soviets honored their repeated offers to finance the dam then "we can make a lot of use of it in propaganda with the satellite bloc: 'You don't get bread because you are being squeezed to build a dam.' "

Allen Dulles wondered what reasons the secretary would offer to the American and Egyptian peoples for his actions.

"I'll put it on the ground that since the offer was made the situation has changed and so on. On the whole it is too big an affair to swing today. I am not going to put it on the lack of peace in the area."

Foster Dulles went on to say that he had already notified the British ambassador that morning. "They were going to phone London and there's no reply so I guess it is all right."

Only two senior associates, Hoover and George V. Allen, were with Dulles when Hussein arrived for his appointment. Hussein was ebullient and there was some preliminary chitchat.

"Hussein began by saying he was greatly concerned by the Russian offers and the expectations they raised," recalled Allen. "He eulogized the High Dam, emphasized Nasser's strength of vision and said how much he, Hussein, wanted the U.S. to do it. He showed that he realized we had problems. But he touched his pocket and said, 'We've got the Soviet offers right in our pocket.' This gave Dulles his cue. Eisenhower had said often that the first person to say such a thing, he'd tell him to go to Moscow.

"Dulles did not read the statement but more or less paraphrased it. Dulles' reply was kindly in tone. He said we had seriously considered it and realized how important it was. But frankly, he said, the economic situation makes it not feasible for the U.S. to take part. We have to withdraw our offer."

Hussein was crushed. He left the fifty-minute meeting declining to talk with waiting reporters.

A few minutes later, Dulles called Knowland and gave him the news. "I just had a talk with the Egyptian ambassador on the Aswan Dam project and told him we are not in a position to go ahead with the dam offer.

"It will be interesting to see what happens," continued Dulles as he stood on the brink of the biggest crisis of the Eisenhower Administration. "In all probability when Nasser goes to Moscow he will sign up some agreement with the Russians. I told the ambassador that the Egyptians, having just won their independence, ought to be pretty careful.''

In another telephone call to his brother, Dulles said he thought that Hussein had "handled himself surprisingly well and with dignity."

But it was Egypt's dignity that Nasser now felt compelled to vindicate.

• •

Nasser had just finished his talks with Tito and Nehru on the summer resort of Brioni and was flying back to Cairo with Nehru when he heard the news. An aide came out of the cockpit and handed the Egyptian leader a résumé of the press release distributed immediately after Hussein's session with Dulles. Without saying a word to Nehru, who was sitting next to him, Nasser got up and walked to the back of the plane and showed the cable to Foreign Minister Mahmoud Fawzi and Mohamed Heikal, the journalist.

"This is not a withdrawal," said Nasser. "It is an attack on the regime and an invitation to the people of Egypt to bring it down."

Indeed, there was an uncanny similarity between the statement and the way the Eisenhower Administration had denied aid to Iran's Mohammed Mossadegh three years earlier. The President's tart denial had been leaked to the press and Mossadegh's position was weakened just prior to the CIA-sponsored coup that had returned the Shah to the throne.

Nasser bitterly noted that the State Department release stressed friendship to the people of Egypt and asserted that "the United States remains deeply interested in the welfare of the Egyptian people." That sounded to Nasser suspiciously like a direct appeal to Egyptians to get a new leader who might be better able to deal with the great United States.

"This method was quite obvious," said Nasser later. "We have had many years of experience with it."

When Nasser finally showed the cable to Nehru, the Indian leader said, "Those people, how arrogant they are."

Nasser's plane landed at Cairo airport around midnight and he went directly home without making a public comment on Dulles' renege. But he was furious. He deeply resented the condescending way in which the release questioned "Egyptian readiness and ability to concentrate its economic resources upon this vast construction program." His lacerated pride was outraged at the public insult, at the rude rebuff after giving in to all the bank's demands. He was humiliated and felt publicly rejected and scorned.

Less than twenty-four hours after Washington's withdrawal, London also withdrew from the dam project. The World Bank had no choice but to follow.* Bank president Eugene Black had wanted to proceed with the project and was disappointed at Dulles' renege and appalled at the way it was handled.

"Imagine going to the Chase Bank and asking to borrow ten thousand dollars," he said, "and then reading in the newspapers that you were turned down on the grounds that your credit was no good." In fact, he asserted, the bank had carefully examined Egypt's economy and had determined that it was strong enough to support building the dam under the terms the bank was proposing.

• •

Washington's plan to undermine Nasser included other plots beyond the dam renege. The day after Dulles' action, Bill Eveland, the undercover CIA agent, met in Washington with Allen Dulles and Herbert Hoover, Jr., and heard some of the details. Eveland had spent the past two months in the Middle East trying to determine whether the British desire for a coup was the only way to stop the leftward drift of Syria toward Cairo and Moscow. Eveland had reported that he found enough "indigenous anti-Communist elements" in Syria to halt the drift without a coup. If these elements were supported by the United States and Britain, he claimed, the anti-Communists could prevail.

The Dulles brothers had other ideas. They had worked up an ambitious secret program to strengthen the West's position and weaken Nasser. Their strategy was comparatively simple. They would nurture America's ties with a coterie of Middle East countries: Iraq, Jordan, Libya, Saudi Arabia and Syria. With Libya to the west and Sudan to the south, both pro-Western, such an alliance would completely surround Nasser with pro-Western nations. On an informal level, it would have the same strangling effect on Egypt that Britain envisioned with its Baghdad Pact. But unlike the pact, it would not be a formal arrangement, which was open to parochial attack by such countries as Israel. This would be an alliance only in the sense that it was a grouping of countries suspicious of Nasser and inclined to be friendly to the West.

The first step was to increase American influence in the countries sur-

---

* The dam was finally constructed with the help of a $554 million loan by the Soviet Union and the work of thirty-five thousand Egyptian laborers and two thousand Russian technicians; it was dedicated in 1971, the year after Nasser died.

rounding Egypt by whatever means possible. With Iraq, Libya and Sudan that was not a problem. All three countries in one form or another were so closely allied with the West that their support could be counted on. Jordan, Saudi Arabia and Syria were different.

Jordan's King Hussein had proved his tough independence by kicking out Glubb Pasha; he would have to be bought.

Saudi Arabia's King Saud was flirting with Nasser and lavishing his money indiscriminately in bribes to enemies of his family's traditional foes, the Hashemites of Jordan and Iraq; he would have to be cowed.

Syria was in total disarray with British, French, Russian and American agents all competing with leftist, moderate, rightist, Islamic, anti-Zionist and nationalist forces to determine the complexion of a stable government; a leader would have to be found.

The plan was born partly as a reaction to the heavy pressure London was exerting on Washington to take extreme actions in the region. It was both less rash than Britain's desire to overthrow the governments of Saudi Arabia, Syria and Egypt, and more attuned to U.S. national interests. That specifically meant protecting Saudi Arabia with its vast oil fields and America's large interests there. As Foster Dulles advised the CIA early in the planning: "No success achieved in Syria could possibly compensate for the loss of Saudi Arabia."

Eveland's target area was Syria, where he was to encourage anti-Communist politicians to "stem the leftist drift," as his orders read. One of his duties was to be sure that American money controlled the first refinery that Syria proposed building in the northern city of Homs. It was from there that the Iraq Petroleum Company's pipeline from the Mosul-Kirkuk fields of Iraq went on to terminate at the ocean. Syria planned to build the refinery astride the pipeline so it could produce for its own needs and save the costs of importing fuel, a major expense for a country that was starved for foreign-exchange reserves.

Syria had invited Russia and Czechoslovakia to tender bids for the refinery, much to the dismay of London and Washington and the Anglo-American oil companies that owned the pipeline. It was feared that Communist involvement in the project would make the pipeline vulnerable to blockage or diversion of oil destined to Western Europe. Additionally, two American oil companies, Standard Oil of New Jersey (Exxon) and Mobil, owned part of the Iraq Petroleum Company, and they were skittish about how Communist involvement in the refinery might affect their profits.

Clearly it was in the West's interests to build the refinery, but Washington had a problem. It was almost impossible to shake any aid out of Congress for an Arab country, as the furor over the Aswan dam had recently proved. So the Dulles brothers had come up with a solution of questionable legality, as Eveland learned in his meeting July 20 with Hoover and Allen Dulles. Congress would be bypassed. The CIA would subsidize the refinery with its secret funds to make sure that an American company could underbid any Communist offer.

On his way back to Syria, Eveland stopped in London where he met again with the secret service's George Young, the man who was hotly advocating Britain's destabilizing policy in the Middle East. Britain and Iraq were going ahead with their plans to stage a pro-West coup in Syria, he informed Eveland. Then the British intelligence officer complained to Eveland for a half hour about Washington's foot-dragging in joining Britain in its covert operations.

From London, Eveland flew on to Beirut where he met on July 23 with peripatetic Kim Roosevelt, who was in the area inaugurating the CIA's new policy to contain Nasser. Roosevelt informed Eveland that the man he should work with to build up anti-Communist Syrian politicians was Mikhail Ilyan, a leader of the National Party and former foreign minister. Ilyan was rich, a landowner, and well connected. But he was a Christian, which meant he was more effective behind the scenes than trying to compete openly with Moslem rivals. "He will be the key to the operation," said Roosevelt.

When Eveland inquired whether Saudi and Egyptian intrigue and bribes could be neutralized in the Syrian political scene, where they played a dominant role, Roosevelt replied that he thought that could be accomplished. King Saud now looked on the Egyptians as a threat, Roosevelt said, adding that he would be flying on to see the king "to encourage him to recognize that the future of Saudi Arabia depended on U.S. support. I have good reason to believe that Saud will do what's best for his country and our oil interests there. There are now ways for us to control expenditures of Saudi money."

As for the Egyptians, "Nasser had been stunned by our refusal to finance the Aswan dam, which damaged Egyptian prestige in the Near East. Now that Egypt's president realized that the United States could be tough and was prepared to counter his disruptive activities, Nasser would have to pay attention to his own serious domestic problems."

"And will there be a coup to topple Nasser as the SIS [Britain's Secret Intelligence Service] proposed?" asked Eveland.

"Certainly not yet," said Roosevelt. "We'll watch him carefully and concentrate on creating a friendly bloc of Iraq, Syria, Saudi Arabia and Jordan."

But Gamal Nasser had other plans.

. .

Mohamed Heikal telephoned Nasser the morning after Dulles' renege and found the Egyptian president still furious.

"Dulles and Eden were deceiving us all the time," complained Nasser. "They pressed us for peace with Israel, they pressed us for pacts and all they wanted to do was to increase their own influence. We are going to build the High Dam by ourselves and we will do anything to make it possible."

Heikal asked him about an old proposal to divert half of the Suez Canal revenues for the purpose.

"Why only half?" snapped Nasser.

Later that day Nasser asked his intelligence people for a report on British forces in the area. That night he sat down and with pencil and paper wrote: "Appreciation from the point of view of Mr. Anthony Eden." Before he finished he had covered nearly six pieces of paper with his speculations about what would happen if he did the unthinkable: nationalize the Suez Canal Company, Europe's lifeline to Middle Eastern oil.

Nasser's first conclusion was an accurate one: "Eden will behave in a violent way." Through thirteen more points, the Egyptian leader looked at all the possible results that could stem from nationalizing the canal. He doubted that Eden would launch a full-scale invasion. Perhaps, mused Nasser, he would try to send battleships into the canal. That could easily be countered.

Nasser, underestimating Mollet's and Eden's hatred of him, considered it unlikely that France would join any action since it was so involved in Algeria. And he doubted that Eden would involve Israel, since that would ruin Britain's fragile position among the Arabs. "Israel may try but Eden will refuse. He will prefer to keep it European." He estimated that both Washington and Moscow would stay out.

Finally, after receiving a study of British forces in the region (two infantry brigades, three paratroop battalions, two air squadrons on Cyprus, all tied down by the EOKA guerrillas; the 10th Armored Division in Libya and Jordan), Nasser concluded that Britain's forces around Egypt were too small to support an invasion. He calculated that it would take two months for Britain to mobilize an invasion force. "We came to the conclusion that in these two months, through diplomacy, we could reach a [peaceful] settlement," he recalled. But, he wondered, "Can we gain two months by diplomacy? If we succeed we shall be safe."

On July 23, Nasser met with members of the Revolutionary Command Council and put before them three proposals: "To nationalize the canal, to nationalize fifty percent of the canal, or to give an ultimatum that if they don't finance the High Dam we will nationalize the canal." The idea of an ultimatum was quickly discarded. Nasser and his colleagues concluded that "if we give an ultimatum, the answer will be another ultimatum. They will say: If you nationalize, we will use force. They would put us in a corner."

Once that option was out of the way, the decision to go the whole way was easy. "We decided that, rather than nationalize fifty percent, it is better to nationalize completely."

The next day Nasser finally spoke out publicly about Dulles' renege during ceremonies opening a new oil pipeline at Mostorod, five miles north of Cairo. "Our reply today is that we will not allow the domination of force and the dollar," he declared. "I will tell you Thursday, God willing, how Egypt has acted so that all its projects—such as this project —may be projects of sovereignty, dignity and not those of humiliation, slavery, domination, rule and exploitation. The projects which we draw up will build our national economy and at the same time build our sovereignty, dignity and independence."

With rage in his voice, Nasser declared: "When Washington sheds every decent principle on which foreign relations are based and broadcasts the lie, smear, and delusion that Egypt's economy is unsound, then I look them in the face and say: Drop dead of your fury for you will never be able to dictate to Egypt."

Soviet Ambassador Yevgeni D. Kiselev was in the audience, nodding in apparent approval of Nasser's remarks. Afterward, he told newsmen that Moscow certainly would finance the High Dam if Egypt wanted.

• •

While Kiselev talked with the press, Nasser was preparing for a more significant meeting. He had seen Mahmoud Yunis, the efficient chief of the Egyptian Petroleum Authority, at the ceremony and asked him to come to the presidential offices in Cairo afterward. Yunis, 46, and Nasser had at one time been fellow instructors in the army staff college and Nasser trusted him and admired his abilities.

267

When Yunis walked into the president's office that afternoon, Nasser said simply: "I am going to nationalize the Suez Canal Company."

"I was stunned," recalled Yunis, "I kissed him on both cheeks. I was unable to speak."

Nasser told Yunis that it was going to be his job to lead the actual take-over. He could have his pick of any number of men he needed. Yunis had only two days to map out a plan and recruit the people since Nasser had already publicly declared that he would have his answer for Washington on July 26. The take-over had to be accomplished peacefully and the canal kept open to traffic in order to avoid giving the Western powers any dramatic reason for reacting precipitously. Nationalization was legal since the company was an Egyptian one, but that would not stop Britain if there were bloodshed. Finally, everything had to be accomplished in complete secrecy.

Nasser and Yunis agreed that the best time to seize the company was during Nasser's scheduled speech Thursday in Alexandria celebrating the fourth anniversary of the abdication of King Farouk. Yunis and his handpicked group of men were to spring into action when Nasser gave the code by mentioning Ferdinand de Lesseps in his speech. It was a nice touch. Many Egyptian workers had perished (Nasser claimed 120,000; the company said 1,390) building de Lesseps' canal and he was widely despised by Egyptians.

• •

Nasser arrived in Alexandria about 4 P.M. on July 26 and immediately held a Cabinet meeting. It was the first time civilian members of the Cabinet were told; only some of the officers who had taken part in the coup four years earlier had been informed. Several of the civilians were nervous and frightened by the idea, but the Cabinet unanimously approved the seizure.

While Nasser was briefing the Cabinet, Yunis and his squads were fanning out along the Nile in preparation for taking over the company's four major installations. Yunis had chosen his thirty men with care. They were mainly civilians, all personally known to him, professors and accountants, and a few army engineers. They were divided into four teams, one to go to Port Said, at the northern end of the canal; one to Port Suez, at the southern end; and one to stay with Yunis in Ismailia, where the canal company's headquarters was located. The fourth team, made up of Yunis' aides in the Petroleum Authority, was in Cairo, where the company also maintained an office.

Only three of Yunis' assistants were in on the secret. The others were given a packet with two envelopes inside, the first to be opened when they arrived at their destination; it carried directions to specific streets. The second envelope was to be opened only when they heard Nasser mention de Lesseps' name over the radio; it revealed their mission.

"In order to assure absolute secrecy and obedience, I told them that one man in each group, unknown to the others, had instructions to shoot on the spot anyone who violated secrecy or failed to carry out orders," said Yunis. "This made a hard impression. Some of them sweated."

Two other men in on the secret were Major General Ali Ali Amer, Nasser's closest friend and eastern commander of the Egyptian Army, and Mohammed Riad, governor of the Canal Zone. General Amer was under orders to move his troops if Yunis needed them. Governor Riad's assignment was to gather up the chiefs of the company's three operating divisions and take them to Yunis in Ismailia after the company had been seized.

While Yunis and his men prepared to strike, thousands of Egyptians began jamming into Liberation Square, a vast plaza that owed its unplanned existence to British naval guns; they had pounded the area into rubble seventy-four years earlier during the conquest of Egypt. There was a festive, expectant atmosphere as the Egyptians waited for Nasser to deliver his promised answer to Dulles. By sunset the crowd was estimated to number a quarter million people, foreign dignitaries in front, facing the balcony from which Nasser would speak, and behind them teeming hordes of Egyptians, some wearing flowing gallabiyas and white turbans. Members of the Cabinet soon filled the chairs on the balcony of the bourse building, the same balcony where the assassination attempt had been made on Nasser's life nearly two years earlier. Since then much had happened to the young leader. He was now firmly in control of his country, he was a statesman of world renown, and now he was taking the extraordinary step of standing up to the combined power of England, France and America.

Shortly after 7:30 P.M. Nasser walked onto the balcony. He was wearing a dark business suit with a handkerchief in his breast pocket and carried a cluster of notes in his left hand; he had been so busy he had not had time to write out his speech. But that was of little concern to him. He knew exactly what he wanted to say.

At 7:41 P.M. Nasser began his speech by paying an elaborate tribute to Colonels Salah Mustafa, the Egyptian military attaché in Jordan, and Mustafa Hafez, a commander stationed in Gaza. Both men were involved in *fedayeen* operations against Israel and both were killed in mid-July by parcel bombs sent by Israeli intelligence. Only four days earlier, Nasser had attended Mustafa's funeral with the slain soldier's father.

Calling Israel a "stooge of imperialism," Nasser declared: "They strengthened Israel so that they can annihilate us and convert us into a state of refugees. We shall all of us defend our nationalism and Arabism and we shall all work so that the Arab homeland may extend from the Atlantic Ocean to the Persian Gulf."

As Nasser began his long oration, Yunis' men tore open their first envelope and proceeded to their destinations, waiting with great expectation for Nasser to utter the code word, de Lesseps.

Nasser was masterful. He spoke for the most part in the vernacular of the street, abandoning the flowery constructions of classical Arabic, and the Egyptians loved it. He poked fun, was by turns derisive and boasting as he delivered a litany of ignominies, some of them more fanciful than real, that Egypt had suffered under British rule and during the frustrating struggle it had had to wage since then to buy weapons to defend itself against Israel. He heaped scorn on the Arab "stooges and supporters of imperialism," meaning Iraq, and added: "You know them all, and I need not tell you about them. If I mentioned their names I would be creating a diplomatic or political crisis."

The crowd loved it. It interrupted him frequently with wild applause, roared with laughter at his gibes and listened in rapt silence to his catalogue of successes Egypt had enjoyed since the overthrow of Farouk.

As the minutes turned to hours, Nasser still had not mentioned de Lesseps. Yunis and his men waited, the tension mounting. A full moon had risen over the banks of the canal. The hands of the clock were moving toward 10 P.M. Nasser was comparing Washington's generosity to Israel against its stinginess toward Egypt. He tore apart the State Department press release, charging that it was aimed at deposing him and embarrassing Egypt. He defended Egypt's economy with facts and figures, and recalled that World Bank president Black had insisted to him that the bank was not political and had no connection with the United States. But, Nasser pointed out, the bank was political because it could not take any action without the approval of its managing board and "this managing board is composed mainly from Western countries moving in the orbit of the United States."

Then came the moment. "I gazed at Mr. Black, who was sitting on a chair, and I imagined that the person seated before me was Ferdinand de Lesseps. [Applause.]" During the next few minutes, Nasser worked de

270

Lesseps into his speech twelve more times just to be sure that the signal had not been missed. He spent considerable time retelling the story of how de Lesseps had used conscripted Egyptian labor to build the canal and how Egypt lost its 44 percent of the canal shares to the British government in 1875. This economic dependence soon gave Britain political dominance, said Nasser, charging that the West had sought the same kind of control with the dam loan.

"Today we are not repeating the past. The Suez Canal Company became a state within a state, one which humiliated ministers and ministries and which humiliated everyone. This canal is an Egyptian canal. It is an Egyptian limited company. Britain forcibly took away from us our right in it, namely, forty-four percent of the company's shares. In return for the one hundred twenty thousand who perished in digging it and for the money spent on building it, we get one million pounds, or three million dollars. [Yet] the Suez Canal, which according to decree was constructed for the benefit of Egypt, yields thirty-five million pounds in annual revenue, or one hundred million dollars.

"We shall never repeat the past, but we shall eliminate the past. We shall eliminate the past by regaining our rights to the Suez Canal. [Applause.] This money is ours and this canal belongs to Egypt, because it is an Egyptian limited liability company. [Applause.]

"We shall build the High Dam and we shall obtain our usurped right. [Applause.] We shall build the High Dam as we desire. We are determined. Thirty-five million pounds annually is taken by the canal company. Why not take it ourselves? [Applause.]

"Therefore I have signed today and the government has approved the following: [Applause.] A resolution adopted by the president of the republic for the nationalization of the world company of the Suez Canal. [Prolonged applause.]' "

Nasser then read the decree nationalizing the canal company. It was a flawlessly legal document putting forth Egypt's right to nationalize. Nasser was beating the West at its own game. He was staying scrupulously within the law. The crowd loved it. He was repeatedly interrupted by tidal waves of joyous, near hysterical applause.

Then Nasser announced the astonishing news that the take-over was already in progress. "While I talk to you at this moment some of your Egyptian brethren are proceeding to administer the canal company and conduct the affairs of the canal company. Right now, at this very moment, they are taking over the canal company—the Egyptian canal company, not the foreign canal company. They are now carrying out this job

271

so that we can make up for the past and build new edifices of grandeur and dignity.'' The crowd went wild.

Yunis and his men performed their task faultlessly. Not a shot was fired, no one was injured. They simply walked into the various canal company installations and announced: "In the name of the government of Egypt, I inform you that the Suez Canal Company is nationalized and I have come to take over the premises."

The dream of nearly a century had come true. Egypt was finally the master of its own canal.

A surge of joy and pride swept through Egypt and the whole Arab world. Nasser's already high prestige soared to new heights.

PART THREE
THE
EXPLOSION

July 26 to March 16, 1957

CHAPTER XIV

Israelis Have Something to Lose

HAMMARSKJOLD

ANTHONY EDEN heard of Nasser's nationalization of the Suez Canal Company in the midst of a royal dinner at 10 Downing Street for King Faisal of Iraq and Prime Minister Nuri es-Said. Eden and another British guest, Viscount Salisbury, as Knights Companions of the Most Noble Order of the Garter, wore the sash and knee britches of their order, the embodiment of empire. It was as they were eating, at about 9 P.M. Thursday, that a Foreign Office messenger climbed the stairs to the tasteful Georgian room and ruined the party.

"I told my guests," recalled Eden. "They saw clearly that here was an event which changed all perspectives, and understood at once how much would depend upon the resolution with which the act of defiance was met. Our party broke up early, its social purpose now out of joint."

Nuri es-Said, the loquacious Iraqi leader, was outraged that Nasser had not deigned to inform him of his move even though the two were bitter enemies. "Hit him, hit him hard, and hit him now," implored Nuri. As he and the king were ushered out of the residence, they passed a bust of Benjamin Disraeli, the prime minister who was responsible for Britain's purchase of a controlling interest in the canal. "That's the old Jew who got you into all this trouble," Nuri cracked. But he received no answering smile from Eden. The current prime minister was in no mood for banter.

Eden immediately summoned his senior ministers, the chiefs of staff of the armed services, and the ambassadors from France and the United States. Aldrich was on holiday and his place was taken by the chargé

275

d'affaires, Andrew Foster. By around midnight the formal meeting got under way in the downstairs Cabinet room with Eden's pronouncement ringing in every participant's ears: "The Egyptian has his thumb on our windpipe."

Eden told the meeting that "this is the end. We can't put up with any more of this. By this means Nasser can blackmail us, he can put up the canal dues, he'll run it very badly, this will absolutely stifle our trade, it will be impossible. Our whole position demands strong action. I want to seize the canal and take charge of it again."

A legal adviser informed Eden that "you know he's doing nothing illegal in nationalizing the canal."

"I don't care whether it's legal or not, I'm not going to let him do it," answered Eden. "He's not going to get away with it."

Lord Louis Mountbatten, First Sea Lord of the Admiralty, was at the meeting and related that "Eden became very fierce. He ordered the chiefs of staff to do an all-night session and then prepare plans for seizing the whole of the Suez Canal militarily."

The emergency meeting lasted for two hours and at five o'clock that Friday morning Foster sent his report to Washington. "Cabinet takes an extremely grave view of situation and very strong feelings were expressed, especially by Eden, to the effect that Nasser must not be allowed to get away with it. . . . The question confronting Cabinet tonight was of course extent to which U.S. would go in supporting and participating in firm position vis-à-vis Nasser in terms of economic sanctions and, beyond that if necessary, military action. . . . Cabinet decided to have chiefs alert British commanders in Mediterranean to situation. Chiefs were instructed to produce soonest a study of what forces would be required to seize canal and how they would be disposed if military action became necessary. . . . As meeting broke up Lloyd told me he himself was moving toward conclusion that only solution lay in a Western consortium taking over and operating the canal, establishing itself if need be by military force."

Eden was outraged at Nasser's action, appalled at the threat it posed to Britain's economy and empire, and resolved to do what he had been wanting to for months: slap down the young leader of the Nile.

"This was the challenge for which Eden had been waiting," observed Anthony Nutting. "Now at last he had found a pretext to launch an all-out campaign of political, economic and military pressures on Egypt to destroy forever Nasser's image as the leader of Arab nationalism."

Britain was in an uproar. Nasser was widely compared with Hitler and the canal with the Rhineland. The London *Times* warned that Nasser's action was "a clear affront and threat to Western interest . . . the time has arrived for a much more decisive policy." It added: "An international waterway of this kind cannot be worked by a nation with low technical and managerial skills such as the Egyptians." The *Star* pointed out that "the canal is an oil pipeline, an economic lifeline." The *Daily Sketch* said it was an opportunity for the government to "prove that its legs are not completely palsied by getting up on them and raising hell." The *Daily Mail:* "Hitler on the Nile." The *News Chronicle:* "The British government will be fully justified in taking retaliatory action." The *Herald:* "No more Hitlers." The *Mirror* suggested that Nasser study the fate of Mussolini. In succeeding days, the prestigious *Times,* sensing the tunes of glory, carried such editorial headlines as "Time for Decision," "A Hinge of History" and "Resisting the Aggressor."

In the House of Commons the day after Nasser's nationalization, Eden vowed that the government would act "with firmness and care. The unilateral decision of the Egyptian government to expropriate the Suez Canal Company, without notice and in breach of the concession agreements, affects the rights and interests of many nations."

Though the nationalization was entirely within Egypt's legal right, Labor leader Hugh Gaitskell endorsed Eden and vowed his party's support for a firm policy. "On this side of the House, we deeply deplore this high-handed and totally unjustifiable step by the Egyptian government," he declared. Liberal Party leader Clement Davies seconded Gaitskell's remarks and termed the nationalization a "deplorable action." Labour member Reginald Paget compared Nasser's "technique" with Hitler's and questioned whether Eden was "aware of the consequences of not answering force with force until it is too late." At the end of the session, the *Manchester Guardian,* the only newspaper not to jump aboard the jingoistic bandwagon, reported: "Indignation was the unanimous verdict at Westminster . . . there were no recriminations, no blame from the Opposition."

The national sentiment was perhaps best expressed by Churchill to Lord Moran, his physician: "We can't have that malicious swine sitting across our communications."

Eden held another meeting of his Cabinet, with the chiefs of staff attending, on July 27 and in the evening sent Eisenhower a militant cable.

"If we take a firm stand over this now we shall have the support of all the maritime powers. If we do not, our influence and yours throughout the Middle East will, we are convinced, be finally destroyed. My colleagues and I are convinced that we must be ready, in the last resort, to use force to bring Nasser to his senses. For our part we are prepared to do so. I have this morning instructed our chiefs of staff to prepare a military plan accordingly."

Even though he was set on waging war against Nasser, there was no way for Eden to do it immediately. To his chagrin, Eden learned from his military chiefs that Britain's war preparations would take some time to materialize. "It was deeply humiliating," recalled Eden's press spokesman, William Clark, of Eden's meeting with the chiefs of staff. "In effect, the prime minister said there had been an act of aggression against us and he wished to respond forcefully and immediately. What could the chiefs of staff recommend? Their answer was ill-prepared but perfectly clear: We could do nothing immediately."

Nasser had been right. There were not enough forces in the Middle East. It would take at least six weeks to get together a force sufficiently strong to attack Egypt.

Eden also received a disappointment when the Foreign Office reported back to him on the research he had ordered into the legality of Nasser's action. A lawyer brought the legal department's study to Eden on Friday, saying that Nasser's action was indeed perfectly legal so long as he did not close the canal to shipping. Eden read the report, tore it up and flung it in the lawyer's face.

• •

Eden's temper and his health had disintegrated further. By July, he was taking many pills. His violent moods and peculiar behavior were the gossip of the corridors of power. "The political world is full of Eden's moods at No. 10," wrote Lord Moran in his diary on July 21. "All this is known to Winston, and he is anxious about the future. He sees that things cannot go on like this for long. At the back of his mind, as I keep finding out, is the disconcerting fact that he put Anthony where he is."

Nasser's nationalization of the canal aggravated further Eden's unsettled state. From now until he succumbed to his passion for war, he was out of sync with his old cautious, compromising self. He was obsessed, a driven man, his vast experience and intellect reduced to tunnel vision. At the end of the tunnel was Nasser.

• •

President Eisenhower arrived at his office at 8:10 A.M. that Friday and, after two brief meetings, called in Herbert Hoover, Allen Dulles and

Colonel A. J. Goodpaster, his military aide, to discuss the canal nationalization. Hoover was acting secretary of state while Dulles was touring Latin America; he currently was in Lima to attend the inauguration of Peru's new president, Dr. Manuel Prado. Eisenhower was clearly angry and unhappy with Nasser.

"This action is not the same as nationalizing oil wells, since they exhaust a nation's resources, and the canal is more like a public utility," said the President. He wondered whether Nasser had acted legally.

Hoover indicated he had, adding: "Nasser's speech is a sustained invective in the most violent terms against the United States and its officials containing many inaccuracies."

"We must challenge these inaccuracies," said Ike.

"The basic problem is that the British will want to move very drastically in this matter," said Hoover, "because of the worldwide impact on their position, including their relations with other countries."

Eisenhower too thought London would act. (He still had not received Eden's telegram, which arrived only at 4 P.M.) He noted Britain would act because of the "large block of stock they hold and the importance of shipping through the canal."

"It will be necessary to make a statement this morning," said Hoover. He thought it should "be in terms of 'viewing with grave concern,' not giving details."

The President agreed, stressing that "we should give no hint of what we are likely to do." The statement should point out that Nasser's speech is full of inaccuracies, Ike added. "It should also make clear our great interest in the canal since the commerce of the West with the East passes through it. The statement should bring out that we regard the matter with the utmost seriousness and are consulting with others affected. There should be one sentence making clear that Nasser's speech was full of misstatements regarding the United States."

Eisenhower told Hoover to draft the statement, "the shorter the better. Discuss it with Secretary Dulles by phone and then bring it to me."

After receiving Eden's intemperate cable, Eisenhower telephoned Vice President Nixon and told him: "This thing in the Mediterranean looks pretty bad. Herbert Hoover is busy on it. Meanwhile, if you have a chance tell Bill Knowland and Lyndon Johnson [Senate majority leader], on a very confidential basis—explaining that we don't want to be out in front in being tough—that this might develop into something and we don't want them astonished. We may need a little help. This is Security Council stuff. I won't stand by and let our nationals be abused."

That same day Eisenhower received cables from Paris reporting that the French reaction was even more militant tnan the British. The French government, the press and the people were up in arms against Nasser. Foreign Minister Pineau called Egyptian Ambassador Kamal Abdel Nabi into his office and accused Nasser of "an act of plunder." Nabi refused to accept a French note detailing France's case against Nasser, calling it "inadmissible and unacceptable."

Pineau publicly stated that France would not "accept the unilateral action of Colonel Nasser." Prime Minister Mollet went even further in the days ahead and called Nasser an "apprentice dictator" whose methods were similar to Hitler's: "the policy of blackmail alternating with flagrant violations of international agreements." Mollet said publicly that Nasser's *The Philosophy of the Revolution* should have been titled *Mein Kampf*. He announced that France had decided upon "an energetic and severe counterstroke." The National Assembly passed a resolution calling Nasser a "permanent menace to peace."

• •

The leaders of Britain and France were itching for a fight. Both countries agreed to have their military commands work up joint invasion plans. Pineau planned to fly to London on the weekend and Eden requested that Eisenhower send a representative so the Big Three Western countries could act in concert. With Dulles still in Peru, Ike chose the department's No. 3 man, veteran diplomat Robert Murphy.

Murphy met with the President and Hoover Saturday morning and within hours was on an airplane to London. "The president was not greatly concerned and there was no talk of recalling Dulles from Peru," Murphy said. Eisenhower told him: "Just go over and hold the fort. See what it's all about."

As usual, Eisenhower was at his coolest in a crisis, though he later admitted: "I did not view the situation as seriously as did [Eden]; at least there was no reason to panic."

Basically, the President recalled, "Murphy was to urge calm consideration of the affair and to discourage impulsive armed action. While I agreed that it would not be difficult to seize and operate the canal at the time, the real question would be whether such action would not outrage world opinion and whether it could achieve permanent, soundly based stability. Should nationals of Western countries be seized or mistreated, of course, such an event would change the complexion of the problem and warrant any action that might be necessary. But in the situation as it then stood Murphy was to represent my conviction that any sweeping action taken regarding Nasser and the canal should not be an act of the 'Big Three Club.' In addition, I wished to avoid any effort by our allies, the French in particular, to relate Nasser's action to the Arab-Israeli quarrel.''

After his meeting with Murphy, the President flew off to Gettysburg for a three-day weekend.

Ike's calm did not mean that Washington was underestimating the explosive potential of the situation. In a message Saturday to the Sixth Fleet, the chief of naval operations, Admiral Burke, warned that "it is probable that there will be no concerted military action for at least several days but there is always a possibility with existing tense situation and emotional people that an incident may occur in Egypt which will require prompt action to protect U.S. nationals. State has not requested ambassador to evacuate U.S. nationals from Egypt but be prepared to execute Egyptian evacuation plans on short notice.''

• •

Eisenhower could afford to take a somewhat relaxed attitude toward the canal crisis because direct American interests were few. Only 2.7 percent of the ships using the canal were American registry, the government had no financial interests in the canal company and the U.S. was totally independent in meeting its oil needs. The only major U.S. investments were in the oil states. ARAMCO, in Saudi Arabia, was totally American-owned, and the Kuwait Oil Company was 50 percent American. Lesser shares were held in other oil companies that, for the most part, were dominated by British owners.

By contrast, Britain and France were both hostages to the canal. Both countries depended heavily on canal-shipped oil. Oil tankers heading for Europe had comprised two-thirds of the canal traffic in 1955. Two million barrels of Middle East oil went to Europe each day, with 1.2 to 1.3 million going through the canal, the rest by pipeline from the Middle East.

Britain was especially vulnerable to any threat to the canal. It was the canal's largest user. Of the 14,666 ships that passed through the canal in 1955, one-third were British and two-thirds belonged to NATO nations. Some sixty thousand British troops passed through the canal annually, traveling to and from Britain's bases east of Aden. A cutoff of canal traffic would quickly bring Britain to its knees: two-thirds of its oil came through the canal.

"Ever since Churchill converted the Navy to the use of oil in 1911,

British politicians have seemed indeed to have had a phobia about oil supplies being cut off, comparable to the fear of castration," observed historian Hugh Thomas.

Beyond that, Britain's 44 percent of the company shares made it the largest single shareholder. Nine of the company's thirty-two directors were British and the annual dividend to London was about $8 million.

France's interest was heightened by the fact that de Lesseps had not only built the canal but its blue-chip shares were still traded on the Bourse and the company's headquarters was in Paris. The shares closed at $260 before Nasser's speech; the next day they plummeted, losing 21 percent of their value. A majority of the shares were owned by private French citizens. More important, the majority of France's oil came through the canal.

• •

Eisenhower of course was acutely aware of the heavy dependence of Britain and France on the canal, and especially their need to receive oil through it. "The economy of the European countries would collapse if those oil supplies were cut off," he had confided to his diary earlier that year. "If the economy of Europe would collapse, the United States would be in a situation of which the difficulty could scarcely be exaggerated."

In a letter to Winston Churchill, Eisenhower repeated the observation. "The prosperity and welfare of the entire Western world is inescapably dependent upon Mideast oil and free access thereto. This is particularly true of all Western Europe, and the safety and soundness of that region is indispensable to all the rest of us. These facts should provide such a clear guidepost for all our policies, actions, efforts, and propaganda in the region that we would allow nothing to weaken the solidarity of our unified approach to our common problems."

• •

Nasser's popularity was never so high in Egypt as it was now. He returned to Cairo on Saturday aboard a train garlanded with flowers, ribbons and strings of lights. Cheering, joyous crowds thronged the route, and he was delayed at every village by delirious children and adults who swarmed to the train, reaching out to touch his hand. Occasionally he pulled his handkerchief from his breast pocket and waved it, extending his arms in an Eisenhower-like victory sign.

Cairo welcomed him with exuberance. Tens of thousands of frenzied

Cairenes jammed the two-and-a-half-mile route from the train station to the Presidency, causing him to take seventy-five minutes to reach his office. From the balcony of the Presidency Nasser spoke to the throng. The violent European reaction to nationalization showed that Britain and France had no plans to turn over the canal to Egypt in 1968, said Nasser, referring to the date when the canal had been scheduled to be open to purchase by Egypt. "Why should Britain say that this nationalization will affect shipping in the canal? Would it have affected shipping twelve years hence?

"The noise that we expected arose in London and Paris without any justification except imperialist reasons, the habits of sucking the blood of nations and stealing their rights. As for the impudence of France and the French foreign minister, I shall not reply to this. The French foreign minister was rude to the Egyptian ambassador in Paris yesterday. I shall leave it to the struggling Algerians to teach France a lesson in behavior."

Anwar Sadat, a member of the original junta and now editor of the daily *Al Gomhuriya,* also spoke to the crowd about "conceited cowards like Eden and Pineau and the rest of the felonious stupid horde." After the speeches, Sadat joined Nasser and said, "If you had consulted me, I would have told you to be more careful. This step means war and we are not ready for it. The weapons we have, we've only just received. We've not been adequately trained to use the new weapons. Our training has been British, and we haven't had time to change our military thinking, our military orientation, from Western to Eastern. But now that this decision has already been taken, of course, we should all support you. And I shall be the first to do so."

Nasser was careful to the point of fastidiousness in acting legally and in making sure that traffic through the canal continue unimpeded. He wanted by all means to avoid giving the West an excuse to accuse him of violating the 1888 Convention of Constantinople that guaranteed free passage through the canal. "It is very important to distinguish between nationalization, which is an internal right of the Egyptian government, and violation of international agreements," observed Sadat's newspaper on July 29. The new Suez company announced at the end of its first day that forty-nine ships had navigated the canal. That was four better than the average.

The only other pretext that was likely to be believed by the world as a sufficient excuse for war was coercive Article V contained in the nationalization decree. The article made it a crime punishable by imprisonment for employees of the old canal company to leave their jobs. Nasser had included that injunction out of fear that Britain and France would urge their nationals to leave, thus throwing the company's operations in chaos and giving the Western powers an excuse to intervene with the claim that Egypt was incapable of operating the canal. But by the end of July, Egypt announced that any employee who wanted to leave could do so after giving the obligatory one-month notice. Nasser also reaffirmed that "nationalization of this company in no way affects Egypt's international obligations. The freedom of shipping in the Suez Canal will in no way be affected. There is no one more anxious than Egypt to safeguard freedom of passage and the flourishing of traffic in the canal."

In London, when Anthony Nutting pointed out to Eden that Britain might not actually have any worry about the canal staying open since it was now in Egypt's best interests to collect as many tolls as possible, the prime minister "merely replied that I should know that the capacity of the Arabs to cut off their nose to spite their face was infinite."

• •

Bob Murphy arrived in London late Saturday night and met the next day with Selwyn Lloyd and Christian Pineau, the latter having flown in that morning. Murphy found the conversation of the foreign ministers restrained and he heard nothing specific about the allies' plans beyond Lloyd's assertion that Britain was ready to use force if necessary. The American diplomat learned far more that evening from two old friends, Chancellor of the Exchequer Macmillan and retired Field Marshal Harold Alexander. Murphy and Macmillan had worked as the American and British political advisers to General Eisenhower during the war, and Murphy also knew Alexander from that period.

"I was left in no doubt that the British government believed that Suez was a test which could be met only by the use of force," recalled Murphy. "I was told that the French saw eye to eye with the British on the necessity of making a stand, and that they were prepared to participate in a military operation. Macmillan and Alexander conveyed the impression of men who have made a great decision and are serene in the belief that they have decided wisely." Both men insisted to Murphy that "Nasser has to be chased out of Egypt."

Macmillan complained that if Nasser was not backed down "Britain would become another Netherlands." (The Dutch ambassador had a sense of humor and merely laughed when he eventually heard the remark.)

After the dinner, Murphy, convinced that Britain was ready to go to war, hurriedly sent off a report to Eisenhower, which Ike received Sunday in Gettysburg. By the time Murphy awoke Monday morning, the President's answer was awaiting him. It advised him that Dulles was returning from Peru and would be sent to London.

Dulles arrived back in Washington that Sunday afternoon and told reporters: "The Egyptian action purporting to nationalize the Suez Canal Company strikes a grievous blow at international confidence. The action could affect not only the shareholders who, so far as I know, are not Americans, but it could affect the operation of the canal itself and that would be a matter of great concern to the United States as one of the maritime nations."

Later, after briefings on the crisis, he talked with Nixon by telephone, telling the vice president: "It is bad. The British and French are really anxious to start a war and get us into it. I'm doing the best I can to make them realize they may have to do it alone."

In another phone call, this one to Democratic Senator Mike Mansfield, Dulles had to try to calm the legislator's bellicose mood. "I hope we don't give in to Nasser as he has all the attributes of an unstable dictator," said Mansfield, who was not known for his hawkishness. "We should act closely with the British and the French and take determined action."

"I don't know that we want to plunge into a war," countered Dulles.

"We can't let him get away with it," insisted Mansfield.

Big Bill Knowland, on the other hand, was far more cautious though he enjoyed a reputation for aggressiveness. Just before Dulles left for London, Knowland told him on the phone that he hoped the British and the French would not start something "which needs our help. I don't think public opinion would be ready to support that."

The sense of crisis, of impending violence, was palpable.

• •

Events moved rapidly. Over the weekend, London and Paris froze the sterling assets of Egypt, and insisted on paying their canal tolls to banks in Britain and France. This had the effect of denying Egypt payment of tolls since the money went into frozen accounts. On Monday, Eden won loud applause from both sides of the House when he replied to a question about the recent British sale of two destroyers to Egypt: "I do not know where they are, but I think that we can leave it to the Royal Navy. It will take care of them wherever they are." He declared Egypt could not be allowed "unfettered control" of the canal. Its operations must be conducted by an international authority, "upon this we must insist. Nothing less can be acceptable to us."

By now, there was no doubt left in Eden that he had to act with force against Nasser. He and Macmillan both sent most secret messages Monday night to Eisenhower saying the government had made a "firm and irrevocable" decision to "break Nasser." Hostilities would be started as soon as possible, probably in about six weeks, with no intermediate or less drastic efforts to be given a chance.

The President was appalled. "Such a decision was, I thought, based far more on emotion than on fact and logic."

Eisenhower returned to the White House from Gettysburg shortly after 9 A.M. that Tuesday, July 31, and a half hour later began a long meeting with Dulles, Hoover and State Department legal adviser Herman Phleger. Soon they were joined by Treasury Secretary Humphrey, Chief of Naval Operations Burke, Deputy Secretary of Defense Reuben Robertson, Assistant Secretary of Defense Gordon Gray and the CIA's Allen Dulles.

Eden's shocking message was studied and restudied as the President and his top officials sought a way to divert the Briton from an action that they thought would bring worldwide condemnation down on Britain and the West. Even though Eisenhower and the others harbored no affection for Nasser, the idea of force was repellent.

"I can scarcely describe the depth of the regret I felt in the need to take a view so diametrically opposed to that held by the British," recalled Eisenhower. "Yet I felt in taking our own position we were standing firmly on principle and on the realities of the twentieth century. I felt it essential to let the British know how gravely we viewed their intentions and how erroneous we thought their proposed action would be."

During the meeting, which lasted until 10:56 A.M., it was decided that Dulles should leave at once for London to meet with Eden in an effort to gain time and personally give him a letter from Eisenhower.

The President's letter was blunt. He wrote that before any military action could take place there had to be a meeting of the signatories of the canal convention of 1888. "I cannot overemphasize the strength of my conviction that some such method must be attempted before action such as you contemplate should be undertaken. If unfortunately the situation can finally be resolved only by drastic means, there should be no grounds for belief anywhere that corrective measures were undertaken merely to protect national or individual investors, or the legal rights of a sovereign nation were ruthlessly flouted. A conference, at the very least, would have a great educational effect throughout the world. Public opinion here, and I am convinced, in most of the world, should be outraged should there be a failure to make such efforts. Moreover, initial military successes might be easy, but the eventual price might become far too heavy."

The President pointed out to Eden that if Britain did attack, it could not automatically count on U.S. forces joining in since Congress would have to approve such an action and it was currently adjourned. It could be reconvened, but it would not likely sanction force unless "there would be a showing that every peaceful means of resolving the difficulty had previously been exhausted. Without such a showing, there would be a reaction that could very seriously affect our people's feeling toward our Western allies."

Eisenhower concluded by noting that though Eden had written that the decision to use force had already been taken, he hoped that "you will consent to reviewing this matter once more in its broadest aspects."

The letter was sent to Dulles around one o'clock, but then Ike had second thoughts about the wording of the paragraph about Congress being reconvened. "He twice called the secretary saying that he feared his first version intimated too strongly possibility of calling special session of Congress," recorded Eisenhower's secretary, Ann Whitman. "He dictated revised page two to me, which was sent over barely in time for secretary to make his scheduled departure."

• •

Though Eisenhower opposed the immediate use of force, he strongly sympathized with Eden's predicament. "Nasser and the Suez Canal are foremost in my thoughts," he wrote Swede Hazlett. "Whether or not we can get a satisfactory solution for this problem and one that tends to restore rather than further damage the prestige of the Western powers, particularly of Britain and France, is something that is not yet resolved. In the kind of world that we are trying to establish, we frequently find ourselves victims of the tyrannies of the weak.

"In the effort to promote the rights of all, and observe the equality of sovereignty as between the great and the small, we unavoidably give to the little nations opportunities to embarrass us greatly. Faithfulness to the underlying concepts of freedom is frequently costly. Yet there can be no doubt that in the long run such faithfulness will produce real rewards."

The joint chiefs of staff voiced other ideas the same day that Dulles left for London. "The joint chiefs of staff are seriously concerned with the implications of the recent Egyptian nationalization of the Suez Maritime Canal Company,'' they declared in a memorandum for the secretary of defense. ''They consider this Egyptian action to be militarily detrimental to the United States and its allies. Among the military implications of this action are those affecting the continued United States control of military bases and facilities in the general area; the future of the Baghdad Pact organization; the economic and military strength of European nations and therefore of NATO; the French position in North Africa; the free flow of shipping through the Suez Canal; and those affecting the United States security interests if Nasser's arbitrary action is tolerated and a further precedent for such arbitrary action thereby established.''

The chiefs strongly recommended that the canal company be placed in friendly hands. If that did not occur, then ''the United States should consider the desirability of taking military action in support of the U.K., France and others as appropriate.''

The military leaders also issued a cautionary warning: ''The joint chiefs of staff desire to point out that Israel may be tempted to capitalize on the situation by taking unilateral action inimical to U.S. interests. Any such unilateral action should be prevented.''

Washington that same day joined London and Paris and froze all Egyptian assets. But for the moment that was as far as Eisenhower was willing to go.

The only things that now stood between the determination of the leaders of Britain and France to go to war were Dwight Eisenhower and Foster Dulles, or so it seemed. In reality, it was the unpreparedness of the British and French military that was delaying war. This reality underlay everything that happened during the next three months.

• •

As Foster Dulles flew to London, Britain and France were gathering their cumbersome military machines together into a strike force. The nearest deepwater harbor capable of supporting a seaborne landing force was Malta, a thousand miles from Egypt. The chiefs of staff had to admit to Eden that Britain could wage an all-out war or it could fight a guerrilla uprising, as in Cyprus, but it was not prepared to launch an immediate amphibious landing. Though the country spent 10 percent of its budget on defense and had 750,000 men and women under arms, it had neither enough troops in the region to attack nor the equipment and trained troops to launch war immediately against Egypt.

Ike celebrates his election victory early on Nov. 7, 1956, at the Sheraton Hotel in Washington shortly after the fighting stops in Egypt (38).   38

40

39

A worried President Eisenhower at the
White House shortly after Israel attacked
Egypt on Oct. 29, 1956 (39); Adm.
Arleigh Burke (40); Lord Mountbatten
(41). Sunken ship blocks Suez Canal
Nov. 1, 1956 (42).

41

42

43 Israeli troops advance toward the Gaza Strip on Nov. 2, 1956 (43); Ben Gurion helps erect barbed-wire fences at a settlement opposite the Gaza Strip shortly before the Israeli attack (44).

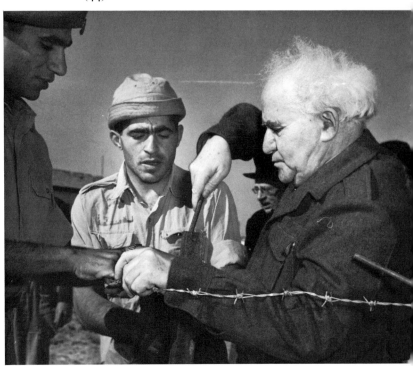

44

Jubilant Israeli troops display Egyptian flag after occupying Egypt's Abu Ageila
stronghold in the Sinai, Nov. 4, 1956 (45). Egyptian and Palestinian prisoners
rounded up in the capture of the Gaza Strip in early November 1956 (46).

Labour leader Hugh Gaitskell (47). In London, a crowd gathers in Trafalgar Square during a Labour protest against the war one day before the British and French troops parachute into Egypt on Nov. 5, 1956 (48).

Moshe Dayan and victorious Israeli troops at captured Sharm el Sheikh at the tip of the Sinai peninsula, Nov. 6, 1956 (49); Secretary-General Dag Hammarskjöld of the United Nations tells a news conference in New York that the fighting in Egypt will end at 7 P.M. EST, Nov. 6, 1956 (50).

50

Israeli tanks near the Suez Canal (51); ships and helicopters of the Anglo-French invasion force attack Egypt, Nov. 6, 1956 (52).

British paratroopers drop on Port Said on Nov. 5, 1956 (53); burning oil tanks in Port Said caused by air and naval bombardment on Nov. 6, 1956 (54).

Victims of the Anglo-French air and sea attack on Port Said, Nov. 6, 1956 (55, 56); a view of the devastation at Port Said (57).

"You see! Now you can understand what it means to have satellite trouble!"

London *Daily Express* cartoon showing Eisenhower and Khrushchev, Nov. 28, 1956 (58).

Canadian Major General
E. L. M. Burns, commander of
the United Nations Treaty
Supervisory Organization in the
Middle East (59).

In the aftermath of the Anglo-French-Israeli attack. Egyptian nationalists vented their anger by destroying the statue of Ferdinand de Lesseps, builder of the Suez Canal, in Port Said on Dec. 24, 1956 (60).

Sinai road plowed up by withdrawing Israeli troops who destroyed roads and facilities in the Sinai when they returned captured territory to Egypt on March 16, 1957 (61).

Menachem Begin, leader of the ultranationalist Herut Party, speaks out in Tel Aviv against Israel's return of captured Egyptian lands, March 8, 1957 (62).

Ben Gurion, Moshe Dayan and Shimon Peres after the war (63); Danish troops of the United Nations Emergency Force (UNEF) guarding a position near the Suez Canal following the withdrawal of Anglo-French forces (64).

64

65

66

U.N. Ambassador Henry Cabot Lodge (65); Lady and Sir Anthony Eden with Eden's successor, Harold Macmillan (66); a mature Gamal Abdel Nasser in 1967 (67).

67

In some cases, Egypt, with its new Czech weapons, was now even better armed than Britain, though its forces were still not adequately trained to use them. It had MiGs, Ilyushin bombers and medium tanks. Egyptian troops were equipped with the good Czech semiautomatic assault rifle; Britain had only World War II breech-loading rifles. The British had no airborne antitank gun, and only two landing ships capable of carrying amphibious troops. It had only five squadrons of ancient Hastings and Vickers Valetta troop-carrying planes, barely enough to lift a single parachute battalion and its equipment.

Planning for the invasion of Egypt started July 28. France sent its top military men to London on that date to meet with their counterparts and during the weekend a secret joint military command was established. By the time Dulles was flying to London, the French were able to inform Britain that they were ready to devote two divisions, the 10th Parachute and the 7th Light Mechanized, to the enterprise. On the same day, the British Admiralty announced that certain unspecified naval movements had been ordered. On Wednesday, the day Dulles arrived in London, the War Office reported that "precautionary military measures" were being taken.

During the early days of August more military announcements poured out of London and Paris. The Admiralty announced that three aircraft carriers currently at Portsmouth were being sent to the Mediterranean; H.M.S. *Bulwark* (22,000 tons), *Theseus* (13,190 tons) and *Ocean* (13,190 tons). A partial mobilization of twenty-five thousand men and prolonged service for conscripts due for discharge were also decreed. A proclamation of "great emergency" was rushed to the Queen, who was attending the races at Goodwood. (It was later snickered that she signed the proclamation on the rump of a horse.) British subjects were warned to leave Egypt unless they had "compelling reasons" for staying.

At the same time, Paris announced that its Mediterranean fleet was being assembled at Toulon. It included the aircraft carriers *Arromanches* (14,000 tons) and *Bois-Belleau* (11,000 tons), the battleship *Jean Bart* (35,000 tons), the cruiser *Georges-Leygues* (7,600 tons), two light cruisers, four heavy destroyers, seven frigates, six submarines and smaller vessels. The French also warned their nationals to leave Egypt.

Israel was anxious to join in the looming war, but "at this point the participation of Israel was totally excluded," recalled Abel Thomas. "We even decided, at the request of the British, not to inform the Israelis of our plans. But we did let them know that something precise was in preparation, confirming news reports."

• •

Dulles began discussions immediately on his arrival in London with Eden, Lloyd and Pineau. The customary roles of Dulles and Eden were now reversed. Dulles, the brinksman whom Europeans for years had criticized as being too bellicose, was now preaching peace and patience; Eden, the compromiser and negotiator, wanted war.

There was no mistaking the aggressive atmosphere in London. *The Times,* in words echoing those of Eden in his first cable to Eisenhower, editorialized: "Quibbling over whether or not [Nasser] was 'legally entitled' to make the grab will delight the finicky and comfort the fainthearted, but entirely misses the real issues." Macmillan flatly declared to Dulles that Britain would be finished as a world power if Nasser won: "This is Munich all over again." Macmillan, like Eden and most members of the Cabinet, was of the prewar generation that had been scarred by the experience of Britain's hesitations in opposing Hitler's march toward war. Almost to a man, they were now confusing the 1930s with the 1950s, Hitler with Nasser.

Dulles had his work cut out for him, and he performed it masterfully. He argued long and convincingly that there was a need to "mobilize world opinion" before any military action could be taken. He counseled patience. He argued that Britain and France and the United States join together to convene an international conference of maritime nations to discuss the problem and decide on a solution.

Despite his admonitions against war, Dulles could not help sharing his sympathy with the British and French attitude and at one point he told Eden that "a way must be found to make Nasser disgorge what he is attempting to swallow."

Eden, in his desire for war, leaped on the sentence as an endorsement of Anglo-French war plans. "These were forthright words," Eden later declared. "They rang in my ears for months." But Murphy, who knew Dulles well and heard him make the remark, said Eden exaggerated its importance. "That type of statement was a relief from the pressures and was to be taken with a warehouse full of salt," Murphy observed, noting that Dulles often made outrageous remarks which he did not mean. "He was entirely capable of suddenly ejaculating in the midst of a critical situation: 'It's about time we started throwing bombs in the marketplace!' "

Still, in Eden's feverish state, it was a mistake that tended to obscure in the prime minister's mind just how determined peace candidate Eisenhower was to oppose force. Eden's passion so clouded his reason that after reading Ike's forceful letter he concluded that "the President did not rule out the use of force." True, but there were so many qualifiers in the letter that only Eden in his blind hatred of Nasser could have missed the point.

Observed Bob Murphy: "The prime minister had not adjusted his thoughts to the altered world status of Great Britain, and he never did."

After thirty-six hours in London, Dulles was able to leave with the issuance of a joint declaration—which he had written on the plane on the way over—calling for a meeting of the major maritime powers starting August 16 in London with Britain as the host.

Dulles had accomplished as much as he and Eisenhower had hoped. The mere fact that the Big Three had met and approved an international gathering as the next step, and not immediate war, tended to lessen tensions. By August 3, both parliaments in Britain and France had gone into summer recess, which put a halt to all the blustery rhetoric of the legislators and also helped dampen passions. Suddenly the threat of war seemed less imminent. When Dulles arrived back in Washington, he said: "We do not want to meet violence with violence." It seemed as though the dogs of war had been kept under leash.

But all that was on the surface. Underneath, war plans were going forward. The day after Dulles left London, General Sir Hugh Stockwell was recalled from Germany, where he was commanding the 1st Corps of the British Army of the Rhine, and was made task force commander of the British invasion force.

Staff officers labored day and night on an invasion plan and on August 10 Stockwell was able to present to Eden a detailed scenario to accomplish his order "to be prepared to mount operations against Egypt to restore the Suez Canal to international control." Eden approved it with smiles. D-day was secretly set for September 15.

• •

Although unaware of the details of the secret military planning now proceeding at a breakneck pace, Eisenhower and Dulles were uncomfortably aware of Eden's and Mollet's passion to wage war. Eisenhower's and Dulles' strategy was to divert their European allies from war by a series of delaying maneuvers. Various schemes were discussed. Perhaps, Dulles suggested to the President in a telephone call August 6, Eisenhower could go to the London Conference to lend more importance to it. But that would be "awkward in that other heads of government may feel

they have to go too. Going to Egypt would be entirely out of the question." Eisenhower wondered about meeting Nasser somewhere out of
Egypt, perhaps Rome. Dulles pointed out that the French were particularly concerned that the United States do nothing to build up Nasser's
prestige.

"If you go to meet him it would be a bitter defeat of all their hopes,"
said Dulles. "We [Washington against London and Paris] are working at
cross-purposes here. They are not anxious to find a peaceful way out—
they do not think there is such a way."

Well, said Eisenhower, "if there is any clear chance of doing some
good I will go. I could stay for a few days and still get back in time to
make my [Republican] Convention speech on the twenty-fourth."

Meanwhile, the Administration already was being pestered by Britain
to provide it with material for its expeditionary forces. London had asked
to purchase some radio electronic equipment, and on August 9 Assistant
Secretary of Defense Gordon Gray called up Dulles and asked whether it
should be authorized. "If we specifically approve it there may be other
requests and we may be in the position of endorsing the expedition," said
Gray. "And if we don't, it may appear we are not giving them the proper
support."

"I would agree to the request because it's relatively unimportant,"
said Dulles. "But put in a caveat so it won't establish a precedent."

• •

Eisenhower and Dulles, ever careful to keep a bipartisan cast to foreign
policy, now tried to enlist several Democratic senators to join the U.S.
delegation to the London Conference. Lyndon Johnson, Mike Mansfield,
Walter George and William Fulbright had all been invited. But it was an
election year, the issue could be explosive, especially among conservatives and Israel's supporters, and they all prudently declined. As part of
the same effort, Ike and Dulles held a full-scale bipartisan briefing August
12, a Sunday, for the top leadership of the House and Senate.

The tone of the briefing was grim and unanimously anti-Nasser. The
President opened by noting that "things are not going so well as to give
unbounded hope for a peaceful solution." He cited Nasser's anti-West
statements, the Egyptian leader's written ambition "to unite the Arab
world and if possible the Moslem world, and to use Mideast oil and the
Suez Canal as weapons against the West." Nasser's ambitions sounded,
said Eisenhower, "much like Hitler's in *Mein Kampf,* a book no one
believed."

292

Dulles concurred. Britain's and France's immediate reaction had been to use force, he said, but he went to London and told them that "the immediate use of force would alienate world opinion since they had not yet made their case." But, he added, "the United States cannot be unsympathetic to the British and French views in the light of Nasser's ambitions. Fulfillment of Nasser's ambitions would result in reducing Western Europe literally to a state of dependency and Europe as a whole would become insignificant. Britain and France cannot let Nasser have a stranglehold on the canal."

Republican Senator H. Alexander Smith wondered whether "any change of leadership in Egypt might bring in a person even worse than Nasser."

"Nasser is the worst we've had so far," replied Dulles, referring to Nasser's "Hitlerite" personality.

Representative Dewey Short commented that Nasser seemed to be "playing the old Hitler game," and Senator Styles Bridges interjected that Nasser had to be stopped "before he really gets started."

"We are finally convinced that he is an extremely dangerous fanatic," said Dulles. "If he can get by with this action, the British and French are probably right in their appraisal of the consequences." He added later that the allies thought of Nasser as "a wild man brandishing an axe and that they do not have to wait for the blow to fall."

Lyndon Johnson was indignant. "Haven't we had enough experience with this type of situation to realize that we can't deal with this colonel and shouldn't we face up to it and say so to our allies? We should tell them they have our moral support and that they should go on in."

Eisenhower agreed that "We can't accept an inconclusive outcome leaving Nasser in control." He later emphasized that he "wanted everyone to understand clearly that we do not intend to stand by helplessly and let this one man get away with what he is trying to do. The United States will look to its interests."

On that note, the secretary of state took off for the conference of maritime powers in London.

• •

After a two-and-a-half-month period of relative calm following Hammarskjold's April visit, violent incidents began breaking out again along Israel's frontiers. Secretary-General Hammarskjold had devoted much of his time since April seeking a solution and he was becoming disillusioned and impatient. He was particularly unhappy with Ben Gurion, who in public spoke of Israel's desire for peace but in private refused to take measures to keep the frontiers quiet. Israeli troops, in violation of the armistice, were still occupying the vital El Auja demilitarized zone south of the Gaza Strip, refusing to permit U.N. observers in the area or to allow meetings of the Mixed Armistice Commission to be held in the El Auja headquarters. Israeli patrols again were operating provocatively close to the armistice lines, and Israeli soldiers were building fortifications in demilitarized zones along both the Egyptian and Syrian sectors.

Hammarskjold had returned to the Middle East in July, arriving there on the nineteenth, the day Dulles pulled out of the dam loan. With everyone's attention diverted by that crisis, the secretary-general accomplished little, and after a week of futile talks with both sides, he returned to New York. As tensions increased and the violence of incidents escalated in August, Hammarskjold's disappointment with Ben Gurion became acute.

In a cable to Burns on August 7 he complained about continued Israeli construction of fortifications in demilitarized zones. "This situation, which has dragged on for very long, will not only put the Israelis in a very bad position but also seriously reflect on policy of UNTSO. Israelis should consider that they have something serious to lose by continuing operations undermining authority of UNTSO. I am likewise concerned by Syrian work in northern demilitarized zone. The Israelis should not be surprised by such moves on the Syrian side with the freedom they have granted themselves. They cannot attack the Syrians while on the other hand disregarding your requests.

"I further would like to check with you my impression of a degeneration of Israeli discipline along the Gaza Strip. The number of cases where Israelis violate cease-fire in that region seems to be mounting and show increased frequency. The Israelis must understand that such a policy will eliminate all possibilities for us to discipline the other parties and will finally put them to blame."

In a letter to Ben Gurion, Hammarskjold warned that if Israel did not soon halt its aggressive policies he would have to issue a public report. His letter produced no result and with increasing exasperation and frustration he watched the region disintegrate. On August 17 Israelis raided inside Egypt and killed nine Egyptians. Hammarskjold again wrote to Ben Gurion: "If you blame us for the inability of the U.N. organs to assist, you should not, on the other hand, stall on such cooperation as would increase our possibilities to be of help. We have not been able, in the last few months, to register much of a cooperative attitude from your side in relation to our efforts.''

What Hammarskjold did not know was that Ben Gurion—like Eden and Mollet—wanted war. All of Hammarskjold's letters and efforts were in vain. War was now a national policy of all three countries.

• •

The first shiploads of the new French weapons had arrived in Israel during the night of July 24 and were unloaded in great secrecy. The sharp Anglo-French reaction to Nasser's nationalization of the canal two days later brought jubilation to Israel's leaders. Now Nasser's days looked numbered. Dayan wanted to attack Egypt immediately while the consternation caused by the nationalization occupied the world's attention.

He visited Ben Gurion on August 2 and proposed three plans of attack: take over the Sinai Peninsula and the Suez Canal, capture Sharm el-Sheikh, or occupy the Gaza Strip. Ben Gurion protested that the French arms were just starting to arrive. But Dayan, who had a soldier's appreciation for the relative strength of the two armies, believed that Israel was stronger than Egypt even without the French weapons. "I assured him that from what I knew of our Army, we could gain our objectives even without the arms we had been promised by France."

Ben Gurion calculated that fewer casualties would be suffered by Israel if it waited until more French arms were received. He no doubt also was already considering the possibility that France might in some way be brought into Israel's war plans, for when Dayan asked if he should honor a French request for information about Israeli ports and airfields, Ben Gurion answered: "If the French want such information, we must provide it willingly. Altogether we must treat them as brothers all along the line."

When Dayan expressed the hope that Britain would attack Egypt, Ben Gurion dampened his ardor by declaring that Eden would not attack without U.S. support. "There is no hope of that scoundrel Dulles supporting any daring action against the Arabs and the Russians."

Five days later Dayan's dreams of conquest took a step closer to becoming true. French Defense Minister Bourgès-Maunoury, during a meeting with Shimon Peres in Paris, asked how long it would take Israeli forces to sweep across the Sinai. About a week, answered Peres. Would Israel be willing to attack Egypt in concert with France? asked Bourgès. Certainly, answered Peres. The meeting was the first open indication to the Israelis that there might be the hope of warring against Egypt in collusion with France. No more was mentioned of the pregnant matter during August while the diplomatic ballet danced itself out.

• •

The centerpiece of America's diversionary efforts was the London Conference, which opened August 16 in stately Lancaster House, over-looking the tranquil gardens of Green Park. Twenty-two nations were in attendance, the top sixteen users* of the Suez Canal and the original signatories to the Convention of Constantinople, which guaranteed free access of all shipping to the canal.

How dramatically the world had changed since the convention had been signed in 1888, six years after Britain's conquest of Egypt and nine years before Queen Victoria's fabulous Diamond Jubilee, was stunningly evident in the formidable titles of the original signatories. Among them, they made up the cream of the great and proud rulers of the nineteenth century. They were Her Majesty the Queen of the United Kingdom of Great Britain and Ireland, Empress of India; His Majesty the Emperor of Germany, King of Prussia; His Majesty the Emperor of Austria, King of Bohemia, etc., and Apostolic King of Hungary; His Majesty the King of Spain and in the name of the Queen Regent of the Kingdom; the President of the French Republic; His Majesty the King of Italy; His Majesty the King of the Netherlands, Grand Duke of Luxembourg, etc; His Majesty the Emperor of all the Russias; His Majesty the Emperor of the Ottomans. Now only Britain and the Netherlands retained ruling royal families and those had severely diminished power. But if the titles were now different, the purpose for the gathering in London of the rep-resentatives of the original signers was the same: how to protect the wealth and privileges of their nations.

Egypt, although invited, stayed away. At a press conference teeming with three hundred reporters and photographers on August 12 in Cairo, Nasser explained his reasons, charging that Britain, France and the United States had conspired "to starve and terrorize the Egyptian peo-ple. The three powers immediately froze Egyptian assets and funds in their banks. Britain and France mobilized their reserves and officially announced that their troops and fleets were on the move. The Egyptian government strongly deplores these measures, and regards them as a

*Australia, Britain, Ceylon, Denmark, Ethiopia, France, India, Indonesia, Japan, New Zealand, Norway, Pakistan, Persia, Portugal, Sweden, United States.

threat to the Egyptian people to make them surrender part of their territory and sovereignty to an international body, which in fact is international colonialism."

Nasser reiterated his pledge that Egypt would operate the canal efficiently and fairly. He noted that since nationalization 766 ships had safely
navigated it. Egypt was capable of operating the canal and, he vowed,
Egypt would not accept any international control over its operation of
the canal. He pointed out that forty-five nations had used the canal in
1955, and therefore the London conference was not truly international.
He also found it strange, he added, that to his "complete surprise the
British government extended an invitation to consider matters concerning the Suez Canal, which is an integral part of Egypt, without any consultation with Egypt." Nasser then referred to a nationally televised
speech Eden had made August 8 in which the prime minister had brutally
attacked the Egyptian by declaring: "Our quarrel is not with Egypt, still
less with the Arab world; it is with Colonel Nasser."

Said Nasser, "The British prime minister spoke: 'We don't trust Nasser. It is Nasser we quarrel with.' Very well, if these people have no
trust, there is no reason to go to London for talks."

• •

The opening of the conference at 10 A.M. Greenwich Summer Time
was met with massive protests in the Arab world. Arabs observed five
minutes of silence for the "assassination of liberty." Twenty-four-hour
general strikes closed shops and emptied streets throughout Egypt, Jordan, Lebanon, Libya and Syria and to a lesser extent in Iraq, Morocco,
Sudan and Tunisia. Saudi Arabia remained unaffected, though its government had, like all Arab nations, including pro-British Iraq, endorsed Nasser's nationalization.

Representatives to the conference immediately coalesced into two
blocs, as expected. The Big Three bloc, led by Foster Dulles, had the
support of eighteen of the representatives; the pro-Nasser group included
only Ceylon, India, Indonesia and the Soviet Union.

In the diplomatic thrust and parry that continued until August 23, when
the conference finally ended, India's V. K. Krishna Menon was the main
combatant for Egypt, with the Soviet Union acting as his second. He was
the brilliant, darkly handsome and exceedingly disliked, in the West,
acting foreign minister of India. Even Eisenhower, who usually could
find a kind word for anyone, despised him. "Krishna Menon is a menace
and a boor," Ike confided to his diary. "He is a boor because he con-

ceives himself to be intellectually superior and rather coyly presents, to cover this, a cloak of excessive humility and modesty. He is a menace because he is a master at twisting words and meanings of others and is governed by an ambition to prove himself the master international manipulator and politician of the age."

The core of the debate was over what kind of international group should be created to help Egypt operate the canal. Menon proposed a group so loosely knit that it would have no influence at all. It would be "a consultative body of user interests with advisory, consultative and liaison functions" and its existence would be "without prejudice to Egyptian ownership and operation."

Dulles wanted something amounting to a supercompany that would have actual operating control of the canal. His proposal was so blatant that Eisenhower cabled him on August 19 with the warning that "Nasser may find it impossible to swallow the whole of this as now specified." He suggested that Nasser be offered the right to appoint the actual operating officer, "subject to board approval."

Dulles shot back a cable pointing out that he was unlikely to get British and French approval of such a proposal, adding: "I doubt whether we should make at this stage concessions which we might be willing to make as a matter of last resort in order to obtain Egypt's concurrence."

Eisenhower was repentant. "I understand the box you are in," he cabled back. "I will approve your decision and support you in whatever action you finally decide you must take."

Dulles' proposal carried 18 to 4, and the conference ended. The vote had no force, of course, and merely represented a statement of the position of the West and its allies. An eight-hundred-page text of the proceedings was sent to Egypt for Nasser's edification. It is doubtful that he ever read it.

But the conference did accomplish one important thing, as did the Big Three parley earlier, and that was to dampen war passions. The American strategy was working, at least outside the offices of Anthony Eden and Guy Mollet. The powerful British Labour Party, which originally had given Eden unqualified support, now had calmed down and served notice that it would agree to the use of force only if the imbroglio were first referred for conciliation to the United Nations. An even more serious sign of slipping support for Eden's war policy began appearing in public opposition. Eden got his first taste of it as he and Clarissa Churchill celebrated their fourth wedding anniversary August 14 by attending a showing of the topical diplomatic comedy *Romanoff and Juliet*. When they returned to 10 Downing Street they found about five hundred demonstrators shouting: "We want peace." "Go to the United Nations."

Eden observed wryly: "We ate our supper to a noise like a palace revolution. Strange wedding bells, but it seemed a fitting epilogue to our play."

Less than a month had passed since the West had exploded in indignation at Nasser's nationalization of the Suez Canal, but the British press's jingoistic reaction to kick back was already being replaced by a more thoughtful attitude of trying to settle the crisis by means other than violence. The London *Daily Mirror* dropped from the ranks of the sword rattlers and accused the editors of hawkish papers, notably *The Times,* of being "cardboard heroes" who in the 1930s had appeased Hitler but now demanded "savage and instant revenge" against a small country.

This developing split in the country's support was portentous for Eden. Had he been able to attack Egypt immediately, there was little doubt that he would have been cheered by his countrymen. But as passions cooled, so did his support. Doubts began to occur, and with them came questions about the role of Britain in the 1950s and the wisdom of embarking on a nineteenth-century policy of gunboat diplomacy.

The growing skepticism was manifest by the end of the London Conference. Suddenly Dulles, who was widely disliked and distrusted in Europe as a Cold Warrior, was being hailed as a man of peace. "For almost the first time, Mr. Dulles is popular in Europe," reported *The New York Times* on August 24. "Europeans have long suspected Mr. Dulles of a too great willingness to go to the brink of war, as he once described it. Now, it appears to many that Britain and France were approaching the brink over Suez, and Mr. Dulles proved a restraining influence."

On the same day that the conference ended, Ike was nominated at the Republican Convention and hailed as a leader of peace.

• •

The ending of the London Conference found the West at an impasse. Egypt had simply ignored the results, Britain and France were not yet able to launch an invasion, and the United States was left desperately seeking a way to resolve the crisis. Dulles rose to the occasion by suggesting another time-consuming diversion. He urged that a committee of the conference representatives go to Nasser and personally present the majority view to him. The group comprised Australia, Ethiopia, Iran, Sweden and the United States, and its head was florid, outspoken Robert

G. Menzies, 61, Australia's prime minister and an unabashed defender of Eden's policies. Before the opening of the London Conference he had set forth his anti-Nasser views in a TV speech in London, declaring: "To leave our vital interests to the whim of one man would be suicidal. We cannot accept either the legality or the morality of what Nasser has done."

His choice as leader of the committee was the worst possible. It meant the mission would be an almost certain failure, which Eisenhower was beginning to suspect might be the hidden intention of both Britain and France. Ike was right.

Nasser, in trying to keep up his posture of reasonableness, agreed to see the Menzies mission on September 3. But before the group even arrived in Cairo a number of provocative moves were made by the Anglo-French leaders. The dispatch of French forces to Cyprus to "protect" French nationals was announced August 29. The next day Britain and France issued warnings to their nationals to leave Egypt and three other Arab countries as well, Jordan, Lebanon and Syria.

"By now I was wondering at times whether the British and French governments were really concerned over the success or failure of the Menzies mission," recalled Eisenhower. "Such evacuation hardly showed an intent to work for a peaceful solution."

The State Department was coming to the same conclusion. "In the course of a conversation yesterday you asked whether I personally thought the British and French were bluffing in connection with their military preparations," William M. Rountree, a top Dulles aide, wrote the secretary of state on September 1. "The weight of evidence appears to indicate the British and French military movements go far beyond a war of nerves [and] are preparations for actual hostilities on a large scale. The British and French attitude toward negotiations with Nasser seems to be that they expect a rejection of the eighteen-nation proposal and insist upon that rejection coming quickly rather than engaging in pro-tracted negotiations. It could be said that their actions indicate they ac-tually desire such a rejection, presumably in the belief that a settlement based upon the eighteen-nation proposal would not entirely meet their requirements. Until we know more of actual British and French inten-tions we should not permit ourselves to support any act in the United Nations which would do no more than set the stage for military interven-tion."

Worried, Eisenhower wrote another long letter to Eden on September 2 "to remove from Anthony's mind any possible misapprehensions as to

300

the convictions of the American government and people.'' The letter was polite but firm. ''I am afraid, Anthony, that from this point onward our views on this situation diverge. I must tell you frankly that American public opinion flatly rejects the thought of using force.'' The President pointed out that he and Eden faced two separate problems, the canal and ''to see that Nasser shall not grow as a menace to the peace and vital interests of the West. We have friends in the Middle East who tell us they would like to see Nasser's deflation brought about. But they seem unanimous in feeling that the Suez is not the issue on which to attempt to do this by force.''

Eden answered with what the President found to be a ''disturbing'' letter. ''I can assure you that we are conscious of the burdens and perils attending military intervention,'' Eden wrote. ''But we have many times led Europe in the fight for freedom. It would be an ignoble end to our long history if we tamely accepted to perish by degrees.''

Eden was by now totally obsessed with the specter of Nasser destroying Britain's empire. About the time of his latest letter to Ike, he told U.S. diplomat Loy Henderson: ''I would rather have the British empire fall in one crash than have it nibbled away.''

Eisenhower answered Eden's letter on September 8 with a mollifying but nonetheless straightforward message maintaining his opposition to force. ''Whenever, on any international question, I find myself differing even slightly from you, I feel a deep compulsion to re-examine my position instantly and carefully. But permit me to suggest that when you use phrases in connection with the Suez affair, like 'ignoble end to our long history' in describing the possible future of your great country, you are making of Nasser a much more important figure than he is.

''We have a grave problem confronting us in Nasser's reckless adventure with the canal, and I do *not* differ from you in your estimate of his intentions and purposes. The place where we apparently do not agree is on the probable effects in the Arab world of the various possible reactions by the world.'' The President wrote that Eden's belief that Nasser was becoming the leader of Islam was a ''picture too dark and is severely distorted.''

At the same time, Ike added, ''We do not want any capitulation to Nasser. We want to stand firmly with you to deflate the ambitious pretensions of Nasser. [But that] can best be assured by slower and less dramatic processes than military force.'' Among such methods, Eisenhower said, were economic pressures against Egypt, promotion of a users' organization to run the canal, establishment of alternative oil routes, and

"Arab rivalries . . . which can be exploited if we do not make Nasser an Arab hero. Nasser thrives on drama. If we let some of the drama go out of the situation and concentrate upon the task of deflating him through slower but sure processes such as I described, I believe the desired results can more probably be obtained."

Eisenhower concluded by assuring Eden that "we are not blind to the fact that eventually there may be no escape from the use of force. But to resort to military action when the world believes there are other means available for resolving the dispute would set in motion forces that could lead, in the years to come, to the most distressing results. With warmest regard, as ever your friend."

Eden was disappointed by the letter and complained that it had obviously been written by the secretary of state. "The only thing that's true to Ike in that is his signature and that's illegible," Eden snapped. Actually, Eisenhower had written the letter and then asked Dulles for his suggestions. Dulles smilingly cut one paragraph that read: "It took your nation some eighteen years to put the original Napoleon in his proper place, but you did it. You have dealt more rapidly with his modern imitators." Dulles observed that force had been used against Napoleon. Eisenhower, grinning, agreed to the deletion.

• •

The Menzies mission arrived in Cairo September 2 to a polite welcome and met the next day with Nasser. It was not a happy meeting. Menzies was all bluster and threats. "I explained to him the strength of opinion in both London and Paris, and added, in substance, 'I am not making any threats but frankness as between two heads of government requires me to offer my personal opinion that you are facing not a bluff but a stark condition of fact which your country should not ignore,' " reported Menzies. "Nasser assured me that he did not treat the British action as a bluff."

Recalled Nasser: "When Menzies began to threaten I closed the papers in front of me." He told Menzies: "We have nothing to discuss with you." It was only through the intervention of Loy Henderson, representing Dulles, that the meeting was saved. But the conclusion was predictable.

Nasser had all the arguments on his side. "What is your problem?" he asked. "Freedom of navigation? I'm ready to discuss that. Tolls? I'm ready to discuss that. The British press charges I'm trying to build an empire? We can discuss that too if you want—but I will not discuss

Egyptian sovereignty. Perhaps you would like to discuss British fears that I'm going to cut off their lifeline of empire? If I did that, it would mean war with Britain. Do you think I'm crazy enough to do that? And if I was so crazy how could the international board that you propose prevent me from doing it in any case?"

There was no serious answer. Menzies' mission soon ended in failure. It was devastatingly ridiculed by journalist Mohamed Heikal. He mockingly proposed in *al-Akhbar,* Cairo's largest newspaper, that Australian sheep should be internationalized, not the canal. "Those who use woolen clothes made of the wool of Australian sheep have the right to consider the future of this wool according to the principle of the London Conference, which says that the users, not the owners, have the primary rights." The analogy was too close for comfort.

The mission ended in mutual dislike between the Australian and Nasser. "So far from being charming, Nasser is rather gauche, with some irritating mannerisms, such as rolling his eyes up to the ceiling when he is talking to you and producing a quick, quite evanescent grin when he can think of nothing else," complained Menzies.

An Egyptian reporter described Menzies as "blunt, hostile, and arrogant . . . like a bull in a china shop. He was often drunk and he sweated profusely. We began to refer to him as the Australian mule."

Menzies did not move Nasser one jot closer to bowing to the West's desires. But he did unwittingly buy time. Menzies remained in Cairo until September 10. The original date for invasion by the Anglo-French forces was the fifteenth, but that had been delayed until September 26. Now another way to buy time had to be discovered by Eisenhower and Dulles.

303

CHAPTER XV

We'll Be Plastered as Assassins and Baby Killers

MOUNTBATTEN

WHATEVER HIS FAULTS, Foster Dulles was never accused of lacking ingenuity. While Eden and Mollet searched desperately for an internationally acceptable pretext to go to war with Egypt, Dulles applied all his formidable energies and legal prestidigitation to sidetrack them. He was inventive and ploddingly patient, repeatedly offering up diplomatic alternatives to the violence the allies wanted. When the Menzies mission collapsed, with no other result than rancor on both sides, the persistent secretary of state came forth with yet another diplomatic dance for gaining time.

Dulles' latest idea was little more than a slapdash proposal to create an organization of the users of the canal, comprising initially the eighteen Western-bloc members of the London Conference. Since the Soviet Union had not been part of the majority, that country would be conveniently left out. The purpose of the organization was not quite clear but that was one of its virtues. The suggested members would first have to meet to decide the function of the new organization, a process guaranteed to consume more time. Tentatively, Dulles thought that the users might establish a group that would parallel the old canal company and participate with Egypt in assuring the efficient operation of the waterway.

Eden and Mollet had other ideas. They reluctantly accepted Dulles' proposal for a users' association, since they had little choice if they wanted to demonstrate to Washington and the world that they were exhausting all peaceful means before resorting to war. But privately they were hatching other plots.

304

On the day of Menzies' departure from his failed mission in Cairo, Mollet and Pineau flew to London for talks with Eden and Lloyd. Afterward, they said that the talks had made them determined "to resist, by all appropriate means, any arbitrary interference with rights established under national agreements [and had] discussed the further measures to be taken." There in fact had been no interference with canal shipping since Nasser's nationalization, but it was indicative of their flushed state of mind that they continually invoked the image.

Behind their public statement, Eden and Mollet took secret decisions aimed at bringing the crisis to the violent head they sought. They ordered the old Suez Canal Company to release all its non-Egyptian pilots from their contracts, thus freeing them to depart. This step, the European leaders confidently anticipated, would create havoc at the waterway and render Egypt incapable of handling shipping through the canal, thereby giving them a pretext to intervene. They also decided to take the dispute to the United Nations, where they expected it to founder under a Soviet veto. This would have the effect of clearing one more diplomatic hurdle to war.

Their plan was simple if diabolical. They would exhaust all the obvious alternatives to war as soon as possible. That way they still might be able to launch their war on schedule. The invasion date, put back again by planning complications, was now set for October 1.

With their decision to withdraw the foreign pilots, Eden and Mollet had a reasonable expectation that they might soon get their pretext for war. It was yet another goad to make Nasser react rashly. If Nasser tried to retaliate, Lloyd confided to Anthony Nutting, that will "give us a casus belli."

• •

Eden presented Dulles' users' plan to an emergency meeting of Parliament on September 12 as though it were his own idea. His explanation of its purpose made it sound like a formula for war, not an effort at conciliation. Under the plan he expounded, the users of the canal would hire their own pilots, collect tolls, and then if Egypt refused to cooperate, it "will once more be in breach of the Convention of 1888." The Labour Party was by now in a rebellious mood, suspicious of Eden's motives and responsive to growing antiwar feeling among the populace. Labour members greeted Eden's description of the users' organization with shouts of "Deliberate provocation" and "What a peacemaker!"

Unperturbed, Eden carried on above the uproar. "For this country, military action is always the last resort, and we shall go on working for a peaceful solution so long as there is any prospect of achieving one. But the government are not prepared to embark on a policy of abject appeasement. The government must be free to take whatever steps are open to them to restore the situation.''

Labour leader Hugh Gaitskell made an impassioned response, declaring that the government was "saber-rattling. Either the government seriously intended to use force—and what the prime minister said this afternoon certainly seems to suggest that—or they could be simply bluffing. If they intend to use force in this way—that is, in the absence of any deliberate provocative action by Colonel Nasser or aggression by him—simply to get a solution to this problem, I say that the consequences to this country will be disastrous. Conservatives must understand this. In ignoring the [U.N.] Charter and taking the law into our own hands, we are reverting to international anarchy.''

Conservatives remained solidly behind Eden during the hot and often raucous debate. "Weakness or faintheartedness now can mean carnage for our children within years,'' declared Sir Victor Raikes.

For Dulles, sitting in his office in Washington, such hyperbole and the warring interpretation Eden had given to the users' plan were additional evidence that the Briton was searching for an excuse to go to war. "I'm embarrassed because Eden kind of knocked this whole plan down,'' he said to a colleague later that day. "I think Eden went a little out of bounds. He wants to show [the canal] is a lifeline and it can't be cut—and so justify war. This is where our policy splits.''

Dulles also had a telephone conversation with British Ambassador Sir Roger Makins about authorship of the users' plan. "We would like to give you all the credit for it but Lloyd does not think you want it.''

"I don't,'' replied Dulles.

"Our official line has been and will be that this is a plan jointly prepared.''

Dulles agreed, but Eden's press spokesman, William Clark, indiscreetly gave the game away in London with a clever pun. The plan, he told correspondents, had a *"foster* father.''

Dulles emphasized the pacific purposes of his plan at his press conference the next day. If Nasser fails to cooperate, he declared, "we don't intend to shoot our way through. Then we intend to send our boats around the Cape.''

The remarks were a blow to Eden and a boost to the Labour Party in the second day of debate in London. Gaitskell picked up the secretary of state's remarks and used them as the basis to demand a no-war pledge from Eden. When the prime minister equivocated, Gaitskell impatiently leaped to his feet and insisted with a mocking paraphrase of Dulles that Eden answer whether "he is prepared to say on behalf of Her Majesty's Government that they will not shoot their way through the canal."

"I said that we were in complete agreement with the U.S. government about what to do," replied Eden evasively. Cries of "Answer!" "Answer!" rang through the aroused House. Finally Eden was forced to offer a very cautiously worded pledge that he would take the dispute to the United Nations before force was used.

The incident caused a further deterioration in Eden's relations with Dulles, leaving the prime minister bitter and resentful. Dulles' remark, Eden complained, was "an advertisement to Nasser that he could reject the project with impunity. Such cynicism towards allies destroys true partnership."

Eden's excessive reaction was due to more than the discomfiture Dulles' statement caused him in the House. It also came from the fact that Dulles, by his quick maneuvering, had once again outwitted him on the diplomatic front. He had destroyed another of Eden's schemes to go to war. Eden was left in search of another pretext.

•   •

There was a growing thunderhead on Eden's horizon, this one potentially far more threatening than Foster Dulles. The shift taking place in the public's attitude against going to war was accelerating. Six weeks had now passed since nationalization, a period of great pronouncements and pretentious posturing. Yet no great event had occurred. Nasser was acting reasonably. The canal was open and operating efficiently, trade was going on unhindered, and there were no shortages of oil or other evidence of a national emergency. The public's ardor was cooling as rapidly as its skepticism about the justness of war was increasing.

This tidal change was obvious in the vote of confidence taken at the end of the September emergency meeting of Parliament. Eden was supported 319 to 248, but the vote was almost along straight party lines. Labour's firm opposition to force reflected the changed atmosphere in the country.

The change was even permeating Eden's own Cabinet. His minister of defense, Sir Walter Monckton, 65, one of the leading House lawyers and a supporter of Israel, was also having doubts about Eden's belligerent actions. When he was shown plans for the invasion, he expressed his doubts by commenting: "Very interesting, but how do we actually start this war?"

That of course was Eden's central problem, which was aggravated by Nasser's continuing reasonableness and the smooth operation of the canal.

• •

The difficulty of navigating the 101-mile canal had been greatly exaggerated by the old canal company over the years, creating the image that if the foreign pilots left, the whole waterway would be rendered impassable by the incompetence of the Egyptians. Both Eden and Mollet thought that the departure of the foreign pilots would "constitute embarrassment to Nasser, and thus a pressure point against him," in the words of Pineau. But when the old company notified the pilots that they could leave, the reverse happened.

There had been 205 pilots on the day of nationalization, including 61 French, 54 British and 40 Egyptian. They and all the hundreds of other support personnel were warned by the company that they would lose their pensions if they remained beyond September 15. On that date, some six hundred foreign canal employees departed. Risk insurance for canal cargoes was increased 250 percent by Lloyd's of London.

Mahmoud Yunis, who had taken over the canal during Nasser's speech, saved the situation for Egypt. He had been anticipating the move and in the weeks previous had conducted an active campaign to recruit new pilots. He hired twenty-six Egyptians, most of them navy captains, scoured other waterways around the world for pilots and had streamlined operating procedures to make piloting easier. The first day of sailing without the old pilots, forty-two ships safely transited the canal. The jubilation that this success represented for the new company and Egypt gave Nasser's cause yet another powerful boost in morale. Lloyd's of London dropped its risk premium within the month.

"[Now] any thought of using force, under these circumstances, was almost ridiculous," observed Eisenhower.

• •

In the eyes of the world, center stage of the Suez affair was the diplomatic activity being created daily by Foster Dulles. But the most visible activity was the least important. Behind the scenes, hidden from view of the public, was unfolding a bizarre chiaroscuro of intrigue and collusion.

On one level Britain and France were joined together in building up a military force to attack Egypt. But they also continued with their own schemes, going their separate ways to weaken Nasser. Britain was deeply involved in its clandestine operations to depose Nasser and stage a coup in Syria. France moved to strengthen its secret alliance with Israel. The United States carried forward its plan to build up an informal alliance of anti-Nasser nations. Washington also now decided that the British had been right about Syria and launched its own misguided James Bond operation to stage a coup there.

All this scheming occurred simultaneously with Dulles' dramaturgy, contributing to the confusion and fantasy atmosphere pervading the crisis. So many issues—the canal, Arab nationalism, Western colonialism, anti-communism, Eisenhower's political campaign, the Arab-Israeli conflict—were now entangled in the drama that it was near impossible to identify the game much less the players.

• •

Ben Gurion and Moshe Dayan were attending a general staff meeting in Tel Aviv on September 1 when a "most immediate" message arrived. It was from the Israeli military attaché in Paris and he had a startling question from the French to relay. Would Israel be interested in taking part in an Anglo-French war against Egypt? The Israeli leaders did not have to waste time considering the idea. The country would indeed like part of the action, Ben Gurion cabled to Paris. Within six days, Major General Meir Amit, Dayan's chief of operations, met in the Paris home of Colonel Mangin with Vice Admiral Pierre Barjot, the deputy commander of the joint command of the Anglo-French invasion forces, and discussed in more detail what role Israel might play. "Admiral Barjot made it clear that his questions at this stage were only for enlightenment, though he was asking them on the assumption that appropriate political conditions might arise in the immediate future for Israel to take part in the operations," observed Dayan.

Shimon Peres flew to Paris on September 19 to pursue war talks with Defense Minister Bourgès-Maunoury. Dayan had told Peres that he should set three conditions for cooperation with the French. First, France should officially invite Israel to take part in talks so that the Jewish state was treated as "an ally with equal rights"; second, the war should not be such that it might involve Israel in a conflict with Britain, which had a defense treaty with Jordan; and third, Israel wanted as its reward the possession of Sharm el-Sheikh and a number of areas in central and northern Sinai.

309

Peres met twice with Bourgès, who informed the Israeli that the Cabinet had approved the initiation of high-level talks with Israeli officials on joint war plans. Peres returned to Israel the next day, September 25, and reported to Ben Gurion that "the British and French had made up their minds, though had not yet reached a formal decision, to undertake joint military action to nullify the nationalization of the Suez Canal. France would like Israel to be a full and equal partner in the operation [but] Britain would be opposed to any idea of cooperation or direct contact with Israel—or at least have serious reservations about such an association."

"[This] radically changes the position," replied Ben Gurion. "We must now weigh this more serious move very carefully." To his diary, he confided: "This was our first opportunity to find an ally."

At a Cabinet meeting that same day Ben Gurion received permission to send a secret delegation to Paris to embark on formal talks on colluding with France to wage war against Egypt.

• •

The atmosphere was now further clouded by an escalation of the vicious round of attack and counterattack along Israel's frontiers. Violence increased sharply in late August and through September, capturing world attention and bringing the wrath of Dag Hammarskjold down once again on Ben Gurion. The Israeli leader persistently refused to allow U.N. observers in the El Auja area, which Israeli troops continued to occupy in defiance of the armistice agreement. In a cable to Chief of Staff Burns, Hammarskjold instructed him to tell Ben Gurion that if observers were not soon allowed in El Auja then "Israel goes on record as considering itself free from the obligations under the armistice agreement. I must also note that the stand now taken as to observer arrangements represents a further serious departure not only from compliance with the armistice agreements but also from the expressed wishes of the Security Council. This move is so serious as to make a report to the Security Council necessary."

Hammarskjold's threat to go public with his charge of Israeli violations of the armistice had no effect on Ben Gurion. Instead, the prime minister pursued his retaliation policy with renewed vigor. In clashes on August 30, two Israelis and thirteen Egyptians were killed. By September, the violence extended to the Jordanian border, which split Jerusalem in half and intruded like an axe into the center of Israel.

While on a mapping exercise close to the border, six Israeli soldiers were killed and four wounded by Jordanian troops on September 10; three Israeli civilians were slain at an oil-drilling camp inside Israel two days later. Israel struck back on the eleventh and the thirteenth with heavy military raids that took the lives of thirty Jordanians.

Fears were spreading that Israel and Jordan might get into an all-out war, but General Burns discounted such speculation in a September 14 cable to Hammarskjold. He noted that many Egyptian camps in the Sinai were empty, indicating that two of Egypt's three Sinai divisions had been withdrawn to protect the canal. Burns thought that if Israel attacked anyone it would be Egypt.

But attention continued to focus on the Jordanian border because of the escalating incidents there. On September 23, a Jordanian soldier whose brother had been killed by Israelis earlier in the month went berserk and attacked a group of one hundred scientists attending an Israeli archeological congress. The archeologists had gathered within four hundred feet of the border in Jerusalem when the soldier fired his Bren at them, killing four and wounding seventeen. The next day an Israeli woman and a farmer were also killed in separate incidents involving Jordanians.

Israel was gripped with fury. Golda Meir discounted the possibility that the shooting of the archeologists resulted from the soldier's grief. "She was not interested in fact that orders not to open fire were given to Jordan Army," Burns reported to Hammarskjold on September 24. "She was not prepared to accept an excuse that undisciplined Jordanian soldiers disobeyed orders. Nor were recent shooting incidents the consequences of Israel policy of retaliation." The foreign minister told Burns that the "Jordan Army was undisciplined and fed on propaganda that Israel was to be destroyed. If Jordanian government had no control somebody would have to take over."

Burns warned: "Situation very tense. Jordanians expecting to be attacked any day."

Hammarskjold replied to Burns the same day with a stinging indictment of Israel's retaliatory policy. "Of course, it should not be any surprise, but I note with regret that the Israeli government can never transcend its one-sided view of how matters may be straightened out. When has Israel ever admitted any responsibility or expressed regret in the cases where their people, unprovoked, have violated the cease-fire? It should follow that they admit that their retaliation policy is no better means for re-establishment order than the U.N. operations which they so high-handedly reject. But it seems impossible to make them see that they cannot maintain on the one side that threats to use military force, and excessive military reprisals, are effective means to achieve a change of policy, and on the other hand that the incidents which have occurred for the last one and a half years all are expressions of the other government's policy.''

Israel's retaliation for the attack on the archeologists came with devastating force the next day, but not before a futile attempt by Burns to stop it. He had heard rumors that Israel was prepared to attack and tried unsuccessfully to get in touch with Ben Gurion and Meir. Finally he reached Arthur Lourie, acting director-general of the Ministry of Foreign Affairs. Lourie said he knew of no plans to retaliate but offered to try to respond to Burns's request for constraint. He later telephoned Burns to tell him that he had "been unable to reach Mrs. Meir or Mr. Ben Gurion, nor had he been able to find any of the Israeli Army authorities who could give the necessary assurance.''

At that time, both Ben Gurion and Meir were in a Cabinet meeting at which the war collusion talks with France were being approved. Also approved was a massive retaliatory attack against Jordan.

It came in the dark against a police fortress near Husan, just south of Jerusalem. When the large Israeli force, estimated as a regiment, finally withdrew, it left behind thirty-nine Jordanian bodies, including a twelve-year-old girl, and eleven wounded policemen and civilians. The police building and a schoolhouse were destroyed.

Hammarskjold was upset. He sent Ben Gurion another letter condemning Israel's policy of retaliation. Hammarskjold of course had no way of knowing that there was more to Israel's harsh attacks that month than just retaliation. The raids not only satisfied Israel's passion for revenge but they diverted attention away from its border to the west with Egypt. If the Jewish state was going to wage war against Egypt with France, then it could veil that intent by creating tension to the east with Jordan.

• •

The invasion plan jointly embarked on by Britain and France was running into more delays. It had been postponed to October 1 primarily because the political leaders had decided too many casualties would be suffered if troops stormed the beaches and the crowded streets of Alexandria in World War II style. The new objective was to launch a police-type action against Port Said, a seedy, less populated town on the northern terminus of the canal. This change necessitated a massive amount of new work for the harried joint staffs trying to contend with the innumerable details involved in an invasion that was being compared to a "minor Normandy." Naval disembarkation orders, for instance, were so complicated that they were as thick as the London telephone directory.

The force that Britain and France were assembling was impressive by the standards of gunboat diplomacy. There were eighty thousand troops, fliers and seamen assigned to the enterprise, more than two hundred British and thirty French warships, nearly eighty merchant ships, hundreds of landing crafts and twenty thousand vehicles. Five British aircraft carriers and two French were also in the attack force. In addition to the fighter planes from the aircraft carriers, there were a British medium and a light bomber force committed to the armada.

The British contribution was greatest (fifty thousand, which was more Englishmen than Wellington commanded at Waterloo) and an Englishman was chosen as commander. He was General Sir Charles Keightley, who was the Commander-in-Chief, Middle East, and as his deputy was a Frenchman, portly Vice Admiral Barjot. This division of command was carried through the lower subordinate staffs. General Stockwell was in charge of the landing force, and his deputy was prickly but brilliant Major General André Beaufre, a veteran of France's Indochina wars and currently commander of the rebel-ridden Constantine East zone near the Algerian-Tunisian border.

Beaufre was critical of the new plan urged on by Eden and worked out by the British chiefs of staff. The planners had decided that instead of making an opposed landing they would first take forty-eight hours to destroy the Egyptian Air Force and then bomb economic targets like petroleum depots, bridges, and railway stations. This phase would last for eight to ten days during which a massive "aero-psychological" campaign would be conducted to break Egypt's will to fight. That was supposed to be accomplished by dropping leaflets and haranguing the populace from airplanes equipped with loudspeakers.

"Indubitably, we were now in cloud cuckoo-land," complained Beaufre. "The theory was that under this pressure the defense would collapse and signs of war weariness appear."

It was only after the Egyptians had been too cowed to fight by the swashbuckling display of Western technology that troops would land unopposed. That was the heart of the new plan: "land without opposition."

"When I read that sentence, I could hardly believe my eyes," said Beaufre. "We were going from one extreme to the other. How could one hope to reduce resistance to nil and how could one know the result beforehand? Finally, and even more important, how could one expect world opinion to leave us free to bomb Egypt for 'eight to ten days at least' without intervening? It all seemed to me perfectly childish and very dangerous.''

Nonetheless that was the plan adopted. Working day and night in London in the dingy bombproof section of the War Office deep underground between Whitehall and the Thames, the joint staff produced the necessary revisions.

The first code name for the invasion had been Hamilcar, after the Carthaginian general, but it had to be changed when the French started painting their vehicles with the identification mark ''A'' while the British were using ''H.'' Only then was it realized by the British planners that Amilcar was the French spelling of Hamilcar. The operation was then renamed Musketeer, presumably after Dumas, and in its latest permutation was now called Musketeer Revised.

The planning problems were symptomatic of the deluge of difficulties that plagued all stages of the operation. British and French equipment was not interchangeable, few soldiers on either side knew the other's language and there were such annoying incompatibilities as the French using centigrade thermometers while the British used Fahrenheit. The troops all had to be fitted out in scarce tropical gear, and vehicles were to be painted yellow for easy identification but the French discovered it would take more of that paint than France produced in a year.

The essence of the operation now was the psychological warfare effort. British Brigadier Bernard Fergusson was quickly flown off to Cyprus to take charge of it. His staff of two dozen reservists was unfamiliar with the printing machinery on which they were to print the leaflets to drop on Egypt and as a result the presses frequently broke down. Only one plane equipped with loud-hailers could be found, and it was in Kenya. When it finally arrived on Cyprus it was discovered that during a refueling stop in Aden someone had stolen the public-address system. Arabs who were hired to broadcast anti-Nasser propaganda from Britain's clandestine Cyprus radio station quit in protest and only Palestinians with accents barely understandable to Egyptians could be found to make the broadcasts.

More serious than all of these compounding problems was the lack of a deepwater port in the region. The only adequate harbors were Malta, nearly six days' sailing time from Port Said by the slower troop transports, and Algiers for the French, which was even farther away. Such distances created a fatal gap between the time of a declaration of war and the arrival of the troop ships. During that period the Egyptians could strengthen their fortifications and, more important, work on world opinion to deflect the Anglo-French invasion.

This handicap resulted from Eden's insistence that the war must start with an ultimatum. It would naturally be so worded that Nasser would have to turn it down. Then, but only then, could the Anglo-French force move. It was a transparent cover to his real intentions, but Eden was adamant in maintaining the diplomatic niceties with the fiction that Britain attacked only after all else had failed. That should satisfy Eisenhower, Eden hoped, and maintain Britain's relations with other Arab states. Such legal fastidiousness was a sign of the weakness of Britain's moral position and Eden's failure as a leader. He was a sad, flawed figure, all grandiose on the outside but without confidence inside. Yet he stubbornly resisted all advice.

Even with the invasion landing place moved to Port Said, the casualties were likely to be horrendous, and the enormity of the potential slaughter was impressed on Eden by Lord Mountbatten, who by now was strongly against launching a war. He and a number of senior military leaders had become appalled at the whole idea of an invasion into a populous area. Mountbatten, one of Britain's most distinguished military men and a member of the royal family, took his doubts to Eden.

"Do you realize the only places we can land in Port Said are in the built-up area?" he said to Eden. "Do you realize that in order to land with safety we'll have to have preliminary bombardment by ships? Do you realize the naval gun trajectory at close range is practically flat? All our six-inch guns from the cruisers will go bursting into the town. And as for the great fifteen-inch guns of the French battleship *Jean Bart,* think of the mess they're going to make, think of the casualties and horrors, think of all the photographs the Egyptians will take. We'll be plastered round the world as assassins and baby killers. It's a horrible thought."

Eden was unmoved and ordered planning to continue.

• •

The enervating effects of Eden's gall-bladder operations and of the many pills he was taking were claiming their toll on his physical reserves and mental faculties. His temper, always volatile at the best of times, was now giving way to uncontrollable tantrums with the slightest provocation. An example of his deteriorating state, according to biographer Leonard Mosley, supposedly occurred in a seriocomic confrontation with military historian B. H. Liddell Hart. Eden had asked the respected military expert to help in drawing up plans for the campaign against

Egypt, but then had rejected four successive strategies. When he asked for yet another version, Liddell Hart had boldly sent back the original—and now Eden liked it.

"Captain Liddell Hart, here I am at a critical moment in Britain's history, arranging matters which may mean the life of the British empire," lectured Eden. "And what happens? I ask you to do a simple military chore for me, and it takes you five attempts—plus my vigilance amid all my worries—before you get it right."

"But, sir, it hasn't taken five attempts. That version, which you now say is just what you wanted, is the original version."

In the ensuing silence, Eden's face reddened, then he threw an old-fashioned inkwell at the historian. Liddell Hart watched for a moment as the blue stains spread through his light summer suit, then he stood up, grasped a wastebasket, jammed it over the head of the prime minister and walked out.

• •

In a crisis that had more than its share of silliness, no aspect of it was barmier than that which was about to be carried out by the intelligence services. The capacity of the spies to create mischief seemed as endless as their inability to accomplish anything positive. The CIA again was the star performer in the opéra bouffe that now began unfolding.

Kim Roosevelt had hinted to the CIA's Bill Eveland earlier that the agency thought it had a strong enough hold over King Saud to pressure Saudi Arabia into the informal anti-Nasser alliance Washington was fostering. In late September, to his astonishment, Eveland learned what this supposed lever was. It entailed a plan to convince Saud that if he were not more forthcoming the West would cut off his oil revenues. How this was to be done was at first kept from Eveland.

The man delegated to carry out the scheme was once again Robert Bernerd Anderson, the same one who had failed in his secret mission to Nasser and Ben Gurion earlier in the year. Flying in a special White House plane, Anderson picked up Eveland in London and then in great secrecy flew on to the U.S. base at Dhahran. They drove to Riyadh where they had an audience with King Saud and his top advisers in the king's palace. Saud was seated on a throne in a large hall dominated by great chandeliers. At least twenty-five high-backed chairs stretched out on each side of Saud's throne. His advisers sat on his left, the American delegation on his right. Anderson did the talking.

After delivering a flowery salutation from President Eisenhower, he averred that Nasser's nationalization of the canal was a threat to the Arab nations, and particularly to Saudi Arabia. It could, he added ominously, render "Saudi Arabia's petroleum worthless."

Saud replied that Nasser's action had been simply to claim what belonged to Egypt. Anderson countered that if shippers lost faith in the canal they would have to find costly alternate routes and then the king's oil would bring in less revenues. There might even be a war, which would stop the flow of Saudi oil, added Anderson. Then he came to his pièce de résistance.

According to Eveland, Anderson said: "Your Majesty must understand, we've made great technological advances and are now on the threshold of sources of power that will be cheaper and more efficient than oil. It might be necessary for us to ensure that our allies are self-sufficient and free from threats of blackmail."

What, asked the king, would the Europeans substitute for oil?

"Nuclear energy."

The meeting ended.

That night Anderson and Eveland had dinner with the king and his retainers, but there was no table conversation and the dinner ended early. Shortly after midnight Anderson was summoned to meet with Prince Faisal, the power behind the throne. Faisal, no fool, told Anderson that his threat was completely foolish and the Saudis were unimpressed.

The bluff had not worked.

Another secret mission had come to an end. According to Eveland, the plot had been the brainchild of Howard Page, a senior executive of the powerful Standard Oil of New Jersey, one of the owners of ARAMCO. Page personally sold the idea to Eisenhower, claimed Eveland.

The ignoble end of the Anderson mission did not prevent other clandestine schemes in the region from continuing. As part of the plan to build up anti-Nasser states, the CIA at this time put King Hussein on its private payroll. The arrangement was finally exposed in 1977 when news accounts reported that millions of dollars had been funneled over the years to Hussein under a program called NOBEEF. That was Kim Roosevelt's coded invention, standing for "beef up Jordan"; the NO, in CIA code, meant Jordan. The CIA now, in effect, was funding its own aid program to Jordan out of sight of congressional critics.

In Syria, Eveland learned in the beginning of October that Washington had opted to support Britain in overthrowing the pro-Nasser government. Eveland was instructed to urge the conservative Syrian plotters to act by late October.

Eveland's first duty was to collect 500,000 Syrian pounds (about $165,000) and deliver it to his Syrian contact, landowner Mikhail Ilyan. Eveland went to the Middle East regional finance office of the CIA in Beirut and collected a suitcase full of used Syrian notes, put the case in his car trunk, drove to Damascus and met Ilyan at the New Omayyad Hotel. The money would be used to pay army colonels, politicians, newspapermen and others to support the coup, Ilyan assured Eveland. But more than money was needed. Ilyan and his conspirators wanted assurance that America would back the coup once it started and would offer immediate diplomatic recognition to the new conservative government.

The assurance, Ilyan added, would have to come from President Eisenhower in a public statement echoing his April 9 declaration: "America would observe its commitments within constitutional means to oppose any aggression in the Middle East." Eveland was doubtful, but he cabled the request to Allen Dulles. The next day he had an answer. The statement would be made between October 16 and October 18 by Foster Dulles.

Ilyan accepted that promise, and preparations began in earnest toward staging a coup. The target date was set for the end of October.

• •

Invitations to join Dulles' users' association went out to the eighteen Western-bloc members of the London Conference on September 15, touching off reactions in Cairo and Moscow. Nasser, during an address that day to graduating cadets of the air academy at Bilbeis, charged that the proposed association was "in truth [an organization] for declaring war. It is impossible to have two bodies to regulate navigation through the canal." Sarcastically, he added: "By the same token we should be able to get together a number of countries and say we are forming an association of the users of the Port of London and all ships bound for London would pay to it. [Applause and laughter.] This is an association to usurp rights, to usurp sovereignty, to proclaim war." Moscow called the proposed association "a great provocation against Egypt" and warned that attempts to impose it by force "would lead to immense destruction in the Suez Canal and the oil fields. The U.S.S.R., as a great power, cannot stand aside from the Suez problem."

Despite such protests, the founding meeting of the Cooperative Association of Suez Canal Users (CASU), as Dulles' proposal was now known, opened September 19 in London. All eighteen countries sent their foreign ministers and Dulles himself traveled across the Atlantic for the third time in seven weeks to head the American delegation.

The secretary of state was acutely aware of how delicate his job was, for on the same day the conference opened he received another of the National Intelligence Estimates that had been regularly reporting on the war intentions of Britain and France. "The majority of the British Cabinet, especially Prime Minister Eden, and virtually all the members of the French Cabinet, are convinced that the elimination of Nasser is essential to the preservation of vital Western interests in the Middle East and North Africa," said the estimate, the product of the CIA, the State Department, and all the intelligence staffs of the Pentagon.* "They are gravely concerned with the dangers of appeasement and probably believe that forceful action against Nasser offers the only real hope of arresting the decline of their positions. The attitude of the U.S. will continue to be of very great importance. The U.K. and France fully recognize that a resort to military force against Nasser without at least implicit U.S. support would involve risks [stemming from the Soviet Union] which they would hesitate to assume alone. On the other hand, there are limits to the U.S. restraining influence."

While Britain and France pressed hard for the founding of an association that would collect canal tolls and provide its own pilots, in effect assuming operation of the canal, Dulles quickly quenched the idea. "Membership in the association would not, as we see it, involve the assumption by any member of any obligation," he told the opening meeting. He expressed the hope that members would pay their tolls to the association but then added: "This action, I emphasize, would be entirely a voluntary action by each of the member governments, if it saw fit to take it." As for the association pilots, "Obviously if Egypt makes it obligatory to use only pilots that are chosen by it, then I do not see that the pilots of the association would practically have very much to do and that part of the plan would have collapsed." In effect, Dulles was admitting the new association would have no meaningful powers.

Dulles was aware that even if the proposed association had tried to force its own pilots on Egypt, Nasser had already thought of a riposte. In a message from the U.S. Embassy in Cairo, Dulles had been informed that Nasser had bragged to the Ethiopian ambassador on September 18 that he had a way to thwart use of CASU pilots. "If a users' association

*The Army, Navy, Air Force and joint chiefs of staff, plus the FBI and the Atomic Energy Commission; all served on the National Intelligence Board.

convoy arrived to use the canal, he would not shoot at it," said the report. "[He] would merely move in another convoy, so that any ensuing blockage would be CASU's fault for failing to get clearance from the Egyptian canal authority."

Given such realities and Dulles' tepid expectations for the association, the meeting limped to an unproductive conclusion on September 21, but not before a comic debate. It centered on the acronym CASU. Dr. Joseph M. A. H. Luns, foreign minister of the Netherlands, thought it lent itself to such word plays as CASU belli. He suggested the acronym be CASCU. The Portuguese delegate objected, saying in his language "CASCU is something which really is not mentioned." (One definition of it is testicle.) Pineau also objected, noting it was "extremely derogatory" in French, sounding like the term for ass-breaker.

Finally the name Suez Canal Users Association (SCUA) was agreed to. Soon staffers at the American Embassy in London were pronouncing it SCREW-YA. SCUA was officially founded October 2 at an ambassadorial-level meeting in London and soon faded into deserved oblivion, but not before causing an even wider rift between Eden and Dulles.

It came about when Dulles was asked at a Washington press conference the same day of SCUA's official founding whether the new association would have "teeth." "There is talk about the 'teeth' being pulled out of it," said Dulles. "[But] there were never 'teeth' in it, if that means the use of force."

A news bulletin of Dulles' remarks was taken in to Eden at No. 10 Downing Street. With him was Nutting who was imploring the prime minister to keep close relations with America. When Eden read Dulles' comments, he "flung the piece of paper at me across the table, hissing as he did so, 'And now what have you to say for your American friends?' I had no answer. For I knew instinctively that this was for Eden the final letdown. We had reached breaking point."

• •

While SCUA slowly sank out of sight, Eden and Mollet went ahead with their plan to take the dispute to the U.N. despite opposition from Dulles. The secretary of state had solid reasons for his opposition to taking the matter to the Security Council. A secret study by the State Department in early September had tartly concluded that the West had no case worth presenting to the Security Council and Dulles thought the matter could only end badly. He had talked Eden and Mollet out of going to the United Nations earlier in the month, but at the end of his latest

London trip the two European leaders acted while the secretary of state was flying back to Washington. They introduced the matter before the Security Council on September 23. Dulles did not hear of it until he disembarked from his plane. He was not happy.

"It is a deplorable situation," Dulles complained in a telephone conversation with U.N. Ambassador Henry Cabot Lodge.

"It is a device [by Britain and France] aimed at placating world opinion and the Labourites," replied Lodge. "The U.S. cannot support it because force is the only alternative. It indicates willingness to scrap the U.N.—go through it and have a showdown."

The Anglo-French action now confronted Dulles with the awkward question of how to vote in the Security Council if Egypt or one of the Eastern members introduced a resolution condemning force. Britain and France would be left in the embarrassing position of having to veto it. But Dulles was determined to save America such embarrassment. He warned Lodge to be prepared to vote for an antiforce resolution even though it meant splitting from America's allies.

British and French U.N. officials, resentful of America's opposition, now stopped consulting with Washington. Confusion reigned. "We are anxious to play along with them," Dulles explained to a colleague in a telephone conversation, "but it's hard when we don't know what they are up to and they won't consult with us."

The split between the allies was emphasized by Eden's conspicuous efforts to keep in close consultation with Mollet. This was glaringly apparent on September 26 when Eden and Lloyd flew to Paris for overnight talks with Mollet and Pineau. The Britons found their French counterparts in "great spirits and very belligerent." During his stay in Paris, Eden sent a report to Rab Butler, whom he had left in charge of the government. "My own feeling is that the French, particularly Pineau, are in the mood to blame everyone including us if military action is not taken before the end of October. They alleged that the weather would preclude it later. I contested that."

The invasion date had again been pushed back, this time to mid-October in deference to the United Nations, which was going to hear the Anglo-French case starting October 5. It would hardly look good for England and France to be landing troops in Egypt while they were before the Security Council arguing that Nasser's regime was a threat to peace.

During the Paris talks, the French leaders did not confide to Eden their growing collusion with Israel. For the moment, the relationship remained the exclusive secret of Paris and Tel Aviv. By dealing covertly with

Israel, France was assuring itself that it would have its war one way or another. If the British backed out—the French never completely trusted perfidious Albion—then Mollet could still go to war in collusion with Israel.

The attack on Egypt was now only a matter of time.

CHAPTER XVI

Eden Is Looking
for a Pretext

PINEAU

THE FRENCH CABINET DECISION to initiate talks with Israel about warring against Egypt received a prompt response in Tel Aviv. A high-level delegation left Israel within five days aboard the discomforts of a converted World War II French bomber, and by Sunday, September 30, just three days after Eden's visit, serious talks were under way about launching a Franco-Israeli war against Nasser.

Meeting secretly in the Montparnasse home of Colonel Louis Mangin, Defense Minister Bourgès-Maunoury's trusted aide, the two sides talked for two days. The Israeli group was headed by Foreign Minister Meir and Chief of Staff Dayan; the French, by Pineau and Bourgès. In an opening forty-five-minute survey of the situation, Pineau explained that France thought the best time to attack was in mid-October when the Mediterranean was still calm and before the U.S. presidential election. He believed that war at that time would go unopposed by Eisenhower because the President would not want to split openly with America's allies on the eve of the election, or alienate Jewish voters by opposing Israel.

Pineau explained the many problems facing the Anglo-French planners of Musketeer Revised, though he was careful not to reveal any of the details of the invasion plan. The immediate difficulty, said Pineau, was the United Nations. It was scheduled to hear the Anglo-French case against Egypt for about a week, starting October 5. In addition, it would be at least October 15 before the British Cabinet would make its decision on whether to press ahead with the invasion of Egypt.

Pineau admitted that the French were unsure how the British would

323

act. "Eden is looking for a pretext to justify intervention," but he was being held back by Washington and mounting opposition within his Cabinet, said Pineau. Britain might back out. If so, would Israel be interested in warring against Nasser with France? Pineau asked.

It was an unparalleled offer for the tiny Jewish state and, as Dayan recalled, "We wholeheartedly agreed."

Golda Meir had a series of detailed questions about how the superpowers might act, and especially what Britain's attitude would be toward Jordan. Would Britain honor its defense treaty with Jordan if Israel captured the west bank of the Jordan River?

"You ask me to be an oracle," protested Pineau. "If we are here together, it's precisely because we're not sure of anything." But, he added, his estimate was that Britain probably would intervene against Israel if it tried to capture the west bank.

Meir wondered whether Washington should be informed of their talks.

"No," replied Pineau. "Dulles has done everything to delay action. We must not put them in a position of having to say yes or no since they could only say no because of the oil lobby. That would get us into a much more difficult situation than if we hadn't consulted them."

Dayan urged that France and Israel go to war as soon as possible. "The Egyptian Army is totally devoid of any military experience and it hasn't had time to be instructed in the use of the Russian arms," he said. "If we wait we will have to face an Egyptian Army trained by Russian cadres and adapted to ultramodern arms.

"In any event," continued Dayan, "as matters stand now Israel believes it can totally destroy the Egyptian Air Force in three weeks by using only half the planes we have now. If France intervenes, the destruction can be much faster."

The meeting adjourned for lunch in a dining room dominated by the stern portrait of the host's father, General Charles Emmanuel Mangin, hero of the World War I battles at Verdun and the Marne. Under his gaze, French and Israelis now plotted an action that could lead to another war, perhaps even World War III.

The afternoon talks concentrated on military planning. Since Britain's role remained undecided, the two sides plotted with the assumption that Britain would stay out or enter only later. If that happened, however, Britain might deny use of its Cyprus airfields to France. Were Israel's fields suitable to handle French planes? What were Israel's military needs? It was decided to send a French military delegation to Israel to answer the many questions facing the conspirators.

Dayan met the next day with tall, patrician General Paul Ely, the chief of staff, in the secrecy of Mangin's home. Ely greeted him warmly and asked how France could help supply Israel with more arms. Dayan asked for a squadron of transport planes, one hundred Super Sherman tanks, three hundred half-tracks, one thousand bazookas, three hundred four-wheel-drive vehicles capable of negotiating the sandy wastes of the Sinai and fifty tank transporters. Israel had no need for more fighter planes. It had already received sixty Mystère IV's—though Washington was led to believe there were only twenty-four—and less than two weeks earlier Canada had finally agreed to sell Israel twenty-four Super Sabre jets with U.S. concurrence. (It was only later in the month that U-2 reconnaissance planes finally spotted the large number of Mystères, causing a surprised Eisenhower to remark dryly that the planes apparently had a "rabbitlike capacity for multiplication.")

Ely assured Dayan that France would meet Israel's requirements. But Dayan wanted more than just equipment. He also sought assurances of French air cover, supporting naval units and a diversionary landing by French forces. Ely indicated that France would favorably consider providing such assistance.

Before Dayan left, Ely interjected a sour note into the harmonious talks. He advised Dayan that it would be best for Israel to attack Egypt first rather than wait until France alone or France and Britain attacked. Otherwise, he added, it would look as though Israel were rapaciously taking advantage of the Western attack. Dayan was upset. To attack first was not an attractive proposition to Israel since it would make the country look like the lone aggressor. The question was left hanging, a disturbing echo in Dayan's mind.

Dayan reported to Ben Gurion immediately on his return to Israel on the night of October 1, and the prime minister was not happy. He was disturbed about the suggestion that Israel strike first and uneasy with the unpredictability of the British. He wanted a night to think through the situation. The next day, Ben Gurion told Dayan: "My conclusions are unfavorable, stemming from the assumption that the English will not take part and will not permit the French to operate from Cyprus."

Dayan, though sharing the same misgivings, was anxious not to lose this unique chance to attack Egypt. "It would be easy now to extinguish this tiny flame of [French] readiness to go to war against Nasser, but it will be impossible to rekindle it," he warned Ben Gurion. "Three months ago, we would have regarded a situation in which France was prepared to join us in taking military action against Egypt as a dream."

325

Ben Gurion's doubts remained, but he agreed with his chief of staff not to share them with the French military mission, led by Major General Maurice Challe, that had accompanied the Israeli delegation back to Tel Aviv. This time the Israelis had flown in the comfort of a DC-4, the gift of President Truman to General Charles de Gaulle, who in turn had given it to the Defense Ministry. From now until the outbreak of war, the Israeli colluders made their secret trips to Paris in DC-4 luxury.

That night, October 2, Dayan called a meeting of the General Staff and delivered electrifying news: Israel might soon go to war with Egypt. Though the government had not yet made the final decision, Dayan cautioned, he was issuing an Early Warning to get prepared for hostilities. All officers training overseas were to be recalled, reconnaissance flights and patrols of Egypt were stepped up and preparations were made for the implementation of a general mobilization of Israel's civilian army. The probable date for hostilities was set for October 20.

• •

Foster Dulles was preparing for the October 5 meeting of the Security Council on the Anglo-French complaint against Egypt. In discussing tactics with Ambassador Lodge, Dulles remarked of Britain and France: "We don't know what they are after. The French are eager to get into a fighting war. About the British, it is harder to say. They were ready to go into it. The French think I snatched the British from their clutches. The British Cabinet is divided; I don't know where the balance of power lies."

"They want to destroy Nasser's prestige," said Lodge. Dulles did not argue with him.

In another telephone call the next day, this one with Senate Majority Leader Lyndon Johnson, Dulles admitted: "We don't know what the British and French are up to. They are not very forthgiving in keeping us informed. I don't think we want to give them anything like a blank check on our support for whatever they do. You have any thoughts?"

"I don't know. It is complex."

"I'll find time if you want a full briefing."

"My schedule is extremely busy," concluded the master politician from Texas. This late in the political campaign, Johnson was not about to get the Democratic Party involved in the Suez quagmire.

Indeed, the political implications of the Suez crisis were now becoming threatening, as Ike was strongly reminded October 8 by his press secretary, Jim Hagerty. In a three-page memorandum to the President he discussed possible diplomatic moves. "Somehow the American people and the people of the world expect the President of the United States to do something dramatic—even drastic—to prevent at all possible costs another war." Recalling that Eisenhower had gained attention in his 1952 campaign with his pledge of "I shall go to Korea" to stop the war, Hagerty worried that Suez might provide a similar opportunity for Democratic candidate Stevenson. "I would not like to see the President lose his leadership in the fight for peace in America and throughout the world to the opposition candidate who might conceivably think of saying: 'I shall call on Nasser' or 'I shall call a summit conference on the Suez Canal.' "

Goaded by Hagerty's memorandum, Eisenhower telephoned Herbert Hoover, Jr., and told him that if the U.N. talks were unsuccessful "we should not fail to do something about it, possibly dramatic, possibly even drastic. Suez is probably the number one question in the minds of the American people. The British and the French feel they have got to cut off Nasser, but nothing would make me madder."

Hoover assured him that Dulles "has many things in mind."

Ike said he would like to talk with Dulles but "I never know when he is free and people chase him around if they know the President is calling." He ended the call by telling Hoover that "we ought to think of everything, including having Nehru negotiate."

Hoover agreed, but with a caveat. He acidly noted that he would not mind bringing the Indians into the process—but only if the widely disliked Krishna Menon were left out.

A little later Eisenhower rephrased Hagerty's memorandum and sent it over to Hoover at the State Department. "Dear Herbert, as you could tell from my telephone conversation, I have not any very definite views of what I might do either now or in the future in order to prevent the Suez business from getting out of hand." But, Ike suggested, he might issue a White House statement containing "a frank warning that the United States will not support a war or warlike moves in the Suez area. Of course the British and the French are bitterly against building up Nasser. This concern has been rather overtaken by events since he has already become, mostly as a result of this quarrel, a world figure. If therefore we can think of any plan that we could accept, even though it falls somewhat short of the detailed requirements listed by Britain and France, we might through some clandestine means urge Nasser to make an appropriate public offer.

"A more spectacular thing might be for me to invite a number of nations to a conference, including most of the eighteen who agreed upon the 'London Plan' as well as India, Egypt, Israel and possibly Saudi Arabia. None of the items in this list has been deeply studied; I send it to you more as a clear indication of my readiness to participate in any way in which I can be helpful than as a series of suggestions.''

• •

Lloyd and Pineau flew to New York for the opening of the Security Council debate on October 5, and Dulles met with them before the first session. The European foreign ministers tried to sway Dulles by repeating to him alarming rumors about the Middle East. ''The situation is rapidly deteriorating,'' Lloyd declared. ''Nasser is planning a coup in Libya; there is a plot to kill the king. King Saud is also threatened. Jordan is already deeply penetrated. Syria is virtually under Egyptian control. Nasser is actively assisting EOKA in Cyprus.'' Pineau gave a similar litany of looming doom. He justified the Franco-British military buildup by extravagantly claiming that without ''these precautions the mobs might have been let loose, ships not allowed through the canal and foreign pilots detained in Egypt.''

Dulles was not impressed. He repeated that U.S. policy was firmly against the use of force except as a last resort. The fact that they were meeting at the United Nations was ample proof that that stage had not yet been reached.

In reporting to the President, Dulles said he had asked Lloyd and Pineau the purpose of taking the dispute to the United Nations: ''Was it for war or peace? Pineau and Lloyd replied in effect that they did not believe that any peaceful way existed. They urged the use of force, arguing that only through capitulation by Nasser could the Western standing in Africa and the Middle East be restored.''

The proposed Anglo-French resolution sought to have the council reaffirm freedom of navigation of the canal, and urged Egypt to negotiate ''a system of operation'' of the canal and to cooperate with SCUA. It was essentially a restatement of the principles adopted at the London Conference. When the debate began, Egyptian Foreign Minister Mahmoud Fawzi showed a willingness to compromise, but he charged with some justice that the proposal's purpose actually was to assure that ''the Suez Canal be finally amputated and severed from Egypt.'' Soviet Foreign Minister Shepilov backed Egypt with the declaration that ''reactionary forces were trying to force Egypt to her knees.'' For their part, Lloyd and Pineau demonstrated no interest in compromising; in return, Fawzi, with the Soviet veto assured, stood as firm as they. The meeting appeared headed toward a certain deadlock.

Once again, diplomatic magician Dulles had an alternative plan to consume more time. He encouraged the three foreign ministers to try to work out their differences in private sessions with Hammarskjold acting as mediator. Before they began the talks in the secretary-general's thirty-eighth-floor office overlooking the East River, Hammarskjold told Dulles: "I will be acting merely as a chaperone."

"My understanding of a chaperone is a person whose job is to keep two people apart," replied Dulles. "Your job is to get the parties together."

The foreign ministers managed to agree to a six-point resolution three days later, which the council adopted October 13. The salient point for Egypt was Number Two, which called for respect for Egypt's sovereignty. The other five points were virtually a rehash of the Anglo-French proposal on free passage and negotiated tolls. At the last moment, Britain tried to attach six other points, all prejudicial to Egypt, on instructions from Eden. He ordered Lloyd to press for passage of what amounted to a tougher restatement of the original Anglo-French resolution. Fawzi balked and the Soviets vetoed the new proposal, which no doubt was just what Eden wanted. Hammarskjold's biographer, Brian Urquhart, a career U.N. diplomat, perceptively observed that the veto made it "possible to show Egypt and the Soviet Union publicly allied against the West, thereby relieving Eden and the French government of the unwelcome possibility of a negotiated settlement." Once again Nasser was made to appear as a Communist partisan; opposition to him was opposition to Communism.

Nonetheless, Fawzi, Lloyd and Pineau agreed to meet in Geneva to discuss implementation of the six original points. The date for the gathering: October 29.

• •

At the end of the U.N. meeting, Eisenhower and Dulles were satisfied that their strategy of stalling was paying off. Dulles confided to colleagues that he now believed Anglo-French military plans were "withering on the vine." Eisenhower said at a press conference that "it looks like here is a very great crisis that is behind us. I do not mean to say that we are completely out of the woods, but I talked to the secretary of state . . . and I will tell you that in both his heart and mine at least there is a very great prayer of thanksgiving."

329

Because of his successful delaying tactics, Dulles was again Europe's favorite whipping boy, particularly in Britain. "We do not ask the Americans to do or say anything which would be impossible in an election year," editorialized the Tory *Daily Telegraph* on October 9. "We do not even ask them for a tune which we can echo, for we are perfectly capable of calling our own tune. What we do ask is that they should refrain from blowing now hot, now cold in matters which, as we believe, concern our very existence; and which in the long view may well concern theirs also." In the same paper that day, an article began: "The feeling is becoming widespread that we are being sold down the Suez Canal by America." In the *Daily Express,* also the same day, a front-page cartoon of Dulles carried the caption: "Well, even if he is nothing but a crazy, mixed-up corporation lawyer, at least he could make up his mind exactly which river he is selling us down." *The New York Times,* reporting on the rising anti-Americanism, speculated that its root was frustration over the Suez crisis, which has "demonstrated to the nation, as nothing has before, the rapid decline of Britain's imperial power."

The British were quite right in detecting a certain slippery quality to Dulles' diplomacy those troubled summer months, but they were wrong about its purpose. It was a deliberate way to keep their prime minister from launching them into a war and not, as they suspected, an effort to humiliate or replace them in the Middle East.

• •

Israel now diverted everyone's attention from Dulles' diplomatic gyrations by staging another of its massive attacks, nearly causing a war that no one really wanted. A large force of Israeli troops in half-tracks and tanks, supported by artillery and planes, smashed into the Jordanian village of Qalqilya, northeast of Tel Aviv, in the darkness of October 10 and inflicted widespread death and destruction. "In the village of Qalqilya," reported the United Nations, "observers saw the body of one woman, killed by 120mm mortar shell fragments in her house; the body of one Jordan Army soldier, killed by mortar shells in his house and three wounded persons [a mother and her two children; a third child was killed]. Numerous impacts of 120mm mortar shells and artillery shells were seen in various houses, some of which were severely damaged. The village school was hit by several mortar shells. Fragments of artillery shells and the tails of 120mm mortar shells were found. Twenty bullet holes were seen in the garage door of one house on the main street as well as many other bullet holes on walls along that street and in another

330

house." In addition, the Qalqilya police fortress was blown up by Israeli troops, as was a water-pumping station across the street.

By the time the attackers had withdrawn before the light of dawn, at least forty-eight Jordanians were dead. For the first time, the Israeli raiding party, despite its mighty size, met determined resistance from Jordan's tough Arab Legion. Israel lost eighteen killed, its highest casualty toll since the 1948 war.

Israel claimed the cause of the Qalqilya raid was the slaying of two citrus workers the day before, but U.N. officials had their doubts. On October 3, the day after Dayan issued his Early Warning, Israel walked out of the Jordanian Mixed Armistice Commission meeting with the declaration that there was "no useful purpose in the continuation of routine examination of incidents." Thereafter, Israel no longer requested that border incidents be investigated by the United Nations.

The Israeli action was a prelude to establishing a pretext for war, suspected Chief of Staff Burns. In an urgent message to Hammarskjold on October 5, Burns cabled: "As no complaints can be checked or substantiated by UNTSO without our investigation, it is of course open to Israel, by mere assertion, to build up a list of violations by Jordan which will in her eyes and, failing any contradiction, maybe in the eyes of the world, justify retaliatory or 'punitive' measures. The end result can only be constant feuding across demarcation lines or a resumption of the war."

The savagery of the Qalqilya attack, coming on top of Israel's three large raids the previous month, sent the Arab world into a frenzy. King Hussein urgently requested that Britain honor its treaty obligations and come to Jordan's rescue.

But Eden prudently stalled, since the entry of British forces would have caused a grotesque situation that was almost too absurd to contemplate. "This was a nightmare which could only too easily come true," observed the harried Eden. "Jordan calling for support from Egypt and ourselves, Nasser calling for support from Russia, France lined up with Israel on the other side." And that was only the half of it. Britain was about to collude with Israel and France against Egypt, so it could find itself having to fight with Israel on one front and against it on the other.

Hussein angrily turned to Cairo for help, which finally caused Eden to act. He urged Iraq to send troops into Jordan as a way to strengthen Hussein and prevent the Egyptians from gaining greater influence. But movement of the Iraqi troops touched off stern warnings from Israel, which feared an alliance between Jordan and Iraq. Entry of Iraqi troops into Jordan "would be a direct threat to the security of Israel and to the validity of the Israel-Jordan Armistice Agreement," a government statement warned. Privately, Israeli spokesmen threatened that the country would be justified in taking over the coveted west bank if Iraq intervened.

The tough talk by Israel caused Peter Westlake, the British chargé d'affaires in Tel Aviv, to deliver a stern warning to Golda Meir that Britain would honor its treaty with Jordan if that country was attacked by Israel.

The situation was now about as confusingly entangled as a Molière farce, and Dayan confided to his diary: "I must confess to the feeling that, save for the Almighty, only the British are capable of complicating affairs to such a degree. At the very moment when they are preparing to topple Nasser, who is a common enemy of theirs and Israel's, they insist on getting the Iraqi Army into Jordan, even if such action leads to war between Israel and Jordan in which they, the British, will take part against Israel."

The Iraqi troops issue was dragged like a red herring through the rest of the crisis, causing bitter public exchanges in the United Nations and elsewhere between officials of Britain and Israel. Yet under the surface the two countries were soon to start secretly conspiring with France to attack Egypt.

The Iraqi fracas was not the only grave repercussion caused by the Qalqilya raid. Coming as it did on top of the strong attacks over the previous month, the raid left Jordan so weakened that its existence was now in doubt. King Hussein, humiliated by the raids, was fighting for his throne. Western analysts speculated that Israel, Iraq and Saudi Arabia might at any moment tear Jordan apart, each taking a section of the country for themselves. Israel above all wanted the west bank, that protrusion across the Jordan River that lay in the heart of Palestine.

Possession of it would give the Jewish state straight frontiers much easier to defend than the patchwork left over from the 1948 war, and its capture was one of Israel's long-term strategic goals. Israeli officials constantly queried the French about how Britain would react to their conquest of the west bank, but the answer was always the same. Britain would honor its treaty with Jordan.

Repercussions of the Qalqilya raid extended to Eisenhower. He was indignant at its ferocity and accurately suspected Israel's secret purpose was to hasten the collapse of Jordan and thus to snatch up the west bank. He instructed Dulles "to make very clear to the Israelis that they must stop these attacks against the borders of Jordan. If they continue them, and particularly if they carry them on to the point of trying to take over and hold the territory west of the Jordan River, they will certainly be condemned by the United Nations. Moreover, should there be a United Nations resolution condemning Israel, there will be no brake or deterrent possible against any Soviet move into the area to help the Arab countries."

Despite such warnings, U-2 flights showed by mid-October that Israel was mobilizing, and Washington analysts thought the Israelis planned to attack Jordan. The President recorded in a Memorandum for the Record on October 15 that Ben Gurion's "obviously aggressive attitude" seemed to be inspired by three things:

"(a). His desire to take advantage of the gradual deterioration in Jordan and to be ready to occupy and lay claim to a goodly portion of the area of that nation.

"(b). The preoccupation of Egypt and the Western powers in the Suez question, which would tend both to minimize the possibility that Egypt would enter a war against him promptly, while at the same time it would impede Britain's capability of reinforcing Jordan.

"(c). His belief that the current political campaign in the United States will keep this government from taking a strong stand against any aggressive move he might make."

Eisenhower recorded that he told Dulles to warn Israeli Ambassador Eban that "Ben Gurion should not make any grave mistakes based upon his belief that winning a domestic election is as important to us as preserving and protecting the interests of the United Nations and other nations of the free world in that region. The secretary is to point out, moreover, that even if Ben Gurion, in an aggressive move, should get an immediate advantage in the region, that on a long-term basis aggression on his part cannot fail to bring catastrophe and such friends as he would have left in the world, no matter how powerful, could not do anything about it."

• •

The scheduled talks on the Suez crisis in the United Nations caused Eden once again to postpone the invasion, this time indefinitely. The Anglo-French staff was put to work in early October on a Winter Plan, and it appeared that the use of force by a joint British and French expedition was receding farther into the misty future.

The lack of action was taking its toll on the morale of British troops, particularly the twenty-five thousand reservists called up on short notice and sent away from their families and jobs. They had proudly sailed in early August waving placards: "Look out, Nasser. Here we come." Now, two months later, they were still cooped up on ships or in camps, and on October 4, 5 and 8 troops protested in Malta and Cyprus, leading to the arrest of twenty-one reservists. But Eden on the ninth released a statement saying that "the situation does not warrant the release" from service of reservists.

The protests were symptomatic of the welling opposition to force that was now inundating Britain. The issue divided families, caused angry arguments among friends and threatened to split the country as no other national question since Munich. The early prophecies that Suez was another Munich were proving true in a way that no one had considered.

The pressures on Eden from this growing opposition were considerable. They increased when his respected minister of defense, Walter Monckton, informed him on September 24 that he intended to quit because of his opposition to Eden's war policy. He finally did so in a letter dated October 11 but not announced until the eighteenth, when the official reason given was health problems. Lord Mountbatten had been aware of Monckton's opposition and had urged him to quit and speak out about his reservations. After resigning, Monckton stopped in Mountbatten's office and told him about his action. "Well," said Mountbatten, who as a military leader felt constrained to follow the orders of the government and not voice his criticisms publicly, "now are you going to speak?"

"I can't because he's forced me to accept the post of paymaster general."

"Why, in heaven's name?"

"He doesn't want me to leave the Cabinet. He said if I resign now it would break the government, the government would fall, and it's a good government, Dickie, except for this bit of nonsense going on, and I don't want to be the cause of it falling. I feel by staying in the cabinet I can hold the hotheads."

"Hold the hotheads!" exploded Mountbatten. "There's only one hothead and that's the prime minister. How can you control him unless you go yourself and speak out freely?"

"I've made up my mind, Dickie. It's been difficult enough. Don't bully me."

Mountbatten sadly watched him leave.

Anthony Head, a gifted Conservative who entered Parliament in 1945 and currently was secretary of state for war, was appointed Monckton's replacement. He had no illusions about Eden's policy but carried out his job in a professional way and had no substantial impact on the crisis.

In addition to Monckton's defection, Eden was also faced with Anthony Nutting's opposition to his policy to depose Nasser. Eden's protégé was openly skeptical, and their relations had by now become extremely cool and strained. It was an unwelcome daily reminder to Eden that not only the Labour Party, many of his military commanders and Washington thought his policy wrong, but some members of his own inner circle as well.

These strains took their toll on October 5 when Eden suffered a sudden attack of a "severe feverish chill" in University College Hospital in London. Eden was visiting his wife, who officially was in the hospital for a "24-hour dental checkup," when he was stricken. His temperature shot up to a dangerous 106° and he had to be hospitalized overnight. The cause of the ailment was never explained, but ever since his gall-bladder problems Eden had been subject to these mysterious bouts of fevers, one of the symptoms of amphetamine overdosage. The mounting strains on him could not have helped his weakened condition, and in fact the strains could have been greater than anyone suspected. It was later reported that Clarissa Eden was actually in the hospital because of a miscarriage.

Eden's seizure occurred on a Friday; he was back in his office the following Monday. But now his colleagues observed a strange change in him. He was unusually calm and for the rest of the crisis he never lost his famous temper. The suspicion was that he had been prescribed heavy doses of tranquilizers, which he may have used alternately with pops of amphetamines to maintain his alertness as the crisis ripened. If so, it was a mind-addling combination that would help explain some of his barely rational conduct later on.

Eden felt well enough that week to travel to Llandudno, in Wales, to attend the annual Conservative Party conference and deliver a belligerent speech on Suez. "We have always said that with us force is the last resort, but cannot be excluded. We have refused to say that in no circumstances would we ever use force. No responsible government could ever give such a pledge." The five thousand delegates loved it; they clearly shared his bellicosity.

With such one-sided support still ringing in his ears, Eden received the day after his speech a surprise Sunday visit at Chequers. His visitors were General Challe, recently returned from Israel, and Albert Gazier, the French minister of labor and a close confidant of Mollet. Because of the explosive situation posed by the threat of Iraqi troops moving into

335

Jordan, Mollet had decided it was time to bring Eden into France's plans for collusion with Israel. The French wanted Eden to prevent Iraq from moving its troops into Jordan lest Israel attack and upset the Franco-Israeli plot for warring against Egypt. This Eden quickly agreed to do. Then from General Challe he heard in broad outline what France had in store for Nasser.

Standing before a map of the Middle East, Challe said, "The Israelis here, the Egyptians there. Where is our position? Here on the canal." He described a plan, largely composed by him, of Israel attacking across the Sinai and Britain and France then demanding that "both sides" withdraw from the canal. When Egypt refused, as it surely would since its forces would be in their own country, the Anglo-French force would intervene between the two armies at the canal. Suez would be in their hands. The "Israeli pretext" would be their justification for using force.

Eden was "thrilled at the idea," recalled Challe.

Indeed, the plan was like a divine visitation to Eden. It answered all his hopes. Israel would provide the pretext for force and the force would topple Nasser.

Aside from a private secretary, only Anthony Nutting was with Eden at the meeting with the French officials. He was appalled at the prime minister's obvious enthusiasm for the plan. Eden had promised to give his answer to Paris by Tuesday, forty-eight hours later, but Nutting observed: "I knew then that, no matter what contrary advice he might receive over the next forty-eight hours, the prime minister had already made up his mind to go along with the French plan. We were to ally ourselves with the Israelis and the French in an attack on Egypt designed to topple Nasser and to seize the Suez Canal. Our traditional friendships with the Arab world were to be discarded; the policy of keeping a balance in arms deliveries as between Israel and the Arab states was to be abandoned; indeed, our whole peace-keeping role in the Middle East was to be changed and we were to take part in a cynical act of aggression. In all my political association with Eden, I had never found so unbridgeable a gulf between us."

In his excitement following the meeting with the French, Eden immediately called Selwyn Lloyd, who was still in New York working on the coming meeting in Geneva with Fawzi, and ordered him to fly home at once. Lloyd arrived at the Foreign Office on the morning of the sixteenth and was taken aside by Nutting, who was unhappy and increasingly agitated about the French plan. After explaining the plan, Nutting told Lloyd his reasons for opposing it. Not only would the operation put Britain in the curious position of attacking the victim of aggression, but there was another major concern, Nutting observed. "We should confirm the deep-seated suspicion of many Arabs that we had created Israel, not as a home or refuge for suffering and persecuted Jewish humanity, but to serve as a launching platform for a Western re-entry into the Arab world and a military base, organized and financed by Western governments and Western money, to promote Western 'imperialist and colonialist' designs."

"You are right," Lloyd said. "We must have nothing to do with the French plan."

But during a private lunch with Eden that same day, the prime minister's infectious enthusiasm caused Lloyd to change his mind and support the plan. A stronger or more experienced foreign secretary might have been able to stand up more forcefully to the prime minister, but Lloyd had neither the stature nor the stomach to do so. In their excitement, Eden and Lloyd flew to Paris that same afternoon to discuss with Mollet and Pineau the Israeli pretext. They gave their assent to it during a five-hour meeting in which no other officials took part.

When Lloyd returned to Whitehall the next day, Nutting asked him about the Paris meeting. "He admitted that Eden had confirmed his wholehearted endorsement of the French plan and that further consultations would take place in Paris between French and Israeli representatives," recalled Nutting.

"All I could do, and this I did, was to tell him very solemnly that, if we went through with this plan, I would have to resign. I could not stay in the government if it meant being a party to this sordid conspiracy."

• •

General André Beaufre, the French land commander of the invasion forces, had heard of the Israeli connection before Eden, and he was not happy. It meant drawing up yet more plans, and in addition, he suspected Israeli motives. The Challe mission to Israel at the beginning of October had "returned delighted with the dynamism of this attractive young nation; its members were enthusiastic of intervention at all costs and under any conditions," recalled Beaufre. "However, it soon proved that their enthusiasm had been deliberately inspired by the Israelis, who were being more artful than our people realized. The Israelis, for instance, had painted them a glowing picture of Egyptian weakness and of their own confidence in the success of their plan. But this was mere bait; basically they were only too well aware of the difficulties of the problem and they were trying to obtain from us that support which was completely essential

337

to them." France would have to provide Israel with naval bombardment and naval cover of the coast and the major port of Haifa, air support and supply, and the destruction of the Egyptian Air Force.

"The support required was limited but vital to the success of the operation," observed Beaufre. "The French therefore had to be won over. I very soon perceived that the Israelis had completely succeeded."

Beaufre learned of Israel's involvement on October 8 or 9 in a message from Vice Admiral Barjot that outlined "Hypothesis I" (I for Israel). It was assumed that Britain would remain neutral and the extent of French participation would be limited to providing air and naval support for the Israeli thrust across the barren Sinai desert. The landing of French troops was now only a contingency that would be decided on later. Starting October 12, joint Franco-Israeli military talks began in Paris and Beaufre's worst suspicions were confirmed. "The Israelis had no intention of moving up to the canal. On the other hand, they insisted that our landing must be *simultaneous* with their attack. It was therefore clear to me that they were determined to be assured of our political and strategic cover from the outset, and they made no secret of the fact that they would not attack unless assured of British neutrality. The Israeli action would help us not at all. What the Israelis were primarily trying to do was to involve us and there were too many people ready to comply light-heartedly."

Beaufre's worries about the Franco-Israeli plan disappeared on October 18 when General Ely's chief of staff, General Gazin, told him electrifying news: "The decisions have been taken. The British are on the move."

• •

Simultaneously with the preparations for war, which now finally got under way in earnest, the CIA's plot to stage a coup against the leftist government in Syria moved forward. Foster Dulles delivered the promised public statement to the Syrian plotters at his October 16 press conference when he declared that the United States would carry out the April 9 White House declaration to "assist and give aid to any victim of aggression" in the Middle East. That was all the plotters needed to hear to press ahead; they had their assurances of Washington's backing. The CIA's Bill Eveland was informed by Mikhail Ilyan in Beirut that a date had been set for the coup: October 29.

Some members of the Administration now also wanted to move against Nasser. But Eisenhower turned down any attempt to overthrow the

Egyptian leader at the moment because it might inflame the Arab world. Hoover had brought the matter up at a meeting in early October when he referred "to the visit of a group with one of our agencies on how to topple Nasser. I wonder if this is the time to attempt this?"

"An action of this kind cannot be taken when there is as much active hostility as at present," replied Eiswnhower. "For a thing like this to be done without inflaming the Arab world a time free from heated stress holding the world's attention as at present would have to be chosen."

The President seemed to be implying that at some later date he would support a covert scheme to topple Nasser. He was not concerned with the morality of the act but with its timing.

• •

Beyond his worries about what America's allies were up to in the Middle East, Eisenhower was now in the final rigorous days of the presidential campaign. The testing of hydrogen bombs in the atmosphere had become the central issue. Adlai Stevenson scored points by vowing that if elected his first "order of business" would be to seek a worldwide end to all H-bomb testing. He gained more attention by warning that the tests throw up "huge quantities of radioactive materials which are pumped into the air currents of the world at all altitudes and fall to earth as dust or in rain. This fallout carries strontium 90, which is the most dreadful poison in the world."

Eisenhower tried to duck the issue by insisting that scientists had assured him the tests were as safe as possible and that they were indispensable for the nation's security. On October 11, fed up with Stevenson's constant attacks, he said at a press conference: "Now, I tell you frankly, I have said my last words on these subjects. I think I have expressed all that is necessary to express on them for the purposes of any political campaign."

But Stevenson kept hitting the issue, and then the Russians barged into the debate in a ham-handed way. Premier Bulganin sent a letter to Eisenhower on October 17 urging that H-tests be halted. Russians "fully share the opinion recently expressed by certain prominent public figures in the United States concerning the necessity and the possibility of concluding an agreement on prohibiting atomic-weapon tests," said the letter.

The intrusion of the Soviets into the political campaign was bad enough, but Eisenhower was even more furious when Moscow released the text of the letter before it could be translated for him. In an angry note on October 21, the President blasted Bulganin. The letter "departs from accepted international practice in a number of respects. First, the sending of your note in the midst of a national election campaign . . . constitutes an interference by a foreign nation in our internal affairs of a kind which, if indulged in by an ambassador, would lead to him being declared persona non grata in accordance with long-established custom. Your statement with respect to the secretary of state [Bulganin had accused Dulles of distorting the Soviet position on disarmament] is not only unwarranted, but is personally offensive to me. You seem to impugn my sincerity. However, I am not instructing the Department of State to return your letter to your embassy . . . because I still entertain the hope that direct communications between us may serve the cause of peace."

Stevenson was left with little to do except to say he shared "fully President Eisenhower's resentment at the manner and timing" of Bulganin's "interference in U.S. political affairs." If the Russians were out to help the Democrat, they could not have gone about it in a clumsier way.

. .

Amidst these pressures Eisenhower had celebrated his sixty-sixth birthday on October 14 with the receipt of an affectionate note from Foster Dulles. "As another anniversary comes to you, I join with the many millions throughout the world who are thankful for your life and works," Dulles wrote. "I can never adequately express the measure of deep satisfaction which I have had from working so intimately with and under you during these past four years."

Ike took time out to respond with an equally warm note: "Perhaps it is just as well that when we are together our talk must be of Suez or Morocco or South Vietnam. Because I assure you that I am even more tongue-tied than you (and sometimes I blame my inadequacy on my Germanic origin) in trying to tell *you* the rewards I have received from our association."

He also received a birthday greeting from Eden. "Our friendship remains one of my greatest rewards," wrote Eden. "Public life makes one value such a relationship more than ever in these anxious times." Ike wrote back: "I know that nothing can ever seriously mar either our personal friendship or the respect that our governments and peoples have for each other."

In less than a fortnight Eisenhower was going to learn how wrong he could be.

• •

Ever since Eden had approved collusion with France and Israel, information from the Europeans had dried up, particularly from London, which normally was very open with Washington. Eisenhower and Dulles had both noticed the sudden blackout, and Dulles was actively concerned. "I'm quite worried about what may be going on in the Near East," he said in a telephone conversation with his brother, Allen, on October 18. "I don't think we have any clear picture as to what the British and French are up to there. I think they are deliberately keeping us in the dark."

Dulles had no idea just how much in the dark he was being kept. Top officials of Britain, France and Israel were about to meet secretly outside of Paris to cement the final details of their war against Egypt.

• •

As though Washington did not already have its hands full, there now occurred a crisis in a totally unexpected area: East Europe. Mass demonstrations again broke out in Poland on October 19 and the next day spread to Hungary. The demonstrators in both nations were demanding the replacement of pro-Soviet leaders and greater freedom from Soviet hegemony.

There were reports of clashes between Polish and Soviet troops, and the crisis was so acute that Khrushchev led a Soviet delegation to Warsaw on October 19. Khrushchev accused the demonstration leaders of wanting "to sell the country to the Americans and the Zionists after the Soviet soldiers shed their blood here during World War II." Khrushchev left without being able to stem the demonstrations and soon Soviet troops were reported massing at Poland's borders. An expectant atmosphere gripped the world.

But for the Eisenhower Administration, the demonstrations had their bright side. In a telephone call with a friend, Foster Dulles said: "I don't think it is bad for elections that these things are happening." The secretary listening in on the conversation added: "They agreed we should capitalize on it [the Polish demonstrations]."

Publicly, Eisenhower made a comment on the demonstrations that came close to being as provocative as Bulganin's letter. "All friends of the Polish people recognize and sympathize with their traditional yearn-

341

ing for liberty and independence." He added, "Our hearts go out to the captive peoples" of Eastern Europe.

From a political viewpoint, the timing of the uprisings could not have been better for the Administration. Eisenhower and Dulles had been arguing all along that the new Soviet leadership did not significantly change the tyrannical cast of Soviet Communism. Now the peoples in two Eastern-bloc countries were demanding more freedom and in return were being threatened by the possible entry of Russian troops. It all seemed to prove that Eisenhower and Dulles had been right. They planned to use the uprisings to show that democracy was the better system. The world, particularly those emergent nations of the Third World, could now clearly judge for themselves which system offered more freedom. It was an unparalleled chance to score a major point against Communism.

What Eisenhower and Dulles did not know, however, was that Britain, France and Israel were about to ruin this great opportunity.

• •

The time had come for the British, French and Israeli colluders to meet face-to-face, the first and only time representatives of the three nations met to synchronize their war plans. With the utmost secrecy, the various delegations traveled to the spacious and secluded villa of the Bonnier de la Chapelles in Sèvres, just outside Paris. Pineau drove there in his own car in the afternoon of October 22, careful that he was not being followed. The Israeli delegation, headed by Ben Gurion and made up of Dayan and Peres, flew into the military airport of Villacoublay, near Sèvres, and were picked up in an unmarked car by Colonel Mangin. Their landing had been delayed by fog, extending their flight to seventeen hours. By the time they arrived at Sèvres they were weary and tense. Lloyd later that Monday told his colleagues he had a cold and then made his way in secret to the Villacoublay airport and then to Sèvres.

The first meeting got under way at 4 P.M. between the Israelis and the French, who were represented by Mollet, Pineau and Bourgès-Maunoury. Ben Gurion had a surprise for his French hosts: a bold, not to say to French ears fanciful, plan to divide up the Middle East.

"Before all else, naturally, the elimination of Nasser," Ben Gurion declared. But after that he wanted to partition Jordan, with the west bank going as an autonomous region to Israel and the east bank to Iraq. Lebanon would lose its territory up to the Litani River to Israel and certain other parts would go to Syria with the remaining territory becoming a

Christian state. A pro-Western leader would be installed in Damascus. Israel would also take Sharm el-Sheikh at the tip of the Sinai peninsula from Egypt.*

Ben Gurion's plan stunned the French. "If he stuck to his grandiose plan, we realized, we were already at an impasse," observed Abel Thomas, attending as Bourgès' aide. "Or was he trying to back out of dealing with Britain? If so, why then did he come?"

It was a rocky start for the negotiations. Mollet warned that "by trying to embrace too much we will not solve anything. We have an immediate problem to solve. If yes, then it is today that it must be decided or never. It is not in one month, not in six months that the decision must be made —but now."

Ben Gurion was disappointed by Mollet's stern rejection of his regional plan and his pique showed as the talks moved into the substance of the collusion. Eden had insisted to Mollet that Britain would take part only if it had a pretext for war. That pretext was an initial attack by Israel followed by ultimatums to both Israel and Egypt. Only then would England commit its forces.

Ben Gurion objected. He did not like the idea of Israel attacking alone and being held up to the world as the aggressor. It was like Israel being the robber and Britain and France the good-guy cops, he complained.

Ben Gurion was also worried about Israel having to fight alone in the first days before the Anglo-French force moved. Egypt now had Soviet Ilyushin-28 bombers and might use them to bomb Israel's cities before the Anglo-French destroyed the Egyptian Air Force. He also feared that in the interim, while Israel fought alone, the Soviets might send in "volunteers" to help Nasser, thus escalating the conflict into a superpower confrontation.

Pineau emphasized that Britain absolutely would not take part if it did not have its "Israel pretext." Ben Gurion's concerns about security were understandable, Pineau continued, and France was prepared to give Israel military guarantees.

Ben Gurion had other reservations. America should be informed and its approval received before the attack. He also thought the attack should be put off until after the U.S. elections since Eisenhower was campaign-

---

*Actually, the plan was not at all fanciful. In the 1967 war Israel finally did capture the west bank and Sharm el-Sheikh, and in the 1978 invasion of south Lebanon it established its influence up to the Litani River and began openly supporting Lebanese Christians, thus achieving the goal outlined twenty-two years earlier by Ben Gurion.

ing as the peace candidate. After the election, America was more likely to come to Israel's aid if need be, added Ben Gurion.

Mollet dryly cautioned Ben Gurion not to count on prompt U.S. support. He sarcastically said that it seemed to take the country years to understand foreign relations problems: in World War I, America only responded in 1917, and waited from 1939 to 1941 to enter World War II. He said it would probably take another two years for Washington to understand the gravity of Nasser's nationalization.

Bourgès assured Ben Gurion that he could count on the French Navy to defend the shores of Israel and French planes to defend Israeli skies. But, he added heavily, if the campaign were not launched in the next few days France would have to back out. It could not much longer hold its merchant vessels and troops in readiness. "The beginning of November is the final date."

Ben Gurion replied that he was not willing to accept the stigma of attacking first, or of accepting the risks of fighting alone for several days. Under the circumstances, he added, it seemed pointless to stay and he might as well leave in the morning.

Though the two sides appeared deadlocked, the atmosphere between them was friendly and relaxed. That changed when Lloyd and his private secretary, Donald Logan, arrived at 7 P.M. The Britons met first with the French to be briefed on the state of the talks, causing resentment among the sensitive Israelis, who thought Lloyd was trying to snub them. When Lloyd finally joined the Israelis, he recalled, "My first impression was of a roomful of utterly exhausted people, mostly asleep. One young man was snoring loudly in an armchair. Ben Gurion himself looked far from well."

To the Israelis, Lloyd looked sullen. The congenial atmosphere suddenly became chilly. Ben Gurion and Lloyd exchanged a cool handshake. It was obvious that Lloyd was uncomfortable and determined to maintain his distance from the Israelis. Ben Gurion, his memories still alive of the bitter struggle between the British and the Jews in the last days of the Palestine mandate, bristled at Lloyd's presence. He thought that Lloyd tried to treat him "like a subordinate."

Dayan too resented Lloyd, later observing that "Britain's foreign minister may well have been a friendly man, pleasant, charming, amiable. If so, he showed a near-genius in concealing these virtues. His manner could not have been more antagonistic. His whole demeanor expressed distaste—for the place, the company and the topic."

344

Lloyd in fact was not happy having to collude with the Israelis, and it was only his loyalty to Eden and his desperation to bring a conclusion to the drawn-out Suez crisis that accounted for his presence in Sèvres. He was in no mood to bargain with Ben Gurion or the French.

His opening remarks concentrated on the U.N. talks with Egyptian Foreign Minister Fawzi, which he said had all but solved the problem of navigating the canal. But the agreement would not weaken Nasser and in fact would strengthen him. The British government wanted Nasser overthrown, he declared, and thus was willing to attack with France if Israel attacked first.

In his artful way, Lloyd made it sound as though Israel were acting entirely independently, without British encouragement. The British attack would come only as a consequence of the Israeli action, and not in cooperation with it. He maintained this thin line of reasoning even twenty years later in his memoirs. "We had no plan for cooperation with Israel," he wrote. "We had said that we would not defend Egypt, and we had agreed to a French proposal that if Israel attacked Egypt we would intervene to protect the canal. In our military plans, Musketeer and then Musketeer Revised, Israel did not figure. The object would be to prevent fighting for the crossing places over the canal and damage to the many millions of pounds' worth of British ships and cargoes passing through it. If the combatants did not accept our military presence, we would use force. If Nasser accepted our military presence, he would lose prestige. If he did not, we would put into operation Musketeer Revised."

It was indicative of the desperate state of mind of Lloyd and Eden that they could have convinced themselves with this slim jesuitical argument that they were not actually colluding with Israel. But both men went to their graves maintaining it.

Ben Gurion was outraged at Lloyd's transparent attempt to dissociate Britain from Israel, and especially Lloyd's insistence that Israel attack first and be labeled the aggressor. "All of this has as a consequence—if not as an objective—the making of Israel look like an aggressor while Britain and France will look like peace lovers," protested Ben Gurion. "In fact, it is Britain and France who are trying to avoid losing face."

Lloyd responded that it was impossible for Britain to join with Israel to attack Egypt. "We have thousands of British subjects in Arab countries with valuable property, and oil installations of great strategic importance. If there was a joint attack, there might be wholesale slaughter of British subjects and destruction of our installations." He added that Brit-

345

ain could not afford to be branded an aggressor because, he noted pointedly, it "has friends, like the Scandinavian countries, who would not view with favor Britain's starting a war."

"I did not dare glance at Ben Gurion as Selwyn Lloyd uttered this highly original argument," recalled Dayan. "I thought he would jump out of his skin. But he restrained his anger."

Dayan attempted to break the deadlock by suggesting that Israel could stage a paratrooper raid near the canal, giving the Anglo-French a pretext to issue a warning to both sides to withdraw their troops from the canal since their presence threatened its smooth operation. If Egypt turned down the demand for evacuation, as it would surely do, the Anglo-French force could start bombing Egyptian airfields the next morning.

Lloyd insisted that the Israeli action had to be a "real act of war." Otherwise, the Anglo-French ultimatum would appear like aggression. Dayan assured him the Israeli attack would be a real act of war. Lloyd conceded in that case it might be possible to set the time between the Anglo-French ultimatum and the start of the bombing of Egyptian airfields at thirty-six hours. Ben Gurion thought that was too long a time.

The talks ended inconclusively.

Lloyd and Logan left Sèvres about midnight and returned to England. The talks appeared stalled, though significantly Dayan's proposal had accepted Britain's central demand that Israel attack first. But Ben Gurion had been careful not to endorse it, always referring to it as "Dayan's plan." Dayan noted his prime minister's caution and he "feared that his reservation was not just a tactical move vis-à-vis the British and the French, but was really sincere, and that he had many doubts about it." It had been agreed that Pineau would fly to London the next evening to continue the talks with the British.

• •

Before Pineau flew to England, another crisis erupted. Without authority from the central government, the Algerian military command and a French intelligence unit decided on their own to kidnap Algerian rebel leader Ahmed Ben Bella. He was taken from a Moroccan passenger plane scheduled to land in Tunis but that was forced by French planes to land instead at Algiers. It was a flagrant breach of international law and the world press harshly condemned France. Mollet was late to the second-day meeting at Sèvres because he was engrossed in handling this latest crisis.

Amid such extraneous pressures, the French and the Israelis discussed what lures they could give Pineau to take to London to entice Eden to join the collusion. "We would need to equip Pineau with a formula which would determine whether the Suez campaign took place or was canceled," concluded Dayan. "But Ben Gurion had not yet made up his mind whether, in the present circumstances, Israel could join in the war. It was evident that he was disappointed with the meetings so far."

In a private talk with Ben Gurion, Dayan expounded his plan, reassuring the Old Man that Israel could fight alone for thirty-six hours without suffering serious casualties. "I was not sure whether he really believed in the dark picture he kept painting of Egyptian planes wreaking havoc and destruction on Israel's cities or whether he did so for tactical reasons." Dayan told Ben Gurion that under his plan the Israeli Air Force would not go into action except to act as an air cover reserve to guard against Egyptian attacks. "This should encourage the Egyptians to assess our actions as no more than a large-scale reprisal operation, which they would not wish to turn into a full-fledged war," Dayan said. "They were unlikely to cross the border or to bomb Israel's cities and airfields."

Ben Gurion listened carefully to Dayan's plan, but at the end he made no comment. Dayan asked permission to present it to Pineau for relay to Eden. Ben Gurion agreed, providing that "I indicated it was my personal proposal without committing him to it." With that Ben Gurion retired to his room for the rest of the day, leaving Dayan and Peres to continue the talks with Pineau and Bourgès. Pineau carefully wrote down the various points of Dayan's plan, read his notes back to Dayan and then promised that he would use them as the basis for presenting Israel's position in his London talks that evening.

Before Pineau departed, Dayan once again warned him that the plan was his and had not been approved by Ben Gurion. Pineau, suspecting that Ben Gurion was only seeming to hold out for a better deal, replied, "I know, I know how you fellows work." Said Dayan to himself: "I envy him his confidence."

Pineau had dinner with Lloyd in his official residence at Carlton Gardens and about 10 P.M. Eden joined them. Lloyd had returned to London with the feeling that there would be no war because of Ben Gurion's refusal to attack first. But now Pineau presented Dayan's plan and Eden was impressed. He decided that another meeting should be held in Sèvres the next day. Lloyd continued to maintain the fiction that Britain was not colluding with Israel. "I said that I wished to make it clear that we had not asked Israel to take action," recalled Lloyd. "We had merely stated what would be our reactions if certain things happened."

347

Pineau arrived back at Sèvres the next day at 4 P.M. and announced that a British delegation would soon arrive.

In Lloyd's place Britain sent Sir Patrick Dean, who as deputy under secretary of state at the Foreign Office also served as the head of the Joint Intelligence Committee. The same day that he was suddenly ordered to go to Sèvres he was scheduled to host a stag black-tie dinner in his London home for a visiting CIA colleague. Dean's wife did the honors and the CIA agent and his local representative ate without hearing a hint that at the moment Britain was concluding its deal with Israel and France to attack Egypt.

Dayan and Peres had used the morning to get Ben Gurion to finally agree to Dayan's plan. But now the Israeli prime minister wanted one other thing: a piece of paper signed by all three countries outlining their agreement. The paper called for Israel to attack first, for Britain and France to submit "appeals"—not ultimatums, since Ben Gurion objected to Israel being so addressed—to Israel and Egypt the next day, and for the Anglo-French air force to attack Egypt within thirty-six hours. Britain insisted that Israel pledge it would not attack Jordan, which Ben Gurion did in the paper.

The document was signed by Ben Gurion, Pineau and Dean. As Ben Gurion studied the paper, he "was tense, and he made no effort to conceal it," observed Dayan. "He read and reread the articles in the plan with scrupulous care, knitting his brows in furious concentration and murmuring each word to himself. He then neatly folded the paper and placed it in the inside pocket of his jacket."

Ben Gurion had also earlier gotten another piece of paper from Bourgès-Maunoury. "The French government pledges to station on Israeli territory a reinforced squadron of Mystère IV-A and a squadron of F-84 fighter-bombers during the period from the 29th to the 31st of October 1956 so as to assure the air defense of Israeli territory. In addition, two ships from the national navy will dock at Israeli ports during that time."

The time of the Israeli attack was now set. It was for the afternoon of October 29—eight days before America's election.

CHAPTER XVII

An Opportunity to
Settle Accounts

DAYAN

THE FINAL DAYS of October loosed an avalanche of pressing events on the President of the United States and his secretary of
state. The election was less than two weeks away. Hungary and Poland
were near rebellion. Israel was mobilizing. British and French forces
were gathering in the Mediterranean, and communications between those
countries and Washington had all but ceased. There was an atmosphere
of momentous events afoot.

Eisenhower's schedule for the final days of the campaign was packed
with political appearances and speeches, despite his aversion to campaigning, yet Eastern Europe and the Middle East demanded presidential
action. Poland was in tumult, shocking the world with its forceful assertion of independence. Wladyslaw Gomulka, 51, a onetime blacksmith
who had been sacked as first secretary of the United Workers' Party in
1948 during the height of Russia's anti-Tito campaign, was swept back
into power on October 21. With nationalist fervor, Gomulka declared
that all Communist countries had "full independence and sovereignty."
But he prudently added: "Polish-Soviet relations based on the principle
of equality and independence will give the Polish people such deep feelings of friendship toward the Soviet Union that any attempt to sow dis-
trust of the Soviet Union will find no fertile soil among the Polish
people."

The Soviet leaders could live, however unhappily, with such restrained
nationalism. But in Hungary the uprisings took a totally uncontrollable
turn. While Britain, France and Israel colluded in Sèvres, the Hungarian

349

Communist Party Central Committee on October 24 named as premier Imre Nagy, 60, who only the year before had been deposed from that position on charges of being a Trotskyite and Titoist. Nagy, a former locksmith, promised independence from Russia and democratization of the government. But the spontaneous combustion of rebellion had already gone too far. On the same day as Nagy's appointment, tens of thousands of Hungarians, ordinary citizens, students and large numbers of defecting army personnel, rose up against security forces and the hated AVH secret police and attacked government buildings, Communist Party offices, barracks and the Budapest radio station.

By the next day heavy fighting was raging throughout much of the country and large areas of western Hungary fell to the insurgents. At the American Embassy in Budapest, a radio operator managed to get an open line to the State Department and cabled: "Am typing on floor. All in telex room on floor to avoid gunfire. A big battle has just took place in front of legation seems to have gone towards Parliament. Seems all Americans still OK and safe. Street fighting again flaring up with tanks fighting it out at present. Parliament Square crowded with people fighting many Soviet tanks and troops. Intermittent shots heard through night. Quieter towards morning. October 25: Crowds moving in streets, center town especially Pest Danube Riber bank area full of Soviet tanks and troops. Heavy gunfire from Parliament area."

Washington asked: "Do you people believe this fighting is going to spread further?"

"Have no way of knowing but seems very possible that it will spread. Strength of Soviet troops estimated to be one mechanized infantry division. Hungarian troops held in background. Soviet doing bulk of fighting. Some Hungarian troops known to have joined the crowd. American apartment house sprayed with Russian machine-gun fire due to presence of insurgents firing from roof. All Americans and domestic help safe in basement."

Correspondent John MacCormack of *The New York Times* had witnessed the fighting around the Parliament and then sought refuge in the embassy. He got on the telex and told Washington that the earlier demonstrations had become "something like a small war after Russian troops had been called in to 'restore order' " on the twenty-fourth. The next day Parliament Square "was strewn with dead and dying Hungarian men and women shot down by Russian tanks. The massacre in front of Parliament occurred after some hundreds of demonstrators had come to it in trucks, armored cars and even riding on top of Russian tanks. They shouted to this correspondent: 'The Russians are with us.' The Russian tank crews smiled and waved. This love feast became first a disappointment and then a tragedy. Some ten minutes later another Russian tank roared up and opened fire on the crowd. I saw dozens of prone bodies and a number of wounded men and women. The tanks fired not only their machine guns but their big guns. The insurgents were unarmed."

As darkness approached on the twenty-fifth, the telex operator reported to Washington that "thousands of Hungarians gathering in front of American legation again shouting for Russians to leave. They are still gathering. Mass demonstration carrying Hungarian flags and black flags running over 2,000 have sung Hungarian anthem and appealed for help. In speech just delivered on radio, Imre Nagy has promised that as soon as arms laid down, Soviet troops now (repeat now) fighting will be withdrawn to former position in Hungary and that negotiations will be started to have all Soviet troops withdrawn."

. .

Hungary was suddenly drawing Washington's attention away from the Middle East. At a Friday meeting October 26 of the National Security Council, the 301st since Ike took office, Hungary was the prime topic, though as the President noted, the nation's top security officials had a large plate of troubles to pick from. "We had a scattering of reports from around the globe, all disquieting. There were rumors—which turned out to be false—of the assassination of the king of Jordan; news of riots in Singapore and of serious unrest in Morocco, Tunisia and Algeria. But the compelling news continued to be Hungary." That would soon change.

The CIA's Allen Dulles reported on the latest fighting between Soviet troops and Hungarian "freedom fighters." Now that blood was flowing in the once-placid streets of Budapest, the question facing the world was whether the West was going to intervene on the side of the rebels. For years, the twenty-eight transmitters of Radio Free Europe, which operated under the guidance of the CIA, had broadcast provocative programs into Eastern Europe denouncing the evils of Communism and extolling Western freedom. Eisenhower had employed that same message in his first campaign, saying, for instance, in August 1952: "The American conscience can never know peace until these [enslaved] people are restored again to being masters of their own fate. Never shall we desist in our aid to every man and woman of those shackled lands who is dedicated to the liberation of his fellows."

As Eisenhower well knew, unilateral intervention by U.S. troops over such a distance was out of the question. But Washington could not be sure that the leaders in the Kremlin really believed that. Allen Dulles told the meeting that Khrushchev had recently been seen at a diplomatic cocktail party in Moscow and he had "never looked so grim. His days may well be numbered."

"I doubt," replied Eisenhower, "that the Russian leaders genuinely fear an invasion by the West." Nonetheless, he recalled, "We knew this was a dangerous moment—that the Communist leaders in Moscow were doubtless searching their souls for answers to painful questions: Could they permit a Gomulka to rule in Poland after what happened in Hungary? Could they permit a loosening of control in the satellites?" If the Russians lost their grip, Eisenhower warned the council, they might "resort to extreme measures, even to start a war. This possibility we must watch with the utmost care."

Then Eisenhower turned to the issue that in the final days of his campaign would become inextricably intertwined with the Communist uprisings: the Middle East. Foster Dulles told the council of "very worrisome" events in Jordan, including the rumor that Hussein had been assassinated. The rumor had originated as an official announcement in Paris and probably had been planted by French intelligence in an effort to help Israel in its scheme to fool Washington and Cairo into believing that Israel's war preparations were against Jordan rather than Egypt.

In another meeting that same day, Allen Dulles convened the CIA's Watch Committee assigned to decipher the cloudy events unfolding in the Middle East. Clues were accumulating, and they were both obscure and at the same time alarming. France and Israel were obviously up to something, but so too were France and Britain. Were all three in the thing together? From Tel Aviv, Dulles' agents reported that Moshe Dayan had briefly been out of the country; from Paris, that senior Cabinet members were unavailable; from London, that the normally open exchange of intelligence information had dried up completely. The CIA's liaison officer to British intelligence, Chester L. Cooper, reported that his usual warm welcome at the Joint Intelligence Committee meetings in London had turned frigid. "When [the meetings] were held I was excused after a few moments of embarrassed anodyne discussion," he reported. "There seemed to be a sudden noticeable cooling of relationships." Another alarming clue was the interception of an increased amount of radio traffic between Tel Aviv and Paris, a telling prelude to modern battle.

Dulles added to all these darkening portents a report received over the weekend from the U.S. ambassador in Paris. It said that France, Britain and Israel planned to attack Egypt, but not until after the U.S. election. The information carried extra weight because it came from Ambassador Dillon's old friend Jacques Chaban-Delmas, minister of state in the French Cabinet. The Dillons had owned the Château Haut-Brion vineyards for three generations in Bordeaux, the family seat of Chaban-Delmas, and the two men were longtime mutual admirers. Chaban-Delmas told Dillon of the "joint action," about which he actually knew little, because the Frenchman wanted to reassure Washington that France was not trying to jeopardize Eisenhower's chances in the election. It was the only leak about the collusion between Britain, France and Israel before they went to war.

Despite Dillon's report, Allen Dulles, like just about everyone else, found it difficult to believe that the three countries were embarked on such a feckless enterprise. Perhaps it was possible to imagine that France and Israel were up to something, he said, since they were both fighting the Arabs. But Britain? Why should it link itself with Israel and risk its relations with Iraq, the Persian Gulf emirates and Jordan? It was difficult to imagine that Britain would join in an underhanded alliance with Israel at the expense of its relations with the Arabs and Washington too.

Yet the evidence seemed persuasive. The armed forces of the three countries were obviously moving toward a war footing, though whether together or separately was uncertain. Richard Bissell, who had developed the U-2 program, displayed high-altitude pictures showing British convoys assembling in Malta and Cyprus. There were also pictures of French military supplies being loaded onto ships in Marseilles and Toulon. It did not appear, observed Bissell dryly, "that the allies were gathering in the Mediterranean for a regatta."

Another analyst, Robert Amory, a Harvard lawyer and now deputy director of the CIA, noted that Eden was so furious with Nasser that he would probably be willing to join anyone to overthrow the hated Egyptian. Amory was especially well connected in Britain. His distant cousin and close friend was Derick Heathcoat Amory, minister of agriculture in Eden's Cabinet, and Bob Amory frequently visited him. Aside from all the rumors in Britain about imminent action, Amory had reports from Tel Aviv that Israel's mobilization was massive. He was convinced that there would soon be a war.

James Angleton, the agency's Israeli expert who prided himself on his connections with Mossad, disagreed. "Amory's remark may sound alarming but I think I can discount it," declared Angleton. "I spent last evening and most of the early hours with my friends, and I can assure you that it's all part of maneuvers to impress the Jordanians. It certainly is not meant for any serious attack. There is nothing in it. I do not believe there is going to be an attack by the Israelis."

Amory, who distrusted and disliked Angleton, bristled at Angleton's remarks. He felt Angleton was being used by the Israelis. "Allen," Amory snapped, "you've got to choose between me and my people and this co-opted Israeli operative."

Early the next day Amory attended a State Department meeting with a dozen or so top officials, including Allen Dulles. Foster Dulles was going to make his only direct campaign effort that Saturday evening in Dallas with a speech reviewing the world situation. Copies of the speech were placed before each of the participants and Dulles read it carefully. When he got to the section on the Middle East, he read a passage indicating that the U.S. could not guarantee a peaceful outcome.

Most of the officials around the table nodded in agreement. Amory objected. "Mr. Secretary," he said, "if you say that and war breaks out twenty-four hours later, you will appear to all the world as *partie prise* to the Israeli aggression—and I'm positive the Israelis will attack the Sinai shortly after midnight tomorrow."

Allen Dulles remarked with some emotion: "That's much stronger than the Watch Committee's conclusion yesterday."

"Okay," replied Amory. "I'm sticking my neck out. I'm only a six-teen-thousand-dollar-a-year CIA official, but I'm prepared to lay my job on the line that there's a war coming tomorrow or the day after."

Foster Dulles removed the reference; he later thanked Amory.

•   •

Moshe Dayan was doing everything he could to hide Israel's intentions from the world. On his return October 25 from Sèvres, he had immediately set in high gear the mobilization of 100,000 men during a meeting that same evening with his General Staff. He was not at liberty to reveal the collusion, but he got the point across by telling his officers that Britain and France might attack Egypt. If they do, he added, "we should behave like the cyclist who is riding uphill when a truck chances by and he grabs hold. We should get what help we can, hanging on their vehicle and exploiting its movement as much as possible, and only when our routes fork should we break off and proceed along our separate way with our own force alone."

Dayan ordered the intelligence branch to intensify rumors that Iraqi troops had moved into Jordan and to leak word that Israel was about to attack Hussein's kingdom. Israeli agents were so efficient that Dayan noted with satisfaction the next day that "in operations they claim that intelligence is so successful that they have begun to believe their own rumors."

To reinforce the deception, Israeli troops were moved openly to the northern and eastern borders facing Syria and Jordan. Combat units selected for the real war were transported stealthily southward toward the Sinai. A number of soldiers and officers were given leaves so that they could be conspicuously at home with their families and friends for the Friday-evening Shabbat and the traditional rounds of Saturday visits that Israelis pay to each other. The army men were told to be highly visible. The purpose was to create the impression by their presence away from the borders that the atmosphere was relaxed and that the reservists were being mobilized as part of training maneuvers. The ruses were highly effective.

• •

Dwight Eisenhower was also busy that Saturday, though not in the way he would have preferred. Among his morning appointments was a meeting with Mr. and Mrs. Jackson Wheeler of Los Angeles, their daughter, Judy, and their son, Charles. Charles, noted the President, was "the youngest Eagle Scout in the history of Scouting." The demands of the campaign went on regardless of the perilous state of the world.

Foster Dulles later called on Eisenhower to report that the Hungarian revolt was still spreading. "Large sections of the Hungarian armed forces have gone over to the dissidents, and throughout the countryside there are large areas in opposition to the regime," Dulles told the President. "Signs of condemnation of the Communists are arising all over Europe. In Italy, Spain, and France there are strong demonstrations for the Hungarians."

The two men then talked about the Middle East. "Recent reports have come in of a considerable mobilizing of the military in Israel," remarked Eisenhower. Dulles suggested that he communicate directly to the Israeli government.

It was clear now that no Iraqi troops had moved into Jordan, despite Israeli insistence that they had, and Eisenhower's message emphasized that fact. "So far as I am informed," Eisenhower cabled Ben Gurion, "there has been no entry of Iraqi troops into Jordan. I must frankly express my concern at heavy mobilization on your side." He added pointedly: "I renew the plea that there be no forcible initiative on the

355

part of your government which would endanger the peace and the growing friendship between our two countries."

Eisenhower that Saturday honored a campaign pledge to have a complete physical examination to prove he was capable of carrying on for four more years. At 2 P.M., the President set off for Walter Reed Hospital for twenty-four hours of tests and rest.

Dulles was on his way to Dallas, but before he left he made one last attempt to pierce the mystery of the belligerent moves by Britain, France and Israel. The U.S. ambassador in London was instructed to see Foreign Secretary Selwyn Lloyd and ask him directly about British intentions. Then Dulles had Israeli Ambassador Abba Eban summoned off the golf course of the Woodmont Country Club near Washington for an emergency meeting.

Eban and his deputy, Reuven Shiloah, rushed to the State Department and found Dulles "surrounded by an anxious retinue of advisers looking hard at a map in the middle of the room." Eban noticed that "the map portrayed the Israeli-Jordan armistice boundary, and nowhere touched Sinai." Eban knew about Israel's plotting with France, but he too was ignorant of the British involvement.

"The secretary's mood was somber," recalled Eban. "From U.S. ambassadors in the Middle East, including Edward B. Lawson in Israel, reports had come of great Israeli troop concentrations amounting to virtual mobilization. Dulles replied with frank skepticism to my argument that Israel was, after all, faced by grave danger."

"What have you to worry about?" Dulles asked. "Egypt is living in constant fear of a British and French attack. Jordan is weak. It is now clear that the Iraqis are not going to enter Jordan. On the other hand, if it is Israel that is planning to attack, it is perhaps because your government regards the present time as suitable."

Recalled Eban: "I promised to convey what he had said, but added an expression of regret that 'the United States government has not shown a greater degree of faith in Israel's basic intentions.' "

His report to Tel Aviv, noting the map in Dulles' room did not show Egypt, was greeted with satisfaction.

• •

Dayan was still maintaining the deception that Israel was about to attack Jordan. He ordered U.N. observers stationed at the disputed crossroads near El Auja removed. "Better that they complain of being ordered to move than that they should report the concentration of our forces preparing for action," Dayan wrote in his diary on October 27.

The mobilization of Israeli civilian reserves proceeded with deception. They were told the enemy was Jordan. "This deceptive explanation ties in with the news and articles which have been appearing in the press in the last few days," observed Dayan. "The prospects are good that we may succeed in camouflaging the true purpose of the mobilization."

French war equipment was pouring into Israel. Two hundred trucks with front-wheel drive arrived that day "and saved the situation," reported Dayan. There had been 13,013 civilian trucks called up in the mobilization but maintenance on them had been so poor that only 60 percent were fit for service.

In Tel Aviv, British Ambassador Sir John Nicholls called on Ben Gurion and again warned that England had every intention of honoring its defense treaty with Jordan. If Israel attacked Jordan, he declared, England would move against Israel. Ben Gurion replied: "I think you will find your government knows more about this than you do." Sir John reported the exchange in a cable to Whitehall. Before it was distributed Ben Gurion's rejoinder was cut from the circulated copies.

· ·

In Dallas, Dulles made a point of telling the Republican audience that events in Hungary proved the "weakness of Soviet imperialism," adding, "All who peacefully enjoy liberty have a solemn duty to seek, by all truly helpful means, that those who now die for freedom will not have died in vain." On the Middle East, he was cautious: "I cannot predict the outcome. The situation is grave. There are complicating and disturbing factors unrelated to the canal itself. But if the governments most directly concerned, those of Britain, France and Egypt, with help from the United Nations, do come to agree, they will have written an inspiring new chapter in the agelong struggle to find a just and durable peace."

· ·

Reports continued to flood Washington about Israel's mobilization. Eban repeatedly assured the State Department that it was all defensive. But radio traffic between Paris and Tel Aviv was increasing dramatically and Eisenhower noted that "we believed this had real significance."

The reports were so ominous that Dulles, after returning from Dallas, spent Sunday in his office. At 5:38 P.M., he telephoned Eisenhower, who

357

had just returned with a clean bill of health from his overnight stay at the hospital, and told the President that he thought American nationals should be evacuated from Egypt, Israel, Jordan and Syria, all told about sixty-five hundred persons.

"Will this exacerbate the situation?" asked Eisenhower.

"I don't think so. It may lead to some anti-American demonstrations, and if the British strike, it will lead to the inference that we knew about it. But I think it will not basically make the situation more serious." They agreed to send out the order that night.

"I just cannot believe Britain would be dragged into this," exclaimed Eisenhower.

Dulles said he had talked with both the British and French embassy officials and "they profess to know nothing at all. The Britisher said he had some information that they had acted to warn the Israeli against attacking Jordan. Their ignorance is almost a sign of a guilty conscience, in my opinion."

While still in the hospital, Eisenhower had sent another urgent cable to Ben Gurion, saying he had received reports that Israel's mobilization was almost complete. "I have given instructions that this situation be discussed with the United Kingdom and France, which are parties to the [1950 Tripartite] Declaration, requesting them to exert all possible efforts to ameliorate the situation." The cable ended forcefully. "Again, Mr. Prime Minister, I feel compelled to emphasize the dangers inherent in the present situation and to urge your government to do nothing which would endanger the peace."

Now, in his telephone conversation with Dulles, the President wondered if there had been an answer from Ben Gurion. There had not. Ben Gurion had no intention to answer anything from Washington until after Israel launched its war.

• •

In Israel, Ike's latest cable had been received with a certain smugness. It proved, observed biographer Bar-Zohar, "how mistaken the United States President was in his assessment of the situation."

Ben Gurion that Sunday went before the regular meeting of the Cabinet in Jerusalem and formally sought its endorsement for launching war the next day. The coalition Cabinet approved, except for the members of the leftist Mapam faction; they formally opposed but agreed to share responsibility for the sneak attack if the rest of the Cabinet favored it.

The pressure on Ben Gurion was intense. He was worried about Israeli casualties, about Egyptian bombing attacks on Tel Aviv and other Israeli cities, and about the reliability of his European allies. He still did not trust the British and was nagged by doubts whether they would maintain their pledge to attack Egypt and thus relieve opposition to the Israeli attackers. The intense strain of the past weeks finally felled him after the Cabinet meeting. His temperature shot up to 103° and after returning to his Tel Aviv home he collapsed in bed. Still, he continued his chores. Members of the opposition parties, all except the Communists, were called to his bedside to hear the news that Israel was going to war. Even his old nemesis, Menachem Begin, was summoned to his side. Though the two men disliked each other, Begin was so thrilled at the news that he warmly congratulated Ben Gurion.

By now signs of the mobilization had become so obvious that, following the Cabinet meeting, Israel announced late Sunday that it had called up reservists as a "precautionary measure." The reasons given included the entrance of Iraqi forces into Jordan, a false rumor that Israeli intelligence was still putting out, and renewed *fedayeen* attacks, which was also false. Dayan noted in his diary that the statement was "calculated to draw attention to the Jordan border as the source of tension and the likely scene of military conflict."

French supplies continued to arrive. That day the last of two squadrons of Mystère and Super Sabre jets flown by French pilots landed, ready to protect Israeli skies against Egyptian bombing attacks. The Red Mogen David, Israel's Red Cross, issued appeals for blood donors.

• •

Eisenhower was scheduled to make a campaign swing on Monday through Miami, Jacksonville and Richmond, and he was troubled about leaving Washington at such an anxious time. "If I did call off the southern trip, though I don't think it's necessary to do so, it would be misunderstood," Ike said to his speech writer, Emmet John Hughes. "There'd be political yapping all around that the doctors *really* found I was terribly sick and ready to keel over dead."

They were sitting in the President's office, discussing the next day's speeches, but Ike's attention kept returning to the strange events evolving in secrecy in the Middle East. Eisenhower was, observed Hughes, "dismayed, baffled and fearful of great stupidity about to assert itself." Said Eisenhower: "I just can't figure out what the Israelis think they're up to. Maybe they're thinking they just *can't* survive without more land.

But I don't see how they can survive without coming to some honorable and peaceful terms with the whole Arab world that surrounds them.''

Turning to the reports about French complicity, Eisenhower grew heated. "Damn it, the French, they're just egging Israel on—hoping somehow to get out of their *own* North African troubles. They sat right there in those chairs three years ago, and we tried to tell them they would repeat Indochina all over again in North Africa. And they said, 'Oh, no. That's part of metropolitan France!'—and all that damn nonsense.''

Hughes left to work on the speeches. When he returned a short time later he found Eisenhower more upset than before. The latest reports reflected mounting suspicion that Britain was with France in encouraging Israeli aggression. "I just can't believe it,'' said Eisenhower. "I can't believe [the British] would be so stupid as to invite on *themselves* all the Arab hostility to Israel. Are they going to *dare* us—dare *us*—to defend the Tripartite Declaration?''

Hughes noted that "from the viewpoint of Israel, the timing looks superb: Russia is deep in satellite trouble, Britain and France are straining at the leash for a crack at Nasser, and the U.S. is in the middle of a national election. Thus, the chance looks golden.''

Sighing deeply, Eisenhower slowly walked out of the room.

• •

In London that evening Ambassador Winthrop Aldrich finally got a chance to carry out his orders to confront Selwyn Lloyd about what was going on. The two men had dinner. Aldrich asked Lloyd directly about the Israeli mobilization. Lloyd replied that Britain did not know any details and added that only the day before his ambassador in Tel Aviv had warned Israel not to attack Jordan. Was Israel going to attack Egypt? Aldrich asked. With a straight face Lloyd claimed that Her Majesty's Government had no information.

Washington still had no idea that the Sèvres meeting had taken place, but by late that evening of October 28 there was finally enough evidence for the Intelligence Advisory Committee to conclude with confidence that Egypt was going to be Israel's target. Warnings that Israel would attack Egypt "in the very near future" were immediately sent to Eisenhower and all U.S. unified commands. It was the first official recognition that Israel would attack Egypt rather than Jordan. The war was less than twenty-four hours away.

Eisenhower was in his office by 7:35 Monday morning, preparing for his campaign trip. At 8 A.M. Dulles telephoned, saying there was nothing new on Israel's mobilization. Ambassador Lawson had seen Ben Gurion earlier and "felt definitely Ben Gurion was not talking frankly to him."

"At least things on both fronts—Hungary and Israel—seem a little better this morning than last evening," said Eisenhower, relieved that a major war had not broken out yet.

"We have gained twenty-four hours," replied Dulles philosophically.

• •

At U.N. headquarters about that hour, a Strictly Confidential cable from Burns to Hammarskjold arrived, warning that "the Israeli partial mobilization and the explanation given indicate a heightening of the danger of an all-out war. It is noteworthy that they mention renewal of Egyptian-directed *fedayeen* activity first among reasons for mobilization. As UNMO [U.N. Military Observers] investigations are refused there is nothing to stop Israel military forces from grossly exaggerating circumstances of any incident to provide occasion for retaliation."

• •

At that moment in Israel, where it was seven hours later than in Washington, paratroopers were gearing up for a strike deep in the Sinai desert. Other Israeli troops were massed along the southern border, waiting for the signal to attack. Israeli pilots and the two squadrons of French fliers were making last-minute checks on their Mystère, Super Sabre, Ouragan and Meteor jets and piston-driven Mustangs and Mosquitos.

That same morning Dayan had met with Ben Gurion, still bedridden, to discuss the wording of the official announcement that would be released after the attacks began. Dayan's formula was that it "should be firm and threatening, but it must reveal nothing of our true intentions." After many rewrites, Ben Gurion finally approved a brief statement that said: "The Army spokesman announces that Israel Defense Forces entered and engaged *fedayeen* units in Ras en Nakeb and Kuntilla, and seized positions west of the Nakhl crossroads in the vicinity of the Suez Canal. This action follows the Egyptian military assaults on Israeli transport on land and sea designed to cause destruction and the denial of peaceful life to Israel's citizens." There had been no aggressive action by Egyptian troops, but the assertion served as a face-saving excuse.

During the rush of events that morning Dayan took time to ponder Eisenhower's two telegrams to Ben Gurion. "It is apparent that [Eisenhower] thinks the imminent conflict is likely to erupt between Israel and

361

Jordan and that Britain and France will cooperate with him in preventing this,'' Dayan wrote in his diary. ''How uninformed he is of the situation!''

About the time that Eisenhower was leaving for his campaign trip, Dayan was back in his underground command post in Tel Aviv where he and his operations officers had moved in preparation for war. The atmosphere was one of high excitement, especially among senior officers. Dayan observed that there was a feeling of ''an opportunity to settle accounts, that the day we've been waiting for has arrived, when at last there can be release for the pent-up bitterness they have harbored for the eight years since the establishment of the State of Israel, eight years of Arab threats to destroy Israel.''

• •

Reports from the Middle East arriving in Washington were becoming urgent, though not more enlightening. Dulles summoned French and British diplomats to his office to question them about developments, about which they knew nothing, and to instruct them to advise their governments that the use of violence now would ruin the West's condemnations of Russia's actions in Hungary. The West would lose a great opportunity to exploit Soviet troubles if attention were diverted from the rebellion in Hungary, Dulles observed. He then ordered Assistant Secretary for the Near East William Rountree, who had recently replaced George Allen, to invite Israeli Ambassador Abba Eban back to the State Department again to see if he might be able to offer some clarification of the mystifying events.

Eban only that morning had received an answer from Israel to his request for more information about the mobilization. ''It was not clear,'' Eban had cabled, whether ''Israel had been the victim, not the author, of the situation.'' In reply, Eban was advised ''to describe the situation as arising from 'security measures' and to stress that there was no connection between what we were doing and the conflict of other powers with Egypt.''

Eban went to the State Department and sat in Rountree's office again emphasizing the defensive nature of Israel's actions. Donald Bergus, head of the Palestine Desk, entered at 3 P.M. and handed a note to Rountree, who read it out loud. Israel was attacking Egypt.

With sarcasm, Rountree said to Eban: ''I'm certain, Mr. Ambassador, that you will wish to get back to your embassy to find out exactly what is happening in your country.''

362

• •

Ben Gurion and Dayan were at last having the war with Nasser that they had so long anticipated. Though they were pledged by the Sèvres agreement to open hostilities with a "real act of war," they moved cautiously into the shadowing emptiness of the Sinai desert. Except for small bands of roving Bedouins and a strip of settlements along the coasts, the Sinai had no civilian population and few roads. The first phase of their attack was carefully designed to appear as another retaliatory raid, a blow not sufficiently strong to provoke an Egyptian bombing attack on Israeli cities. The full force of Israel's assault was being held back for thirty-six hours until the promised attack by Royal Air Force planes against Egyptian airfields. Even though two squadrons of jets manned by French pilots were deployed in Israel to counter Egyptian bombers, Ben Gurion and Dayan were taking no chances. They were pitting three divisions against Egypt's one, plus a ragtag unit called the Palestine Division, which General Beaufre described as being "of little account."

Israeli pilots opened hostilities at 3:20 P.M. Middle East time by flying four World War II vintage piston-driven Mustangs barely twelve feet from the Sinai desert floor and cutting with their wings and propellers the few Egyptian telephone lines.

With Egyptian communications confounded, the limited Israeli assault snapped into action. The lead brigade was the 202nd Paratroop, commanded by aggressive Colonel Ariel Sharon, leader of the secret commando Unit 101. The main body of Sharon's armored force of three thousand men moved across the Egyptian border at Kuntilla, in central Sinai, at 4 P.M., routing five lightly armed Egyptian observation posts.

At about the same time, sixteen U.S.-made C-47 cargo planes filled with 395 Israeli paratroopers were lumbering across the Egyptian border at five hundred feet to avoid Egyptian radar. The paratroopers were from the 1st Battalion of Sharon's brigade, and their leader was every bit as tough as Sharon. He was Lieutenant Colonel Rafael ("Raful") Eitan, a farm boy from the Galilee, short, taciturn and merciless, who later became chief of staff in Begin's government. The C-47's were escorted by ten Israeli Meteor jets from Hazor Air Base, which was under the command of flamboyant Ezer Weizman.

At 4:59 P.M., as dusk was deepening the shadows among the magically swirled dunes of the desert, the C-47's popped up to fifteen hundred feet at the eastern edge of the jagged granite mountains of the Mitla Pass and the paratroopers jumped. Because of pilots' error, the billowing silk parachutes landed the elite troops several miles east of the entrance to the pass and they were forced to march for two hours across the harsh land before taking up their positions.

There was no opposition. Their drop and march were unobserved by Egyptian troops. By 7:30 P.M. Eitan and his troops had dug in and established blocking positions and ambushes on the only two roads in the wasteland. Shortly after nightfall, three Egyptian vehicles happened by with soldiers going off on leave. The Israeli paratroopers destroyed one vehicle and its passengers, but the other two escaped to report the presence of Israeli troops nearly seventy miles inside Egyptian territory.

At nine that evening six French Nordatlas cargo planes flying out of Cyprus dropped supplies to the Israeli battalion, including eight jeeps, four 106mm recoilless rifles, two 120mm mortars, ammunition, medicine, food and water.

Two hours later, Israel's Foreign Ministry announced that the country was engaged in "security measures to eliminate the Egyptian *fedayeen* bases in the Sinai Peninsula. . . . It is not Israel which has sought to encompass Egypt with a ring of steel with the announced and flouted purpose of annihilating her at the appropriate moment."

• •

As the war started, Air Force Colonel Ezer Weizman pondered the profound doubts that plagued Israel. For the average Israeli, Weizman wrote, "deep down in his heart there was some hidden fear, filling his world with gnawing doubts: Were Israel's victories in the War of Independence a true expression of her collective ability? Did they represent the essence of every value belonging to our persecuted people? Did they indicate the superiority of the Israeli Jew in his homeland, or were they some fleeting 'miracle,' like luck, which is governed by chance? Did we just exploit the enemy's temporary weakness, which occurred in one war but will not recur? . . . Only a further military contest could prove it beyond all doubt."

• •

Forty minutes after word of Israel's attack was broadcast, Dulles telephoned Cabot Lodge at the United Nations. "The Israelis have moved into Egyptian territory. We don't know yet in what force or whether it is a raid from which they will retire. The British and French are coming in and we will see if they will act in the U.N. calling upon the Israelis to withdraw."

Dulles added: "Partly it is to smoke them out to see where they stand."

In another call to an aide, Dulles said, "It looks so bad we may have to stop our aid [to Israel]. They don't think we would do that."

At 5:45 P.M., Admiral Radford called Dulles, advising that "our assessment is it is going to get bigger as soon as daylight comes, if not tonight. We don't think it can be stopped."

To Senator Knowland, Dulles said: "My guess is [the Israeli attack] has been worked out with the French at least and possibly with the British. We thought they would attack Jordan. We are asking for a Security Council meeting tomorrow and have asked the British and the French if they would join us. We took action to evacuate American civilians that we will need money for."

"That's no problem," answered Knowland.

•   •

Swift communications was not one of the greater strengths of the Eisenhower Administration. The joint chiefs of staff, the CIA and the State Department learned of the Israeli attack not by official channels but through an Associated Press news bulletin sent worldwide at 3 P.M. EST. Eisenhower, out campaigning, did not hear of it until 6 P.M.—nine hours after the fact—when his plane, *Colombine,* landed at Richmond, Virginia, the last of his three scheduled political stops that Monday. With his usual coolness in a crisis, the President went ahead with his routine speaking engagement before heading back to Washington. By the time he landed at the capital at 7 P.M., his calm had been replaced by a roaring rage at the Israelis.

Already awaiting him at the White House were his top security officials, the two Dulles brothers, Defense Secretary Charles Wilson, Chairman Radford of the joint chiefs of staff and others. Eisenhower ordered Foster Dulles to send a scathing cable to the Israelis. "All right," the President said, "Foster, you tell 'em, goddamn it, we're going to apply sanctions, we're going to the United Nations, we're going to do everything that there is so we can stop this thing."

Later Eisenhower recalled that "we just told [the Israelis] it was absolutely indefensible and that if they expect our support in the Middle East and in maintaining their position, they had to behave. . . . We went to town right away and began to give them hell."

365

But still there was no clear idea of how the Israeli attack related to the Anglo-French buildup of invasion forces. Several officials at the White House emergency meeting thought that Israel was merely engaged in a probing action. Others thought that the Israeli troops would move rapidly to the Suez Canal and the whole thing would be over in three days. Foster Dulles disagreed with both views.

"It is far more serious than that," he said. "The canal is likely to be disrupted and the oil pipelines through the Middle East broken. If these things happen we must expect British and French intervention. In fact, they appear to be ready for it and may even have concerted their action with the Israelis."

Radford added: "There are rumors that the British, French and Israelis have made a deal with Iraq to carve up Jordan. The French and British may think that, whatever we may think about what they have done, that we have to go along with them."

Defense Secretary Wilson speculated that "the Israelis must be figuring on French and British support, thinking that we are stymied at this pre-election period, and the U.S.S.R. also because of its difficulties in Eastern Europe."

"I don't care in the slightest," injected Eisenhower, "whether I am re-elected or not. I feel we must make good on our word," he added, referring to the Tripartite Declaration of 1950. "In these circumstances, we cannot be bound by our traditional alliances. Instead, we must face the question of how to make good on our pledge."

Radford said the matter should be handled "on the basis of principle," and Eisenhower agreed.

"We should let the British know at once our position," said the President, "telling them that we recognize that much is on their side in the dispute with the Egyptians—but that nothing justifies double-crossing us. I cannot conceive that the United States would gain if we permitted it to be justly said that we are a nation without honor. If the British get into this operation they may open a deep rift between us. If the British back the Israelis they may find us in opposition. I don't fancy helping the Egyptians but I feel our word must be made good."

Dulles observed that "there has been a struggle between the French and us to see who will have the British allied with them in the tense situations in the Middle East and North Africa. I think there is still a bare chance to unhook the British from the French."

The meeting adjourned after an hour with the decision to invite to the

366

White House the British chargé d'affaires, J. E. Coulson. Ambassador Makins had left for a new assignment earlier in the month and the new ambassador had not yet arrived, leaving Coulson in charge of the embassy. He arrived shortly after 8 P.M. and Eisenhower and Dulles met with him.

"The prestige of the United States and the British is involved in the developments in the Middle East," Eisenhower told Coulson. "I feel it is incumbent upon both of us to redeem our word about supporting any victim of aggression. Last spring, when we declined to give arms to Israel and to Egypt, we said that our word was enough.

"In my opinion, the United States and the United Kingdom must stand by what we said. In view of information that has reached us concerning Mystères and the number of messages between Paris and Israel in the last few days, I can only conclude that I do not understand what the French are doing."

"I do not know about the messages," interjected Coulson.

"If I have to call Congress in order to redeem our pledge I will do so," said Eisenhower. "We will stick to our undertaking."

"Would the United States not first go to the Security Council?" asked Coulson.

"We plan to get to the United Nations the first thing in the morning— when the doors open, before the U.S.S.R. gets there," shot back the President.

Dulles warned that some of the Baghdad Pact countries had called on him earlier and had "asked me what the U.S. is going to do to redeem its pledge."

Eisenhower interrupted, obviously agitated at how damaging a British attack would be. "We had had a great chance to split the Arab world," he said. "Various of the countries were becoming uneasy at Egyptian developments. I don't know what Sir Anthony is thinking, but I'm certain that it is important that we stick together. Please communicate my ideas urgently to London and assure Lloyd and Anthony that we wish to be with them."

Then the President added forcefully: "I will not betray the good word of the United States, and I will ask Congress if necessary to redeem our pledge." Again he was referring to the Tripartite Declaration's pledge to oppose aggression in the Middle East.

About the same time Eisenhower was talking with Coulson, press secretary Hagerty was issuing a strong statement telling the world what Ike

367

was telling the British chargé: "The United States has pledged itself to assist the victim of any aggression in the Middle East. We shall honor our pledge."

Still later that evening Eisenhower had another meeting that did nothing to assuage his anger at Israel. A group of prominent Republicans called on him and said that for the first time in the campaign they thought he might lose. Their reasoning was that Israel had "committed aggression that could not be condoned," recalled Eisenhower. "Perhaps it would be necessary for the United States, as a member of the United Nations, to employ our armed force in strength to drive them back within their borders. If this turned out to be the case, much of the responsibility would be laid at my door. With many of our citizens of the eastern seaboard emotionally involved in the Zionist cause, this, it was believed, could possibly bring political defeat."

At the end of his meeting with the worried politicians, Eisenhower remained resolved to get the Israelis out of Egyptian territory. "I thought and said that emotion was beclouding their good judgment," recalled the President. He pressed on without hesitation his opposition to aggression in the Middle East—despite his regard for his World War II British allies and the threat posed to his re-election by the U.S. partisans of Israel.

• •

As usual the first victims of the war were the innocent. Arabs living within Israel were putatively citizens with most of the rights of Jewish Israelis, but on October 29 they were put under curfew to start at 5 P.M. and to last till 6 A.M. The *mukhtar* (headman) of Kfar Kassem, a village inside Israel near Tel Aviv with two thousand Palestinians who were known for their friendliness to Israeli rule, protested. Many families were still out in the fields or in surrounding towns working and had no way of receiving warnings of the curfew, he complained. The Israeli Border Police, known as the most ruthless of the country's troops, nonetheless set up roadblocks. After 5 P.M. they stopped all villagers returning to Kfar Kassem, lined them up along the road and shot them. Men, women and children were cut down. Of sixteen olive pickers returning in one truck, only a sixteen-year-old girl survived; all but two of them were women, one of them eight months pregnant. When it was over, by 6 P.M., forty-seven men, women and children had been slaughtered.

Israel also took advantage of the confusion of the start of the war to grab hold of a small village in the demilitarized zone on the Syrian border. Some seven hundred Arabs were forced across the Banat Yaqoub bridge

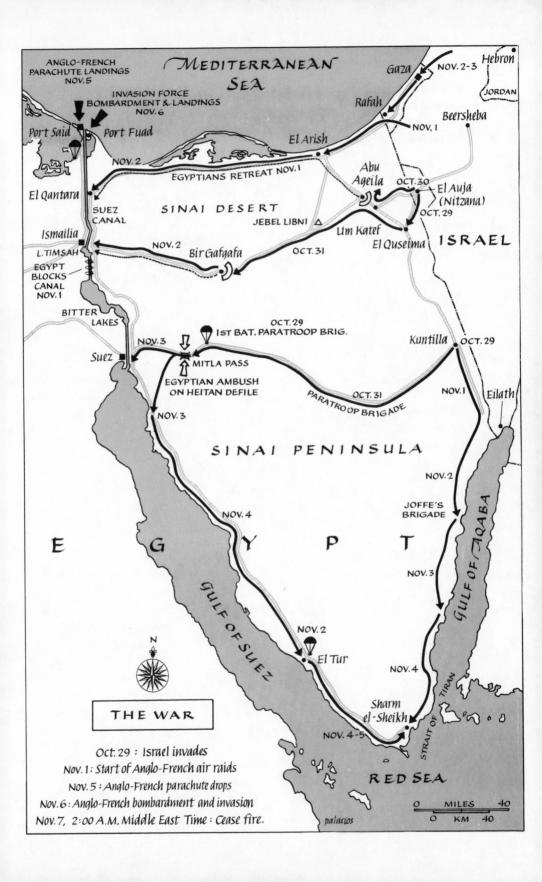

ANGLO-FRENCH
PARACHUTE LANDINGS
NOV. 5

MEDITERRANEAN
SEA

Gaza
NOV. 2-3
Hebron

JORDAN

INVASION FORCE
BOMBARDMENT & LANDINGS
NOV. 6

Rafah

NOV. 1
Beersheba

Port Said
Port Fuad

El Arish

Abu
Ageila
OCT. 30
El Auja
(Nitzana)

NOV. 2
EGYPTIANS RETREAT NOV. 1

OCT. 29

El Qantara

SINAI DESERT

SUEZ
CANAL

JEBEL LIBNI △

Um Katef
El Quseima
ISRAEL

Ismailia

L. TIMSAH

NOV. 2
Bir Gafgafa
OCT. 31

EGYPT
BLOCKS
CANAL
NOV. 1

BITTER
LAKES

OCT. 29
1ST BAT. PARATROOP BRIG.

Kuntilla
OCT. 29

NOV. 3

Suez

MITLA PASS

NOV. 1
Eilath

EGYPTIAN AMBUSH
ON HEITAN DEFILE

OCT. 31
PARATROOP BRIGADE

NOV. 3

SINAI PENINSULA

NOV. 2

NOV. 4

JOFFE'S
BRIGADE

E   G   Y   P   T

NOV. 3

GULF OF AQABA

GULF OF SUEZ

NOV. 2

El Tur

NOV. 4

N

Sharm
el-Sheikh

THE WAR

NOV. 4-5

STRAIT OF TIRAN

Oct. 29 : Israel invades
Nov. 1 : Start of Anglo-French air raids
Nov. 5 : Anglo-French parachute drops
Nov. 6 : Anglo-French bombardment and invasion
Nov. 7, 2:00 A.M. Middle East Time : Cease fire.

RED SEA

0   MILES   40
0   KM   40

palacios

into Syria and most of the homes in their village were razed by bulldozers and plowed under. Israel had had its eye on the strategically located village for years. Now it was Israel's.

The war had barely begun.

CHAPTER XVIII

Ugly and Unsmiling

LODGE

TUESDAY DAWNED with a gathering sense of unreality. The crisp October light did nothing to dispel the shock and incredulity created in Washington by the Israeli attack and the ominous silence of Britain and France. Unquestionably some devious plot was unfolding, but its dimensions and even its participants remained unclear. By any rational standard, Britain should not be involved in collusion with Israel in the Middle East. Yet accumulating evidence indicated to Washington that it was. Dwight Eisenhower was bewildered and anxious.

The President's face was drawn and his eyes heavy with fatigue when he arrived at his White House office shortly after 8 A.M. on October 30 and telephoned Foster Dulles. The secretary of state said he had just been talking with Cabot Lodge, who related to him a disturbing encounter. Lodge had been at the Metropolitan Opera House the previous evening when he learned of Washington's decision to demand a Security Council meeting to request Israel's immediate withdrawal from Egyptian territory. Britain's U.N. ambassador, Sir Pierson Dixon, was also at the opera and Lodge informed him of the U.S. plan. "Lodge said that while Dixon was normally an agreeable fellow, last night it was as though a mask had fallen off. He was ugly and unsmiling," Dulles reported. "When asked if Britain would live up to the 1950 [Tripartite] Declaration, he said: 'Don't be so damned high-minded.' " The declaration, declared Dixon, was "ancient history and without current validity."

Eisenhower noted that "none of the newspapers seem to look on the situation with the same urgency that the Administration does."

371

"You probably read the early editions," replied Dulles.

At a meeting later that Tuesday morning, Eisenhower, Dulles and Herbert Hoover were still confused about Britain's role in the Israeli attack. "We still hope the British will join us" in submitting a U.N. resolution against Israel, Dulles said.

"Have the French been given the opportunity to join with us?" asked Ike.

They had, said Dulles, but "neither yesterday nor this morning had they shown any evidence of desire to act rapidly on the matter."

An International News Service bulletin was brought to the President, saying, mistakenly, that the landing of British and French troops in Egypt was imminent.

"I wonder if the hand of Churchill might not be behind this inasmuch as this action is in the mid-Victorian style," said Eisenhower. "In my judgment the British and the French do not have an adequate cause for war. Egyptian action in nationalizing the canal is not enough to justify this."

"The British were practically in agreement with Egypt at the recent U.N. meeting, but they've been delaying any resolution since then," observed Dulles. "This is not a question of the Suez. It really is a question of Algeria for the French and of their position in the Persian Gulf for the British." He added with uncanny precision: "I think the odds are high that the British may be evicted from Iraq and that the pipelines may be blown up. It may be necessary for us to make major adjustments in our oil situation soon."

"The British may think they can settle the matter quickly and thus have their oil supply continue without interruption," said Eisenhower. "If oil is cut off and American ships take the route around the Cape, the oil supplies of Western Europe will be greatly cut down."

Hoover noted that "the British may be estimating that we would have no choice but to take extraordinary means to get oil to them."

Dulles agreed. "Their thinking might be that they will confront us with a de facto situation in which they might acknowledge that they have been rash but would say that the U.S. could not sit by and let them go under economically."

"I don't see much value in an unworthy and unreliable ally," snapped Eisenhower. "The necessity to support them might not be as great as they believe."

Dulles agreed but he was worried. "There's the danger of our being drawn into the hostilities as we were in World Wars I and II—with the difference that this time it appears that the British and French might well be considered the aggressors in the eyes of the world engaged in an anti-Arab, anti-Asian war. I've been greatly worried for two or three years over our identification with countries pursuing colonial policies not compatible with our own.''

Earlier in the morning, Eisenhower had written a long personal message to Eden and now he had Dulles help with its editing so it could be sent off urgently. He hoped that there was still a chance to divert the British from a course that seemed sure to lead to disaster.

''I address you not only as head of Her Majesty's Government but as my longtime friend who has, with me, believed and worked for real Anglo-American understanding,'' Ike wrote. ''Certain phases of this whole affair are disturbing me very much. I should like to ask your help in clearing up my understanding as to exactly what is happening between us and our European allies—especially between us, the French and yourselves.''

The President cited the French sale of arms and warplanes to Israel ''in violation of agreements now existing between our three countries,'' increased radio traffic between Tel Aviv and Paris, Dixon's ''completely unsympathetic'' behavior the previous night and his claim that the Tripartite Declaration was no longer valid. Eisenhower emphasized that no one had told him the declaration was dead.

''All of this development, with its possible consequences, including the possible involvement of you and the French in a general Arab war, seems to me to leave your government and ours in a very sad state of confusion. It is true that Egypt has not yet formally asked this government for aid. But the fact is that if the United Nations finds Israel to be an aggressor, Egypt could very well ask the Soviets for help—and then the Mideast fat would really be in the fire. . . . We may shortly find ourselves not only at odds concerning what we should do, but confronted with a de facto situation that would make all our present troubles look puny indeed.

''Because of all these possibilities, it seems to me of first importance that the U.K. and the U.S. quickly and clearly lay out their present views and intentions before each other, and that, come what may, we find some way of concerting our ideas and plans so that we may not, in any real crisis, be powerless to act in concert because of misunderstanding of each other. With warm personal regards.''

About the time this letter was sent, one from Eden arrived. Ike later described the exchange of messages as ''a sort of transatlantic essay contest.'' Eden wrote that Britain felt ''no obligation'' to go to Egypt's aid under the Tripartite Declaration. "Nasser and his press have relieved us of any such obligation by their attitude." Eden claimed that action by the U.N. was not likely to be "rapid or effective" and maintained that "decisive action should be taken at once to stop hostilities."

After reading Eden's message, Eisenhower acidly observed during a meeting with aides that "the British case would be improved if the Egyptians had not simply nationalized the canal and then operated it effectively."

It was obvious to Eisenhower and his aides that Eden was not being candid, nor was he sharing his plans with Washington. Something fishy was going on. But what? The meeting broke up on a note of deep anxiety.

Twenty minutes later, at 11:36 A.M., Dulles telephoned Ike to say that Eden at that moment was announcing in the House of Commons the landing of British and French forces in the Suez Canal area. It was another false report. What Eden was announcing at that moment was the ultimatum agreed on at Sèvres to be issued to both Egypt and Israel to remove their troops from the canal. It was rude of Eden to make such an important announcement without prior notification to Washington.

Eisenhower exploded. "The White House crackled with barrack-room language the like of which had not been heard since the days of General Grant," reported columnist James Reston.

"I think it will probably be necessary to make clear publicly that we have not been, and are not now, associated with the French and the British in their activities," Ike told Dulles.

In the afternoon, press secretary Jim Hagerty released a prepared statement to the news media that pointedly noted the President received his first information of the ultimatums "through press reports."

Eisenhower also sent stern, identical messages to Eden and Mollet, addressed simply "Dear Mr. Prime Minister." The President expressed his "deep concern at the prospect of this drastic action. It is my sincere belief that peaceful processes can and should prevail."

The original text expressed an "earnest request" that Britain and France desist from violence, but Eisenhower suggested to Dulles over the telephone that be changed to the "unwisdom of taking this action." He explained he did not want "to put it in the form of a prayer that would not be answered—in other words, to save ourselves, if we can, from a complete slap in the face. I don't think it will make much difference either way [since I doubt] either country will pay any attention."

But, he added, "I think we almost have to send it. At least it establishes us before the Arab world as being no part of it."

In the end, the message was sent without any request and simply expressed the President's concern.

Dulles said he thought the Anglo-French ultimatum was "about as crude and brutal as anything I have ever seen."

Eisenhower had not yet read it and so Dulles told him about it. "It's pretty rough," agreed Eisenhower.

"It is utterly unacceptable," exclaimed Dulles.

"They haven't consulted us on anything," complained the President. He again worried about the Russians. "Where [else] is Egypt going to turn?"

In another conversation, Dulles said he suspected that Eden was going to try to claim that the Tripartite Declaration was no longer in force. "He never said any of this publicly," said Eisenhower. "I want him to know that we are a government of honor, and we stick by it."

The confusion and uncertainties of the rapidly unfolding events were getting Eisenhower down. "The only thing I can see we can do is keep our hands off," he said. "After all, we will not fight" Britain and France. "They are our friends and allies and suddenly they put us in a hole and expect us to rescue them."

Another message arrived from Eden, this one finally telling Eisenhower officially about the ultimatums and the putative reasons behind them. The news wires had already carried much of the information taken from Eden's remarks in the House. "Knowing what these people [Egyptians] are, we felt it essential to have some kind of physical guarantees in order to secure the safety of the canal," Eden wrote. Disingenuously, he added that haste was necessary because "the Israelis appear to be very near to Suez."

"We should have had this message yesterday," Eisenhower remarked to Dulles.

"If we had had it yesterday, we might have stopped them," replied Dulles. (Eden later admitted that indeed he had not sent the message earlier because "I didn't want to give time for Ike to ring up and say: 'Dulles is on his way again.'")

In another meeting that day, this one with the head of the Office of Defense Mobilization, Arthur Flemming, Eisenhower discussed the likely effects on the world oil supply if Britain and France attacked Egypt. "I'm inclined to think that those who began this operation should be left to work out their own oil problems—to boil in their own oil, so to speak," said Eisenhower. "They will be needing oil from Venezuela and around the Cape and before long they will be short of dollars to finance these operations and will be calling for help. They may be planning to present us with a fait accompli, then expect us to foot the bill. I'm extremely angry with them.''

"I think we should not help the British and French in these circumstances unless they ration their consumption of oil," said Flemming. "Our studies indicate we should have no problem satisfying our own requirements.''

"In that case I see no reason why we should ration oil," said Eisenhower. He instructed Flemming to investigate whether tankers from the Navy could be used to help Britain's shipping problem "in case we should decide to do so.''

Later that afternoon Ike's speech writer, Emmet Hughes, found the President "torn between anxiety and, I fear, overoptimism. More calm (as usual) than either White House staff or State Department—all of whom are whipping themselves into an anti-British frenzy.'' But Eisenhower told Hughes he was not optimistic at all. "I'm afraid the British'll come out of this with more loss of face. What are they going to do—fight the whole Moslem world?

"I've just never seen great powers make such a complete mess and botch of things. Of course, there's nobody, in a war, I'd rather have fighting alongside me than the British. But this thing? My God!''

•   •

Guy Mollet and Christian Pineau had flown to London the morning after the Israeli attack to play out the charade decided on a week earlier at Sèvres. The ultimatum that would be sent to Egypt and Israel had already been drafted and approved at Sèvres, but now the Anglo-French leaders went through the motions of conferring on what they would do.

U.S. Ambassador Aldrich, meanwhile, had been instructed to question Lloyd directly about British plans, but throughout that Tuesday morning he was put off repeatedly by the foreign secretary. Finally, at 4:45 P.M., Aldrich was called to Whitehall by Sir Ivone Kirkpatrick, permanent undersecretary of the Foreign Office, and was handed a copy of the ultimatum. Aldrich was stunned. It was clear to him now that Lloyd had outright lied to him two nights earlier when he denied British involvement with Israel. Aldrich complained that the ultimatum demanded both sides pull back ten miles from the canal, which would mean Egyptian troops would be 110 miles inside their own territory while Israeli troops would be nearly 100 miles inside Egypt. Aldrich said Egypt could not possibly accept it. Kirkpatrick responded with a shrug of the shoulder. Eden, he informed the startled ambassador, was at that moment informing the House of the ultimatum.

Eden's announcement to the House was met with a frigid silence. The Tories, as if in embarrassment, stared straight ahead and the Labourites seemed frozen in horror. Finally Labour leader Hugh Gaitskell blurted out: "I think it would be unwise if we were to plunge into any lengthy discussion." But he could not constrain himself. He wanted to know if the United States had been consulted. How about the United Nations? And why was there an absence of any mention by Eden of the Tripartite Declaration? "I would like him to tell us the government's attitude to that declaration now," said Gaitskell.

Eden barely seemed to hear the questions as he lounged languidly on the front bench, his striped-trousered legs propped up on the table and his eyes staring at the ceiling. When he finally answered, he was less than candid. "Certainly the spirit of the Tripartite Declaration—and more than the spirit—operates in our minds. It is also true that Egypt's own attitude to the Tripartite Declaration has been, to say the very least, equivocal."

A vote of confidence was taken, and Eden barely won. It was along straight party lines, 270 to 218. When Eisenhower heard the count, he confessed: "I could not dream of committing this nation on such a vote."

In France, the National Assembly gave Mollet a robust majority of 368 to 182 in approving his policies.

The simple fact that action had finally been taken seemed to lift, however temporarily, a great burden from Eden and some of the senior members of his Cabinet, which had approved his actions. Eden was "almost boyish, reminiscent of a young officer of the First World War, very calm, very polite, the captain of the first eleven in a critical match," according to historian Hugh Thomas. Harold Macmillan, 62, who had predicted that Washington would "lie doggo" and allow Britain to attack Nasser, was like the "young Macmillan of the thirties again, hat thrown in the air."

• •

In the United Nations that Tuesday, the world was treated to an extraordinary spectacle. Britain and France vetoed a resolution submitted by their traditional ally, the United States. The resolution had called for Israel to withdraw its troops. The Soviet Union then submitted essen-

377

tially the same resolution and Britain and France again vetoed. It was the first time the two countries had cast vetoes in the history of the United Nations.

British and French diplomats had not been informed of Eden's and Mollet's plans and many of them were deeply shocked and disturbed by the ultimatums and the vetoes, U.N. Ambassador Pierson Dixon among them. Though his reaction at the opera had seemed to indicate he knew about the plan, he actually did not and he was greatly upset. "The effort of concealing these feelings and putting a plausible and confident face on the case was the severest moral and physical strain I have ever experienced," he recalled. The French U.N. ambassador, Bernard Cornut-Gentille, had a nervous breakdown during the U.N. debates. British ambassador to the Soviet Union, Sir William Hayter, thought of resigning. He had been at a Kremlin party when a copy of the ultimatum arrived at his embassy. "I could not believe my eyes," he said. "I began to wonder if I had drunk too much at the Kremlin. The action we were taking seemed to me flatly contrary to all that I knew, or thought I knew, about British policy."

The envoy most uncomfortable was Humphrey Trevelyan in Cairo. He heard of the ultimatum only late in the afternoon when one of his officers came by his office and said: "I think you had better come down the corridor and see what is coming over the ticker." Commented Trevelyan: "It was the British government's ultimatum, which had presumably been delivered to the Egyptian ambassador in London, since it had not been delivered through me." The ultimatum had been handed to the Egyptian and Israeli ambassadors in London and Paris at 4 P.M. Trevelyan was summoned to Nasser's office to receive Egypt's response that evening.

Foreign Minister Mahmoud Fawzi was with Nasser, and he later said, according to Anthony Nutting, that "in all his diplomatic experience he never saw an ambassador so shocked and bewildered by his instructions."

Nasser appeared relaxed and seemingly at ease when Trevelyan entered. "I have your ultimatum," said Nasser.

"But it does not say ultimatum," replied Trevelyan. "It says 'communication.' According to my text, the purpose of the intervention is to stop the fighting and protect the canal."

"We can defend the canal and tomorrow we shall be defending it from more than the Israelis," replied Nasser, ending the meeting.

The ultimatum gave Egypt and Israel each twelve hours to "withdraw" their troops from the canal area. Israel gladly accepted as planned, since it had no troops closer than about thirty miles to the canal. Nasser naturally refused. The ultimatum was scheduled to expire at 6 A.M. the next day, Cairo time.

• •

Ambassador Trevelyan awoke Wednesday expecting to find the embassy surrounded by troops and the atmosphere crackling with war tensions. Instead, everything appeared normal. The ultimatum deadline had come and gone and nothing had happened. Ship convoys were placidly transiting the canal. The only sign of unusual activity was the stream of buses that plied the desert road to Alexandria throughout the day carrying Americans leaving the country.

Out of sight, the vast Anglo-French armada, the ships loaded with troops, began steaming from the docks in Malta and Algiers on the six-day sail to Egypt.

• •

In Hungary too there was a deceptive lull. The riots and fighting of the previous week had come to a standstill, leaving many villages and cities in the hands of the anti-Soviet nationalists. Premier Nagy had abolished one-party rule and demanded the withdrawal of Soviet troops from Hungarian territory. By Wednesday, the rebels seemed in a strong position. Soviet tanks began moving out of Budapest, and Nagy rashly declared that Hungary would withdraw from the Warsaw Pact, maintain strict neutrality between East and West, and seek the protection of the United Nations. Unlike Gomulka in Poland, Nagy was going too far too fast for the comfort of the Kremlin leaders, but he was still unaware of that. For the moment, it looked as if he were winning.

The euphoric atmosphere was reinforced with the release from prison of Josef Cardinal Mindszenty, 64, the Primate of Hungary who had been sentenced to life in prison in 1949 for his anti-Soviet activities. He was let out of Felsoepeteny Castle by the Army and returned in triumph to Budapest. "The revolution has triumphed," declared Imre Nagy on October 31. "We will tolerate no interference in our internal affairs."

• •

In the Sinai, Israel unleashed the full might of its attack against Egypt. After the parachute landing at Mitla Pass, Israel launched a three-pronged assault across the Sinai sands. The Jewish state entered the war with forty-five thousand well-trained men against Egypt's thirty thou-

379

sand, including the ragtag Palestine Division, and 155 warplanes, not counting the 60 French jets, against 70 operational Egyptian combat planes.

Even with their great advantage of surprise, numbers and equipment, the attackers quickly ran into unexpectedly tough resistance. Impetuous "Arik" Sharon had stormed across the border late Monday with his 202nd Paratroop Brigade in a wild dash across the center of Sinai to relieve the brigade's 1st Battalion at the Mitla Pass. Sharon's force over-ran several lightly defended outposts and finally joined up at the Mitla Pass with Eitan's 1st Battalion at 10:30 P.M. Tuesday. At first light on Wednesday, Sharon inspected Eitan's positions and found they were much farther east of the entrance to the pass in open desert than he thought safe. He requested permission from headquarters to move to the entrance but it was denied. The nearest Israeli troops were eighty miles away and an Egyptian armored brigade was operating near Bir Gafgafa, just fifteen miles to the north. Headquarters did not want Sharon to call attention to his force. Frustrated, Sharon tried a ruse. He radioed for permission to send a reconnaissance unit into the pass, and this was granted. But again he was warned not to engage in any large-scale action.

Sharon was convinced he would not meet stiff resistance in the pass since the Egyptian troops stationed there, the 5th and 6th Battalions of the 2nd Brigade, had been bombed and strafed heavily Tuesday afternoon by Israeli jets. He rashly decided to ignore headquarters and put together a large force to enter the steep-sided pass. Three companies on half-tracks supported by three French AMX tanks and four 120mm mortars were formed under Major Mordechai Gur. At around 12:30 P.M., Gur's force moved into the eastern entrance of the pass and then entered the Heitan Defile, a three-mile-long section of sheer cliffs that at its narrow-est was only fifty meters wide. It was there that the Egyptians were lying in wait.

The Egyptian battalions had suffered few casualties in the previous day's air attacks and now their troops were hidden in caves cut in the walls of the pass and in previously prepared rifle pits along the tops of the high ridges. Gur's force was hit hard almost as soon as it penetrated the defile. The leading two half-tracks were quickly knocked out. As their troops scattered they were pinned down by intense rifle and machine-gun fire. Gur, in the third half-track, dashed past the two immobilized vehi-cles only to have his vehicle slip into a wadi and get stuck.

The Egyptian fire was hellish. An ammunition truck, a fuel truck and three other Israeli vehicles were hit and exploded into flames. As the patrol raced through the defile it lost or suffered damage to another half-track, a tank, an ambulance and a jeep. Bodies of the dead and wounded and the burning carcasses of vehicles littered the defile's passage.

Gur had no communications with Sharon and a runner had to be sent back to inform the commander of Israel's heavy casualties. Sharon responded by sending two reinforced companies to the rescue. After two and a half hours of heavy hand-to-hand fighting, the Egyptian force was finally flushed from its hideaways. But the cost had been great. Israel lost 38 men killed and 120 wounded. The Egyptian casualties were 150 killed, some of them after they had been taken prisoner.

The second and third prongs of the Israeli attack went south toward Sharm el-Sheikh and west across the desert north of Sharon's paratroops. The southern attack was launched by the 9th Mechanized Brigade under the command of Colonel Avraham Yoffe. Its first day of operations had less to do with fighting than in negotiating the rugged, roadless terrain down to the tip of the Sinai Peninsula.

The other task force, the one attacking west, north of Sharon, had a considerably harder time. It met fierce Egyptian resistance at the desert junction of Abu Ageila, a barren intersection on the main El Arish-Ismailia road about fifteen miles west of the frontier from El Auja. The force was commanded by Colonel Yehudah Wallach and was composed of the 4th and 10th Infantry Brigades and the 7th Armored Brigade.

Wallach's group stormed out of the vital El Auja demilitarized zone that Israel had taken over the previous year on the night of the twenty-ninth and quickly overcame weak resistance at several lightly manned outposts along the frontier. But its progress was not as rapid as the overall commander of the Sinai forces, Brigadier General Assaf Simhoni, would have liked. Early on the thirtieth Simhoni committed the tanks of the 7th Armored Brigade, in direct violation of an order from Dayan.

Dayan had not wanted a large deployment of tanks in Egyptian territory until it was certain that Britain and France were joining the war. Thus he had ordered Simhoni to hold the 7th in reserve until the dawn of the thirty-first. If the British and French backed out, a serious consideration even at this late date, then Dayan could withdraw his troops and maintain that Israel had simply indulged in yet another of its reprisal raids. But Simhoni was ignorant of the collusion with Britain and France and, with the aggressiveness typical of the Israel Defense Forces, he sent his tanks into battle right at the start of the attack.

Dayan was furious, but typically pragmatic. "What has been done is done," he wrote in his diary. "If indeed the advance of this armored brigade into the Sinai leads to increased Egyptian activity, particularly in the air, there is nothing we can do now to prevent it. Better, then, at least to extract the maximum advantage.'' He ordered the tanks to attack.

An advance guard of the 7th had already attacked at Um Katef, an eastern outpost of Abu Ageila, and had been twice repelled by deadly accurate antitank fire. The unit had lost several tanks and half-tracks, and suffered casualties as well. Dayan now decided that the main force of the 7th should bypass Abu Ageila and capture the Ismailia road at a point behind Abu Ageila at Jebel Libni. The assault on Abu Ageila was assigned to the 10th Infantry Brigade and a pickup brigade comprising infantry, half-tracks and a battalion of Sherman tanks commanded by Lieutenant Colonel Avraham Adan.

The lead infantry battalion of the 10th led the attack Tuesday night but it was quickly repelled by fierce fire from the dug-in Egyptian troops. It spent the rest of the night trying to regroup and pull its troops together to await the arrival of the rest of the elements of the attack force. It took Adan's Sherman tanks to capture the Abu Ageila crossroads early the next morning. But the heavily fortified outposts around the crossroads remained in Egyptian hands that Wednesday.

• •

The expiry of the ultimatum had passed at 6 A.M. Wednesday and still the promised bombing attacks by British and French planes had not yet occurred by noon. That meant the Egyptian Air Force remained intact and capable of launching a lethal assault on Israel's cities. There was great anxiety in Tel Aviv. Ben Gurion was worried and his doubts about Eden's reliability as a fellow schemer were rising. He had never trusted Eden, and as the minutes passed he was beginning to lose his confidence in the whole enterprise. If Eden backed out now, Israel would stand alone as an aggressor and exposed to the wrath of all the Arab nations and the world.

By midafternoon, Ben Gurion's trepidation was overflowing. The Anglo-French bombing raids were now eight hours late, and perhaps never would come. After a heated argument with Dayan, he ordered Israeli troops pulled out of the Sinai. Dayan resisted, arguing that the attack would come, but Ben Gurion insisted. As a compromise, Dayan ordered Israeli forces to suspend offensive operations and go into a mobile defensive posture until further notice. Israel would fight only when it had the assurance that Britain and France had joined the fray.

The Old Man, still suffering from flu, waited in his modest Tel Aviv home with his anxiety and apprehensions mounting.

• •

The Anglo-French bombing attacks had been delayed for two unforeseen reasons. The first came because the planners had slated the attacks to take place at night in order to avoid plane losses. Orders had to be reissued and schedules straightened out before the first wave of bombers could take off in daylight. Then, to his horror, Eden learned from Trevelyan that fifteen U.S. transport planes were lined up at Cairo-West Airport waiting to evacuate Americans; in addition, some three thousand Americans evacuating to Alexandria were using the road adjacent to the airport. Eden hastily ordered Defense Minister Anthony Head to stop the bombers at all costs. They were turned back only at the last minute before dropping any bombs.

Sorting out all this confusion took more time. It was not until 7 P.M., Cairo time, twenty-five hours since the ultimatums had been delivered and thirteen after their expiry, that the bombers flying from Malta and Cyprus began unloading their deadly cargoes on Cairo-West and other Egyptian airfields. The bombers used no bombs greater than one thousand pounds in order to avoid excessive casualties. The population had been warned of the attacks by the British propaganda radio on Cyprus, now christened the Voice of Britain, and by leaflets. The bombers' work was to pock the runways of the airfields, leaving the Egyptian warplanes stranded, to be finished off by carrier planes. For the next two days two hundred Canberras, Venoms and Valiants, and forty French Thunderstreaks, bombed economic targets in Egypt and wiped out much of the Egyptian Air Force on the ground.

• •

While the bombers were performing their destructive duties in Egypt, the increasingly uneasy members of the Labour Party in London were still in the dark about Eden's invasion plans. They had been made extremely suspicious by Eden's earlier fudging about the Tripartite Declaration and by the stunning news that Britain had joined France in vetoing the American resolution in the United Nations. Thus the Wednesday session of Parliament was tense and the comments from Labourites took on a new acerbity. Their mood was not improved by Eden's continued evasiveness. Despite repeated questions about Britain's military plans, Eden refused to even admit whether force might be used.

In growing irritation, Gaitskell declared: "This is really a fantastic situation. Not only Opposition members but the whole House and the whole country are waiting for an answer to this question. I ask the prime minister again—I do not ask him to disclose troop movements—I ask him simply to tell the House, the country and the whole world whether the decision has been finally taken that British and French troops shall invade the canal zone."

Eden again refused to give a straight answer, which finally convinced Gaitskell that Eden had indeed decided to invade. "All I can say is that in taking this decision, it is the view of the Opposition that the government have committed an act of disastrous folly whose tragic consequences we shall regret for years because it will have done irreparable harm to the prestige and reputation of our country," declared Gaitskell.

As suspicions gelled into conviction, the Labourites bombarded Eden and Lloyd with more questions. Lloyd, to his discredit, lied on the House floor when he was asked directly by Gaitskell whether there had been "collusion" between Britain, France and Israel. "It is wrong to state that Israel was incited to this action by the government," replied Lloyd. "There was not a prior agreement between us about it."

Then Lloyd dropped a bombshell. He officially announced, just before the session adjourned at 10:29 P.M., that the commencement of aerial operations against Egypt had begun. The House disbanded in disarray.

• •

Eden had another shock that day, this one far more severe than the near-bombing of Americans living in Egypt. His protégé Anthony Nutting resigned in protest over the government's Suez policy. The harried prime minister called Nutting to his office within minutes of receiving his resignation letter. Nutting tried to explain his opposition to Britain's collusion and the dangers it posed to the country's relations with the Arab world. By colluding, Nutting warned, "we would convince the entire Arab world that they had been right all along in believing that we had created Israel as a beachhead from which we would one day return to re-establish ourselves in the Middle East.

"It was a painful encounter. As I looked him in the eye, he looked away. Already, I felt, he knew that he was beaten, having tried and failed to act out of character."

The meeting ended with the former protégé thoughtfully offering to keep his resignation secret as long as possible so as not to exacerbate his mentor's political difficulties. The two old colleagues shook hands and Eden said with a smile, *"Tout casse sauf l'amitié.* I hope, in spite of all this, that we shall see something of each other in the future."

That was the last time Nutting saw Eden.

• •

The CIA's plot to stage a coup in Syria was ruined by Israel's invasion. An angry and red-faced Mikhail Ilyan confronted agent Bill Eveland in Beirut and declared: "Thanks to God I'm alive to see you and say what a terrible thing you and your government did. The Israelis are right now headed for the Suez Canal! How could you have asked us to overthrow our government at the exact moment when Israel started a war with an Arab state?"

Eveland was dismayed. "My protests that I'd been ignorant of the Israeli plan fell on deaf ears."

Thus another CIA plot fizzled out.

• •

Eisenhower, his anger subsided, was feeling a bit depressed but more mellow Wednesday toward his British allies. "We should not be too bitter," he advised Senator Knowland, who had telephoned from California. "It is difficult for us to put ourselves in their shoes. I think they made a bad error from their own viewpoint. I think it is the biggest error of our time, outside of losing China. I am afraid of what will happen. But don't condemn the British too bitterly."

Eisenhower's mood no doubt was buoyed by early reports of enthusiastic support for his Administration's position in the United Nations. Cabot Lodge told Dulles about it, and the secretary of state had suggested Lodge call the President because "he is blue this morning." Lodge did and reported to Ike that "never has there been such a tremendous acclaim for your policy. Absolutely spectacular." Hammarskjold had handed Lodge a note during the council debate the previous day that said: "This is one of the darkest days in postwar times. Thank God you have played the way you have. This will win you many friends." The ambassador from Colombia had told him that the twenty-one Latin American countries were "behind the President as never before." Support had been received from diplomats from Africa and Asia, from Europe and Canada, from newsmen and busboys, typists and elevator operators. Lodge said: "A New Deal Democrat in the Secretariat—who has been

385

there for eleven years and has always looked at me with a jaundiced eye
—said, 'You make me proud to be an American.' "

Somewhat wistfully, Eisenhower said, "Too bad this story can't be
given to the press for all of the United States to hear. But it probably
would embarrass the persons mentioned, especially the diplomats."

• •

The Administration's immediate problem was to speak in one voice of
moderation and rein in the hotheads such as Vice President Nixon. He
called Dulles early that Wednesday morning and said he wanted to "hit"
the Suez crisis in the waning days of the presidential campaign. Dulles
cautioned him that he should be moderate but Nixon did not like that.
"What's wrong with condemning Britain and France?" he asked.

"Nothing particularly—if it's in moderation," said Dulles. "We are of
the same civilization, the same beliefs and so on. The President has said
throughout he wants to do what is right regardless of the election. He will
not sacrifice foreign policy for political expediency."

"How do you analyze it politically?" asked Nixon.

"You are the political expert," said Dulles.

"We will lose some Israeli votes," said Nixon. They agreed there were
not many of those for the Republican Party anyway.

Dulles then alluded to Hungary and, typically, found in it evidence that
the Soviets were losing the competition with the West. "This is the
beginning of the collapse of the Soviet empire," he said with exaggerated
delight.

The lesson of Suez, he added, was the end of "the idea that we can be
dragged along at the heels of the British and French in policies that are
obsolete. This is a declaration of independence. For the first time they
cannot count upon us to engage in policies of this sort."

Later in the day, Dulles talked with Lodge again to coordinate strategy
at the United Nations. If a resolution to condemn Britain and France was
introduced by Yugoslavia, then Lodge should vote for it, Dulles instructed. "Will [the British] violently attack us if we vote?"

"Dixon told me he would attack us if there were a resolution of condemnation," said Lodge. "He is so emotional and that idiot Randolph
Churchill is hanging around so the atmosphere is jumpy." Nonetheless,
Dulles ordered Lodge to vote against America's allies, a courageous act
in the face of certain condemnation by U.S. Anglophiles and others just
before the election.

．．

By this time, Eisenhower had decided to cancel the rest of his political campaign and deliver an address to the nation. Dulles was charged with providing the speech, but when it reached speech writer Emmet Hughes at 3:15 P.M. Wednesday it was too rambling to be used. Eisenhower said he needed a whole new speech. The nationwide telecast was scheduled for 7 P.M.

Hughes was in near panic. He telephoned Dulles to come to the Cabinet Room so he could read the new speech as Hughes rewrote it. Recalled Hughes: "We go past 6:00 still dictating, typing, pencil-editing, with Dulles reviewing text as it comes back from typewriter. He is ashen gray, heavy-lidded, strained. His shoulders seem to sag as he murmurs: 'I'm just sick about the bombings . . . the idea of planes over Cairo right now!' "

Eisenhower, typically, was the calmest person in the White House. While his speech writer and secretary of state sweated over the speech, the President sauntered out to the South Lawn and practiced golf shots for forty-nine minutes.

Just forty-five minutes before TV time, Hughes rushed to the President's bedroom to show him the final draft of the speech. Ike read it aloud while he dressed in a gray suit, warning Hughes at the beginning that "I want to be sure we show clearly in here how vital we think our alliances are. Those British—they're still my right arm."

Ike liked the fifteen-minute speech and a quarter hour before the start of the telecast he arrived in the Oval Office. Hughes was there underscoring with grease pencil the parts of the speech to emphasize, handing the President one page at a time. "It's four minutes before seven as I hand him last page," wrote Hughes. "He clutches them, jesting, 'Boy, this is taking it right off the stove, isn't it?' "

As Hughes and the nation watched expectantly, Eisenhower began his speech. Hughes thought, "No moment since Korea has seemed so charged with war peril. Even technicians around cameras were hushed and anxious. Press was edgy with expectancy." Ike's voice was strong and confident, his face calm and serious. He told the nation that he had not been "consulted in any way about any phase" of the Anglo-French-Israeli attacks, and that he thought them "an error." But, he added, "to say this is in no way to minimize our friendship with these nations, nor our determination to maintain those friendships. We are fully aware of

387

the grave anxieties of Israel, of Britain and France. We know that they have been subjected to grave and repeated provocations." Nonetheless, "the United Nations represents the soundest hope for peace in the world."

On Hungary, Ike applauded Russia's withdrawal of its tanks from Budapest. He disavowed any "ulterior purpose" of U.S. policy in the Hungarian crisis. He said he wanted to "remove any false fears that we would look upon new governments as potential military allies," thus trying to assure Moscow that Washington did not consider Hungary's withdrawal from the Warsaw Pact as the first step to its entry into NATO.

The necessity of mentioning Hungary with the Middle East in the same speech was, as Dulles had mentioned to Eisenhower earlier, "a great tragedy." But the fact was that "the British and French are doing the same thing as the Soviets," said Dulles. The Anglo-French action could not have occurred at a worse time. Their attack obscured in the eyes of the world the differences between the two systems.

Despite the necessity of linking the Middle East with Hungary, the speech was a great success for Eisenhower.

• •

With bombs dropping over Cairo and other Egyptian cities, the House of Commons reconvened Thursday, November 1, with the Labourites in a seethingly rebellious mood. It had been a grave error for Eden not to inform Labour leader Gaitskell of his plans, as was custom in the British system, and now members of the Labour Party felt not only shocked at Britain's aerial war against Egypt but personally affronted at Eden's autocratic manner. The House was charged with tension. Cries of "fascists," "cowards" and "murderers" rang through the chambers as one of the stormiest sessions in the long history of the House of Commons got under way.

When Eden entered the House loud booing broke out. Defense Minister Head began the debate by reporting on the bombing raids but was greeted by catcalls and derisive remarks from the Opposition. Yellow-bearded Labourite Sydney Silverman caused an uproar when he interrupted to inquire if a declaration of war had been issued. Insults were screamed, arms waved and fists shaken. "At one point the chances of fighting actually breaking out between members was very real, so intense were the passions on each side," reported Lord Kilmuir. The session degenerated into pandemonium. Speaker William Morrison was so frustrated in his futile efforts to restore order that he stalked off the dais with

388

his white wig waving and his black robes flying. It was the first time a Speaker had suspended a session in twenty years.

The debate resumed half an hour later but the mood remained ugly and bitter. When Eden re-entered he was again booed and greeted with shouts of "resign!" He repeatedly tried to explain away his policy but failed. Even his effort to connect Suez with Munich and World War II fell flat. "I come back to the personal accusation that I was too much obsessed by the events of the 1930s and was, in consequence, old-fashioned," he said to the resentful House. "However that may be, is there not one lesson of that period which cannot be ignored? It is that you best avoid great wars by taking even physical action to stop small ones."

Fiery Labourite Aneurin Bevan expressed the predominant mood in an impassioned speech in which he reminded the House that in 1940 Britain also had stood alone. But, he added softly, "then we had honor on our side." He compared Britain's ultimatum to Egypt with Germany's to Norway in 1940. "We have only to substitute Egypt for Norway. It is exactly the same thing. It is the language of the bully."

With perhaps more insight into Eden's deteriorating physical and mental state than he realized, Bevan observed that "I have not seen from the prime minister in the last four or five months evidence of the sagacity and skill he should have acquired in so many years in the Foreign Office. I have been astonished at the amateurishness of his performance. There is something the matter with him."

A Labour motion of censure failed 324 to 255. Eden had again won on strict party lines. But the blooming suspicions about his fitness to lead and the passions riled up by the bombings of Egypt were spreading through the country. Britons of every class and political persuasion were caught up in the uproar. Families and friends fought over the issue, protesters marched and orators screamed. It was turning into a national shouting match, and the target of most of it was now not Nasser but Anthony Eden. He was becoming a direly besieged prime minister.

• •

At the same time Eden was undergoing his ordeal in the House of Commons, Eisenhower and Dulles were meeting with the National Security Council in Washington. The urgent and deeply disturbing question before them was to decide on what action to take in the United Nations, which was scheduled to consider the Suez matter at 5 P.M. The Eisenhower Administration was suddenly faced with choosing between guilty allies and an injured and weak country supported by the Soviet Union.

389

"If we are not now prepared to assert our leadership in this cause, then leadership will certainly be seized by the Soviet Union," declared Dulles. "But asserting our leadership would involve us in some very basic problems. For many years now the United States has been walking a tightrope between the effort to maintain our old and valued relations with our British and French allies on the one hand and on the other trying to assure ourselves of the friendship and understanding of the newly independent countries who have escaped from colonialism. Unless we now assert and maintain this leadership, all of these newly independent countries will turn from us to the U.S.S.R. We will be looked upon as forever tied to British and French colonialist policies.

"Basically we have almost reached the point of deciding today whether we think the future lies with a policy of reasserting by force colonial control over the less developed nations, or whether we will oppose such a course of action by every appropriate means.

"It is nothing less than tragic that at this very time, when we are on the point of winning an immense and long-hoped-for victory over Soviet colonialism in Eastern Europe, we should be forced to choose between following in the footsteps of Anglo-French colonialism in Asia and Africa or splitting our course away from their course.

"Yet this decision must be made in a mere matter of hours—before five o'clock this afternoon."

Dulles' grave words sent an electric shock through the meeting, and sparked a heated discussion of what alternatives the country had.

The President wondered whether it was necessary for the United States to introduce a resolution. Perhaps the secretary-general could do it?

"Resolutions will either be introduced by the United States or by the Soviet Union," Dulles declared flatly.

Treasury Secretary Humphrey wondered whether "our resolution could not simply demand that the United Nations determine who was the aggressor." That reminded Eisenhower that the U.S. was still providing Israel with aid.

"It seems a little foolish to me," he commented, "for people who know as much as we do about what is going on to continue to give, as a government, assistance to Israel." He added: "What we must now do is to agree among ourselves what the United States should do."

Then, straying from the subject, he remarked, no doubt to everyone's surprise since the matter was well known: "I had never realized that the

Arab states had consistently afforded the U.N. inspectors access to their boundaries so that inspections could be consistently made. It was the Israelis who had refused similar inspection rights on their side of the boundaries." For a President, who had been presiding for nearly four years over the most critical decisions of U.S. Middle East policy, it was a remarkable admission.

Special Assistant Harold Stassen returned to the main discussion by suggesting that the country limit its action to seeking a cease-fire in the United Nations. After all, he added, "a number of mistakes have already been made. The Soviets made a grave error in putting arms in the hands of the Egyptians. Egyptian seizure of the Suez Canal was a grave error, in turn, and the Suez Canal is an absolutely vital lifeline for the British."

Eisenhower retorted by observing that "transit through the canal has increased rather than decreased since the Egyptians took over."

Dulles added with emotion that a cease-fire resolution had already been vetoed by Britain and France. "What the British and French have done is nothing but the straight old-fashioned variety of colonialism of the most obvious sort," said Dulles.

"Even so," replied Stassen stubbornly, "it seems to me that the future of Great Britain and of France is still the most important consideration for the United States. American public opinion will be divided if we go on with our plan against Britain, France and Israel." Turning to the President, he said pointedly: "You might not succeed in gaining congressional support for your long-term policies if U.S. action in the current crisis divides our people. We must keep the U.S. people united and we will certainly not succeed in doing this if we split away from Britain and France and acted on the assumption—which I do not believe correct—that these two powers are going downhill."

Eisenhower did not agree. "My emphatic belief is that these powers are going downhill with the kind of policy that they are engaged at the moment in carrying out," he retorted. "How can we possibly support Britain and France if in doing so we lose the whole Arab world?"

Humphrey again proposed that America limit its U.N. resolution to a request to determine the aggressor, to which Dulles responded impatiently that "we would very soon find in the U.N. who is the aggressor if we permit the Soviet Union to introduce its resolution. This resolution would certainly declare that Britain and France were the aggressors, and the Soviet resolution would win by acclamation. As a result, we lose our leadership to the Soviet Union."

By now, the President's advisers were badly split and the argument washed back and forth inconclusively. Finally the frustrated President broke in and asked, "What is the argument really about?"

Turning to Dulles, Eisenhower said he agreed that the U.S. had to have a moderate resolution. "Do we need to do anything beyond this?"

"I think the best thing I can do," replied the wearied secretary of state, "is to go back to the State Department and work in quiet."

Eisenhower finally ended the meeting by stating that "we must go now and see what we can do about this business. My idea is to do what is decent and right, but still not condemn more furiously than we have to. Secretary Dulles is dead right in his view that if we do not do something to indicate some vigor in the way of asserting our leadership, then the Soviets will take over the leadership from us."

As his parting remark, Eisenhower said: "I told Anthony Eden a week ago that if the British did what they are now doing and the Russians got into the Middle East, the fat would really be in the fire."

Later, Dulles telephoned Lodge and said he was going to join him in Manhattan that afternoon. "It is getting so confused I just can't meet the alternatives that might arise adequately over the telephone," he explained.

By now the Administration knew the broad outlines of the collusion. Foreign Minister Pineau had spilled the plot to Ambassador Dillon earlier that day in Paris. This knowledge of the collusion made the protests that the ambassadors of Britain, France and Israel voiced that night in the General Assembly seem all the more hypocritical. Even those not in the know were repelled by the weak case presented by the conspirators. After exhaustingly debating until 4:20 A.M., the Assembly voted 64 to 5 for a U.S.-sponsored resolution calling for a cease-fire, withdrawal of troops behind armistice lines and, pointedly, the halt of the movement of troops into the area. At that moment, the Anglo-French invasion force was sailing toward Egypt. Only two Commonwealth nations joined the three colluders in the vote: Australia and New Zealand. It was the greatest majority any resolution had ever received in the General Assembly.

The mood of the British and the French was resentful and it was not improved later when they tried to enlist Washington in jointly offering a strong resolution condemning Russia for its actions in Hungary. "This is a mockery," Dulles told Lodge in a telephone conversation, "for them to come in with bombs falling over Egypt and denounce the Soviet Union for perhaps doing something that is not quite as bad."

392

• •

It was only when the bombs started falling on Egypt that Nasser finally realized that Britain and France were not bluffing and actually planned to invade. He had assumed up to then that all their threats and movement of troops were empty gestures to intimidate him. Thus his first reaction when Israel had attacked in the Sinai was to send some of the withdrawn Sinai troops back across the canal. Now, facing imminent invasion from two of the mightiest European nations, each of which in its time had occupied Egypt in the previous century, Nasser ordered all Sinai forces to come to the defense of the heartland. "We must begin this very night," Nasser told General Abdel Hakim Amer as bombs starting raining on Cairo's airfields late on October 31.

The next day Nasser gave a rousing radio speech which rallied the nation as never before. "We shall fight bitterly, O compatriots. We shall not surrender. We shall fight in defense of Egypt's honor, freedom and dignity. Each one of you is a soldier in the National Liberation Army. Orders have been given for the issue of arms. Let our motto be: 'We shall fight, not surrender. We shall fight, we shall fight; we shall never surrender.' "

At the moment when Britain and France had expected the Egyptian populace to begin cracking under the terror of the bombings and turn on their leader, Nasser began handing out guns. The bombings, though carefully kept away from civilian targets, were nonetheless having the same counterproductive result that they had had in London during the Nazi aerial war. They were stiffening civilian resolve and morale. During the rest of the crisis, Nasser was greeted by shouts repeating his defiant motto as he drove through Cairo streets.

On Thursday, Nasser broke diplomatic relations with Britain and France, seized all British petroleum companies, and ordered all British and French citizens to register with local authorities within three days. All of these measures, reported the London *Times* correspondent, took place "with courtesy and helpfulness on all sides."

Most importantly, Nasser ordered the blockage of the canal, the very thing the Anglo-French action was designed to prevent. The 347-foot *Akka,* a rusting U.S. surplus landing ship, had already been loaded with cement preparatory to scuttling at one of the narrowest points in the northern section of the canal. The man in charge of the *Akka* was Colonel Haney Amin Hilmy II, chief of staff of the Eastern Command. He was doubly determined to perform his job well, for it was his grandfather who had been chosen to perform a similar task in 1882, but he had waited too long and the British invaders sailed into the canal and captured Egypt.

At 2:20 P.M. November 1 Radio Cairo announced the sinking of the *Akka* athwart the waterway just south of Lake Timsah. Other ships also were sunk and soon the canal was completely closed off with the litter of fifty vessels lying on the bottom of the shallow waterway. The whole putative purpose of the invasion was now destroyed—yet the invasion fleet sailed on.

. .

Nasser's order for the immediate withdrawal of his troops from the Sinai began Egypt's own Dunkirk-type rush to save its Army. Nasser rightly perceived that one of the goals of the attackers was to draw the bulk of Egypt's Army into the Sinai and trap it there for easy slaughter by Israel. When the bombs started falling, he recalled, "I saw the whole conspiracy. The Israeli attack was intended only to drag our main forces to Sinai to be cut off there by the occupation of the canal area. Thus the enemy would realize two objectives: first, to destroy our forces east of the canal completely after depriving them of air support, and second, to occupy Egypt without meeting organized resistance once Egypt was deprived of the Army."

The withdrawal from Sinai began within three and a half hours after the first Anglo-French bombs fell and lasted through the next night. Major elements of the Egyptian forces managed with success to camouflage their withdrawal and began moving toward the canal the first night. One force was designated to remain until the next night to act as a block for the retreating soldiers at Abu Ageila. The fortifications were manned by a strong unit consisting of the 17th and 18th Battalions of the 6th Brigade, the 3rd Field Artillery Regiment, and the 94th and 78th Antitank Batteries, plus a jeep-mounted reconnaissance company and two reserve companies. All were under the command of Brigadier Saad Din Mutawally, a tenacious fighter. His men had successfully beaten off repeated attacks by the Israeli troops. But two battalions of the 10th Brigade got lost in the darkness of October 31 and in the words of Dayan spent most of the night "slogging up and down the resistant sand dunes." Dayan was so angry at the force's poor performance that he relieved Colonel Shmuel Gudir on the spot and appointed Colonel Israelial to command the 10th Brigade.

Late in the afternoon of November 1, the defenders of the Abu Ageila defensive complex systematically destroyed as much of their equipment as possible. They went about their task carefully so as not to tip off the Israelis that they were preparing to evacuate their positions. Israeli forces now controlled the three axes across the Sinai, and so the Egyptian troops had to abandon all their heavy equipment and wade over the steep sand dunes northwest to the El Arish road paralleling the Mediterranean. By 7:30 P.M. nearly all of the soldiers were out and on their perilous way. Left behind were one company of infantry and one crew of a 25-pound artillery piece. This small unit fired from different positions throughout the night to fool the Israelis into believing that the positions were still fully manned. By dawn on Saturday they too pulled out after first burying the breech of their gun and destroying as much of the remaining equipment as they could.

The Egyptian evacuation successfully eluded the attention of the Israelis. After the last troops had pulled out, Colonel Adan's Sherman tank battalion captured two Egyptians and sent them to the Um Katef stronghold with a demand that the garrison surrender. The prisoners went there but found the place deserted. Meanwhile, the 37th Mechanized Brigade, which had been repulsed in trying to take Um Katef, heard rumors that the position had been deserted and went to investigate. What it found were the two Egyptians, who again were taken captive by the brigade.

Adan's tanks were waiting for the prisoners to emerge with a white flag of surrender. Instead, they saw a column of tanks without any flag of truce. They immediately assumed the Egyptians were trying to break out and opened with deadly fire from about 1,100 meters. Eight of the 37th's twelve tanks were instantly knocked out and the two forces were preparing for a slugfest when an Israeli reconnaissance plane noticed the tragic encounter and notified the two brigades that they were fighting each other. It was the last battle of Abu Ageila.

Israel now controlled all of the vital northern half of the Sinai, and Egyptian forces were conducting a massive withdrawal, soldiers fleeing pell-mell across the sands while officers frantically tried to save equipment and the Army from destruction. Israel had already shifted its attention to the northern coastal plains of fig trees and orange groves, of white sandy beaches and the populated Gaza Strip.

• •

In Washington, Dwight Eisenhower composed a long letter to his friend Swede Hazlett. After discussing the political campaign ("The Stevenson-Kefauver combination is, in some ways, about the sorriest and weakest we have ever had run for the two top offices in the land"), Ike turned to the "terrible mess" in the Middle East. The Administration had realized, he wrote, that Ben Gurion might try to take advantage of the precampaign period to launch a war "because of the importance that so many politicians in the past have attached to our Jewish vote. I gave strict orders to the State Department that they should inform Israel that we would handle our affairs exactly as though we didn't have a Jew in America. The welfare and best interests of our own country were to be the sole criteria on which we operated.

"I think that France and Britain have made a terrible mistake. Because they had such a poor case, they have isolated themselves from the good opinion of the world and it will take them many years to recover. France was perfectly coldblooded about the matter. She has a war on her hands in Algeria, and she was anxious to get someone else fighting the Arabs on her eastern flank so she was ready to do anything to get England and Israel in that affair. But I think the other two countries have hurt themselves immeasurably and this is something of a sad blow because, quite naturally, Britain not only has been, but must be, our best friend in the world."

Ike also deplored the "opportunities that we have handed to the Russians. Every day the hostilities continue the Soviets have an additional chance to embarrass the Western world beyond measure."

The President ended on an irascible note. "If you have any bright ideas for settling the dispute, I, of course, would be delighted to have them. From what I am told, Walter Lippmann and the Alsops [columnists Joseph and Stewart] have lots of ideas, but they are far from good—about what you would expect from your youngest grandchild."

· ·

The General Assembly's demand for a cease-fire was immediately accepted by Egypt, leaving the British and the French in an awkward position. What was now left of the stated purpose of their "police action"? If there were no combatants, why were they bombing Egypt and allowing their naval task force to continue to sail slowly across the Mediterranean? Washington's speedy sponsorship of the cease-fire resolution had put the conspirators in an extremely difficult spot.

Pineau flew to London on November 2 to concert the two governments' answer to the General Assembly. Pineau, Lloyd and Eden seemed incapable of recognizing the flimsiness of their position, or else were so exhausted by the weeks of scheming and explaining that they were devoid of any ingenuity. At any rate, they insisted, despite all the evidence to the contrary, that they were convinced the "police action must be carried through urgently to stop the hostilities," as their joint statement said. But, their statement added, the two countries would turn over their police duties to a U.N. force if the United Nations formed one.

• •

The idea was largely Lloyd's, and it represented the first retreat from the ambitious dreams of glory hatched two weeks earlier at Sèvres. The euphoria of action had already dissipated. Though the French were still gung-ho, Eden and Lloyd were losing their nerve. They were drained and exhausted by domestic opposition and the continuous round of meetings, consultations and challenges in the House of Commons. The U.N. debates put another sapping strain on them because of the five-hour time difference between London and New York. The debates went into the New York night and Lloyd and Eden had to be available at 2 and 3 A.M., or even later, to approve strategy.

The strain, the sleeplessness, the worry and doubts, the public uproar, were already taking their toll, particularly on the frail Eden. Pineau found the prime minister "ulcerous" over America's cease-fire resolution. "The prime minister is no Churchill," observed Pineau. "He has neither the tenacity nor the steel nerves. The test, instead of strengthening him, exhausts him. It is not yet a 'breakdown,' but we are not far from it."

• •

By the weekend, the Egyptian Eastern Command reported the withdrawal of its troops from the Sinai completed. Thousands of men had managed to escape, but there were still thousands more straggling in the cruel heat of the desert, being taken prisoner or dying of dehydration and exhaustion.

The victorious Israeli Army had already overrun the few forces left in the strategic Rafah salient and captured the Gaza Strip itself with its 200,000 refugees. Ben Gurion was fully recovered from his flu and was now exultant. He ordered Dayan to demand that the U.N. observers in the Strip be ordered out. When some of his colleagues openly worried about the U.N.'s reaction, Ben Gurion chided them. "Why are you so worried? So long as they are sitting in New York and we in Sinai the situation is not bad!"

Israel's war aims were complete except for one last objective: the capture of Sharm el-Sheikh. Colonel Yoffe's brigade was still working its

397

way down the roadless eastern coast where the rugged granite mountains reached right to the edge of the water of the Gulf of Aqaba. From the west, an element of Sharon's force skirted the Mitla Pass and was converging on the Egyptian garrison as well. The Egyptian commander, Colonel Rauf Mahfouz Zaki, explained to headquarters that he had no transportation for his thousand-man force and requested permission to defend his post. Nasser personally gave his approval, though it was apparent that Israel could launch overwhelming forces against the outpost. The battle was still two days away.

. .

Foster Dulles was at home that Saturday night, November 3. He and his wife, Janet, had played backgammon and gone to bed around 10 P.M. A few hours later Dulles awoke with a severe abdominal pain and called an ambulance and his aide Bill Macomber. When Macomber arrived he found the ambulance attendants trying to carry Dulles' large bulk down his home's narrow winding staircase. "He was in real pain at this point and he said: 'Let me get down,' " related Macomber. "He just sat on the steps and eased himself down by sitting on one step at a time all the way down. They put him in the ambulance and I drove Mrs. Dulles in my car right behind it. I remember I was a little irritated because there was hardly a car on the street and the ambulance stopped at every red light. There wasn't a car left or right anywhere, and they just stopped. And then also—incredible—the driver got lost going out to Walter Reed."

The diagnosis was soon made. Foster Dulles had abdominal cancer.

. .

Syria broke diplomatic relations with Britain and France on November 3, and the Iraq Petroleum Company pipeline crossing Syria was blown up. It was jointly owned by Britain, France and the United States. An entirely American-owned line, the Trans-Arabia Pipeline (TAPline), remained untouched. Britain's and France's supply of oil was slowly being strangled.

Arab nations and Third World countries were overwhelmingly declaring their support for Nasser, and condemning the colluders. At home, Nasser had never been so popular. He was wildly cheered whenever he went into the streets.

The twin objectives of the Anglo-French plan had already failed within the first five days of the start of the plot hatched at Sèvres. The oil was drying up and Nasser was surviving with a vengeance. But still the Anglo-

French armada sailed toward Egypt. Its scheduled arrival was on November 6.

.   .

Eden that November 3 Saturday afternoon attended an extraordinary session of the House of Commons. He announced that Britain and France had decided to step aside once a U.N. force was formed. But meantime, he added, the police action had to continue. Gaitskell wondered if British troops would be part of the U.N. force.

"We would naturally not expect to be excluded from it," replied Eden. "We are not burglars."

"The prime minister is perfectly right," replied Gaitskell tartly. "What we did was to go in to help the burglar and shoot the householder."

Gaitskell had had enough. Eden had to go, he said. "If the country is to be rescued from the predicament into which the government have brought it, there is only one way—a change in the leadership of the government. We must have a new government and a new prime minister."

Eden that night went before national TV to try to summon up support for his policy, which was rapidly being exposed as disreputable. His speech was largely a rehash of his earlier justifications except for a telling personal note. "All my life I've been a man of peace, working for peace, striving for peace, negotiating for peace. I've been a League of Nations man and a United Nations man, and I'm still the same man."

But he was not.

The day before, Mountbatten, in desperation, had sent Eden a forceful letter. "My dear prime minister," Mountbatten wrote, "I know that you've been fully aware over these past weeks of great unhappiness at the prospect of our launching military operations against Egypt. It is not the business of the serving officer to question the political decisions of his government, and although I did not believe that a just and lasting settlement of any dispute could be worked out under a threat of military action, I did everything in my power to carry out your orders. Now, however, the decisive step of armed intervention by the British has been taken. Bombing has started and the assault convoy is on its way from Malta. I am writing to appeal to you to accept the resolution of the overwhelming majority of the United Nations to cease military operations, and to beg you to turn back the assault convoy before it is too late, as I feel that the actual landing of troops can only spread the war with untold misery and worldwide repercussions. You can imagine how hard it is for me to break with all service custom and write direct to you in this way. But I feel so desperate about what is happening that my conscience would not allow me to do otherwise."

On the same day as he addressed the House, Eden called Mountbatten and said: "My dear Dickie, thank you so much for your letter. I do appreciate having a friend who speaks his mind."

"Are you going to let me turn back the assault convoy?"

"I'm not obliged to take your advice, you know," answered Eden.

"Of course you're not obliged to take my advice," responded Mountbatten. "But may I nevertheless turn back the assault convoy?"

"No, certainly not," replied Eden. "No, no." Then he hung up the phone.

• •

The pressures on Eden mounted Saturday when the U.N. General Assembly went back into emergency session and Israel, without advance warning, announced that it had accepted the cease-fire. Now there could be no justification for the invasion. Britain and France, reported Dayan, "almost jumped out of their skins."

Ben Gurion's action was prompted by the fear that Britain, even at this late date, would not follow through with the invasion. That would leave Israel as the lone aggressor. It was, Dayan said, a "cold calculation that it is better for Israel not to appear alone as an aggressor who disturbs the peace and ignores U.S. resolutions; it is better that Britain and France should be with her on this front."

Urgent requests were made by British and French officials to Ben Gurion to withdraw his cease-fire. He finally reluctantly did the next day, claiming the fighting had to go on because "*fedayeen* attacks continue." Actually, there was no fighting at all, though Colonel Yoffe's force and Sharon's paratroopers were still moving secretly toward Sharm el-Sheikh.

• •

At the U.N. early Sunday morning, two resolutions were finally adopted, a Canadian call for the forming of a U.N. Mideast force and an Indian resolution demanding a cease-fire within twelve hours.

Hungary was also on the General Assembly's docket, but action was delayed when the Soviet ambassador reported that negotiations with the rebel government were going on for the withdrawal of Russian troops.

Then, as dawn approached in Hungary, the world was delivered another great shock. The calm in Hungary was shattered when a Soviet fist of steel suddenly smashed Budapest. Two hundred thousand troops and four thousand tanks rolled into the city's streets and blasted all opposition before them. No resistance was tolerated. Buildings and bodies were crushed alike in the orgy of indiscriminate killings. By the end of the day fifty thousand Hungarians were dead and wounded in Budapest's streets. Similar acts of brutality were carried out in other cities where rebels had taken control.

By 3 A.M. in New York, it was already obvious that the Soviets were indulging in a bloodbath. The Security Council went into emergency session at that time—forty-five minutes after the General Assembly's vote on forming a U.N. Mideast force—to consider a U.S. resolution against Russia. Within thirteen minutes a resolution was passed demanding that Russia stop its killing and withdraw its troops; the Soviet Union vetoed it, the seventy-ninth veto cast by Moscow.

. .

The world was now on the brink of disaster. Russian troops were slaughtering Hungarians, Egyptians by the hundreds were perishing in the Sinai, Israeli troops were brutally occupying the Gaza Strip, and America was torn between its opposition to Britain, France and Israel in the Middle East, in which Moscow joined Washington, and its condemnation of Russia in Hungary. Through it all, the mighty Anglo-French armada of well over two hundred warships sailed inexorably toward its destiny in Egypt.

For Eisenhower, the choice of how to divide his time between the two crises was painful but simple. No matter how dramatic the events in Hungary, there was nothing short of a major war that could directly influence events there. Hungary sadly was, in the last analysis, an internal Communist affair. Suez was an internal affair of the West, and far more threatening to the United States. There the nation's oldest and strongest allies were pursuing a policy contrary to Washington and enormously damaging to Western unity. The Atlantic Alliance, NATO itself, were endangered. The President somehow had to halt the Anglo-French expeditionary force and as quickly as possible mend fences with America's allies. Eisenhower's efforts now were fully directed toward that cause.

. .

In Trafalgar Square, protesters to Eden's policy gathered by the thousands that Sunday afternoon shouting "Eden must go!" and carrying

placards proclaiming "Law Not War" and "Stop Eden's War." Labourite Aneurin Bevan told the throng: "Are we prepared to accept for ourselves the logic we are applying to Egypt? If nations more powerful than
ourselves accept this anarchistic attitude and launch bombs on London,
what answer have we got?"

Lloyd, meeting with Eden in No. 10 Downing Street, noted that "there
was a steady hum of noise [from Trafalgar Square] and then every few
minutes a crescendo and an outburst of howling and booing."

Five hundred extra policemen had to be detached to keep the crowd
orderly. When the demonstrators tried to descend on No. 10, eight bob-
bies were injured fighting them back. The country was up in arms against
Eden.

• •

The French suspected Eden's resolve was wavering under such pressures, and during that Sunday Pineau and Bourgès-Maunoury flew to
London to urge him to take prompt action. They had earlier proposed
that French paratroopers land that same day at Port Said with the help of
Israeli troops. But Eden was appalled because that would destroy the last
shred of pretext and he had vetoed the plan. Now Pineau and Bourgès
warned him that there would be no pretext left at all if they did not act
immediately. They proposed a joint paratroop landing take place the next
morning to assure that some Anglo-French troops were in place before it
was obvious to everyone that there was absolutely no justification for
their presence. Since the fighting was essentially over between Egyptian
and Israeli troops, the reason they would give for their assault was to
assure the withdrawal of Israeli troops from Egyptian territory.

Eden agreed, and the two countries announced they were going into
Egypt to force Israeli troops out of Egypt. Ben Gurion was outraged. It
made Israel look intransigent and the British and French like white-hatted
rescuers. He cabled his Paris embassy to tell the French: "They have no
authority to make such announcement and am amazed that our friends in
France are party to such a proposal." The French patiently tried to
explain to Ben Gurion that only such a pretext could make Britain agree
to an early invasion. But Ben Gurion was not mollified. To remove as
much taint as possible from his country, Ben Gurion once again announced acceptance of the cease-fire Monday morning. It came at the
same time as six hundred British paratroopers descended on Port Said
and five hundred French jumpers landed just to the south of the port.
That same morning Israeli troops, supported by air cover and outnum-

bering the Egyptian defenders by better than three to one, stormed the Sharm el-Sheikh bastion and captured it. All fighting in the Sinai was over—but not at Suez.

• •

The Anglo-French attack brought an immediate response from the Soviet Union in the form of an extraordinary proposal from Premier Bulganin. On Monday, one day before the U.S. election, he suggested in an impudent letter that America and the U.S.S.R. join forces against Britain, France and Israel. Bulganin warned that "if this war is not stopped, it is fraught with danger and can grow into a third world war." He then had the audacity to propose that Russia and America "crush the aggressors" since their two countries had "all modern types of arms, including atomic and hydrogen weapons and bear particular responsibility for stopping war."

Eisenhower was enraged, and publicly termed Bulganin's proposal unthinkable. He warned that if any other troops moved into the region the United States would oppose them.

Privately, he was worried. "The Soviet Union might be ready to undertake any wild adventure," he warned Herb Hoover. "They are as scared and furious as Hitler was in his last days. There's nothing more dangerous than a dictatorship in that frame of mind."

In this time of crisis, Eisenhower especially missed the ailing Foster Dulles. Hoover, his background limited almost entirely to the oil business, was not an adequate replacement, as Eisenhower later confided to Dulles. His burdens had been increased by Dulles' illness, he said, because the people at the State Department "are accustomed to leaning on someone and set up long conferences several times a day."

Dulles had undergone a three-hour operation, but within four days he was ensconced in Walter Reed's presidential suite, which Ike had thoughtfully given him, and was on the telephone to the officials of the State Department. Soon he was receiving and reading the important cables and speaking frequently with Hoover over the telephone and offering his advice to the President. Eisenhower was happy to receive it.

• •

Bulganin sent threatening letters to Britain, France and Israel on the same day as his letter to Eisenhower. He indirectly threatened to use missiles against London and Paris. To Eden, Bulganin wrote: "In what position would Britain have found herself had she been attacked by more

403

powerful states possessing all types of modern weapons of destruction? Indeed, such countries, instead of sending to the shores of Britain their naval or air forces could have used other means, as for instance rocket equipment." A similar threat was contained in his letter to Mollet.

In a tough letter to Ben Gurion, Bulganin accused Israel of "acting as a tool of foreign imperialist powers" and warned that "Israel is playing with the fate of peace, with the fate of its own people, in a criminal and irresponsible manner." He added that Ben Gurion was placing "a question upon the very existence of Israel as a state. We expect that the Government of Israel will come to its senses before it is too late and will halt its military operations against Egypt." He announced that the Kremlin was recalling its ambassador.

• •

British and French paratroops were now in Egypt and the armada was about to land the main invasion force on Egyptian soil. The Soviet Union could not have had a better cover for its brutality in Hungary. While Moscow rattled missiles in self-righteousness over Suez, its troops were systematically crushing any resistance in Hungary. "The slaughter has been continuous of men, women and children, with hospitals and clinics included among targets," cabled the U.S. Embassy in Budapest.

Piteous appeals were pouring in on Washington. Clare Boothe Luce, the ambassador to Italy, sent an emotional cable directly to Eisenhower. "Franco-British action on Suez is a small wound to their prestige but American inaction about Hungary could be a fatal wound to ours. Let us not ask for whom the bell tolls in Hungary today. It tolls for us if freedom's holy light is extinguished in blood and iron over there. Then a long dark night of cynicism, futility and despair will fold over great parts of Europe and the world."

The anti-Russian National Peasant Party of Hungary sent Eisenhower a message pleading for his support because "the next few critical days will determine whether we enter on a path of peace and liberation or whether we shall increase the appetite of aggression and proceed to a certain world catastrophe."

Ambassador Dillon warned from Paris that "reaction in France to events in Hungary is extremely violent. There is widespread feeling that U.S. lacks interest in Hungarian people and is concentrating on Middle East to exclusion of all else. Hungarian-born French correspondent for *Paris-Match* reports intense fighting Budapest with over fifty Soviet tanks put out of action. He very emotional over slaughter and lays large share of blame on U.S. because of Radio Free Europe broadcasts inciting population to revolt, followed by refusal of concrete help from U.S."

. .

It was true that the CIA had for years been encouraging resistance to the Russians and even planned in the early 1950s for clandestine military action inside East Europe. Caches of sanitized weapons were still hidden throughout Europe. Now that the time for revolt had come, émigré Hungarians contacted their CIA case officers and pleaded for the weapons, but in the sobering light of the brutal Soviet reaction, the CIA belatedly realized that any such operation would be suicidal. As for direct U.S. intervention, it could mean thermonuclear war, and that was unthinkable.

This cold reality crushed Frank Wisner, the CIA's fervently anti-Communist deputy director for plans, head of the second most powerful post within the agency. His Cold Warrior enthusiasms had encouraged CIA agents to foment instability in East Europe, and by chance he was in Vienna when the first of the avalanche of 200,000 frightened emigrants began pouring out of Hungary in a desperate attempt to escape the Soviet juggernaut. Wisner listened to the horror stories of Russian tanks crushing bodies in the streets, of the heroic struggles of unarmed Hungarians fighting Soviet armor, and he was appalled. Shortly afterward he had a nervous breakdown and later killed himself.

The CIA's Bob Amory, who also was deeply involved in East European operations, was "sick at heart" over the slaughter and developed an ulcer. But he refused to concede that the CIA shared any responsibility in the Hungarian tragedy. He placed that with Eisenhower and Dulles for failing to accept his suggestion that they threaten Russia with nuclear warfare unless the Soviets pulled their troops out of Hungary. He and his wife later sponsored a Hungarian refugee, "by way of expiation," explained Amory.

. .

In the midst of such hysteria Eisenhower kept his calmness. It was the eve of the election and all the accumulating pressures of the campaign and the past eight days in the Middle East and East Europe were at a bursting point. The dawning horror of the brutality of the Soviet actions in Hungary and the Soviet threats to Britain, France and Israel increased the pressure intolerably.

"We must stop this before we are all burned to a crisp," said a despairing high official in the State Department.

"It would be difficult to exaggerate the extreme tension that gripped the United States Government," reported *The New York Times*. "It goes without saying that the thought of nuclear war was urgently in many minds."

To his speechwriter, Hughes, Eisenhower remarked: "If those fellows start something, we may have to hit 'em—and, if necessary, with *everything* in the bucket."

The world seemed closer that night to a catastrophic nuclear war than at any time in history.

CHAPTER XIX

The Law of the Jungle
Has Been Invoked

GAITSKELL

THE VAST ARMADA that had been sailing toward Egypt for nearly a week arrayed itself off Port Said in the predawn darkness of November 6. More than two hundred ships, from aircraft carriers down to small landing boats, were at their battle stations awaiting first light. The invasion that Eden had wanted so long was finally about to take place.

Yet even at this late hour Eden was having qualms about the destruction that was soon to be unleashed on the defenseless Egyptians. Mountbatten's warnings about the terrible power of the big naval guns had convinced Eden at the last moment to order that no guns larger than 4.5 inches be used in the bombardment of the shore prior to the troop landings. The order meant the main 15-inch batteries of the battleship *Jean Bart* and of the cruisers could not be used. In the tense moments before the mighty force was about to strike, another order arrived from London. It suspended all naval bombardment. This was too much for the men whose lives were about to be endangered. Without a bombardment the landings could turn into a bloodbath for the Anglo-French troops. The commanders decided to ignore the latest order and, at the first light of dawn, they commanded all but the big guns to open fire. The palm-fringed beaches of Port Fuad and Port Said were raked with "naval gunfire support," as the bombardment was euphemistically referred to in reports to London.

As the naval guns boomed, flights of screaming jets swooped out of the sky and blasted away with machine guns, rockets and bombs. The beach

407

was soon obscured by smoke. "As the shells landed, the smoke was pin-pricked with flashes, while here and there, fierce red flames showed where the lines of wooden beach huts were on fire," wrote D. M. J. Clark, a gunnery control officer in the task force. "The thud of guns added to the confusion, and screaming aircraft plummeted earthward, their guns and rockets blasting."

This softening-up phase lasted for forty-five minutes for the naval guns and ten minutes for the planes. Then, with even the sands burning, the British stormed ashore at Port Said and the French at Port Fuad to the south. The British landed 13,500 men and the French 8,500. The British used a new technique in war for the first time that Tuesday. It was the employment of helicopters to get men and materiel ashore rapidly, a technique that was to be perfected by America in Vietnam a decade later. Within an hour and a half, twenty-two helicopters from the *Theseus* and the *Ocean* lifted four hundred men and thirty-three tons of materiel into the battle zone.

The Egyptians briefly fought fiercely, though organized opposition by the Army soon melted away in the face of the overwhelming might of the invaders. Many civilians had been armed and to the landing troops everyone from small children to old ladies was a potential guerrilla. Houses had to be taken one at a time while children lobbed grenades from the upper stories and snipers fired from hidden nests.

The British troops displayed a humane concern for the civilians rare in warfare. Gunnery officer Clark was impressed with the "downright decency of men who, while being shot at, walked from cover to help old women to safety, to carry babies out of harm's way, to quiet hysterical women and to help wounded enemies who, a moment before, had been yelling and firing with all the abandon of drunks at a shooting gallery."

The French troops were more traditional in their barbarity. Pierre Leulliette, a French paratrooper with the invading forces, observed: "Port Fuad is a pretty town, mostly European, but the destruction is so complete that everything has taken on a tragic mask. Palm trees are blazing like torches. The whole city reeks of fire, grease, metal, gasoline, powder, and carrion. The huge American warehouses along the wharf had been broken into, first by the Egyptians, and then by us. For several weeks, whiskey and turkey are the staples of our diet. The looting of the warehouses goes on for days. We find all sorts of strange objects, from Swiss cuckoo clocks to American ashtrays. Tremendous all-day drinking parties. There were quite a few women raped in the city, and even some

408

very young girls, also a number of shops were looted and some Europeans' apartments wrecked.''

• •

Not far from the warships of the Anglo-French armada were the fifty ships of the powerful U.S. Sixth Fleet. They had been engaged in the evacuation of 2,086 Americans from the eastern Mediterranean up until November 4 and now had withdrawn to allow the British and French to carry out their invasion. It was an odd situation for the men of the three navies, normally the closest of allies. But now America was standing aloof and nobody could predict what might happen in the extremely volatile situation.

Chief of Naval Operations Admiral Burke had warned the fleet to be ready for anything. If fighting broke out among the allies he was convinced the American fleet would prevail. But it would be bloody, he cautioned.

"We can stop them but we will have to blast hell out of them," Burke warned the State Department. "If we are going to threaten, if we're going to turn on them, then you've got to be ready to shoot. We can do that. We can defeat them. The British, the French and the Egyptians and the Israelis, the whole goddamn works of them we can knock off. But that's the only way we can do it.''

The pressures on Eden to bow to the U.N. demand for a cease-fire were multiplying mightily. The raucous British press was again up in arms. The prestigious *Economist, Observer* and *Manchester Guardian* were all calling Suez "Eden's war." The liberal *News Chronicle* characterized his decision to use force as "folly on a grand scale. There can be no further confidence in a man who has brought his country to such a dangerous state of ignominy and confusion." The *Daily Mirror* thundered: "There is NO treaty, NO international authority, NO moral sanction for this desperate action.''

There had been two more resignations of protest from Eden's official family, his press secretary, Bill Clark, and Sir Edward Boyle, financial secretary to the Treasury. Now even Harold Macmillan, who all along had been one of the most hawkish of the inner circle of senior Cabinet officials, suddenly became a dove. At the Cabinet meeting that Tuesday morning of the invasion, Macmillan reported that there had been a run on the pound and gold reserves had fallen by 100 million pounds in the last week. The government did not have enough funds to keep the pound at its $2.78 exchange rate for long, and the U.S. was refusing it access to additional funds. Unless there was a cease-fire, warned Macmillan, he could "not anymore be responsible for Her Majesty's Exchequer." This sudden switch later caused Labourite Harold Wilson to jeer at Macmillan as "first in, first out of Suez."

The withholding of funds by Washington was deliberately aimed at making Britain agree to a cease-fire and to remove its troops from Egypt. Britain had substantial sterling in the International Monetary Fund, but Washington as the largest depositor had the final say on withdrawals. Until Eden relented, the country would be faced with a mounting financial crisis. It was the last straw.

Britain was being universally condemned, the canal was in ruins, oil was cut off, Nasser was stronger and the British pound was growing weaker at a precipitous rate. Rab Butler, a close friend of Treasury Secretary Humphrey from the days when Butler had been Chancellor of the Exchequer, telephoned Washington and personally pleaded with Humphrey for a loan. Humphrey had an attractive package ready for him—a $1.5 billion loan with interest payments deferred—but only on one basis. There had to be a cease-fire and withdrawal.

Eden, his policy in wreckage, suddenly capitulated. He and his Cabinet reluctantly took a half step toward the inevitable. They agreed that a cease-fire should begin that night at midnight (2 A.M. Wednesday, Cairo time). Less than eighteen hours after the main body of the Anglo-French force had landed, the fighting would stop.

• •

Now Eden faced the unpleasant task of breaking the news to his French co-conspirators. He telephoned Mollet that afternoon while the premier and Pineau were meeting with West German Chancellor Konrad Adenauer. Pineau spoke with Eden.

"I hear a broken voice, that of a man who has exhausted the limits of his own resistance and is ready to let himself drown," recalled Pineau. "In substance he says, it is no longer possible. We must stop. The pound has dropped again and we risk panic."

Pineau asked Eden for a delay, even just two more days.

"We won't hold for two days."

"Try," exclaimed Pineau. "We are with you."

"I've already accepted," said Eden.

Pineau thought "the phrase sounds like a death knell."

Eden asked: "And you? You accept, don't you?"

By this time Mollet was back on the phone, desperately trying to bargain for time. Finally he told Eden that he must first consult his Cabinet.

There was a long silence as Mollet hung up the phone. Then Adenauer, in gentle tones, broke the silence. He advised Mollet to accept the cease-fire. A few hours later, after some bitter opposition from diehards, the Cabinet approved the cease-fire.

The great Anglo-French invasion was finished almost before it had begun.

• •

Eisenhower heard the news around noon on that busy election day. He telephoned Eden to express his delight, and to offer some advice. He urged Eden to set no conditions to the cease-fire and to support a neutral force being created by the United Nations.

Eden agreed, saying he thought the force would have to be a large one. "I hope you [American troops] will be there," he said. "Are we all going to go?"

Now the badgered prime minister was in for one more disappointment. He had already declared in the House of Commons that British troops would be part of the U.N. force. He very much wanted that as a face-saving gesture to prove that the whole expedition had not been a total fiasco. But Eisenhower, aware that Nasser would never accept Britain as part of the force, was also afraid that if Britain was included then Russia would try to contribute troops too.

"I will tell you what I am trying to get at," replied Ike. "I don't want to give Egypt an opportunity to begin to quibble so that this thing can be drawn out for a week. I would like to see none of the great nations in it. I am afraid the Red boy is going to demand the lion's share. I would rather make it no troops from the Big Five. I would say, 'Mr. Hammarskjold, we trust you. When we see you coming in with enough troops to take over, we go out.' "

Eden asked for time to think over Eisenhower's suggestions. "If I survive tonight I will call you tomorrow," he said, referring to his scheduled appearance in the House of Commons that evening to explain the cease-fire. "How are things going with you?"

"We've been giving all our thought to Hungary and the Middle East," replied Ike. "I don't give a damn how the election goes."

Shortly after midnight, Ambassador Dillon called on Mollet with a message from Eisenhower repeating the suggestions he had made to Eden. Pineau was also present. The French leaders did not quite understand how much was implied by Eisenhower's request that "the U.N. proposal for the cease-fire and the entry of U.N. troops are being accepted without conditions." Did that mean immediate evacuation of the Anglo-French forces? Dillon suggested Mollet telephone Eden, which he did.

Eden told Mollet that was impossible. Their troops could not be taken out before a U.N. force arrived. But Eden by now had seen the wisdom of Eisenhower's concern that the big powers stay out of the U.N. force. He explained to Mollet the President's reasoning, emphasizing the liabilities of having Soviet troops stationed in the Middle East. Mollet agreed. France would not seek to be part of the U.N. peace force.

America and its allies were at last beginning to act in concert again, and none too soon for now Russia began stirring. Reports of Soviet planes moving into the Middle East were circulating and there were rumors that Russian "volunteers" might soon arrive in Egypt. The danger of a great-power confrontation suddenly was looming larger and was more significant and frightening than the crisis in the Middle East.

• •

Eisenhower was deeply concerned. The reports reaching Washington about Soviet intentions were unrelievedly bleak. Allen Dulles told the President that election day that the Soviets had promised Egypt they would "do something." But what? Ike and his spymaster tried to guess. The most likely move, they decided, would be for the Soviets to fly planes into Syria, where they could threaten Israel and quickly go to the assistance of Egypt. Eisenhower ordered U-2 reconnaissance flights over the area.

If the Soviets actually began moving, the President observed, a major war could erupt.

It was with such foreboding thoughts on his mind that Ike prepared to go through the ritual of casting his ballot. He and Mamie drove the eighty miles to their Gettysburg home, voted and then rushed back to the capital in a helicopter. He was greeted by unconfirmed reports of unidentified aircraft overflying Turkey, a natural route for Soviet planes flying into the Middle East. The President immediately went into a meeting with Admiral Radford, who handed him a list of twenty-one recommendations worked out by the joint chiefs of staff for increasing U.S. military readiness.

"These should be put into effect by degrees," cautioned Ike, "not all at once, in order to avoid creating a stir."

Troops were not recalled from leave, as the JCS had proposed, but interceptor aircraft were placed on advanced alert, tanker squadrons were deployed, and two aircraft carriers, a cruiser and three divisions of destroyers were all ordered to set sail to the Azores and to be ready to reinforce the Sixth Fleet. Other actions included sending all antisubmarine warfare units to sea, placing the Pacific and Atlantic fleets on increased alert, and issuing a general warning to commands around the world.

Radford was taking no chances, but he was doubtful that the Russians would directly intervene in the Middle East. "For them to attempt any operations in the Middle East would be extremely difficult," he pointed out. "The only reasonable form of intervention would be long-range air strikes with nuclear weapons—which seems unlikely."

• •

Eden went before the House of Commons that evening and announced: "Her Majesty's Government are ordering their forces to cease fire at midnight GMT unless they are attacked." Labourites went wild. They leaped to their feet, cheering in jubilation, waving papers and slapping each other on the back. Tories too stood and applauded their prime minister. But Eden's calvary was not yet over. The leader of the Labour Party demanded the last word.

"There is not a shred of evidence that there was any really serious danger to the canal until we intervened," declared Gaitskell. He quoted a letter in *The Times* which observed that both Britain in Suez and Russia in Hungary described their conduct as police actions. "We have coined a phrase which had already become part of the currency of aggression," wrote the letter writer.

Added Gaitskell: "The truth of the matter is that the law of the jungle has been invoked by the British government and the Russians are following suit."

• •

Thousands of fleeing Hungarians were pouring across the Austrian border and the rebellion was already fading into history. The Soviet Union had thoroughly crushed the uprising, leaving the streets of the cities and towns littered with the dead and dying. Imre Nagy found refuge in the embassy of Yugoslavia; he was later kidnapped by the Russians and executed. The satellites of East Europe settled down to another long night of Soviet domination.

· ·

As the polls closed in the United States, a hush was also falling over the Middle East. All fighting had now ceased in the Sinai and along the canal. Anglo-French troops were still disembarking, but others already were on their way out in observance of the cease-fire and eventual withdrawal. General Stockwell caustically cabled London: "We've now achieved the impossible. We're going both ways at once."

British, French and Israeli casualties had been surprisingly light. Britain lost 16 dead and 96 wounded; France, 10 dead and 33 wounded; and Israel, 189 dead and 899 wounded. Egyptian casualties were never reliably established, and weeks later there were reports still coming into the U.N. about "thousands of wounded and dead bodies all over Sanai." Estimates placed Egyptian casualties at 1,000 dead, 4,000 wounded and 6,000 captured or missing in the battle with Israel, and 650 dead and 900 wounded against the Anglo-French forces, mainly from the heavy destruction caused by the naval bombardment, as Mountbatten had warned.

· ·

Eisenhower won an overwhelming election victory that night, carrying forty-one states and 58 percent of the vote. His jubilation was tempered somewhat by the loss of both houses of Congress and the cancellation of a long-planned postelection golfing holiday caused by the Suez crisis. "He's as disappointed as a kid who had counted all the days to Christmas," observed his secretary.

· ·

Though the fighting at Suez was over, the political maneuvering was not. Eden was desperate to salvage something out of the dismal wreckage of his policies. He telephoned Eisenhower at 8:43 A.M. Wednesday and suggested that he and Mollet travel to Washington for a Big Three meeting. Ike, buoyed by his re-election, readily agreed, adding that "after all, it is like a family spat."

Eden said he would call Mollet with the good news and that they would be in Washington that same evening.

But Eisenhower's chief of staff, Sherman Adams, did not like the smell of the plan. He thought such a meeting would make it appear that America was concerting its Middle East policies with the British and French and ignoring the United Nations. He advised Eisenhower not to hold the meeting.

"I made it clear that there could be no departure from their agreement on the cease-fire," Eisenhower argued back. "Eden asked for the meeting because of the developing threat from Russia."

Agitated by Adams' opposition, Eisenhower called Eden and emphasized that the United States was committed to the U.N.'s plan for a peace force in the Middle East. The purpose of their meeting, he added, would be to "concert our positions in NATO and for the future. If by any chance you and Mollet are not in agreement, it would be very unfortunate to have a communiqué issued which would indicate we are in disagreement."

While Eisenhower was talking with Eden, Hoover walked into the Oval Office. After Ike finished his call, Hoover warned: "We must be very careful not to give the impression that we are teaming up with the British and French." He said he had talked with the recuperating secretary of state and Dulles had said "he was very much opposed to the visit at this time."

Hoover introduced a bit of shocking and, as it turned out, incorrect news. The Soviets had offered Egypt a quarter of a million volunteers. "The Russians are making great efforts to put themselves in the position of liberators. There is a danger of a complete turnabout by the Arabs in this matter. They may place themselves in opposition to Hammarskjold's efforts.

"We have to get out to the world that we have not changed our principles and our position," Hoover added.

Treasury Secretary Humphrey entered the office and joined the discussion, siding against Eisenhower. "I appreciate how hard it is for you to tell a man that you won't talk to him but I think the timing question is overriding," said Humphrey.

"I really looked forward to talking with Eden," said a clearly unhappy President. "I'm quite disappointed."

Nonetheless, he followed the prudent advice of his associates and telephoned Eden again and gave the British leader yet another jolt of bad news: the meeting was aborted.

• •

While Eden squirmed to save his political life, Ben Gurion was exultant with Israel's victory. He delivered a provocative victory speech to the Knesset that Wednesday, declaring that the Sinai was not Egyptian territory and "the armistice agreement with Egypt is dead and buried and cannot be restored to life. In consequence, the armistice lines between

Israel and Egypt have no more validity. On no account will Israel agree to the stationing of a foreign force, no matter how called, in her territory or in any areas occupied by her.''

He was saying, in effect, that Israel now controlled the whole of the Sinai and the Gaza Strip and it meant to keep the ill-gotten territory. The U.N. peace force would not be allowed by Israel into the entire area.

It was now Eisenhower's turn to jump out of his skin. ''This is terrible,'' he said to Hoover of Ben Gurion's speech. In a stiffly worded message, the President wrote Ben Gurion that same day that ''statements attributed to your government to the effect that Israel does not intend to withdraw from Egyptian territory have been called to my attention. I must say frankly, Mr. Prime Minister, that the United States views these reports, if true, with deep concern. Any such decision . . . could not but bring about the condemnation of Israel as a violator of the principles as well as the directives of the United Nations.''

He ended with as stern a warning as friendly diplomacy allows. ''It would be a matter of the greatest regret to all my countrymen if Israeli policy on a matter of such grave concern to the world should in any way impair the friendly cooperation between our two countries.''

Eisenhower was not the only one outraged by Ben Gurion's speech. At the United Nations, Canada's Lester Pearson told Ambassador Eban ''that speech must have been as offensive to the British, the French, the Americans and to us Canadians as it was to the Arabs. If you people persist with this, you run the risk of losing all your friends.''

When a vote was taken that night in the General Assembly for a withdrawal of all foreign troops from Sinai the result was 65 to 1—Israel being the only opposition vote.

In Washington, Hoover called Israeli Minister Shiloah to his office for a dressing down. ''I consider this to be the most important meeting ever held with Israeli representatives. Israel's attitude will inevitably lead to most serious measures such as the termination of all United States governmental and private aid, United Nations sanctions and eventual expulsion from the United Nations. I speak with the utmost seriousness and gravity.''

When Ben Gurion heard about Hoover's tough language, he asked Eban whether it might be possible for him to have a private meeting with Eisenhower. The President, hearing of this request, wondered ''whether Ben Gurion's reputation for balance and rationality was really well founded.''

By the next day, Ben Gurion totally retreated, or so it seemed. He cabled Eisenhower that "we have never planned to annex the Sinai desert" and that Israel would withdraw "upon conclusion of satisfactory arrangements with the United Nations."

The qualifier to Ben Gurion's pledge to withdraw should have alerted Eisenhower that there were more twists and turns on the road to Israel's removal of its occupying troops. But for the moment the President was content to have put out yet another brush fire in a month that had more than its share of potential conflagrations.

• •

By Wednesday it was clear that Eisenhower's unyielding opposition to the attack on Egypt was earning America enhanced prestige. Not only was Lodge reporting commendations from the members of the United Nations but Ambassador Raymond Hare cabled from Cairo that a unique opportunity had been created. "The U.S. has suddenly emerged as a real champion of right," reported Hare. There was a new pro-American mood, he continued, that "adds up to a possible opportunity to re-establish our position in a way which would not have seemed possible only a short week ago."

Eisenhower was buoyed by the reaction. He telephoned Humphrey and said, "If settlement is gone through with we have got to move in to try to repair the damage and to secure the area against the Russians. We have got to help through bilateral treaties and be prepared to spend some money in the ultimate hope of reducing our defense budget. We can gain much through friendships and close ties with peoples of these countries."

He reminded Humphrey that he was meeting the next day with a bipartisan group of legislators for one of his periodical briefings of leading congressmen and he wanted the treasury secretary's approval to pledge "modest amounts" to the Middle East. "I will go back in the Aswan dam. I want these people to see we will deal with them. I'm willing to give a seventy-five-million-dollar loan to Egypt. I want to demonstrate that we will be friends with them."

His vision to reshape America's relations with the Middle East in the aftermath of the British, French and Israeli fiasco was expressed in a memorandum to himself that he wrote during these hectic days.

"We should be promptly ready to take any kind of action that will minimize the effects of the recent difficulties and will exclude from the area Soviet influence. One of the first is to make certain that none of these governments fails to understand all the details and the full implications of the Soviet suppression of the Hungarian revolt. We should, I

417

think, get all the proof that there is available, including moving pictures taken of the slaughter in Budapest. We must make certain that every weak country understands what can be in store for it once it falls under the domination of the Soviets."

In the Middle East he thought that the United States could provide surplus food, limited arms, economic aid, training missions for Egypt and financing of the Aswan High Dam. Economic and military aid, in proportion to what would be granted to Egypt, could also go to Israel. Finally, the United States could negotiate security treaties with Israel and the Arab states. It was an inspired program likely to ensure America's future friendly relations in the region. Perhaps out of the wreckage, a new beginning could be made.

• •

The President and his top officials had twenty-three congressional leaders to the White House Thursday for a wide-ranging review of the turbulent fortnight just past. The crushing of the Hungarian rebellion, Eisenhower pointed out, "served to convict the Soviet of brutal imperialism. This is the opposite of the old situation when neutral nations would never view Russia as being guilty of either colonialism or imperialism, and when Russia would never be disbelieved and we would never be believed. The Hungarian situation warns us again that the Soviet is capable of changing its face almost immediately."

Allen Dulles effectively refuted British and French claims circulating in Washington that their invasion had hurt Nasser's prestige and standing at home. "There is no internal opposition to Nasser," he told the legislators. "There is virtually unanimous revulsion among the Arabs against the French and British attack.

"Soviet intentions remain unclear and potentially threatening," he said. "Nasser has apparently received assurances from the Soviet ambassador in Cairo that Russia is prepared to support Egypt all the way, even risking World War III. Presently there are throughout countries like Syria, Lebanon and Jordan many rumors that the Soviet will intervene militarily. Communist China has announced it cannot stand idly by and there are reports of great numbers of Chinese volunteers [ready to] fight in Egypt."

The Soviets had a variety of moves that they could make, such as sending volunteers to Egypt or making a show of force in the Black Sea, added Dulles, "but it is believed that these moves will be restrained short of war."

Washington's anxieties about Soviet volunteers were eased later that day when a cable arrived from the U.S. ambassador in Cairo, Ray Hare. Nasser had just told him that "you need not worry. I don't trust any big power."

. .

Eisenhower had a long telephone conversation that day with Foster Dulles, who was still in Walter Reed recuperating from his operation for intestinal cancer. Ike had just had a disturbing conversation with Ambassador Lodge. "It seems that [people] at the U.N., particularly many of our European friends, are asking why we are so fretful about France and Britain with a few troops in Egypt while we don't show as much concern about Hungary," said Eisenhower.

"I doubt that the feeling about turning our backs on Hungary exists in any quarter but the French and British," replied Dulles.

Eisenhower said Lodge wanted him to send another note to Moscow protesting the Hungarian slaughter. "I think there have already been too many messages," he said. "I don't want to let Cabot down, but I hate to send messages back and forth when we know they won't pay any attention to them."

Dulles said he was not enthusiastic either. The question is, replied Eisenhower, "are we in danger of putting ourselves in wrong in that we will encourage Ben Gurion and people like that if we don't try to put the same pressure on this fellow [Bulganin]?"

"Well, but you have [put pressure on Bulganin]," replied Dulles.

"I have the feeling that we have excited the Hungarians for all these years and now we are turning our backs on them when they are in a jam," confessed the President.

"We have always been against violent rebellion," pointed out Dulles.

"I told Lodge so but was amazed that he was ignorant of this fact."

Eisenhower decided in the end to send another note to Bulganin, "though I am sure it will have no influence."

The sending of notes was about all the Administration found it could do in Hungary. There were still 200,000 Soviet troops there, some, 3,000 to 4,000 refugees were streaming out of the country daily, and there were 400,000 families homeless and 25,000 dead.

. .

But there were measures the Administration could take against Britain and France in the Middle East. Both Eden and Mollet still desperately wanted to meet with him in a show of Western solidarity, but the President continued to refuse. He sent messages on November 11 to both prime ministers expressing the hope that they might soon meet, but first they had to get their troops out of Egypt and a U.N. force into the country. "After it has been carried out successfully, we should then be able to consider arrangements for a meeting," Ike wrote.

• •

As the days passed without any overt move by the Soviet Union to intervene directly in the Middle East, the sense of crisis dissipated but severe problems remained. By the middle of the month some European countries had already had to begin rationing oil, and shortages for all of Europe would be at the crisis stage within another four to six weeks. It would take three to four months to repair the canal, and the only alternative for Europe was American help. The U.S. had the tankers to move 500,000 barrels a day from South America and it could afford to divert another 350,000 barrels it normally imported from that area, Dr. Arthur Flemming reported to Eisenhower. Such amounts would make up all but 15 to 20 percent of Europe's oil needs; the slack could be covered by conservation.

But, Flemming noted, the situation was tricky. If Washington moved too fast or too openly, the Arab nations might cut off other supplies and further aggravate the situation. The British and French had to get their troops out of Egypt before the emergency oil plan could go into operation.

Europe's oil dependence gave Eisenhower another powerful lever against the British and French and he did not hesitate to use it.

• •

Dag Hammarskjold now had his hands full with the Middle East. He was trying to recruit a United Nations force while negotiating with a highly suspicious Gamal Nasser about deployment of more foreign troops on Egyptian soil. His most difficult problem, however, lay with Israel. From the beginning, Tel Aviv flatly refused to accept any U.N. soldiers. More distressing was the level of Israeli brutality in the Gaza Strip.

Occupying Israeli troops killed at least 275 Palestinians immediately after capturing the Strip during a brutal house-to-house search for weapons and *fedayeen* in Khan Yunis. As reports of the wanton killings filtered out, Israel tried to evict U.N. observers from their post in the Strip, taking away their radio and transmitter. The confrontation became so tense that General Burns had to warn Israel not to use force against his personnel; Hammarskjold followed that up with a message of his own on November 7 "that such steps for Israel would have the gravest consequences."

There was another massive bloodletting on November 12 at the refugee camp at nearby Rafah when Israeli troops stormed through the hovels, rounding up refugees for intelligence screenings. Disorders broke out and 111 Palestinians were killed. "It is a very sad proof of the fact that the spirit that inspired the notorious Deir Yassin massacre in 1948 is not dead among some of the Israeli armed forces," commented General Burns.

The head of the Gaza observer force, Lieutenant Colonal R. F. Bayard of the U.S. Army, reported on the thirteenth that Israeli soldiers were trying to prevent U.N. observers from seeing "actions they are taking against the civilian populace. I have come to the conclusion that the treatment of civilians is unwarrantedly rough and that a good number of persons have been shot down in cold blood for no apparent reason. Many key UNRWA [U.N. Relief and Works Agency] personnel are missing from the camps and are believed to have been executed by the Israelis.

"Many Israeli soldiers have robbed civilians, taking watches, rings, fountain pens, etc., away from the Arabs either in their homes or on the streets. Every vehicle and every bicycle has been confiscated. Private workshops and machine shops have been stripped of all mechanical tools. Many mules and horses have been taken and cloth has been taken from the stores.

"It is unpleasant to witness the treatment of the local populace and particularly to note the indignities directed upon personal friends. . . ."

In another letter, this one on the nineteenth, Bayard reported that the Israeli authorities had rounded up four notables and demanded that they sign a statement saying they desired that Israel "take over and administrate the Gaza Strip." When they demurred, they were forced to sign and then the statement was taken to forty other leading citizens for signing. Israel was getting ready to produce "proof" that its annexation would be welcome in the Gaza Strip.

Bayard observed that the Israeli press was making much of the number of *fedayeen* in the Strip, but "as far as we are able to determine, through quite reliable sources, the *fedayeen* in the Gaza Strip last May numbered approximately 300.

"The Israelis have recently made a housing survey to determine the

421

number of people occupying each house. I presume the next move will be to force people out of their homes or to concentrate several families in one house in order to make houses available to the Israelis."

Dayan admitted to the widespread looting in his diary, saying that "groups of our soldiers and also civilians from the settlements in the region began laying their hands on property. Our military police finally got the situation in hand and stopped it, but not before much damage was done to Arab belongings and much shame to ourselves."

Burns suspected that Israel hoped to annex the Gaza Strip and deport its population, though the government repeatedly denied it had any such plans. "Israelis had a record of getting rid of Arabs whose lands they desired," observed Burns. "I have been credibly informed that what the Israeli authorities really had in mind was to absorb only about 80,000 of the Strip's population. The remainder [about 200,000] would have been persuaded to settle elsewhere, perhaps in the Sinai desert.

"That this is not a slander on the Israeli Defense Forces is, unfortunately, only too well attested by . . . incidents in which they took severe repressive measures against Arab civilians, killing large numbers of them."

• •

Advance parties of the United Nations Emergency Force, UNEF as it immediately became known, began arriving in Egypt on November 15. The first in were the Danish with the Colombians, Indians, Norwegians, Swedish and Yugoslavians soon following. Canada wanted to be part of the force, since it was Canada's Lester Pearson who had spearheaded the U.N. resolution creating the force, but Nasser objected.

Canada had offered as its contingent the Queen's Own Rifles. Nasser feared that the name and the similar uniforms of Canadian and British troops might cause Egyptians to believe that English soldiers were part of the force. Canada finally agreed to withdraw the Queen's Own Rifles and donate instead transport, reconnaissance and administrative units.

• •

Nasser's prestige had never been so high as it was now. *The New York Times* reported on November 17 that he had "pulled a political victory out of his military defeat. He had gained strength in the Arab world instead of losing it. The other members of the Arab League have just pledged themselves to support him fully in any further fighting. The balance of this month's events seems to show an irrevocable loss of prestige and friendship by the British and French.''

· ·

The next day the strains, the anxieties, the rebuffs and defeats finally felled Anthony Eden. He was reported suffering from severe overstrain and confined to his bed.

· ·

Quite suddenly, the crisis was past. The Russians had not moved directly into the Suez quagmire, and though none of the belligerents had as yet withdrawn their troops, it was only a matter of time before they bowed to world opinion and to their need for oil and U.S. aid. The great dangers of another world war were over. Now what remained was to clean up the mess and sort out the tragic destiny of Anthony Eden.

CHAPTER XX

We Have These Socialists to Lick

HUMPHREY

THE RUINS OF ANTHONY EDEN'S DISASTROUS SUEZ POLICY lay exposed and in plain view for all to see. The blockage of the canal and the destruction of the Iraq Petroleum Company pipeline were rapidly taking their toll on Britain's oil reserves. Stocks were so short that rationing had to be imposed, scheduled to start on December 17, the first rationing decree in Britain since the World War II controls that had finally been removed from meat and butter only a year and a half earlier. The cost of the invasion had brought near economic ruin. Gold and dollar reserves fell $57 million in September, $84 million in October and a stunning $309 million in November. Britain desperately needed dollars to pay for oil from alternative sources.

Unless the country's oil needs could soon be met Britain would plunge into a deep depression. The Conservative Party would certainly be blamed and was likely to be voted out of power. Neither Tory leaders nor the Eisenhower Administration wanted this to happen. On November 19, Ambassador Aldrich and Chancellor of the Exchequer Harold Macmillan met to discuss the threatening situation. During their talk, Macmillan put forward a plan to save the Tory government, and, incidentally, put himself in a position to become prime minister. Aldrich was so excited by the proposal that he took the unusual step of calling President Eisenhower directly.

"My guess is correct," Aldrich exulted to Eisenhower.

The President had no idea what he was talking about.

"I guessed there was going to be a change [of the prime ministership]," said Aldrich. "I'll send a message right off to you giving the details. Harold Macmillan is terribly anxious to see you as soon as possible. I'll spell that out in the message too."

After Aldrich hung up, Eisenhower called Hoover and asked him if the State Department had received a message from the ambassador. "The guess is that the Cabinet is completely to be reshuffled," said Hoover, reading from the cable, "and that Eden is going out because of sickness."

Hoover commented: "It is very interesting in that they are putting a proposition up to us. They will either have to withdraw from Egypt and have their Cabinet fall—or else they will have to renew hostilities, taking over the entire canal. Obviously things are very much in the making there.

"I think this is one time to sit tight, awaiting further information."

•   •

Though the messages on the secret negotiations between Aldrich and the leadership of the Tory Party remain classified by the government, transcripts of Eisenhower's telephone conversations make it clear that the Conservative leaders and the Eisenhower Administration now began a secret collusion of their own. Its purpose was to keep the Conservative government in power in Britain. It amounted to a highly unethical meddling in Britain's domestic affairs by Eisenhower.

Only minutes after the President finished talking with Hoover, he received a telephone call from George Humphrey at the Treasury Department. Humphrey told Eisenhower he too had just spoken with Aldrich.

"I want to remind you of our discussion about a 'remote possibility,' " said Eisenhower, apparently referring to Eden's expected fall. "Aldrich says part of it is coming about. There are a lot of conditions we cannot possibly meet."

Replied Humphrey: "I hate to have a man stick in there and go to a vote of confidence and get licked. If they throw him out then we have these socialists to lick."

They agreed to discuss the matter the next day, and at 5:30 P.M. that Tuesday, Humphrey and Hoover joined Eisenhower to talk over the delicate matter of keeping the Tories in power. Humphrey, who as a personal friend of Rab Butler's, the co-leader of the Tories with Macmillan in the absence of Eden, said: "In my opinion Butler would be the stronger of the men being mentioned [to succeed Eden]."

"I always thought most highly of Macmillan," said Eisenhower. "He

425

is a straight, fine man, and so far as I am concerned the outstanding one of the British I served with during the war.''

Aldrich's report had said that the Tories would need a ''fig leaf'' to withdraw from Suez and still remain in power, but he had not spelled out what the fig leaf was. The President and his men now speculated about it. Hoover pointed out that the Tories might want something beyond just help with oil and dollars.

''They might have another idea in mind when they speak of the 'fig leaf,' '' Hoover pointed out. ''They might want us to take the responsibility for obtaining some satisfaction internationally which they can then offer as their reason for leaving the canal.''

Humphrey disagreed. ''I think that if they have the idea we are receptive to a request for help that is all they are looking for.''

The President suggested that a message be sent to Aldrich for relay to the Tories. ''We can simply couch our statement along the lines of 'on the assumption stated by Macmillan—that is, that they will announce at once an immediate withdrawal—they can be assured of our sympathetic consultation and help.' Also Macmillan can meet with me on that assumption.''

But now a puzzling question arose. To whom to send this highly unusual message? Macmillan or Butler or both? Certainly it could not go to Eden or the fractured government. Eisenhower decided to telephone Aldrich for guidance.

''We have been getting your messages and I want to make an inquiry,'' said Ike. ''You are dealing with at least one person—maybe two or three —on a very personal basis. Is it possible for you, without embarrassment, to get together the two that you mentioned in one of your messages?''

''Yes, one of them I have just been playing bridge with. Perhaps I can stop him.''

''I'd rather you talk to both together,'' replied Eisenhower. ''You know who I mean? One has the same name [Butler] as my predecessor at the Columbia University presidency. The other one was with me in the war.''

''I know the one with you in the war [Macmillan],'' said Aldrich, adding: ''Oh, yes, now I've got it.''

''Could you get them informally and say of course we are interested and sympathetic, and as soon as things happen that we anticipate we can furnish a lot of fig leaves?''

''I certainly can say that.''

426

"Will that be enough to get the boys moving?" asked Ike.

"I think it will be."

"You see," said Eisenhower, "we don't want to be in a position of interfering between those two. But we want to have you personally tell them. They are both good friends."

"Yes, very much so," said Aldrich. "Have you seen my messages regarding my conversations with them all?"

"Yes, with at least two," replied the President.

"That is wonderful. I will do this—tomorrow?"

"Yes, first thing in the morning."

"I shall certainly do it. And I will then communicate with you at once. Can do it without the slightest embarrassment."

Eisenhower, ever a stickler on organizational routine, instructed the ambassador to "communicate through regular channels."

The President told Humphrey and Hoover that the way he saw the process unfolding was: "First, we are ready to talk about help as soon as the precondition—French and British initiation of withdrawal—is established; second, on knowing that the British and French forces will comply with a withdrawal undertaking at once, we would talk to the Arabs to obtain the removal of any objections they may have regarding the provision of oil to Western Europe; third, we will then talk the details of money assistance with the British."

• •

The next day Humphrey was still puzzling over what the Tories meant by a fig leaf. He now tended to agree with Hoover that it included more than just money or oil. "It may be something that we have not even guessed," he told Eisenhower in a telephone conversation. "It looks to me like it is up to the British to make the next move. If I were doing it alone, I would stick still now and wait until we hear further from them."

Eisenhower agreed, adding that "somewhere between the British and ourselves there is a vagueness, not a frankness that I would like. We don't get the points cleared up that I would like."

Humphrey said the only way to achieve frankness was to have a meeting with Butler or Macmillan. Eisenhower suggested that an appropriate place for such a meeting might be at the next gathering of the Organization for European Economic Cooperation (OEEC), but Humphrey disagreed. "I'm afraid of the OEEC trying to get in and decide where the money the United States will lend will go. I do not want another Marshall Plan."

The conversation turned to the Middle East. Eisenhower had just met with Tunisian Prime Minister Habib Bourguiba and had been impressed by "his sincerity, his intelligence and his friendliness." The President said he wanted to move fast to get the Anglo-French troops out of Suez because Bourguiba had told him his policy opposing the Anglo-French invasion had won America friends in the Middle East. "I don't want to lose everything we have gained," said Ike. "Bourguiba said he was not going to fall under Nasser and he dismissed Israel as a minor thing."

"We have got to keep working with the Arabs," replied Humphrey. "We are on their side until these fellows [British and French] get out. After that, we ought to be in the position of a neutral friend of both sides so that both can trust us to try to work out a fair deal."

A few minutes later, Eisenhower had a full-scale meeting in his office of his top security officials including Hoover, Humphrey, Allen Dulles and Admiral Radford. The purpose of the meeting, Ike explained, was to "gain an understanding of the sequence of actions planned in the Middle East and the means of dovetailing actions in the fields of oil and finance.

"We must prevent the dissolution of Western Europe. Once withdrawal has begun, we must let the Arabs know that we are going to aid Western Europe financially. We must make sure that Saudi Arabia, Iran and Iraq at least are aware of what we are doing, and give their assent. We must explain a number of points to them very carefully. We must stress the importance of restoring Saud's oil markets in Western Europe.

"We must face the question: What must we do in Europe, and then the question, how do we square it with the Arabs?"

Astonishingly, at this late date the Pentagon representative, Deputy Defense Secretary Robertson, proposed that the United States join the Baghdad Pact. Eisenhower was opposed. "I think that if the British get us into the Baghdad Pact—as the matter would appear to the Arabs—we would lose our influence with the Arabs," responded Ike. "The British could then take a very intransigent stand."

A discussion developed about the relative importance between Western Europe and the Middle East, with Eisenhower and Humphrey agreeing that "Western Europe requires Middle Eastern oil, and Middle Eastern oil is of importance mainly through its contribution to the Western European economy."

Humphrey noted that significant events were soon to transpire in both regions. "The British are facing a financial crisis within ten days," he announced. "I think the sequence of events will be this: The British will start out of Suez in a few days. The British will want to come over here a few days later. This will be the time when we must bargain hard with them. Between those dates we must let King Saud, and even Nasser, know that in starting talks with the British, we have not reversed our stand toward them and that we want an understanding with them prior to the British talks. By December 3 our arrangements must be in hand because that is the date of the British financial announcement.''

• •

It was December 4 before Macmillan went before the House of Commons to announce to a distressed nation that Britain was in a financial crisis. The nation's gold and dollar reserves had plunged from $2,244,-000,000 at the end of October to $1,965,000,000 at the end of November. As a result of such losses, Macmillan said, the price of gasoline had to be raised by a shilling a gallon and the government had to go to the International Monetary Fund and the United States for loans, and to Canada and the United States with requests for waiver of interest payments on past loans. It was a somber announcement that immediately threatened the Conservative Party's hold on the government.

• •

Eisenhower's efforts to keep the Tories in power in Britain were encouraged, however indirectly, by a pleading letter from Winston Churchill. ''There is not much left for me to do in this world, and I have neither the wish nor the strength to be involved in the present political stress and turmoil,'' wrote the aged statesman on November 23. ''But I do believe with unfaltering conviction that the theme of the Anglo-American alliance is more important today than at any time since the war. You and I had some part in raising it to the plane on which it has stood. Now, whatever the arguments adduced here and in the United States for or against Anthony's action in Egypt, to let events in the Middle East become a gulf between us, would be an act of folly, on which our whole civilization may founder.

''There seems to be growing misunderstanding and frustration on both sides of the Atlantic. If they be allowed to develop, the skies will darken indeed and it is the Soviet Union that will ride the storm. We should leave it to the historians to argue the rights and wrongs of all that has happened during the past years. If we do not take immediate action in harmony, it is no exaggeration to say that we must expect to see the Middle East and the North African coastline under Soviet control and Western Europe placed at the mercy of the Russians.''

429

. .

On the same day Churchill penned his letter to Eisenhower, Eden departed for a badly needed three-week vacation in Jamaica where, fittingly, he stayed in the retreat of Ian Fleming, creator of the James Bond spy novels. Nothing in Fleming's fiction surpassed the bizarre events that Eden had recently presided over.

. .

Aldrich cabled from London on the day of Eden's departure that the prime minister had suffered a "breakdown." The press and public, strangely enough, seemed to assume that Eden would return to lead the government, observed Aldrich, but the Tory leaders were at that moment working out the details for getting rid of him. "Eden's present physical and more important psychological condition is such that some wonder whether he may desire to assume role of martyr. Whatever the motivation might be, his resignation would no doubt deflect from British government onus for Suez policy, of which he of course was principal architect. Such action would perhaps enable Tory Party to remain at helm in Britain and would mend U.K.'s strained relations with its allies and friends."

Aldrich tried to put the crisis in a historical context. "From the beginning, extraordinary emotion has pervaded. It results in a kind of extreme retrogression to nineteenth-century attitudes startling as well as disconcerting to those who have known Britain in the twentieth. One reflection of this is the remarkable manner in which Britain has thrown her destiny with France, a country whose political stability and military capacity has been the object of widespread British doubt and disparagement over the years. Again, anti-American feeling is at a very high pitch and yet is accompanied by the somewhat contradictory but nonetheless complacent assumption that the U.S. is bound to come to its senses and pick up the check."

. .

Some Washington officials were thinking of picking up more than a check. Herb Hoover was one. In a conversation with Eisenhower on November 26, Hoover wondered whether "it might be necessary for us to approach the British and say that it looks as though they are through in the Middle East and ask if they want us to try to pick up their commitments."

Eisenhower warned that America should not rashly assume such com-

430

mitments. He added generously, "I think we should give the British every chance to work their way back into a position of influence and respect in the Middle East."

The President was giving the Tories all the fig leaves he could. He ordered Cabot Lodge to ease up on his actions in the United Nations directed at getting the British and French to remove their troops from Suez. And, after receiving private understandings from the Tories that they would soon announce their withdrawal, he ordered emergency oil shipments to begin on November 30 and the start of negotiations for giving Britain the financial help it so desperately required.

Selwyn Lloyd announced the start of withdrawal on December 3. By December 22, all British and French troops were gone from Egypt, their departure loudly cheeredy by ecstatic Egyptians and a triumphant Gamal Abdel Nasser, who was now the undisputed champion of the Arab world.

• •

Israel unilaterally announced its withdrawal from the Sinai on December 2 and the next day began moving back its troops. But there were conditions. The country wanted to keep the Gaza Strip with its rich citrus groves and defensive positions against Egypt, and Sharm el-Sheikh, the choke point of the Gulf of Aqaba, and so it stalled. Israel stated its withdrawal would be in stages. The first stage was to a line about thirty miles east of the canal. Then all movement stopped. At the end of the month another minor withdrawal was staged. Then again movement stopped. Meanwhile, Israel waged a vigorous drive in the United States to drum up support for its retention of the two captured areas.

Eisenhower and Dulles, who had returned to work on December 3, proved just as adamant in resisting Ben Gurion's entreaties as they had earlier in demanding the Anglo-French withdrawal. But Ben Gurion was a tougher customer. He persisted week after frustrating week in defying Washington, the personal pleas of Eisenhower and the entreaties of the members of the United Nations.

Ben Gurion openly declared before the Knesset on January 23 that Israel planned to stay in Gaza and retain all of the west coast of the Gulf of Aqaba. His remarks were greeted with wild cheers of approval by the legislators, who, caught up by their own enthusiasm and massive demonstrations of public support, passed a resolution that "Israel shall keep the Gaza Strip" and called on the United Nations to take care of the refugees. Ben Gurion declared that "the Israel administration of Gaza will be a pilot plant of Israel-Arab cooperation," a statement that elicited

431

no echoing response from the Arabs in the Strip who were suffering under Israel's occupation.

Israel's intransigence caused a developing fury in the Arab world and impatience elsewhere. On February 2 the U.N. General Assembly passed another resolution against Israel's occupation, its sixth, ordering Israel's immediate withdrawal. Ben Gurion refused.

In America Israel's propaganda campaign grew to new heights. It was highly successful and brought forth vocal support from such figures as Eleanor Roosevelt, Harry Truman, and Senate leaders Lyndon Johnson and Bill Knowland. Jacob Javits, just elected to the Senate, organized a group of twenty senators to support Israel's position.

Eisenhower's patience was about at an end. On February 11 he approved the sending of a message to Ben Gurion demanding Israel's "prompt and unconditional" withdrawal from Gaza but promising to support Israel's right of innocent passage in the Gulf of Aqaba. Again Ben Gurion refused, arguing in a return message that "there is no basis for the restoration of the status quo ante in Gaza."

The Administration was besieged with Israel's supporters. Knowland called Dulles on February 1 to defend Israel's case, but the secretary of state countered with a lecture. "If we cannot get the Israelis out of Egypt the Russians will get them out and in the process we will lose the whole of the Middle East. I don't see how we can have any influence with the Arab countries if we cannot get the Israelis out of Egypt. We have tried everything short of sanctions."

Knowland asked whether the administration would go so far as to support a U.N. resolution imposing sanctions on Israel.

"Unless the Israelis go we will probably go along with sanctions," replied Dulles. "That's the conclusion the President came to today."

"I've gone along as far as I can and this will mean the parting of the ways," warned Knowland.

"I think you should study this," pleaded Dulles. "We cannot have all our policies made in Jerusalem."

"I agree, but sanctions are pretty serious," said Knowland. "I would like to know the timing. I want to send in my resignation [as a U.N. delegate] before the delegation votes on sanctions."

Lyndon Johnson sent Dulles a letter complaining that "the United Nations cannot apply one rule for the strong and another for the weak; it cannot organize its economic weight against the little state when it has not previously made even a pretense of doing so against the large state [Russia]."

Even Harry Luce, the owner of Time Inc., got into the act. In a telephone call to Dulles, he declared that it would be "a mistake to vote sanctions against them."

"If we do not go along with sanctions that will be the end of any hope for us in the Middle East," patiently explained Dulles. "We are doing all we can to avoid sanctions. We have no desire for them. I am aware how almost impossible it is in this country to carry out a foreign policy not approved by the Jews. Marshall and Forrestal learned that. I am going to try to have one.

"That does not mean I am anti-Jewish, but I believe in what George Washington said in his Farewell Address that an emotional attachment to another country should not interfere."

Later, in a conversation with Lodge, Dulles complained about the "terrific control the Jews have over the news media and the barrage which the Jews have built up on congressmen."

He complained again about Israeli influence in the Congress in a telephone conversation with his old friend Dr. Roswell Barnes of the National Council of Churches. "I am very much concerned over the fact that the Jewish influence here is completely dominating the scene and making it almost impossible to get Congress to do anything they don't approve of. The Israeli Embassy is practically dictating to the Congress through influential Jewish people in the country."

Barnes wondered whether Ben Gurion would back down.

"A great deal depends on whether Ben Gurion can control our government's policies through the Jewish pressure here," replied Dulles. "The non-Jewish elements of the community have got to make themselves more felt or else there will be a disaster here."

The crisis grew. Week after week, Israel stood up to Washington's pressure and refused to give up its conquests. On February 20, Eisenhower and Dulles hosted a meeting for the congressional leadership of both parties to try to convince them to pass a resolution endorsing the Administration's opposition to Israel's occupation. They refused, much to Eisenhower's disgust. "As I reflected on the pettiness of much of the discussion of the morning, I found it somewhat dismaying that partisan considerations could enter so much into life-or-death, peace-or-war decisions," he wrote in his diary.

Despite the lack of congressional backing, Eisenhower by now was determined to take off the kid gloves and show Israel that he meant business. He sent another stiff cable to Ben Gurion warning that the United States might vote for sanctions in the United Nations and that

433

such sanctions might include not only government but private assistance to Israel, a severe blow since individuals in the mid-1950s annually gave Israel $40 million, all tax deductible, and bought $60 million of Israel's bonds. He also decided to take his case to the country immediately.

Eisenhower went on national television that same night and delivered a tough message to Israel. "Should a nation which attacks and occupies foreign territory in the face of United Nations disapproval be allowed to impose conditions on its own withdrawal? If we agreed that armed attack can properly achieve the purposes of the assailant, then I fear we will have turned back the clock of international order.

"If the United Nations once admits that international disputes can be settled by using force, then we will have destroyed the very foundation of the organization and our best hope of establishing world order. The United Nations must not fail. I believe that in the interests of peace the United Nations has no choice but to exert pressure upon Israel to comply with the withdrawal resolutions."

Ben Gurion voiced his defiance the next day before the Knesset, declaring that "every attempt to impose on us perverted justice and a regime of discrimination will encounter unshrinking opposition from the Israeli people. No matter what may happen, Israel will not submit to the restoration of the status quo in the Strip."

Then the Israeli prime minister made what seemed like a direct appeal to Americans over the head of the Administration. "Our opposition to any injurious proposals by the American government cannot weaken in any manner our feelings of appreciation of and friendship for the American people," he said.

Eisenhower and Dulles were distraught. Israel seemed to be exerting more influence on Congress than was the Administration. "We need very badly to get some more vocal support from people other than the Jews and those very much influenced by Jews," Dulles told Dr. Barnes the day after Ben Gurion's speech. "We are really in an unfortunate position. It is impossible to hold the line because we get no support from the Protestant elements in the country. All we get is a battering from the Jews."

Dulles claimed that almost 90 percent of the mail received at the White House after Eisenhower's speech was Jewish. "Out of that percentage, 10 percent supported the President and 90 percent were against. The significant thing is that practically all the response was Jewish. There seems to be no interest in this situation by others."

434

• •

Six Moslem nations, sensing the Administration's weakness, took matters in their own hands the day after Ike's speech. A resolution was introduced in the U.N. General Assembly by Afghanistan, Indonesia, Iraq, Lebanon, Pakistan and Sudan demanding an end of all aid to Israel if it did not withdraw.

Ben Gurion, buffeted by these various pressures, gave in before the resolution reached a vote. On March 1, Golda Meir, as foreign minister, declared that Israel would withdraw, which it finally did on March 16.

As the Israeli forces withdraw they systematically destroyed all surfaced roads, railway tracks and telephone lines. All buildings in the tiny villages of Abu Ageila and El Quseima were destroyed, as were the military buildings around El Arish.

The destruction was carried out despite repeated protests by Hammarskjold, causing General Burns to comment dryly: "God had scorched the Sinai earth, and His chosen people removed whatever stood above it."

• •

Anthony Eden returned from Jamaica with a glowing suntan and the burning determination to hang on to power. On his arrival at London Airport on December 14, he boldly declared: "I am convinced, more convinced than I have been about anything in all my public life, that we were right, my colleagues and I, in the judgments and decisions we took, and that history will prove it so."

But while Eden preened in public, the press and Parliament were filled with speculation about how much knowledge the prime minister had had of Israel's invasion and whether there actually had been collusion between Britain, France and Israel. There had been so much secrecy and covering up that few people knew the facts. Government spokesmen continued to deny collusion, and on December 20 Eden desperately lied about it in the House of Commons. "I wish to make it clear that there was not foreknowledge that Israel would attack Egypt—there was not."

Eden's days were numbered.

When he had entered the House he was greeted by a stony silence from the Opposition "and the feeblest of cheers from the government benches," recalled Lord Kilmuir. "One loyal Conservative rose to cheer to find himself alone and unsupported. It was a grim and revealing epi-

435

sode." Eden was being subjected to that deadliest of British tortures, a studied indifference.

Gasoline rationing was now in effect, and there were long lines of autos at the service stations. The economy was in tatters. Steel prices shot up 6 percent, which was a significant rise at the time. The country was in an uproar over whether the invasion was right or wrong, whether there had or had not been collusion, whether Eden should stay or go. He tried to tough it out, but his performance was not believable. Dulles and Lodge, during a telephone conversation, agreed that "Eden is good at being a rabbit trying to act like a lion."

Churchill seemed to agree. "To go so far and not go on was madness," he said privately.

Over the Christmas holidays Eden was stricken again with the severe fevers that had laid him low in October. An examination by two specialists resulted in the conclusion that he would suffer such attacks as long as he worked under stress. His end had come. Even if he could outlast the ridicule of indifference he could not survive the fever.

• •

Harold Macmillan was in his Treasury office on January 9 when he was summoned to No. 10 Downing. "Eden was in the drawing room," recalled Macmillan. "He told me with simple gravity, as a matter decided and not to be discussed, that he had decided to resign his office. There was no way out. The doctors had told him the truth about his health and, though he was not a doomed man, it must be the end of his political life. Throughout our short and painful conversation he was as charming and elegant and as dignified as ever."

Eden, who had waited so long to become prime minister, resigned his office that day. He had served less than two years.

Eisenhower sent him a nostalgic and considerate letter the day after his resignation. "I cannot tell you how deeply I regret that the strains and stresses of these times finally wore you down physically until you felt it necessary to retire. To me it seems only yesterday that you and I and others were meeting with Winston almost daily—or nightly—to discuss the next logical move of our forces in the war.

"Now you have retired, I have had a heart attack as well as a major operation, and many others of our colleagues of that era are either gone or no longer active. The only reason for recalling these days is to assure you that my admiration and affection for you have never diminished; I am truly sorry that you had to quit the office of Her Majesty's First

436

Minister. Mamie and I pray that you and Lady Eden will have a long, busy and happy life ahead.''

Eden lived out his life in the House of Lords as Lord Avon, an earldom conferred on him in 1961 by Queen Elizabeth, where, impeccably tailored and coiffed as ever, his speeches were always listened to but rarely acted on. He insisted to the end that his Suez policy had been right, and he never admitted that his government had colluded with Israel.

When he died in 1977, a line in the London *Times*'s obituary neatly summed up his career and might have served as his epitaph.

"He was the last prime minister to believe Britain was a great power and the first to confront a crisis which proved she was not."

EPILOGUE

SUEZ WAS A HINGE point in history. It spelled the end of Western colonialism and the entry of America as the major Western power in the Middle East. It should have served as an instructive warning against similar ill-conceived enterprises, but astonishingly it did not. Only four years later, the CIA launched its disastrous Bay of Pigs invasion, a misguided plan that had elements disturbingly similar to the Suez collusion, most notably the naïve expectation that the invasion would result in a popular uprising against Fidel Castro. The lesson that Nasser's survival, and indeed enhancement, should have taught went completely ignored.

Britain, France and Israel, by colluding and waging an unprovoked war, displayed such contempt for justice and the rule of law that they badly blotched the West's record in its competition against Communism. No longer, after Suez, could the West assert that it was uniquely to be trusted as the champion of man's aspirations for a just world.

The Soviet Union secured its presence in the Middle East after Suez. The pro-West Iraqi regime fell in 1958, and both Iraq and Syria—soon followed by Libya—imitated Nasser's example and turned to the Soviets for aid and arms. Though Soviet fortunes, like American, have had their share of ups and downs over the years (Sadat's expulsion of Russian advisers in 1972 was a blow to Moscow), the Russians now appear so embedded in the Middle East that it seems unrealistic to suppose that any settlement of the region's continuing turmoil could occur without active Soviet support. The very thing that Eden had hoped to accomplish,

438

preventing the replacement of British influence by Russia, is now a fact in the Middle East.

For Britain, the hallucinatory actions of Anthony Eden, normally the most upright of men, demonstrated how easily democratic institutions can be circumvented. Lord Mountbatten was moved to reflect on this sad and scary aspect of Suez shortly before his death. "It was astonishing to me to see what one really persistent man could do if he was prime minister," reminisced Mountbatten. "He never let Parliament know what was going on. He never really let the Cabinet know. We were unable to get our approaches through. I of course failed, as I was bound to, because the chiefs of staff have no standing. One or two of those ministers might have—Monckton, Macmillan himself, Selwyn Lloyd, the real men who negotiated the collusion. They didn't.

"The result was that Anthony Eden was able to go through with one of the most disastrous operations ever, entirely on his own. And we think that we have a secure democracy that can prevent that from happening."

Guy Mollet and his government soon followed the fate of Anthony Eden. Mollet fell in May 1957 to be replaced by a government headed by Bourgès-Maunoury. Mollet had ruled for exactly sixteen months, long enough to further besmirch France's once glorious reputation and spell the eventual doom of the unmourned Fourth Republic. Mollet, who had boldly declared that "France without Algeria is not France," lived to see Algeria gain its independence in 1962; he died in 1975. Bourgès' government lasted only through September. In 1958 Charles de Gaulle returned to power at the head of the Fifth Republic. He maintained France's relations with Israel until 1967 when, upset at continued Israeli hostility to the Arabs and sensitive to his country's need for Arab oil, he ordered arms shipments cut off after the Six Day War. The relationship between the two countries quickly descended into the chill state in which it remains today.

Israel emerged from the Suez crisis as the only seeming winner among the conspirators. The war forced Egypt to open the Gulf of Aqaba to Israeli shipping, with U.S. support, and the stationing of an international force, UNEF, along the Israeli-Egyptian frontier to prevent border clashes. Further, in Ben Gurion's eyes at least, Nasser had been taught a lesson. "This campaign diminished the stature of the Egyptian dictator and I do not want you or the entire people to underestimate the importance of this fact," Ben Gurion said in a speech April 2, 1957, in the Knesset. "I always feared that a personality might rise such as arose among the Arab rulers in the seventh century or like him [Kemal Ataturk] who arose in Turkey after its defeat in the First World War. He raised their spirits, changed their character, and turned them into a fighting nation. There was and still is a danger that Nasser is this man.''

In fact, Israel's victory was hollow. The putative gains were far out-weighed by the psychological venom that resulted from the Suez collusion. The experience encouraged later generations of Israelis to pursue Ben Gurion's hostility toward the Arabs and to repeat the conquest of land by war. The 1967 capture of Sinai and the West Bank by Israel led directly to the 1973 war that shook to the roots Israeli self-confidence and brought upon the world oil shortages, economic misery and an incalculable strengthening of the Arab oil states. In addition, the conquest of the West Bank turned Israel, a nation founded on the precepts of the United Nations and the pursuit of freedom, into an occupying power over the lives of 1.2 million Palestinians. The experience has not been an enriching one for the troubled Israeli soul.

Ben Gurion remained in power until 1963 when he suddenly resigned during a venomous dispute with Golda Meir and the stalwarts of the Mapai faction. He attempted a comeback in 1965 by forming his own party, Rafi, with his two protégés, Moshe Dayan and Shimon Peres, but he was ignominiously defeated. After that he finally retired permanently to his Negev kibbutz and died in 1973, having lived long enough to see the victorious 1967 war and the disaster of the 1973 war. His two young aides, Dayan and Peres, played important roles in Israel after Ben Gurion's final defeat, and Peres, the suave and soft-spoken youngster who pioneered Israel's secret arms deal with France, is now leader of the Labor Party that Ben Gurion led for so long.

After the Suez crisis, Gamal Abdel Nasser's relations with the United States continued to deteriorate until the 1967 war when America openly sided with Israel and he broke all diplomatic ties. He died suddenly of a heart attack in 1970 while relations with America remained severed. Though he had continued to be the foremost spokesman for the Arab cause, his rule had bitter disappointments. He sent Egyptian troops into Yemen in their own costly imperial war, and over the years his suspicions of plots against him—not without foundation—caused him to become increasingly authoritarian.

The bitterest irony, however, was the deleterious effect of the Aswan High Dam on Egypt's people. Since its dedication a year after Nasser's death, it has proved to be an ecological nightmare, causing the proliferation of infectious parasites in the Nile and preventing the natural fertilization of farmlands by silt that now remains trapped behind the dam in

Lake Nasser. A chant recently heard sung by farmers in the Upper Nile expresses the farmers' disillusionment with the High Dam that so long had been Egypt's dream.

> *God destroy your house, Nasser*
> *God burn your family, Nasser*
> *What High Dam, what dam?*
> *It rose and why did it?*
> *It destroyed the soil and the crop*
> *And the land now has no crop*
> *Why Nasser did you destroy us?*
> *God destroy your house, Nasser.*

Eisenhower emerged from the crisis under severe criticism for opposing America's traditional allies, and historians since then have generally been critical of his actions during this period. In fact, his firm insistence that the rule of law be obeyed was one of the high points of his presidency. American behavior during this period won high praise in Arab lands and throughout the Third World, offering the nation a unique opportunity to improve its relations with the emerging nations.

Eisenhower continued to give every indication that he wanted to take advantage of the opportunity. During a conversation with Hoover in late November, he observed that "we are in a period in which we can strengthen our bilateral arrangements with the various Arab countries. I would be prepared to take some bold constructive action." A few days later, on December 1, he spoke by telephone with Dulles, who was soon to end his recuperation and return to his duties, about the subject. "I've been nagging our boys to get ourselves a long-range plan in the Mideast," said the President. "What do we want to do if we are going to exclude Russia?"

Dulles had no answer, nor apparently did anyone else. Despite Eisenhower's desire to take advantage of the unique moment, nothing happened. When Egypt urgently requested food, fuel and medicine to compensate for its war damage, Washington refused. Nasser himself tried to improve relations in December when he met with Ambassador Hare in Cairo and spoke for three hours about his grievances and hopes. Hare reported that "Nasser said the position of the U.S. certainly is greatly enhanced by recent events. He frankly admitted he had never thought the U.S. would really attempt to restrain Israel if it attacked." But Nasser saw little hope of a peace agreement with Israel, explaining,

"The fact is that until 1955 Egypt was the only country in the Arab world where people were not particularly interested in the Israeli problem. But today popular indifference has given way to hate and the reason is Ben Gurion's policy from the Gaza attack to the present."

In Egypt, there was now a legacy of hatred that fully matched Ben Gurion's legacy of aggression.

Nasser was most interested, he told Hare, in building up Egypt's economy and raising the standard of living. "Preoccupation with foreign affairs distracts from the accomplishment of essential domestic reform," the Egyptian leader said.

Hare reported that he found Nasser in a serious and "soul-searching mood. His attitude was . . . one of seeking to be understood even to the extent at times of being actually deferential. As I was leaving Nasser said someone had recommended Washington's Farewell Address as being interesting reading. I observed that if I remembered correctly that was the one in which reference was made to no entangling alliances. Nasser laughed."

But there was little to laugh about. As the months went by with no improvement in relations, it seemed America, as far as Egypt was concerned, took Washington's warning literally. No serious attempt was made by the Administration to improve relations. A large part of the reason was a deep aversion that Westerners felt for the man who had faced down Britain and France, a man who had relations with the Soviet Union and Communist China and was a perceived threat to Israel. Hoover expressed the prevailing mood in America and Europe in a conversation with Eisenhower. "I do not think Nasser can be relied upon in any way."

Such blind prejudice allowed a unique opportunity to slip by. Eisenhower's instinct to take advantage of the opportunity had been sound. But with the need to mend relations with Britain and France, and with Nasser sharing no political support in America, he let inertia take its course. He failed to follow through and demand that his ideas be put into action. Perhaps his doubts about running for re-election had been well founded.

In his second term, as he grew into old age, he had neither the energy nor the imagination that he had displayed in his first term—and the Middle East and America are paying for it today.

None of the issues of the Arab-Israeli conflict that prompted Israel to go to war in 1956 are any closer to solution today than they were then. The peace treaty with Egypt in 1979 was a notable achievement, but it has brought no nearer to a solution the root causes of the conflict: the refugees, Israel's occupation of Arab lands, now including the West Bank and the Gaza Strip, its refusal to define the limits of its state and the refusal of other Arab states to sign a peace treaty. Until these are addressed, it is unlikely that the world has seen the last of Suez-type crises in the Middle East.

NOTES

The bulk of new information in this book comes from three sources: the archives of the Dwight D. Eisenhower Library, the archives of the United Nations and interviews. The Eisenhower Library was a particularly rich source of varied records, diaries, letters, memorandums and transcripts of telephone calls. Memorandums of conversations and the telephone transcripts were especially useful and colorful renditions of the confusion, the attitudes and ideas, the conflicts and disagreements, of the major officials of the Eisenhower Administration at the time of the Suez crisis. For those cases where quotations in the transcripts have been paraphrased, I've taken the liberty of putting them into direct quotes, always attempting to keep their integrity. Likewise, the U.N. archives offered an untapped and valuable record of the period. U.N. personnel represent the only neutral witnesses in the Middle East, where both sides tend to confuse their own interests with reality, which makes facts hard to come by in the region. Thanks to the generous help of my good friend Jan Schumacher I have had access to many previously unpublished letters and reports from the level of the secretary-general's office. Only a veteran U.N. official like Jan could have penetrated the tangled archives of the United Nations and returned with his prey. Finally, interviews provided some new information, most notably on the Anderson mission, but after a span of a quarter of a century, memories grow dim and I have preferred to rely on written records where possible.

I have tried to identify new information by source and date within the text, but when that seemed awkward I put the attribution in the following notes. I have not bothered citing sources for public comments or widely known incidents, but I have noted for the curious the sources of the more outlandish quotations and events that abounded in this curious period.

No one who has researched this bizarre story can avoid paying tribute to

444

former *New York Times* reporter Kennett Love. During the 1960s, at a time when very little of the affair had been documented and much remained cloudy in obfuscation, he managed to be amazingly accurate in his book *Suez: The Twice-Fought War*. The book's circular structure is a researcher's nightmare but the effort is worth it.

PROLOGUE

PAGE
21 "Who's the enemy?": Mosley, *Dulles.*
22 "Our people should": Memo of conversation by A. J. Goodpaster.

CHAPTER I

PAGE
30 A crescent moon: All details of the raid come from U.N. document #S/3373, Mar. 17, 1955.
37 Such common sense: George H. Quester, "Was Eisenhower a Genius?" (*International Security,* Fall 1979), and Fred J. Greenstein, "A Look at New Evidence" (*Political Science Quarterly,* Winter 1979); also note to Dulles, Feb. 6, 1957, and telephone call to Dulles, Oct. 23, 1956.
37 "One of the": Aug. 3, 1956.
38 "The French are": Nov. 18, 1957.
38 Routine and orderliness: Ann Whitman memo to Milton Eisenhower, Aug. 28, 1956.
39 "While I am": Letter to E. E. Hazlett, Nov. 18, 1957.
39 Despite such sentiments: Telephone conversation with Dulles, Mar. 28, 1955.
39 To his diary: May 14, 1953.
40 During talks in: Telephone conversation with Dulles, Jan. 30, 1956.
40 Eisenhower was aware: 1967 Columbia Oral History interview.
41 Thereafter he had: Hoopes, *The Devil and John Foster Dulles.*
41 But anyone who: Diary, Jan. 10, 1956.
41 Others, experiencing his: Eban, *Abba Eban.*
42 The Dulles brothers: Corson, *The Armies of Ignorance.*
42 "When Foster Dulles": Roosevelt interview, Washington, D.C., May 3, 1980.
42 Foster's best friend: Mosley, *Dulles.*
42 "He knew that": *Ibid.*
43 He had been: Hoopes, *op. cit.*
43 It was in: Eisenhower, *Waging Peace.*
44 Byroade's harsh warning: #SS-5-/, *Israel's Fundamental Problems.*

CHAPTER II

PAGE

50 The Qibya raid: Oct. 15, 1953. Diary quotations are from the article "Israeli State Terrorism," *Journal of Palestine Studies,* Spring 1980.

50 "Now the Army": Oct. 16, 1953.

50 Ben Gurion told: Oct. 18, 1953.

51 Eisenhower deplored Israel's: Mar. 8, 1956.

52 "Have you read": Bar-Zohar, *Ben-Gurion.*

52 Sharett did not: *Ibid.*

54 Also in March: Berger, *The Covenant and the Sword.*

61 Ben Gurion perceived: Bar-Zohar, *op. cit.*

62 On February 17: *Ibid.*

63 To the Cabinet: *Ibid.*

65 Ben Gurion also: *Ibid.*

CHAPTER III

PAGE

67 During one noisy: Copeland, *The Game of Nations.*

67 The Gaza raid: Letter, Apr. 19, 1955.

68 "Who can cry": Nutting, *Nasser.*

70 Unhappily for Nasser: Mosley, *Dulles.*

72 Byroade was impressed: Copeland, *op. cit.*

73 Nasser would have: Trevelyan, *The Middle East in Revolution.*

CHAPTER IV

PAGE

74 President Eisenhower warmly: Apt. 8, 1955.

75 Eisenhower's belief that: Apr. 9, 1955.

75 "I feel that": Feb. 3, 1956.

75 At another time: Apr. 7, 1955.

75 And Eisenhower, implicitly: Cable #2683, Nov. 12, 1955.

77 Foster Dulles was: Hoopes, *The Devil and John Foster Dulles.*

78 In Rangoon, Chou: Heikal, *Nasser: The Cairo Documents.*

78 Indeed, as Soviet: Khrushchev, *Khrushchev Remembers.*

79 After the meeting: Heikal, *op. cit.*

81 Trevelyan later reported: Trevelyan, *The Middle East in Revolution.*

81 Repeatedly in June: Love, *Suez: The Twice-Fought War.*

82 Dmitri Shepilov, editor: *Ibid.*

82 The election of: Sulzberger, *The Last of the Giants.*

83 A secret CIA: Parmet, *Eisenhower and the American Crusades.*

84 The next day: Burns, *Between Arab and Israeli.*

84 Several days later: *Ibid.*

86 It was an: Bar-Zohar, *Ben-Gurion.*

87 "Whatever the basis": Sept. 20, 1955.
87 "I need an": Interview with Roosevelt, Washington, D.C., Mar. 27, 1980.
88 Dulles and Hoover: Telephone conversation, Sept. 20, 1955.
88 Dulles summoned Roosevelt: Interview with Roosevelt, Washington, D.C., Sept. 22, 1955.
88 "I fear," Dulles: Sept. 22, 1955.
90 "In those days,": Interview with Byroade, Potomac, Md., Mar. 16, 1980.
90 Roosevelt and Copeland: Copeland, *The Game of Nations,* and interview with Copeland, Washington, D.C., Mar. 19, 1980.
92 Byroade was beside: Byroad interview, Washington, D.C., May 11, 1980.
92 Dulles and Hoover: Telephone conversation, Sept. 27, 1955.
93 Nasser's announcement on: Telephone conversation between Dulles, Allen and Hoover, Sept. 28, 1955.
94 Dulles wanted to: Telephone conversation with Hoover, Sept. 28, 1955.
94 Kim Roosevelt met: Copeland, *op. cit.*
95 Allen arrived conspicuously: Interview with Byroade, Potomac, Md., Mar. 16, 1980.
96 Miles Copeland discovered: Copeland, *op. cit.*

CHAPTER V

PAGE

101 In a telephone: Max Rabb to J. W. Hanes, Jr., memorandum from Hanes to Dulles, Sept. 27, 1955.
101 Dulles obliged, and: Minutes of Cabinet Meeting, Sept. 30, 1955.
102 Oddly, when Sherman: Parmet, *Eisenhower and the American Crusades.*
103 What the Egyptian: Burns, *Between Arab and Israeli.*
104 It was a: Notes of talk with Ben Gurion, Prime Minister of Israel, Nov. 18, 1955, at Jerusalem (unsigned), filed Jan. 14, 1956, in Eisenhower's Diary.
104 Eban, in his: Eban, *Abba Eban.*
105 Within six days: Notes taken during the President's conversation with Governor Adams, Oct. 12, 1955.
106 He told Adams: *Ibid.*
106 During his slow: Ann Whitman notes, Oct. 29, 1955.
107 Dulles and Nixon: Memo of conversation, Oct. 18, 1955.
108 It was reported: Seale, *The Struggle for Syria.*
108 But in Israel: Dayan, *Diary of the Sinai Campaign, 1956.*
109 Following the Summit: Dulles memo to all mission chiefs.
110 Eisenhower also wrote: Letter, Oct. 19, 1955.
111 Because of Eisenhower's: Hoopes, *The Devil and John Foster Dulles.*
111 The President ordered: Ann Whitman Diary notation, Oct. 29, 1955.
111 "Molotov was unresponsive": Eban, *op. cit.*
112 Explained General Burns: Burns, *op. cit.*
113 The Egyptians were: *Ibid.*
114 Burns called on: *Ibid.*
115 Nasser reacted positively: Love, *Suez: The Twice-Fought War.*
117 Once again, Burns: Burns, *op. cit.*

118 But in Burns's: *Ibid.*

118 When he heard: Eveland, *Ropes of Sand.*

118 "Not even the": Eban, *op. cit.*

119 "If a conscious": Ladas to P. Bang-Jensen, Jan. 6, 1956.

CHAPTER VI

PAGE

129 Britain actively supported: Nutting, *No End of a Lesson.*

130 Anderson dressed in: Diary, Jan. 11, 1956.

131 The afternoon before: Diary, Jan. 10, 1956.

132 Dulles performed his: Ann Whitman Diary notation, Jan. 11, 1956.

133 Shortly before Bob: Letter, Jan. 9, 1956.

133 In his diary: Diary, Jan. 11, 1956.

135 He and Roosevelt: Interview with Roosevelt, Washington, D.C., May 23, 1980.

CHAPTER VII

PAGE

138 His feeling about: Telephone call between Dulles and Brownell, Jan. 23, 1956.

139 Dulles' interview produced: *New York Times,* Jan. 14, 1956.

140 Two major topics: Letter to Lewis M. Douglas, Jan. 20, 1956.

140 Secretary of State: Jan. 26, 1956.

140 The message was: Jan. 26, 1956.

140 To one of: Telephone conversation with Livingstone Merchant, Jan. 25, 1956.

140 In a telephone: Jan. 28, 1956.

143 At their first: Hoopes, *The Devil and John Foster Dulles.*

144 "I may be": *Ibid.*

144 Eden and his: Mosley, *Dulles.*

145 His other executive: *Ibid.*

146 The meeting ended: *Ibid.*

147 "I think Eden": *Ibid.*

148 "The Russians paid": *Ibid.*

149 Eden and Dulles: This version of the talks is based on the Memorandum of Conversation, #ETW MC 103, Eden Talks—Washington, Feb. 7, 1956.

154 "The Second World": Lloyd, *Suez 1956.*

154 "Without the United": Moran, *Churchill.*

155 One reason was: Adams, *Firsthand Report.*

CHAPTER VIII

PAGE

157 "You did a": Telephone conversation, Jan. 25, 1956.

157 In his reply: Draft submitted to White House, Feb. 6, 1956.

157 Eisenhower was still: Diary, Feb. 7, 1956.

159 Why, he wondered: Diary, Feb. 13, 1956.

160 "No objection": Memorandum of Record by A. J. Goodpaster, Mar. 5, 1956.

162 Long after the: Horne, *A Savage War of Peace*.

162 The secret arms: Peres, *David's Sling*.

163 "There is the": *Ibid*.

164 "The very idea": *Ibid*.

167 Cause for the: Mail dispatch No. 9, *Weekly Summary of Activities of the MAC*, Feb. 29, 1956.

168 "It often seemed": Burns, *Between Arab and Israeli*.

168 "The prime minister": Note by Hoover to Eisenhower, Feb. 20, 1956.

168 Eisenhower answered the: Letter to Ben Gurion, Feb. 27, 1956.

169 "I'm afraid Nasser": Feb. 28, 1956.

170 But two days: Letter, Mar. 21, 1956.

CHAPTER IX

PAGE

173 In London the: Cable #102, July 7, 1953.

174 After leaving the: Heikal, *Nasser: The Cairo Papers*.

174 Observed Lloyd: "I": Lloyd, *Suez 1956*.

175 Glubb had first: Glubb, *A Soldier with the Arabs*.

177 After that Nasser: Trevelyan, *The Middle East in Revolution*.

178 They spoke of: Ladas to P. Bang-Jensen, Jan. 6, 1956.

178 Ladas observed how: *Ibid*.

179 "It put him": Trevelyan, *op. cit.*

179 When he pressed: Love, *Suez: The Twice-Fought War*.

179 "What an intelligent": Heikal, *op. cit.*

180 "In spite of": Lloyd, *op. cit.*

180 "He thought that": Love, *op. cit.*

180 He found Eden: Nutting, *No End of a Lesson*.

181 "My friends were": Eden, *Full Circle*.

181 Nutting had come: Nutting, *op. cit.*

183 "I knew then": *Ibid*.

185 As late as: Moran, *Churchill*.

186 The fifteen long: Eden, *op. cit.*

CHAPTER X

PAGE

189 The badly shaken: Horne, *A Savage War of Peace*.

190 One cable came: Murphy to the acting secretary, Mar. 3, 1956.

191 That same day: USARMA Paris to ACSI, C-13, Mar. 3, 1956.

192 A third cable: Dillon to secretary of state, #3992, Mar. 2, 1956.

192 Two days later: Memorandum for the Record by A. J. Goodpaster, Mar. 5, 1956.

193 "The Italians even": Weizman, *On Eagles' Wings.*
193 The weekly report: Mail dispatch No. 10, *Weekly Summary of Activities of the MAC.*
197 "He made no": Diary, Mar. 13, 1956.
199 Lloyd told him: Lloyd, *Suez 1956.*
201 Pineau was surprised: Pineau, *1956 Suez.*
201 Dulles later confided: Lloyd, *op. cit.*
203 The challenge in: Eisenhower, *Waging Peace.*
203 British hard liners: Nutting, *No End of a Lesson.*
205 His private secretary: *New York Times,* July 27, 1979.
208 "Nasser took this": Trevelyan, *The Middle East in Revolution.*
208 Eden's protégé, Nutting: Nutting, *op. cit.*
208 On the same: Cable #ALO 382, Mar. 12, 1956.
208 "The French public": USCINCEUR Paris to JCS, #EC9-1479, Mar. 12, 1956.
209 Another noted that: Excerpt of a letter to the President (apparently written by William J. Donovan), Mar. 14, 1956.
210 "The tension along": Mail Dispatch No. 11 *Weekly Summary of Activities of the MAC.*
210 Tensions were aggravated: Burns to Hammarskjold, Mar. 29, 1956.
210 On the sixteenth: Mail Dispatch No. 12, Mar. 22, 1956.
210 "The enclosure you": Eisenhower letter.
211 Dulles had prepared: Memorandum for the President, Mar. 29, 1956.
212 That evening, Eisenhower: Diary, Mar. 28, 1956.
213 Two days after: Telephone conversation, Mar. 30, 1956.
213 Dulles was also: Telephone conversation, Mar. 30, 1956.

CHAPTER XI

214 The anti-American tone: Telephone conversation, Apr. 10, 1956.
215 Out of the: Eveland, *Ropes of Sand.*
217 "The British are": Apr. 4.
218 U.N. observers determined: *Report to the Secretary-General on the Gaza Incident of 5 April 1956,* May 15, 1956.
219 "The investigation team": *Ibid.*
221 He asked his: Telephone call to Wilkins, Apr. 9, 1956.
221 Chairman . . . Joint Chiefs: Telephone call, Apr. 10, 1956.
221 Foster's brother, Allen: Telephone conversation, Apr. 9, 1956.
222 Ben Gurion was: Cable #UNTSO 213, Apr. 12.
222 "I must express": Cable #16, Apr. 12, 1956.
223 In a confidential: Cable #18, Apr. 13, 1956.
224 He was writing: Personal letter, at Beirut, Apr. 15, 1956.
224 In a coded: Cable #SECGEN 5, April 18, 1956.
225 At the height: Memorandum, Goodpaster to Whitman, CAP 548, Apr. 11, 1956.
225 The next day: Telephone conversation with Gordan Gray, Apr. 12, 1956.

226 "Let me know": Telephone conversation, Apr. 17, 1956.

226 The changes in: *Basic National Security Policy,* NSC 5602/1, Mar. 15, 1956.

227 Earlier in the: Diary, Jan. 23, 1956.

228 Eisenhower returned them: Note to Dulles, Apr. 2, 1956.

229 In an "Eyes": Copy of Ambassador Bohlen's message to the secretary of state, Mar. 7, 1956.

230 By mid-April, Churchill: Letter, Apr. 16, 1956.

233 When Allen Dulles: Telephone conversation, Apr. 23, 1956.

234 "Things have so": Thomas, *Comment Israel fût sauvé.*

CHAPTER XII

PAGE

238 When Abel Thomas: Thomas, *Comment Israel fût sauvé.*

239 "Far from having": Eban, *Abba Eban.*

239 Sharett's fall from: Bar-Zohar, *Ben-Gurion.*

240 "The reason B-G": Love, *Suez: The Twice-Fought War.*

241 The U.N.'s General: Burns, *Between Arab and Israeli.*

241 The Nord landed: Thomas, *op. cit.*

245 "Nasser soon must": Cable #2515.

246 But in the: Steven, *The Spymasters of Israel.*

247 In a meeting: Memorandum of Conference with the President by A. J. Goodpaster.

250 "The first days": July 12, 1956.

250 U-2 operations began: Date of the first flight remains classified; I base July 4 as the date on the fact that that is the first date mentioned in the Soviet protest of the flights.

250 Eisenhower worried over: Memorandum for the Record by A. J. Goodpaster, July 10, 1956.

CHAPTER XIII

PAGE

253 He summoned to: Memorandum of Conversation, *U.S.-Egyptian Relations,* #2988, May 17, 1956.

255 In a telephone: May 23, 1956.

258 It was written: Letter from Eli Ginzberg, July 17, 1956.

258 "His face went": Interview with Byroade, Washington, D.C., May 11, 1980.

259 "All right," Nasser: *Nasser: The Cairo Papers.*

261 "Hussein began by": Love, *Suez: The Twice-Fought War.*

262 In another telephone: July 19, 1956.

262 "This is not": Heikal, *op. cit.*

263 "Imagine going to": Love, *op. cit.*

263 Washington's plan to: Eveland, *Ropes of Sand.*

265 "He will be": *Ibid.*

266 Mohamed Heikal telephoned: Heikal, *op. cit.*

266 "We came to": Love, *op. cit.*

268 When Yunis walked: *Ibid.*
269 "In order to": *Ibid.*

CHAPTER XIV
PAGE
275 "I told my": Eden, *Full Circle.*
276 By around midnight: Thomas, *The Suez Affair.*
276 Eden told the: London *Times,* Nov. 5, 1980.
276 Lord Louis Mountbatten: *Ibid.*
276 The emergency meeting: Love, *Suez: The Twice-Fought War.*
276 "This was the ": Nutting, *No End of a Lesson.*
277 The national sentiment: Moran, *Churchill.*
278 "It was deeply": Interview with Clark, Washington, D.C., Nov. 11, 1979.
278 Eden read the: Mosley, *Dulles.*
278 By July, he: Thomas, *op. cit.*
278 President Eisenhower arrived: Memorandum of Conference with the President by A. J. Goodpaster, July 27, 1956.
280 "The President was": Murphy, *Diplomat Among Warriors.*
280 As usual, Eisenhower: Eisenhower, *op. cit.*
281 In a message: Cable 27646, July 28, 1956.
282 Eisenhower of course: Diary, Mar. 12, 1956.
282 In a letter: Mar. 29, 1956.
283 After the speeches: Sadat, *In Search of Identity.*
284 In London, when: Nutting, *op. cit.*
284 "I was left": Murphy, *op. cit.*
285 Later, after briefings: Mar. 29, 1956.
285 In another phone: Mar. 29, 1956.
286 He and Macmillan: Eisenhower, *op. cit.*
286 "I can scarcely": *Ibid.*
286 The President's letter: *Ibid.*
287 "He twice called": Telephone conversation, July 31, 1956.
287 "Nasser and the": Letter, Aug. 3, 1956.
287 The joint chiefs: Memorandum for the secretary of defense, *Nationalization of the Suez Maritime Canal by the Egyptian Government,* July 31, 1956.
289 Israel was anxious: Thomas, *Comment Israel fût sauvé.*
290 Despite his admonitions: Eden, *op. cit.*
290 But Murphy, who: Murphy, *op. cit.*
291 Eden's passion so: Eden, *op. cit.*
291 Observed Bob Murphy: Murphy, *op. cit.*
292 Eisenhower and Dulles: *Notes of Presidential-Bipartisan Congressional Leadership Meeting,* by L. A. Munnich, Jr., Apr. 12, 1956.
294 In a cable: #409, Aug. 7, 1956.
294 In a letter: #416 & #417, Aug. 8, 1956.
294 On August 17: Cable #437, Aug. 18, 1956.
295 He visited Ben Gurion: Dayan, *Story of My Life.*
295 "If the French": Bar-Zohar, *Ben-Gurion.*

295 "There is no": *Ibid.*
295 French Defense Minister: Peres, *David's Sling.* He gives the date as May but it almost certainly could not have occurred that early. Because of official censorship, and perhaps even official tampering, dates of sensitive incidents touching on national security are frequently wrong or misleading in Israeli accounts of this period. Compare for instance Peres' timing of the arrival of the first Mystère IV's in Israel with Weizman's version and that of Bar-Zohar, or Peres' timing for the first contacts with France about colluding for war and Dayan's in his autobiography.
297 "Krishna Menon is": Diary, July 14, 1955.
298 Dulles shot back: Cable to the President, Aug. 20, 1956.
298 Eisenhower was repentant: Letter, Aug. 20, 1956.
300 "By now I": Eisenhower, *op. cit.*
300 The State Department: *British and French Intentions Regarding the Suez,* Sept. 1, 1956.
300 Worried, Eisenhower wrote: Eisenhower, *op. cit.*
302 Eden was disappointed: Nutting, *op. cit.*
302 The Menzies mission: Love, *op. cit.*

CHAPTER XV

PAGE

306 For Dulles, sitting: Telephone conversation with Dr. Flemming, Sept. 12, 1956.
306 Dulles also had: Sept. 12, 1956.
309 Ben Gurion and Moshe: Dayan, *Story of My Life.*
309 Shimon Peres flew: Peres, *David's Sling.*
310 In a cable: #151, Aug. 27, 1956.
311 Fears were spreading: Cable #UNTSO 789, Sept. 14, 1956.
311 "She was not": Cable #UNTSO 867, Sept. 24, 1956.
311 Hammarskjold replied to: Cable #512–513, Sept. 24, 1956.
313 "Indubitably, we were": Beaufre, *The Suez Expedition: 1956.*
315 "Do you realize": London *Times,* Nov. 5, 1980.
315 The enervating effects: Mosley, *Dulles.*
316 The man delegated: Eveland, *Ropes of Sand.*
319 The secretary of: *The Likelihood of a British-French Resort to Military Action Against Egypt in the Suez Crisis,* #30-5-56 No. 198.
320 Soon staffers at: Cooper, *The Lion's Last Roar.*
320 A news bulletin: Nutting, *No End of a Lesson.*
320 A secret study: *British and French Proposals on the Suez Questions, and Comments on,* Sept. 7, 1956.
321 "We are anxious": Conversation with Dr. Flemming, Sept. 25, 1956.
321 The Britons found: Nutting, *op. cit.*
321 During his stay: Lloyd, *Suez 1956.*

CHAPTER XVI

PAGE

323 Pineau admitted that: Thomas, *Comment Israel fût sauvé*.

324 It was an: Dayan, *Story of My Life*.

325 Dayan met the next day: Bar-Zohar, *Ben-Gurion*.

325 Dayan, though sharing: *Ibid*.

326 In discussing tactics: Telephone conversation, Oct. 2, 1956.

326 In a three-page: Oct. 8, 1956.

327 Goaded by Hagerty's: Oct. 8, 1956.

327 A little later: Letter to Hoover, Oct. 8, 1956.

328 Lloyd and Pineau: Lloyd, *Suez 1956*.

330 Israel now diverted: Security Council Report #S/3685, Oct. 17, 1956.

331 The Israeli action: Cable #UNTSO 938.

331 But Eden prudently: Eden, *Full Circle*.

332 Repercussions of the: Memorandum for the Record by Eisenhower, Oct. 15, 1956.

334 Lord Mountbatten had: London *Times,* Nov. 5, 1980.

335 It was later: Love, *Suez: The Twice-Fought War*.

336 Aside from a: Nutting, *No End of a Lesson*.

337 General André Beaufre: Beaufre, *The Suez Expedition 1956*.

338 Simultaneously with the: Eveland, *Ropes of Sand*.

338 Some members of: Memorandum of Conference with the President by A. J. Goodpaster, Oct. 6, 1956.

341 But for the: Telephone conversation with Mr. Yarrow, Oct. 22, 1956.

342 "Before all else": Bar-Zohar, *op. cit.*

343 Ben Gurion's plan: Thomas, *op. cit.*

344 When Lloyd finally: Lloyd, *op. cit.*

344 To the Israelis: Bar-Zohar, *op. cit.*

344 Dayan too resented: Dayan, *op. cit.*

346 Lloyd insisted that: *Ibid.*

348 Ben Gurion had: Pineau, *1956 Suez*.

CHAPTER XVII

PAGE

350 By the next: Unsigned and unnumbered sections one through seven, Oct. 25, 1956.

351 "We had a": Eisenhower, *Waging Peace*.

352 The CIA's liaison: Cooper, *The Lion's Last Roar*.

353 Another analyst, Robert: Mosley, *Dulles,* and interview with Amory, Washington, D.C., Sept. 18, 1979.

354 Moshe Dayan was: Dayan, *Diary of the Sinai Campaign, 1956*.

355 Foster Dulles later: Eisenhower, *op. cit.*

356 Eban and his: Eban, *Abba Eban*.

357 Ben Gurion replied: Thomas, *The Suez Affair*.

359 Eisenhower was scheduled: Hughes, *The Ordeal of Power*.

361 At U.N. headquarters: Cable #UNTSO 1072.

361 That same morning: Dayan, *op. cit.*

362 About the time: Dayan, *op. cit.*

362 Eban only that: Eban, *op. cit.*

362 Eban went to: *Ibid.*

364 As the war: Weizman, *On Eagles' Wings*.

364 Forty minutes after: Oct. 29, 1956.

365 In another call: Telephone conversation with Mr. Holland, Oct. 29, 1956.

365 To Senator Knowland: Oct. 29, 1956.

365 Already awaiting him: Love, *Suez: The Twice-Fought War*.

366 "It is far": Memorandum of Conference with the President by A. J. Goodpaster, Oct. 29, 1956, 8:15 P.M.

368 Still later that: Eisenhower, *op. cit.*

CHAPTER XVIII

PAGE

372 At a meeting: Memorandum of Conference with the President by A. J. Goodpaster, Oct. 30, 1956.

373 "I address you": Cable NIACT #3081, Oct. 30, 1956.

373 About the time: Eisenhower, *Waging Peace*.

374 After reading Eden's: Memorandum of Conference with the President by A. J. Goodpaster, Oct. 30, 1956.

374 The original text: Oct. 30, 1956.

375 In another conversation: Telephonic, Oct. 30, 1956.

375 "We should have": Telephone conversation, Oct. 30, 1956.

375 Eden later admitted: Love, *Suez: The Twice-Fought War*.

375 In another meeting: Memorandum of Conference with the President by A. J. Goodpaster, Oct. 30, 1956.

376 Later that afternoon: Hughes, *The Ordeal of Power*.

378 British ambassador to: Hayter, *The Kremlin and the Embassy*.

378 The envoy most: Trevelyan, *The Middle East in Revolution*.

379 The Jewish state: Dupuy, *Elusive Victory*.

381 The Egyptian casualties: Information from an Israeli military commander who declines to be identified.

382 By midafternoon, Ben: Dupuy, *op. cit.*

385 The CIA's plot: Eveland, *Ropes of Sand*.

385 Cabot Lodge told: Telephone conversation, Oct. 31, 1956.

385 Lodge did and: Telephone conversation, Oct. 31.

386 Later in the: Telephone conversation, Oct. 31.

387 Hughes was in: Hughes, *op. cit.*

388 The necessity of: Telephone conversation between Dulles and Eisenhower, Oct. 30, 1956.

389 At the same: *Discussion of the 302nd Meeting of the National Security Council, Thursday, Nov. 1, 1956* by S. Everett Gleason.

392 "This is a": Nov. 2, 1956.

394 Nasser's order for: Love, *op. cit.*

395 In Washington, Dwight: Nov. 2, 1956.

397 The strain, the: Pineau, *1956 Suez.*

397 "Why are you": Dayan, *Story of My Life.*

398 Foster Dulles was: Mosley, *Dulles.*

399 The day before: London *Times,* Nov. 12, 1980.

402 Eden agreed, and: Love, *op. cit.*

403 Privately, he was: Eisenhower, *op. cit.*

403 In this time: Telephone conversation, Dec. 1, 1956.

404 Piteous appeals were: Cable #2171, Nov. 4, 1956.

404 The anti-Russian National: Nov. 4, 1956.

404 Ambassador Dillon warned: Cable #2188, Nov. 5, 1956.

405 This cold reality: Mosley, *op. cit.,* also Powers, *The Man Who Kept the Secrets.*

405 The CIA's Bob: Interview, Washington, D.C., Sept. 18, 1979.

405 "We must stop": Murphy, *Diplomat Among Warriors.* Murphy describes the unidentified person as a "high-ranking official of the State Department . . . not a career foreign service officer."

CHAPTER XIX

PAGE

407 As the naval: Love, *Suez: The Twice-Fought War.*

408 The French troops: *Ibid.*

409 "We can stop": Mosley, *Dulles.*

410 Unless there was: Thomas, *The Suez Affair.*

410 "I hear a": Pineau, *1956 Suez.*

411 Shortly after midnight: Cable #2238, Nov. 6, 1956.

412 Eisenhower was deeply: Memorandum of Conference with the President by A. J. Goodpaster, Nov. 6, 1956.

412 "These should be": Eisenhower, *Waging Peace.*

414 "We've now achieved": Love, *op. cit.*

414 But Eisenhower's chief: Memorandum for the Record by A. J. Goodpaster, Nov. 7, 1956.

416 It was now: Telephone conversation, Nov. 7, 1956.

416 In a stiffly: Cable #482 Tel Aviv, Nov. 7, 1956.

416 Eisenhower was not: Eban, *Abba Eban.*

416 In Washington, Hoover: *Ibid.*

416 The President, hearing: *Ibid.*

416 By the next: Letter from the Israeli Embassy, Nov. 8, 1956.

417 His vision to: Memorandum, Nov. 8, 1956.

418 The President and: *Bipartisan Legislative Meeting* by L. A. Minnich, Nov. 9, 1956.

419 But there were: Cable #1784 Paris, #3422 London, Nov. 11, 1956.

420 But, Flemming noted: *Cabinet Meeting Minutes,* by L. A. Minnich, Nov. 16, 1956.

420 Occupying Israeli troops: Love, *op. cit.*

421 The confrontation became: Memorandum, Nov. 7, 1956.

421 There was another: Love, *op. cit.*

421 "It is a very": Burns, *Between Arab and Israeli.*

421 The head of: Letter, Bayard to Col. Leary, Nov. 13, 1956.

421 In another letter: Letter, Bayard to Col. Leary, Nov. 19, 1956.

422 Burns suspected that: Burns, *op. cit.*

CHAPTER XX

PAGE

424 "My guess is": Nov. 19, 1956.

425 They agreed to: Memorandum of Conference with the President by A. J. Goodpaster, Nov. 20, 1956.

427 The next day: Nov. 21, 1956.

428 A few minutes: Memorandum of Conference with the President by A. J. Goodpaster, Nov. 21, 1956.

430 Aldrich cabled from: #2866, Nov. 22, 1956.

430 Some Washington officials: Memorandum of Conference with the President by A. J. Goodpaster, Nov. 26, 1956.

432 Lyndon Johnson sent: Feb. 11, 1957.

433 Even Harry Luce: Feb. 11, 1957.

433 Later, in a: Feb. 12, 1957.

433 He complained again: Feb. 19, 1957.

433 Despite the lack: Feb. 20, 1957.

434 "We need very": Telephone conversation, Feb. 22, 1957.

435 The destruction was: Burns, *Between Arab and Israeli.*

435 When he had: Love, *Suez: The Twice-Fought War.*

436 Churchill seemed to: Moran, *Churchill.*

436 Harold Macmillan was: Cooper, *The Lion's Last Roar.*

436 Eisenhower sent him: Jan. 10, 1957.

EPILOGUE

PAGE

439 Lord Mountbatten was: London *Times,* Nov. 12, 1980.

441 Eisenhower continued to: Memorandum of Conference with the President by A. J. Goodpaster, Nov. 23, 1956.

441 Nasser himself tried: Cable #1912 Cairo, four sections, Dec. 17, 1956.

442 Hoover expressed the: Memorandum of Conference with the President by A. J. Goodpaster, Nov. 20, 1956.

BIBLIOGRAPHY

Adams, Sherman. *Firsthand Report: The Story of the Eisenhower Administration*. New York: Harper & Brothers, 1961.

Ambiose, Stephen E. Ike's Spies: Eisenhower and the Espionage Establishment. Garden City, N.Y. Double & Company Inc., 1981.

Astor, Sidney. *Anthony Eden*. London: Weidenfeld and Nicolson, 1976.

Bar-Zohar, Michael. *Ben-Gurion: A Biography*. New York: Delacorte Press, 1977.

Beaufre, André. *The Suez Expedition 1956*. London: Faber and Faber, 1969.

Ben-Gurion, David. *Israel: A Personal History*. New York: Funk & Wagnalls, 1971.

Berger, Earl. *The Covenant and the Sword: Arab-Israeli Relations 1948–56*. Toronto: University of Toronto Press, 1965.

Bethell, Nicholas. *The Palestine Triangle: The Struggle for the Holy Land, 1935–48*. New York: G. P. Putnam's Sons, 1979.

Brecher, Michael. *Decisions in Israel's Foreign Policy*. London: Oxford University Press, 1974.

Burns, Lt. Gen. E. L. M. *Between Arab and Israeli*. New York: Ivan Obolensky, 1962.

Churchill, Randolph. *The Rise and Fall of Sir Anthony Eden*. New York: G. P. Putnam's Sons, 1959.

Cohen, Aharon. *Israel and the Arab World*. Abr. Ed. Boston: Beacon Press, 1976.

Colby, William, and Peter Forbath. *Honorable Men: My Life in the CIA*. New York: Simon and Schuster, 1978.

Collins, Larry, and Dominique Lapierre. *O Jerusalem!* New York: Simon and Schuster, 1972.

Cooper, Chester L. *The Lion's Last Roar: Suez, 1956*. New York: Harper & Row, 1978.

458

Copeland, Miles. *The Game of Nations: The Amorality of Power Politics*. London: Weidenfeld and Nicolson, 1969.

Corson, William R. *The Armies of Ignorance: The Rise of the American Intelligence Empire*. New York: The Dial Press/James Wade, 1977.

Crosbie, Sylvia Kowitt. *A Tacit Alliance: France and Israel from Suez to the Six Day War*. Princeton, N.J.: Princeton University Press, 1974.

Dayan, Moshe. *Diary of the Sinai Campaign, 1956*. London: Sphere Books, 1967.

——*Story of My Life: An Autobiography*. New York: William Morrow and Co., 1976.

Divine, Robert A. *Eisenhower and the Cold War*. New York: Oxford University Press, 1981.

Donovan, Robert J. *Eisenhower: The Inside Story*. New York: Harper & Brothers, 1956.

Dupuy, Trevor N. *Elusive Victory: The Arab-Israeli Wars 1947–1974*. New York: Harper & Row, 1978.

Eban, Abba. *Abba Eban: An Autobiography*. Jerusalem: Steimatzky's Agency Ltd., 1977.

Eden, Anthony. *Full Circle: The Memories of Sir Anthony*. London: Cassell, 1960.

Eisenhower, Dwight D. *The White House Years: Mandate for Change 1953–1956*. New York: A Signet Book, 1963.

—— *The White House Years: Waging Peace 1956–1961*. Garden City, N.Y.: Doubleday & Co., 1965.

Epp, Frank H. *Whose Land is Palestine?* Grand Rapids, Mich.: William B. Eerdmans Publishing Co., 1974.

Eveland, Wilbur Crane. *Ropes of Sand: America's Failure in the Middle East*. New York: W. W. Norton & Co., 1980.

Ewald, William Bragg, Jr. *Eisenhower the President: Crucial Days 1951–1960*. Englewood Cliffs, N.J.: Prentice-Hall, 1981.

Farag, E. S. (trans.). *Nasser Speaks: Basic Documents*. London: The Morssett Press, 1972.

Gerson, Louis L. *John Foster Dulles*. New York: Cooper Square Publishers, 1967.

Glubb, John Bagot. *A Soldier with the Arabs*. London: Hodder and Sloughton, 1969.

Halle, Louis J. *The Cold War as History*. New York: Harper & Row, 1967.

Hayter, William. *The Kremlin and the Embassy*. New York: The Macmillan Co., 1966.

Heikal, Mohamed. *Nasser: The Cairo Documents*. London: New English Library, 1972.

—— *The Sphinx and the Commissar: The Rise and Fall of Soviet Influence in the Middle East*. New York: Harper & Row, 1978.

Hoopes, Townsend. *The Devil and John Foster Dulles*. London: Andre Deutsch, 1974.

Hopkins, Harry. *Egypt, the Crucible*. Boston: Houghton Mifflin Co., 1969.

459

Horne, Alistair. *A Savage War of Peace: Algeria 1954–1962*. New York: The Viking Press, 1977.

Hughes, Emmet John. *The Ordeal of Power*. New York: Atheneum, 1963.

Hutchison, Cmdr. E. H. *Violent Truce: A Military Observer Looks at the Arab-Israeli Conflict 1951–1955*. New York: The Devin-Adair Co., 1956.

Khouri, Fred J. *The Arab-Israeli Dilemma*. Syracuse, N.Y.: Syracuse University Press, 1974.

Khrushchev, Nikita. *Khrushchev Remembers*. Boston: Little, Brown and Co., 1970.

Lloyd, Selwyn. *Suez 1956: A Personal Account*. New York: Mayflower Books, 1978.

Love, Kennett. *Suez: The Twice-Fought War*. New York: McGraw-Hill, 1969.

Lyon, Peter. *Eisenhower: Portrait of the Hero*. Boston: Little, Brown and Co., 1974.

Manchester, William. *The Glory and the Dream: A Narrative History of America, 1932–1972*. New York: Bantam Books, 1978.

Margach, James. *The Abuse of Power: The War Between Downing Street and the Media from Lloyd George to Callaghan*. London: Witt Allen, 1978.

Moncrieff, Anthony (ed.). *Suez: Ten Years After*. London: British Broadcasting Corp., 1967.

Moran, Lord. *Churchill: Taken from the Diaries of Lord Moran*. Boston: Houghton Mifflin Co., 1966.

Morris, James. *Farewell the Trumpets: An Imperial Retreat*. New York: A Helen and Kurt Wolff Book, Harcourt Brace Jovanovich, 1978.

Mosley, Leonard. *Dulles: A Biography of Eleanor, Allen, and John Foster Dulles and Their Family Network*. New York: The Dial Press/James Wade, 1978.

Murphy, Robert. *Diplomat Among Warriors*. Garden City, N.Y.: Doubleday & Company, Inc., 1964.

Nazzal, Nafez. *The Palestinian Exodus from Galilee 1948*. Beirut: The Institute for Palestine Studies, 1978.

Neustadt, Richard E. *Alliance Politics*. New York: Columbia University Press, 1970.

Nutting, Anthony. *Nasser*. London: Constable, 1972.

—— *No End of a Lesson: The Story of Suez*. New York: Clarkson N. Potter, 1967.

Parmet, Herbert S. *Eisenhower and the American Crusades*. New York: The Macmillan Co., 1972.

Peres, Shimon. *David's Sling: The Arming of Israel*. London: Weidenfeld and Nicolson, 1970.

Pineau, Christian. *1956 Suez*. Paris: Robert Lamont, 1976.

Powers, Thomas. *The Man Who Kept the Secrets: Richard Helms and the CIA*. New York: Alfred A. Knopf, 1979.

Robertson, Terence. *Crisis: The Inside Story of the Suez Conspiracy*. New York: Atheneum, 1965.

Sachar, Howard M. *A History of Israel: From the Rise of Zionism to Our Time*. Jerusalem: Steimatzky's Agency Ltd., 1976.

Sadat, Anwar. *In Search of Identity: An Autobiography.* New York: Harper Colophon Books, 1978.

Said, Edward W. *The Question of Palestine.* New York: Times Books, 1980.

Seale, Patrick. *The Struggle for Syria: A Study of Post-War Arab Politics 1945–1958.* London: Oxford University Press, 1966.

Snow, Peter. *Hussein: A Biography.* London: Barrie & Jenkins, 1972.

Stephens, Robert. *Nasser: A Political Biography.* London: Allen Lane/The Penguin Press, 1971.

Steven, Stewart. *The Spymasters of Israel.* New York: Macmillan Publishing Co., 1980.

Stone, I. F. *Underground to Palestine and Reflections Thirty Years Later.* New York: Pantheon Books, 1978.

Sulzberger, C. L. *The Last of the Giants.* New York: The Macmillan Co., 1970.

Thomas, Abel. *Comment Israel fût sauvé.* Paris: Albin Michel, 1974.

Thomas, Hugh. *The Suez Affair.* Middlesex, England: Penguin Books, 1970.

Trevelyan, Humphrey. *The Middle East in Revolution.* London: The Macmillan Co., 1970.

Urquhart, Brian. *Hammarskjold.* New York: Alfred A. Knopf, 1972.

Weizman, Ezer. *On Eagles' Wings: The Personal Story of the Leading Commander of the Israeli Air Force.* Jerusalem: Steimatzky's Agency Ltd., 1976.

Wilson, Evan M. *Decision on Palestine: How the U.S. Came to Recognize Israel.* Stanford, CA: Hoover Institution Press, 1979.

Wynn, Wilton. *Nasser of Egypt: The Search for Dignity.* Cambridge: Arlington Books, 1959.

Index

ABOUT THE AUTHOR

DONALD NEFF was born in York, Pennsylvania, in 1930 and has spent a career in journalism. He has reported for the York *Dispatch,* United Press International, the Los Angeles *Times* and *Time* magazine, where he also served as a correspondent, writer and senior editor for sixteen years. His assignments have included tours in Japan, Vietnam and Israel as well as Texas, California and New York. Among his journalism awards, the most recent is the Overseas Press Club's citation for the best magazine article in 1979 for *Time*'s cover story on "The Colombia Connection."

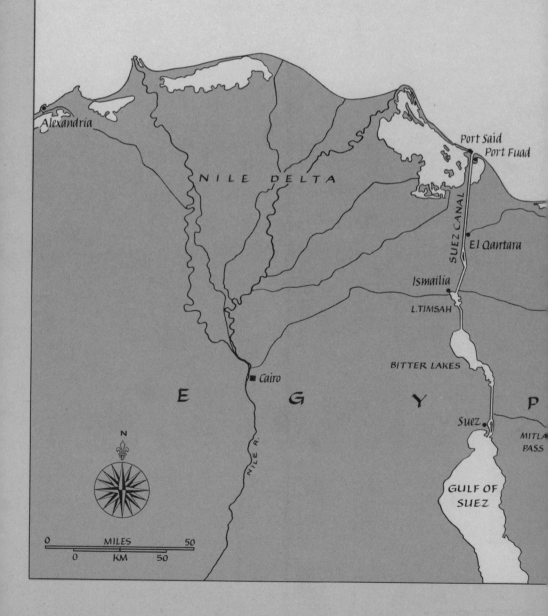

MEDITERRANEAN

Alexandria

NILE DELTA

Port Said
Port Fuad

SUEZ CANAL

El Qantara

Ismailia

L. TIMSAH

BITTER LAKES

E   G   Y   P

Cairo

N

Suez

MITLA
PASS

NILE R.

GULF OF
SUEZ

0   MILES   50
0   KM   50